TOMBS.
TREASURES.
MUMMIES.
Seven Great Discoveries
of Egyptian Archaeology
in
Five Volumes

BOOK FOUR

KV62
The Tomb of Tutankhamen
with
Thirteen Addenda

First published in the United States in 1998 by
Kmt Communications, Inc
Sebastopol, California, USA

Re-published in five volumes in the United States in 2015-17 by
Kmt Communications, LLC
Weaverville, North Carolina, USA

ISBN: 987-1981423385

Book design by the Author in QuarkXpress & Adobe Photoshop

Cover images: Cairo Egyptian Museum

Other Egypt-themed Books by the Author

Imperial Lives: Illustrated Biographies of Significant New Kingdom Egyptians
    Volume One: The 18th Dynasty through Thutmose IV

Intimate Egypt: Black & White Photography of the Ancient Monuments in Seven
    Volumes

Tombs.Treasures.Mummies. Seven Great Discoveries of Egyptian Archaeology

    Book One: The Royal Mummies Caches (TT320 & KV35)

    Book Two: The Tombs of Maiherpri (KV36) & Kha & Merit (TT8)

    Book Three: The Tomb of Yuya & Thuyu (KV46) & The Amarna Cache (KV55)

    Book Five: Complete Catalogue of the Royal Mummies

Ancient Egypt, Modern Hues: Relief Images Digitally Colorized in Two Volumes

T O M B S.
T R E A S U R E S.
M U M M I E S.
Seven Great Discoveries
of Egyptian Archaeology
in
Five Volumes

B O O K   F O U R

KV62
The Tomb of Tutankhamen

Plus
Thirteen Addenda

D E N N I S   C.   F O R B E S

This study is dedicated to

Howard Carter
&
His Team Excavating KV62

Contents

The Tomb of Tutankhamen

Number 62 in the Valley of the Kings

≈ 1922 ≈

"*I fear that the Valley of the Tombs* [sic] *is now exhausted*," wrote Theodore M. Davis in his introduction to *The Tombs of Harmhabi and Touatânkhamanou* (London, 1912), the final volume in the lavishly illustrated series of folio reports he published documenting the impressive discoveries made during his several consecutive seasons excavating in the New Kingdom royal necropolis. He had begun working in the Valley in 1903, and when he quit it in 1912,[1] the American archaeology patron could tally six important royal tombs to his credit — Montuhirkhopshef (KV19), Hatshepsut (KV20), Thutmose IV (KV43), Siptah (KV47), the problematic "Amarna Cache" (KV55) and Horemheb (KV57) — as well as the nearly intact burial of royal in-laws Yuya and Thuyu (KV46), and nine other anonymous uninscribed tombs, one of them (KV56) yielding up a cache of gold jewelry identified with Seti II and the female pharaoh, Tausret.

Another of these anonymous sites (KV58) — a small single-chambered shaft tomb discovered for Davis by E. Harold Jones in January 1909 — contained a handsome uninscribed calcite ushabti and a small quantity of funerary debris,[2] including a collapsed box with numerous fragments of gold leaf bearing the names and figures of kings Tutankhamen and Ay, leading Davis prematurely to conclude (and publish) that he had, indeed, also found the thoroughly robbed tomb of the then-ephemeral third-to-last ruler of the Eighteenth Dynasty. In fact, this site is now believed — despite the presence within of Tutankhamen's name and image, and that of his queen, Ankhesenamen — to represent the caching of fragmentary funerary material which had been looted in antiquity from Ay's royal sepulcher (WV23) in the western branch of the Wadi Bibân el Molûk. The ushabti, in the post-Amarna style, also may have belonged to Ay, part of the suite of grave goods he had prepared as a private citizen prior to his elevation to the throne.[3]

Tutankhamen's presence in the Royal Valley had been indicated initially by Edward Ayrton's happenchance discovery in 1906, under a boulder near the Tomb of Amenhotep II, of a blue-green faience cup bearing the king's prenomen cartouche, no doubt hidden (and

Opposite, Detail of King Nebkheperure Tutankhamen from the golden throne found in the Antechamber of KV62.
Cairo Egyptian Museum

Colorized sketches by Georges Daressy of the engraved scenes & inscriptions on three of the several fragments of gold foil found by the Theodore Davis expedition in a shaft tomb numbered 58 in the Valley of the Kings. At right is a scene depicting the courtier Ay saluting King Nebkheper-ure Tutankhamen, who smites a captive & is saluted also by his queen, Ankhesenam-en. Below, that same royal couple are identified by their cartouches over the sign of Unity of the Two Lands motif. At bottom, Tutankhamen's prenomen & nom-en cartouches are flanked by crowned ur-aei. In part because of these fragments, Davis believed he had found the burial place of Tutankhamen (KV58), despite the fact that the image & cartouche of Ay as king also decorated gold-foil fragments from the same site. Davis, Harmhabi

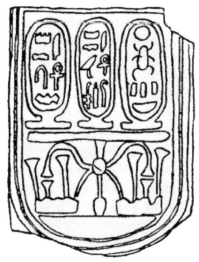

Objects not to relative scale

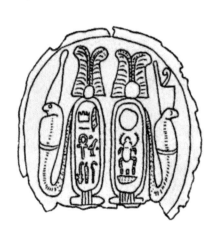

forgotten) by ancient robbers (see Book Three, this series, p. 126). Then on December 21, 1907,[4] the young English archaeologist — clearing limestone chippings from the *gebel* into which were hewn the long known tombs of Seti I and Rameses X — had come upon a roughly rectangular pit[5] cut in the bedrock to a depth of some four feet. From within this space Ayrton's workmen had recovered a quantity of large earthenware pots stuffed to their brims with miscellaneous fu-nerary debris, including stained odd fragments of linen bandaging, nu-merous shards of broken pottery, and several wreaths of dried flowers and leaves, plus reed brooms and some twenty small cloth bags con-taining a crystalline substance. One of the jars also produced a minia-ture gilded-cartonnage mask, of the type often employed to adorn mummified viscera when these were placed in their respective canopic jars.[6] Wrapped around the broken lid of another of the pottery vessels was a cloth head scarf inscribed with the prenomen of Tutankhamen (or as Davis wrote, *"Touatânkhamanou"*) and the reign date of Year 6.

Thus, with the subsequent January 1909 discovery by Jones of shaft tomb KV58 and its Tutankhamen/Ankhesenamen/Ay-inscribed pieces of gold foil, the American dilettante excavator quickly jumped to the conclusion — as was his habit — that this earlier mate-rial (and the Nebkheperure-inscribed small faience cup found stashed under a boulder in 1906) represented all that remained of the funerary furnishings of the second successor to the Heretic, Akhenaten. These items, Davis was certain, had been removed from the little known king's anciently plundered Tomb 58. Thus he was satisfied that he had, indeed, discovered the last royal burial that was to be found in the Wadi Bibân el Molûk, and so pronounced the latter *"exhausted."*

The KV54 jars and their motley contents had been taken to Davis House in the Western Valley and placed in the storage maga-zine there. They were of no intrinsic value to the treasure-hunting am-ateur digger[7] and the next year (at the urging of Harold Jones) he presented them to the Egyptian Expedition of the Metropolitan Mu-seum of Art. The New York group was newly arrived in Luxor, to com-mence work on their concession at Deir el Bahari — which the

Americans were taking over from the British (who had been excavating and restoring that site since the 1890s). Expedition director Herbert E. Winlock graciously accepted Davis's castoffs and shipped the large vessels (several three feet high, with eighteen-inch-wide openings) and their contents back to New York. There in the Museum, each pot was emptied and the various extracted objects examined and dutifully catalogued; and the lot was placed in storage as part of the institution's growing reserve collection of Egyptian artifacts.

It was not until some fifteen years later (1923[8]), after the MMA Egyptian Expedition had found similar — if smaller — vessels with like contents in its own excavations at Deir el Bahari, that Winlock fully realized exactly what it was that the Metropolitan had been gifted with by Davis. The linen head scarf with the Year 6 inscription and Tutankhamen's prenomen (Nebkheperure) already had received a certain amount of scholarly attention, for recording the highest known reign date of Akhenaten's second successor. Now Winlock recognized that the miscellaneous soiled rags deposited in the pots, along with the numerous small bags (which had been found to contain the carbonate-salt material called natron — used as the desiccant in ancient Egyptian embalming), were the refuse left over from the mummification of Tutankhamen. And the American readily concluded that the broken pottery which had filled many of the vessels (some of which subsequently had been pieced back together by Museum conservators to form numerous small dishes, plates and cups, a decanter and several other largish jars of the type used to ferment and store wine and beer) — plus accompanying bits of beef, mutton, fowl and game-bird bones — were the non-consumable garbage from a tomb-site funerary banquet. And there were, as well, the collars of dried leaves and flowers — those few that survived Davis's after-dinner feats of strength[9] — which had been worn by the mourners at said feast, whom Winlock estimated at eight individuals. It was his determination that the Metropolitan's jars contained

Above, Inked inscription on a fringed linen head scarf which sealed one of the many large ceramic jars discovered in the Valley of the Kings by the Davis expedition in 1907. It bears the prenomen (Nebkheperure) of Tutankhamen & the date, Year 6 of the king's reign.

Objects not to relative scale

In December 1907 Edward Ayrton discovered a shallow pit in the Royal Valley, which housed a number of large white pottery storage jars identified with Tutankhamen. These were found to contain a mish-mash of embalming & funerary debris, including floral-&-leaf collars (one at upper right), cloth bags of natron (three, right center) & numerous other broken ceramic vessels (one, right bottom). Theodore Davis — for whom Ayrton was excavating when the find was made — was certain that these materials were all that remained of the grave furnishings from the anciently plundered Tomb 58 in the Valley, which he was convinced had once been the burial place of the then-little-known Tutankhamen. Winlock, Materials/Tut-ankh-Amun

The miniature (15.0 cm. high) painted cartonnage funerary mask, above, was published by Herbert Winlock as having been found in one of the large pottery jars containing materials used in the embalming of King Tutankhamen — as well as debris from the funeral feast attending his interment in the Valley of the Kings — which had been given to the Metropolitan Museum of Art Egyptian Expedition by Theodore M. Davis in 1909. Winlock, Materials/ Tutankh-Amun *Although certainly of the type found in association with canopic viscera bundles, the mask is very unlike anything else associated with the Tutankhamen funerary goods. In all probability Davis substituted it for the miniature gilded-cartonnage mask, above right, which he retained for himself & today is exhibited in the Cairo Egyptian Museum — sharing a vitrine with with his motley finds from KV55, although it certainly does not belong with these. This gilded mask does, however, relate quite nicely to the coffin equipage accompanying the two fetal mummies that Carter would discover in Tutankhamen's tomb, one of which was without a funerary mask.* Intert photo

Opposite & inset, Twenty-two-year-old Howard Carter (1896), when he was employed as an artist & epigrapher at Deir el Bahari, under the direction of Swiss Egyptologist Edouard Naville.
Egypt Exploration Society photos & Author's graphic

what had been cleaned up after those who buried Tutankhamen had departed his tomb, these vessels then having been disposed of by the necropolis priests — along with what remained from the king's embalming — in the rough Valley pit later numbered KV54.

By the time Winlock reached his conclusions, however, it was well-known that Davis's KV58 indeed was not the burial place of Tutankhamen, for that site had been discovered, finally, just a few months earlier — at the end of 1922 — by another excavator, one of Davis's first archaeologists, the Englishman Howard Carter. Carter had been doggedly searching the New Kingdom royal necropolis for Tutankhamen's tomb since 1917, working on behalf of his archaeological patron of more than a dozen years, George Edward Stanhope Molyneux Herbert, the fifth Earl of Carnarvon. That titled Englishman's concession to excavate in the Valley of the Kings had succeeded Davis's in 1914, granting him exclusive digging rights there for a decade. Alas, Davis himself had died at his home in Florida on February 23, 1915, thus never knowing that his published claims three years earlier — to have found Tutankhamen's tomb and so *"exhausted"* the Royal Valley — were mistaken in the extreme.

It will be remembered that it was a young Howard Carter who, as the Antiquities Service's chief inspector for Upper Egypt, had dug for Theodore Davis in the Wadi Bibân el Molûk during the winter seasons from late 1901 through early 1904, finding for him the plundered Tomb of Thutmose IV (KV43) and clearing the already-known but debris-filled Tomb of Hatshepsut (KV20). Carter had first gone to

10

Above left, Framed photo-portrait of George Edward Stanhope Molyneux Herbert, the fifth Earl of Carnarvon, as a younger man.
Highclere Castle

Above right, Arthur Weigall's caricature sketch of a down-&-out Howard Carter, ca. 1909, when he was living in Luxor & eking out a living painting watercolors to sell to tourists, prior to eventually finding employment as the Lord of Carnarvon's archaeologist. Arthur Weigall Archive

Egypt as a teenage artist for the Egypt Exploration Fund (1893-1899), working in turn with Flinders Petrie, Lord Amherst and, finally, Edouard Naville at Deir el Bahari.

After five years at Luxor, working with Davis, Carter was then transferred by Service director-general, Gaston Maspero, from Luxor to Sakkara in the autumn of 1904, exchanging places with James E. Quibell as chief inspector for Lower Egypt. Soon thereafter, however, in January 1905, he became involved in an unfortunate personal confrontation with a group of drunken French tourists, which was to become known in the annals of Egyptology as the Sakkara Affair.[10] Because the strong-willed Carter absolutely refused to apologize or otherwise to express any regrets at all to the French for what he considered fully proper conduct on his part,[11] Maspero was instructed by his own governmental superiors (Sir William Garstin and Lord Cromer, apparently) to reprimand the stubborn young Englishman by relieving him of his important Sakkara post and sending him to Tanta in the Delta: a demotion, as Tanta was definitely a backwater assignment.

Depressed and humiliated, Carter requested a three-month leave of absence from the Service, which Maspero readily granted him. He ultimately undertook his new post in the Delta; but on October 21, 1905, a still-disgruntled Carter tendered his resignation from the Antiquities Service and left its employment, never to return.

He traveled south to Luxor, took up residence there and began a most-uncertain career as a watercolorist, selling his views (chiefly of Deir el Bahari) to tourists and sympathetic friends. He did receive a few professional — though hardly lucrative — illustration commissions,[12] most significantly from his old employer, Theodore M.

Davis (to render several of the more spectacular objects recently found [1905] in the Tomb of Yuya and Thuyu, for the American's 1907 publication of KV46[13]). Carter also stooped to offer his services as a tourist guide.[14] It seemed as if his personal fortunes had fallen as far as they could. And they had. In 1908 fate intervened in Carter's life in the person of an aristocratic fellow countryman, one Lord Carnarvon, who just then very much needed the assistance of a man with exactly the young archaeologist's well-established Egyptological qualifications.

Born at the family estate, Highclere Castle, Hampshire, England, in 1866, George Herbert had succeeded his father as the fifth Earl of Carnarvon in 1890. His inherited fortune was immense, and the young nobleman had occupied his youth chiefly with racing horses and exhibiting some recklessness as an "automobilist." But in 1901, at age thirty-five, he nearly lost his life in a motoring accident in Germany, and was left semi-invalid as a consequence. As part of the regimen to recover his health, the earl visited Egypt in the winter of 1903. There a dormant interest in archaeology was rekindled, and George Herbert embarked on a series of excavations which would fully occupy his winter months for the better part of the next two decades, and the

During his second season excavating in the New Kingdom necropolis of Waset (Thebes/Luxor), the Earl of Carnarvon had the good luck to discover the tomb (numbered TT15) of an early Eighteenth Dynasty mayor of that city, a man named Tetiky. Among the painted scenes decorating its walls was the earliest known depiction (left) of the famous Great Wife Ahmes-Nefertari, mother of Amenhotep I. The chief object recovered from the tomb was a handsome limestone offering table (above). Carnarvon, Five Years

Carnarvon's 1908 discoveries in Tomb 9 in the Birabi included several large, lidded storage jars (one below); the earliest examples of canopics with stoppers fashioned as the heads of the Sons of Horus (bottom right); & a writing board (above) with an historically important inscription relating to the Hyksos. Carnarvon, *Five Years*

rest of his life.

Lord Carnarvon's first dig was undertaken in 1906 at a site allotted him by Gaston Maspero, at the top of the hill called Sheikh Abd el Qurna in the Theban necropolis on the west bank at Luxor. After six weeks of *"day in and day out"* envelopment in *"clouds of dust,"* the English nobleman — who *"knew nothing whatever about excavating"* — succeeded in uncovering only a rather unusual large feline-form wooden coffin containing a mummified cat. Rather than being *"disheartened"* by his lack of much success, Carnarvon found himself *"keener than ever"* regarding his new activity.[15]

For his second season of digging, during the winter of 1907-1908, Carnarvon's concession was expanded by Maspero to include all of the area from Sheikh Abd el Qurna across the Asasif area to the hillside of Dra Abu el Naga. This produced greater results for the earl than he might have hoped for: he discovered the well-decorated tomb of an early Eighteenth Dynasty mayor of Thebes, one Tetiky, which was found to contain important wall paintings dating to the first years of the New Kingdom, including the earliest known contemporary

depiction of the celebrated Ahmes-Nefertari, queen of Ahmose I and mother of Amenhotep I. In addition to a quantity of model coffins of wood and clay containing crude *ushabti* figures, the Tomb of Tetiky (TT15) also yielded up a handsome limestone offering table belonging to the mayor.

Carnarvon's workmen found another tomb — which was dated to the late Second Intermediate Period — during that 1907-1908 season, at a site in the Asasif called Birabi, one numbered 9 in the excavation records. Therein were several large painted red-ware pottery storage jars with conical lids; the earliest examples of canopic jars with stoppers in the form of the heads of the Sons of Horus; and, most importantly, two wooden writing boards (later dubbed "Carnarvon Tablet I" and "II"), the first of which bore a historically very important lengthy hieratic inscription relating to late Seventeenth Dynasty Wasetan King Kamose's struggle to drive the Hyksos foreign rulers out of their strongholds in northern Egypt.[16]

These several discoveries were impressive, indeed; but the astute English earl realized that he was out of his personal depth, archaeologically, and that he needed *"a learned man"* to assist him in dealing with any future such discoveries as those he had just made. Carnarvon turned to Maspero for expert help, and the Frenchman quickly recommended Howard Carter to him. Presumably the Antiquities Service director-general was delighted in having a pretext to entice his former protege back into archaeological activity, if perhaps only temporarily.[17]

It seems that Carter and Carnarvon hit it off at the very outset of their professional association. Simply enough, these disparate men needed each other at that particular juncture in their respective lives. The earl offered the nearly destitute Carter fully gainful employment at what he was well-experienced doing, enabling him to make a dignified return to his former profession; and the full-time services of a field-trained excavator allowed the amateur archaeologist to continue pursuing his new hobby, without the necessity of personally having to

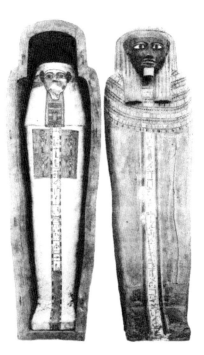

Carter & Carnarvon began excavating together during the winter season of 1909-1910, in the latter's concession in the Wasetan necropolis, specifically the area at the mouth of the bay at Deir el Bahari. On the slope of the northern hill there they located an intact tomb, No. 5, which dated to the Third Intermediate Period & contained the coffined burials of eight adults & one child. Three of the coffins were well-decorated, one of which is seen at left in situ. Another of these (above) dated to the Twenty-second Dynasty & housed the mummy of a male named Padeamen.

Carnarvon, *Five Years*

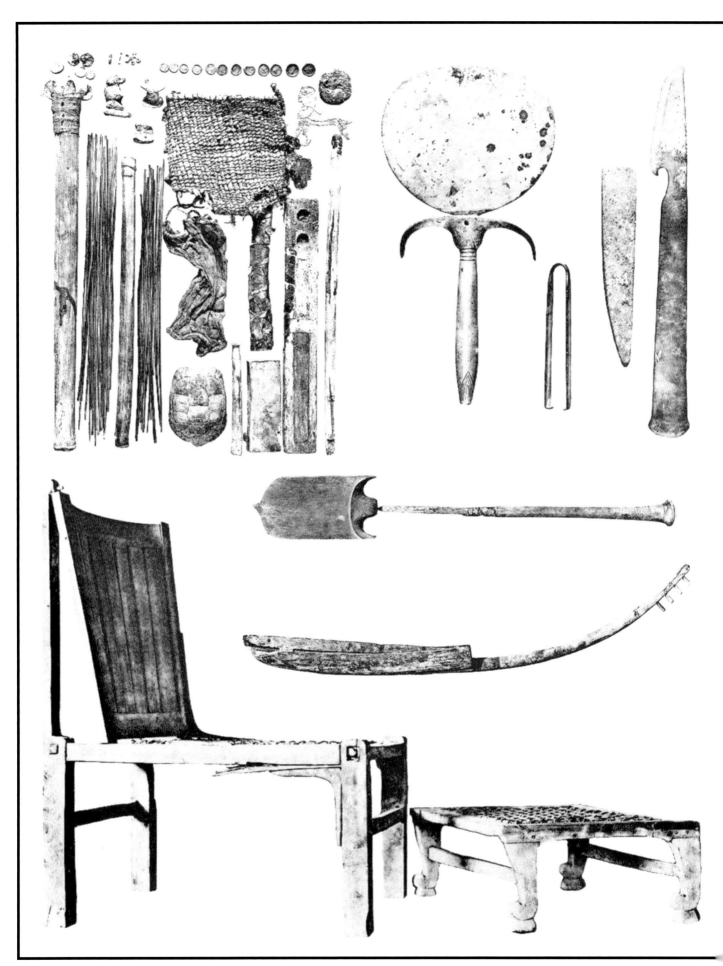

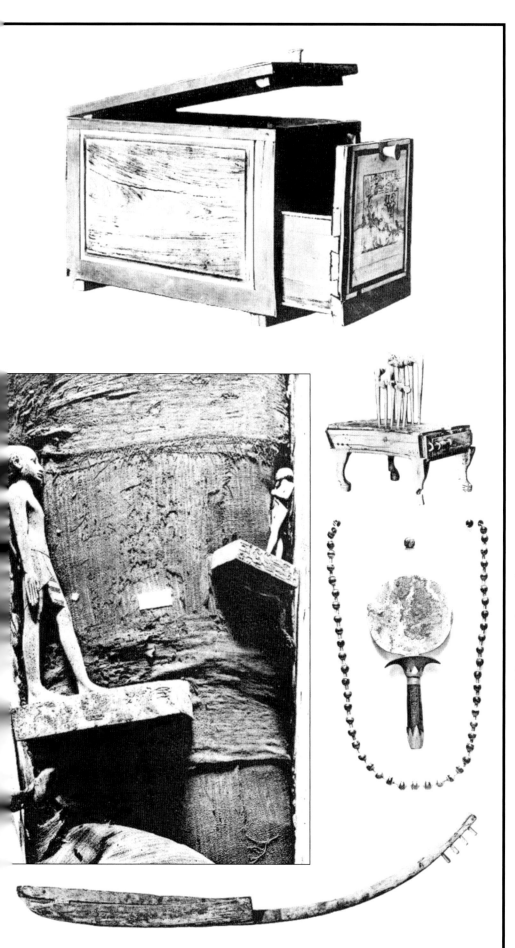

During the winter season of 1909-1910, Carter & Carnarvon excavated in the latter's concession at the mouth of the bay of Deir el Bahari & the immediately adjoining area known as the Birabi, clearing several undisturbed tombs which dated to the Middle Kingdom & the Second Intermediate Period. Objects of note which they discovered include (clockwise from top left): a scribal kit; a bronze shaving set consisting of mirror, razors & tweezers; a wooden toiletries box decorated with the image & name of Amenemhat IV; an especially attractive ivory game board with playing pieces; from Twelfth Dynasty Tomb 25; a gold-&-obsidian necklace & a bronze mirror with gold-inlaid ebony handle; a four-stringed wooden musical instrument; wooden & copper statuettes of two brothers, seen here in situ *with a mummy in the coffin where they were found; a wooden fan stock & handle; wooden headrests; & a wooden chair & accompanying stool.*

Carnarvon, *Five Years*

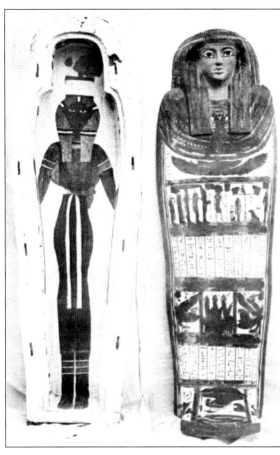

Above, Coffin (lid & basin) of the Lady Irtyru from Tomb 5 at Deir el Bahari, excavated by Carter & Carnarvon during the 1909-1910 season. Of Third Intermediate Period date, it is the finest of the three coffins from the tomb, shared by Irtyru with her husband, Pedikhons, & their son Pedeamen. The basin interior is dominated by a full-face large figure of the goddess Nut. Carnarvon, Five Years

Right, Remains of a rishi-*style found in Tomb 32 of the Second Intermediate Period necropolis at Waset, excavated by Carnarvon & Carter in 1910. When first discovered, the coffin — the finest they had found up until then — appeared in perfect condition; but, when touched, it fell into pieces, & the mummy inside proved to be so badly deteriorated that it could not be saved.* Carnarvon, Five Years

toil *"in clouds of dust."*

    As Winifred, Lady Burghclere, would write years later regarding the association of her brother and Carter: *"Sir Gaston Maspero's advice proved even more fruitful than Lord Carnarvon anticipated. In Mr. Howard Carter Carnarvon obtained the collaboration not only of a learned expert, an archaeologist gifted with imagination...but that of a true friend.... The two men worked together with varying fortune, yet ever united not more by their common aim than by their mutual regard and affection."*[18]

    For the next five winter-seasons (through 1913), Carter and Carnarvon labored in the latter's concession northeast of the mouth of the Deir el Bahari bay, and they enjoyed continuous successes. During 1909-1910 they discovered, halfway down the slope of the northern hill of Deir el Bahari, what would come to be numbered as Tomb 5, and which contained the undisturbed burials of eight adults and one child dating to the Third Intermediate Period; three of the coffins were well-decorated. In 1909 the pair had located in the Birabi what proved to be the unfinished valley temple of Hatshepsut, vaulted-brick tombs of Ptolemaic date and, beneath these, traces of a mortuary temple begun by Rameses IV, but never finished. Under the Hatshepsut foundations, the earl and his archaeologist discovered a series of rock-cut tombs which dated originally to the Middle Kingdom, some of these having been reused in the Second Intermediate Period and the early Eighteenth Dynasty. Many of the burials were intact and yielded a quantity of *rishi*-style coffins and other grave goods of the period.

    One of these Birabi tombs, No. 25, could be dated to the reign of Amenemhat IV of the late Twelfth Dynasty, judging from an intact toiletries box bearing that king's name and image. From the same much-decayed burial came a handsome gold-and-obsidian necklace; a bronze mirror with a gold-inlaid ebony handle; a blue-faience hippopotamus; a gold-and-carnelian amulet; a particularly fine ivory Hounds and Jackals game board and playing pieces; small calcite vases

Lord Carnarvon & his dog at the site of the excavation of rock-cut tombs underneath the foundations of the Valley Temple of Hatshepsut in the Birabi. Activity there took up most of the earl's & Howard Carter's time during the 1910-1914 seasons.
Photo: Griffith Institute

belonging to the toiletries box; and assorted pottery.

The largest and richest tomb found by Carter and Carnarvon in the Birabi was numbered 37 in their sequence. Originally of Middle Kingdom date, it proved to have been reused in the early Eighteenth Dynasty for a cached reinterment of mostly late Second Intermediate burials: *rishi*-type anthropoid coffins in large part, but also rectangular and other varieties of coffins from very early in the New Kingdom. Among the accompanying grave goods were: a shaving set (mirror, razors, tweezers, etc.), dated by associated scarabs to the reign of Amenhotep I; numerous wooden headrests; statuettes of two brothers, one copper, one wood, found together in the same coffin; an intact wooden chair and companion stool; three wooden musical instruments; a wooden fan stock; a scribal kit; toiletry articles; a mechanical toy bird and a bird trap; bead necklaces, bangles and bracelets; numerous scarabs, cowroids and rings; painted wood-panel stelae; writing tablets; and a wide assortment of basketry and ceramic vessels.

In 1912 Carnarvon and Carter jointly published the results of the earl's initial excavations alone and of their subsequent seasons working together, as *Five Years' Exploration at Thebes: A Record of Work Done, 1907-1911*. This is a well-illustrated (eighty plates[19]), fully scientific report, certainly equal to anything being produced in Egyptological literature at the time, and contains scholarly contributions from several of Carter's specialist colleagues: Percy E. Newberry, Georges Legrain, Frank Lloyd Griffith, William Spiegelberg and George Möller. The earl and his excavator continued digging in the Asasif through 1913 and made a few additional interesting discoveries (e.g., tombs 41, 63 and 64); but, regrettably, these finds would never be fully committed to print.

By 1912 the two Englishmen began to grow weary with their *"explorations"* on the Luxor west bank; and it was decided to diversify by extending their operations north to the Delta, which Carter thought might yield promising results. The site he and Carnarvon chose was Sakha, the location of Xoïs of the Graeco-Roman Period. Although they appear to have begun excavating there in March of 1912, they shortly abandoned their efforts, due to the area's heavy infestation with cobras and horned vipers.[20] Whatever Carter and Carnarvon may have found before quitting the site was never published.

Although no doubt disappointed with their wasted effort at Sakha, the pair spent a short second season — spring 1913 — in the Delta, this time at the "Red Mound," Tell el Ahmar, also known as Tell el Balamen, the location of an ancient settlement.[21] The ground there, however, proved extremely difficult to dig; the results of their excavations — in terms of objects found — were, at best, modest and mostly of Graeco-Roman date, consisting of a sculptural fragment, scarabs, amulets, plaques, coins and a pottery jar with a hoard of base-silver jewelry. Carter did succeed in revealing at the water-table level the enclosure wall of a large structure, which he thought was probably a palace or temple.[22] But architectural remains were not what Carnarvon was looking for, nor Carter, for that matter. The earl apparently quickly

The fifth Earl of Carnarvon in a monochrome portrait painted about 1920 by Howard Carter's elder brother, William. "Lordy," as George Herbert was known to the Egyptians, would have been in his early fifties at this time.
Photo: Highclere Castle, Carnarvon Archive

Opposite, Portrait of Howard Carter, painted by William Carter in 1924, when the English archaeologist was 50 years old & at the very height of his professional career. Collection of the Griffith Institute

One of Howard Carter's services to his patron, Carnarvon, was acting as advisor & agent in the purchase of antiquities from dealers in Egypt, for the earl's growing collection at Highclere Castle in England. Among the objects he acquired were three bracelet plaques, above, without provenance but possibly WV22, the Amenhotep III tomb. Carnarvon bequeathed them to the Metropolitan Museum of Art in New York. Authenticity of the Tiye-as-Sphinx plaque has been questioned in recent years. Photos: MMA

lost interest in the unrewarding activity at Balamen and returned to England, to be kept appraised of Carter's meager progress by post.

It should not be surprising that George Herbert, Earl of Carnarvon, was financing archaeological activity in Egypt during the years immediately prior to World War I largely in expectation of finding "objects." While his and Carter's excavations — particularly at Luxor — had so far made contributions to the overall knowledge about Egypt in antiquity, Carnarvon's personal rewards for his considerable expenditures excavating were in the ancient artifacts found in his name, especially those objects of *"beauty and historic interest."*[23] The earl was a collector, after all, and his "share" from the official division (with the Egyptian government, i.e., the Cairo Egyptian Museum) of the finer things found in his concessions was happily added to the growing Egyptian assemblage housed at Highclere Castle.

Agent for the collector was another aspect of Carter's relationship with Carnarvon. In those pre-war years it was still possible legally to purchase Egyptian antiquities in the *suks* of Cairo and Luxor. Competition among European and American collectors (private and institutional) for genuine pieces of high quality was keen; and it was as Carnarvon's expert advisor and purchasing agent in the acquisition of such objects that Carter proved his value beyond those skills he possessed as an excavator. During the fifteen years of their association, Carter judiciously scouted the local antiquities shops and private dealers, made recommendations to Carnarvon, and then bought those pieces which the lord of Highclere Castle wanted for his accumulating collection back home in Hampshire. In fact, George Herbert found it lucrative to engage in occasional antiquities dealing himself, purchasing objects and, in turn, reselling them to fellow collectors *"at a handsome profit."*[24] Besides acting as Carnarvon's antiquities buyer in Egypt, Carter found himself — during the summers back in England — engaged in the capacity as curator of the Highclere collection, meticulously recording the earl's acquisitions and arranging their display; this was a job which the archaeologist apparently took very seriously, producing catalogue volumes in his neat handwriting and fully illustrating them with careful drawings of the objects and their inscriptions.

Following the largely unrewarding spring 1913 campaign at Balamen, Carter joined Carnarvon at Highclere and spent the summer months engaged in his curatorial activities. That autumn he returned to Luxor and "Castle Carter," the commodious domed mudbrick excavation house which the archaeologist had built (with Carnarvon's financing) in 1910, on a low desert rise (Elwat el Diban) at the northern end of Dra Abu el Naga, overlooking the road leading to the entrance to the Valley of the Kings. There he planned his patron's excavation program for the 1913-1914 winter campaign.

Carnarvon had decided to finance one more season probing the sands of the Asasif, which Carter undertook without much enthusiasm and only minor results. At the end of 1913, the Carnarvon concession to the Luxor west bank was relinquished to the Metropolitan Museum Egyptian Expedition, Carter even turning over to the Expedition's director, Ambrose Lansing, his rough reports on the Carnarvon-sponsored work there since 1911. But what next?

In 1912 Carter had been shown — by a local tomb robber — the site of a previously unknown, isolated, empty, large, seemingly royal, undecorated shaft tomb, hidden under a rock behind the ridge of Dra Abu el Naga. It was, on investigation, of the early Eighteenth Dynasty in type; and — because of the associated calcite funerary-jar fragments bearing cartouches of Queen-Mother Ahmes-Nefertari and her son, Amenhotep I, which the excavator had been shown by the tomb robber — Carter was convinced he had chanced upon the burial place of the great ancestress of the New Kingdom, which perhaps she had shared with her son. And now he was determined to clear it thoroughly on Lord Carnarvon's behalf. Which he did during the winter of early 1914. The result was a collection of the rubbish left behind by ancient robbers: fragments of vessels and funerary statuettes in a variety of stones, from which fifty-four individual pieces could be partially reconstructed or otherwise recognized, with several of these bearing the cartouches of Ahmose I; his queen, Ahmes-Nefertari; their son, Amenhotep I; and even a Hyksos king, Apepi, and his daughter, Herath. Historically interesting, to be sure, but not much for the showcases at Highclere.[25]

It was the early summer of 1914, June, that the situation at Luxor changed in a most significant way for the Carnarvon-Carter team. After two relatively unrewarding final seasons there, the seriously ill Theodore Davis gave up his long-time exclusive concession to excavate in the Wadi Bibân el Molûk, and the site was immediately awarded to Lord Carnarvon, who had requested it, but whose initial enthusiasm for the much picked-over New Kingdom royal necropolis may have been something less than Carter's own. Despite Davis's already published assertion that the Valley of the Kings was now *"exhausted"* — an opinion apparently shared by the-soon-to-retire Gaston Maspero in Cairo — Carter held to the view that at least one more kingly sepulcher still waited to be discovered: Tutankhamen's! He was not convinced that Edward Ayrton's and Harold Jones's Nebkheperure-related finds for Davis — the faience cup, the KV54 funerary cache and the meager gold-foil scraps of shaft tomb KV58[26] — proved that king's final resting place already was discovered. Carter believed that the Tomb of Tutankhamen had been missed in turn by Belzoni, Burton, Loret and Davis; and he presumably persuaded his aristocratic patron to the same optimistic viewpoint. The excavator would later recall, *"With all of this evidence before us we were thoroughly convinced in our own minds that the tomb of Tut·ankh·Amen was still to find, and that it ought to be situated not far from the centre of the valley. In any case, whether we found Tut·ankh·Amen or not, we felt that a systematic and exhaustive search of the inner valley presented reasonable chances of success...."*[27]

Carnarvon and Carter were in the process of laying out tactics for an elaborate campaign in the Royal Valley, to commence that winter (1914), when fate intervened with the outbreak in August of World War I. All plans to begin their exhaustive search for Tut-ankhamen *"had to be left in abeyance,"*[28] as British excavation activity in Egypt came to a halt for the time being — although at the outset of the war there was optimism that hostilities would be over by Christmas, 1914.

It was not a question of excavator or earl volunteering for war service (they were respectively forty and forty-eight years old); so, sometime that autumn, Carter returned to Egypt and Luxor. Anxious to activate his patron's Kings' Valley concession, he decided to make a scientific clearance of the long-known Tomb of Amenhotep III (WV22) in the western branch of the royal necropolis — which had been found by Napoleon's Egyptian expedition in the final year of the Eighteenth Century.[29] It is not clear under what authority Carter operated at this time, for there is some question as to whether Carnarvon's Wadi Bibân el Molûk concession also included the Valley's western portion.[30] In any case on February 8, 1915, Carter began his clearance work in WV22, concluding exactly one month later. In the course of this activity, he found the tomb's foundation deposits[31] and a quantity of funerary fragments from the monument's thoroughly decorated but badly damaged interior. Although he later claimed to have made *"a complete clearance"* of Amenhotep III's sepulcher,[32] further clearance and conservation work in WV22 by a Japanese expedition from Waseda University in the 1990s has shown that Carter actually excavated the tomb's rubbish only as far as the well shaft and its associated chamber. Whether some sort of Antiquities Service temporary permit had limited his access to the West Valley to only one month is not known. Certainly he never returned there on Carnarvon's behalf.

By early summer of 1915, Carter was in Cairo and attached to the Intelligence Department of the War Office there, although in a civilian capacity rather than a military one. The exact nature of his work at this time is something of a mystery, and by the following October he was on Department leave and back in Luxor, *"well occupied with drawing and painting."*[33] As his biographer, T.G.H. James, has written, *"The few indications of his war-work suggest that it was intermittent and undemanding. It gave him the opportunity to slip down to Luxor, often for extended periods, to potter around archaeologically, to do a little excavation, to paint, and to keep an eye on what was turning up in the antiquities dealers' shops."*[34]

The next year, 1916, while in Luxor on another of his holidays away from *"war-work"* activities in Cairo, Carter became involved in one of the more romantic exploits of Twentieth Century Egyptology. Having been alerted by locals that a tomb was in the process of being robbed in a remote wadi west of the Theban hills, Carter was led there at night, shinnied down the sheer cliff face on a dangling rope, apprehended and routed the gang of thieves at work, and, by so doing, discovered the unused, rubbish-filled cliff tomb which had been made for Hatshepsut when she was the Great Royal Wife of Thutmose II. Carter subsequently spent twenty days clearing the almost inacces-

sible site, the only "treasure" it contained being the queen's unfinished red-quartzite sarcophagus.[35]

Finally, in the autumn of 1917, Carter's serious activity in Carnarvon's Wadi Bibân el Molûk concession got under way. He wrote, *"The difficulty was to know where to begin, for mountains of rubbish thrown out by previous excavators encumbered the ground in all directions, and no sort of record had ever been kept as to which areas had been properly excavated and which had not. Clearly the only satisfactory thing to do was to dig systematically right down to the bedrock, and I suggested to Lord Carnarvon that we take as a starting-point the triangle of ground defined by the tombs of Rameses II, Mer·en·Ptah, and Rameses VI. The area in which we hoped the tomb of Tut·ankh·Amen might be situated."* [36]

Thus the digging commenced and during the 1917-1918 winter season a considerable expanse was exposed, *"right up to the foot of the tomb of Rameses VI,"* [37] where Carter's workers uncovered the rough remains of a series of ancient tomb-masons' huts sitting atop a mass of quarried limestone chips, indicating to the excavator that the area beneath these crude structures had not been disturbed since the Twentieth Dynasty, and very well might conceal a tomb cut in the bedrock; such a tomb obviously would antedate the nearby monument of Rameses VI. Again, Carter: *"Our natural impulse was to enlarge our clearing in this direction, but by doing this we should have cut off*

One of the badly damaged & recently conserved wall paintings of the Tomb of Amenhotep III, WV22. Discovered in 1799 by the Napoleonic expedition, this large sepulcher in the western branch of the Valley of the Kings had been explored by earlier archaeologists; but Howard Carter decided in 1915 to activate Lord Carnarvon's newly acquired concession to the Kings' Valley by conducting a "full clearance" of the tomb's many chambers, most of which were encumbered with a great deal of rubble & funerary debris. In fact, in his one month of work in the tomb, Carter cleared only as far as the monument's well shaft. He did, however, locate WV22's foundation deposits, which revealed that the tomb had been begun by Thutmose IV, who abandoned it for whatever reason in favor of a site in the main wadi, KV43, which Carter had found for Theodore M. Davis in 1903. George B. Johnson photo

Location of the cliff tomb of Queen Hat-shepsut is indicated by the long oval left of center of t he photographopposite. Led to this spot one night in 1916, Howard Carter rappelled down a rope & routed a gang of tomb robbers at work. He subsequently spent twenty days clearing the unused tomb of debris; the only object of importance it contained was the queen's red-quartzite sarcophagus, below, which was later removed to the Cairo Egyptian Museum. Griffith Institute & Cairo Egyptian Museum

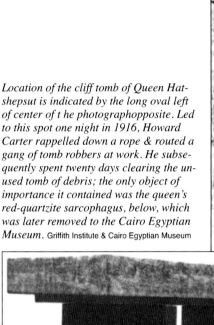

all access to the tomb of Rameses above, to visitors one of the most popular tombs in the whole Valley.[38] Therefore, the decision was made to abandon this spot for the time being and to shift clearance to the bedrock to another part of the delineated triangular area being searched. In any case, the winter season of 1917-1918 had come to a close on February 2nd.

The early months of 1918 saw a crisis in the Carnarvon-Carter association. The already-frail George Herbert nearly died in England that spring from a septic appendix. Additionally, the earl seemed to be growing impatient with Carter's determination to persist in the Valley of the Kings without results. The objects recovered in the first season of Carnarvon-financed activity there were truly minor in the earl's view, consisting mostly of *ostraca*, which were regarded as *"interesting but not exciting."*[39] Carnarvon instructed Carter to find him another Egyptian site, and ultimately they agreed to put in for El Amarna with the Antiquities Service. But Director-General Pierre Lacau — Maspero's successor — flatly turned down Carnarvon's application, stating that this choice site — which prior to outbreak of the war had been under systematic excavation by the Germans, with great successes — was being reserved for the Service itself, with Lacau adding, *"...if we are not able to take it up ourselves in the future, we should grant it to a scientific institution and not to a private individual."* [40] In a further blow to Carnarvon's ambitions as a private digger in Egypt, the Frenchman announced that divisions of objects discovered during excavation would no longer be fifty-fifty between excavator and the Egyptian Museum in Cairo, but rather *partage* thence- forth could require an excavator — private or institutional — to cede to the Museum *everything* found during a dig or clearance that the director-general of the Antiquities Service chose to claim for the national collection.

Carnarvon's bid for El Amarna was dropped. Writing to the earl convalescing at Highclere Castle in early June 1918, Carter recommended several other sites in Middle Egypt; and it was decided for him to undertake a short season at Meir that summer. This was subsequently postponed until the following December, when Carter spent six weeks working there (until January 15, 1919), with even poorer results than had been realized at Sakha and Balamen in the years before the war. Certainly, Carnarvon was less than pleased.

Pierre Lacau (1873-1963), above, was Gaston Maspero's hand-picked successor as director-general of the Egyptian Antiquities Service, following him in that post in 1914. Rather than continue his predecessor's rather liberal policies regarding foreign archaeological work in Egypt, Lacau established that everything found by institutions or private individuals in the course of an excavation could be claimed by the director-general for the collection of the Egyptian Museum in Cairo. Previously partage *("division") had been 50-50 between an excavator & the Museum.* Archival photo

Over the next two years, Carter returned repeatedly to his patron's concession in the Valley of the Kings, clearing hither and yon to the bedrock with only *"interesting but not very exciting"* results, the best of these — from Carnarvon's perspective — being a cache of thirteen large calcite jars found in February 1920 near the entrance to the Tomb of Merneptah (KV8) and bearing the cartouches of that king and his predecessor, Rameses II. Carter remembered that *"...we were naturally somewhat excited, and Lady Carnarvon...insisted on digging out the jars — beautiful specimens they were — with her own hands."* [41]

Without finding much else besides these jars — and some foundation deposits of Rameses IV near the entrance to his tomb (KV2), while breaking ground for a new dump site — Carter had now scoured all of the triangular area where he had been focusing his search for Tutankhamen on Carnarvon's behalf — except, of course, for those several square meters of limestone chips which lay immediately underneath the workmen's huts which had been exposed in the 1917-1918 season. It was decided once more to leave this particular section for a later time when, at the very beginning of an autumn season, it could be cleared to bedrock without inconveniencing visitors to the Tomb of Rameses VI only a few yards away. But even Carter was becoming discouraged with the prospect of finding Tutankhamen's tomb, as he would later write: *"We had now dug in The Valley for several seasons with extremely scanty results, and it became much debated whether we should continue the work or try for a more profitable site elsewhere. After all these barren years were we justified in going on*

Above, Howard Carter's photograph of a cache of 13 large calcite jars in situ, which he located in February 1920, in the Valley of the Kings, near the entrance to the Tomb of Merneptah (KV8); they bore the cartouches of that king & of his predecessor, Rameses II; & hieratic texts on some of the vessels indicated that the lot had originally held oils associated with the funeral of Merneptah. These "beautiful specimens" were the most significant objects found by Carter in his clearance to the bedrock of a triangular area delineated by the tombs of Rameses II, Merneptah & Rameses VI. An Egyptian workman squats by the jars to indicate their scale. Griffith Institute *Below, one of the Merneptah vessels, 35 cm. high, now in the collection of the British Museum.*

with it?" [42]

But go on they did. The next Carnarvon-financed Valley of the Kings activity began in the autumn of 1920, yet again without any investigation of the excavation debris under the workmen's huts. Instead, Carter shifted his clearance efforts to the narrow lateral wadi of the Valley which contained the Tomb of Thutmose III (KV34, found by Loret in 1898). While removing quarried rock chips there over the next two seasons, he came across the beginnings of a low-lying tomb, which Carter theorized originally had been intended for the great warrior-king himself, then abandoned in favor of the elevated cliff-face site at the head of the wadi. Nearby he also came across, in January 1921, foundation deposits belonging to Thutmose III's principal wife, Meritre-Hatshepsut, outside a tomb (KV42) which Carter had excavated in 1900. An historically interesting discovery, perhaps, but certainly not *"exciting."* [43]

One more season? That was the question to be resolved when — in the summer of 1922, shortly after returning to England following yet another unproductive search in the Royal Valley — Carter was summoned to Highclere Castle by his patron. Both earl and excavator dreaded this meeting, for it seems that Carnarvon had made up his mind to call it quits in their hunt for the elusive Tutankhamen; and Carter, for his own part, fully realized that his excavation record in the Valley of the Kings these past several seasons really warranted no other decision. After reviewing the history of their many years working together, and expressing his sincere appreciation for all of Carter's efforts in their joint archaeological endeavors, Herbert announced that, due to the harsh realities of the post-war economy, he would no longer be able to finance what had proved in recent years to be an almost fruitless undertaking.

That should have been it. But Carter — either impulsively, or with careful calculation, having fully anticipated Carnarvon's decision — made a bold proposal to his patron. He produced his map of the Valley with the triangular area of their clearance activity marked out, pointed to the smaller triangular section of a few square meters where the workmen's huts still sat, and said to the earl that until this last remaining bit of ground was also cleared to the bedrock he, personally, would not be satisfied they had truly accomplished what they had set out to do in the Wadi Bibân el Molûk eight years earlier. Thus, Carter stated that, with the earl's permission, he would like to undertake this clearance — one more season's work — at his own expense. If still nothing was found, then he would admit defeat and agree to abandon the Valley. But if, however, he should find something under the huts, that discovery would belong to Carnarvon, as had always been the situation in their relationship.

George Herbert was a sportsman at heart and Howard Carter's proposal appealed to him; except, of course, that the excavator was being far too generous. Yes, there would be one more season in the Valley of the Kings, but at Carnarvon's expense and not his archae-

During his 1917-1918 clearance to the bedrock of a triangular area of the Kings' Valley delineated by the tombs of Rameses II (KV7), Merneptah (KV8) & Rameses VI (KV9), Howard Carter had uncovered the remains of several roughly constructed workmen's huts near the entrance to the latter tomb, seen below. These rested on flakes of quarried limestone, which indicated that the surface beneath the huts had not been disturbed at least since the Twentieth Dynasty. Rather than remove the huts at that time, however, Carter shifted his clearance activities to another part of the designated area, so as not to interfere with access to KV9, one of the most popular tombs in the Valley with tourists. He would not return to this spot, remove the huts & discover what lay beneath them until November 1922. Griffith Institute

Carter's clearance (above) of quarried limestone chips to the bedrock in the relatively small area immediately below the Tomb of Rameses VI (KV9) finally got underway at the beginning of November 1922. This was the only unexplored area in a triangular section of the Royal Valley (as delineated by tombs KV7, KV8 & KV9) he & Carnarvon had been denuding of excavation debris over the preceding several seasons, in hopes of finding a royal tomb, more particularly that of the little known post-Heresy king, Tutankhamen. The site had been covered with the remains of crude stone huts used by workmen preparing KV9 in the mid Twentieth Dynasty. Griffith Institute

ologist's![44]

Once again in Luxor on October 27, 1922, Carter had with him a pet canary just purchased in Cairo. Five days later he began the task of excavating the small area at the northeast corner of the entrance to the Tomb of Rameses VI, where the crude boulder-built huts were situated, mostly still covered up by rock debris. When originally revealed by Carter's workmen a few years earlier, it had been determined that these rough constructions rested on a bed of limestone chips and soil that was about three feet deep. Trenching southward from the Ramesside tomb, by the evening of November 3rd Carter had fully exposed, planned and removed several of the huts, so that the bedrock finally could be laid bare, commencing the next morning.

He would write: *"Hardly had I arrived on the work... November 4th...than the unusual silence, due to the stoppage of the work, made me realize that something out of the ordinary had happened, and I was greeted by the announcement that a step cut in the bedrock had been discovered underneath the very first hut to be attacked. This seemed too good to be true, but a short amount of extra clearing revealed the fact that we were actually in the entrance of a steep cut in the rock, some thirteen feet below the entrance to the tomb of Rameses VI, and a similar depth from the present bed level of The Valley. The manner of cutting was that of the sunken stairway entrance so common in The Valley, and I almost dared to hope that we had found our tomb at last."*[45]

Throughout that day and the morning of the next, Carter's workmen cleared away the surrounding limestone rubble until the demarcations of a rock-cut rectangular stairwell were visible; and, as

Carter would recall, *"It was clear now beyond any question that we actually had before us the entrance to a tomb...*[although] *there was the horrible possibility...that* [it] *was an unfinished one, never completed and never used: if it had been finished there was the depressing probability that it had been completely plundered in ancient times."* [46] Carter ordered his men to begin clearing within the cutting, and step after step slowly came to light. The stairwell had been hewn into a hillock, and, as the fill debris was removed, the western edge receded under the slope of the rock, until it formed a roofed-in passage, finally proving to be six feet wide and ten feet high. At the level of the twelfth cleared step — towards the end of that November 5th workday — the lintel and then the upper part of a doorway were revealed. The latter was *"blocked, plastered, and sealed"* [47] and Carter was ecstatic: *"Our years of patient labour were to be rewarded after all, and I think my first feeling was one of congratulation that my faith in The Valley had not been unjustified."* [48]

The careful archaeologist examined the visible seal im-

The debris-filled cutting in the Valley of the Kings bedrock demarcating the rock-cut stairwell leading to the entrance of the Tomb of Tutankhamen. This photograph was published by Carter as how the stairwell looked when "first seen," *on November 5, 1922; but, because of the visible retaining wall above it, more likely the photo was taken subsequently, probably when the stairs were being cleared a second time, having been refilled with rubble in order to secure the tomb until Carnarvon's arrival in Egypt from England.* Griffith Institute

pressions in the plaster for evidence of who might be buried within the tomb; but he could find no name, only the jackal-and--prisoners stamp of the royal necropolis — indicating at least that the tomb had been made for a person of very high status. Had he cleared only a few inches further down the blocked doorway, Carter would have had his answer regarding the sepulcher's ownership. Instead his attention focused on the doorway's wooden lintel (revealed where some of the plaster had fallen away). He later wrote, *"Under this, to assure myself of the method by which the doorway had been blocked, I made a small peephole, just large enough to insert an electric torch, and discovered that the passage beyond the door was filled completely from floor to ceiling with stones and rubble.... It was a thrilling moment for an excavator. Alone, save for my native workmen, I found myself, after years of comparatively unproductive labour, on the threshold of what might prove to be a magnificent discovery. Anything, literally anything, might lie beyond that passage, and it needed all my self control to keep from breaking down the doorway and investigating then and there. ...It was late, however, and darkness was already upon us. With some reluctance, I re-closed the small hole I had made, filled in our excavation for protection during the night, selected the most trustworthy of my workmen...to watch all night above the tomb, and so home by moonlight, riding down The Valley."* [48]

Lord Carnarvon was in England, and Carter owed it to the earl to inform him immediately of the situation. Accordingly, on the

Upon Lord Carnarvon's arrival in Luxor, November 23, 1922, the tomb site Carter had found in the Valley of the Kings nearly three weeks earlier was reexposed & the rock-cut stairwell fully cleared, revealing a total of 16 steps (right) leading to a sealed doorway, the surface of which had been plastered over & stamped with numerous seal impressions. Griffith Institute

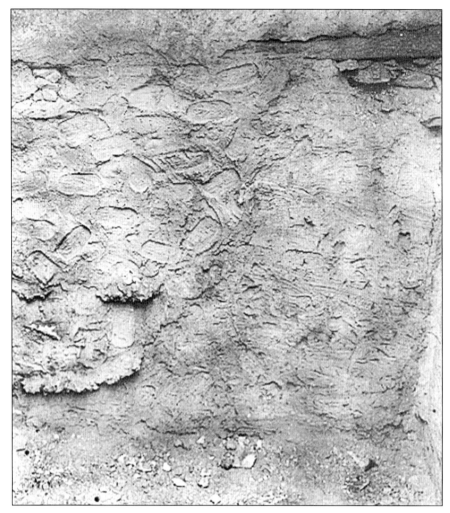

Left, The stamp-covered, mud-plastered sealed doorway at the bottom of the 16 rock-cut steps. Those at the top were of the royal necropolis (jackal-&-prisoners), whereas the ones covering the lower portion of the doorway bore the prenomen of Tutankhamen (Nebkheperure). Note the wooden lintel of the doorway at top right, exposed where the mud plaster had fallen away. Griffith Institute

morning of November 6th, he sent the following cable to Highclere Castle: *"At last have made wonderful discovery in Valley; a magnificent tomb with seals intact; recovered same for your arrival; congratulations."* [49] The excavator would have liked to determine immediately what was behind the sealed door and beyond the rubble-filled passage; but in fairness to his patron, he was forced to await Lord Carnarvon's arrival before proceeding further. To secure the site against interference, he had the excavation refilled to the surface level and then covered with the large boulders from which the workmen's huts had been built. Carter wrote, *"The tomb had vanished. So far as the appearance of the ground was concerned there never had been any tomb, and I found it hard to persuade myself at times that the whole episode had not been a dream."* [50]

Carnarvon arrived in Luxor on November 23rd, accompanied by his daughter, Lady Evelyn Herbert. By the afternoon of the next day, the tomb site had been recleared of the rubble fill and the stairwell fully excavated, revealing a total of sixteen rock-cut steps. With the entire plastered doorway exposed, Carter discovered to his and Carnarvon's delight the several stamped cartouches of Nebkheperure — Tutankhamen! But it was now also apparent that there had been two successive openings and reclosings of the upper part of the

It was apparent to the excavators that the upper part of the door had been reopened & closed again at least twice, indicating that the tomb probably had been plundered on two separate occasions following the king's interment. The stone-blocked robbers' tunnel is seen above. But the fact that it had then been twice resealed by the necropolis authorities held out the promise that something of value had been left behind by the tomb thieves.

Photos: Griffith Institute

Narration continues page 42.

The KV62
ANTECHAMBER
Southeast Corner, *In Situ*

Immediately to the left inside the outer-door of the Antechamber, on its long east wall, the excavators found leaning against one another several gilded wheels that had been anciently dismantled from a group of three gold-plated chariot bodies, which occupied the southeast corner of the room in a jumbled heap. Mixed in with the chariot parts are the disassembled pieces of a portable sunshade, a part of which may be recognized at right in the grided rectangular framework lying in front of the chariot bodies. Among the other objects deposited in this area are chariot yokes, half-a-dozen calcite vessels, basketry, numerous staves, a lidless wooden box painted white &, of course, a realistic, painted life-sized "mannequin" of the king.

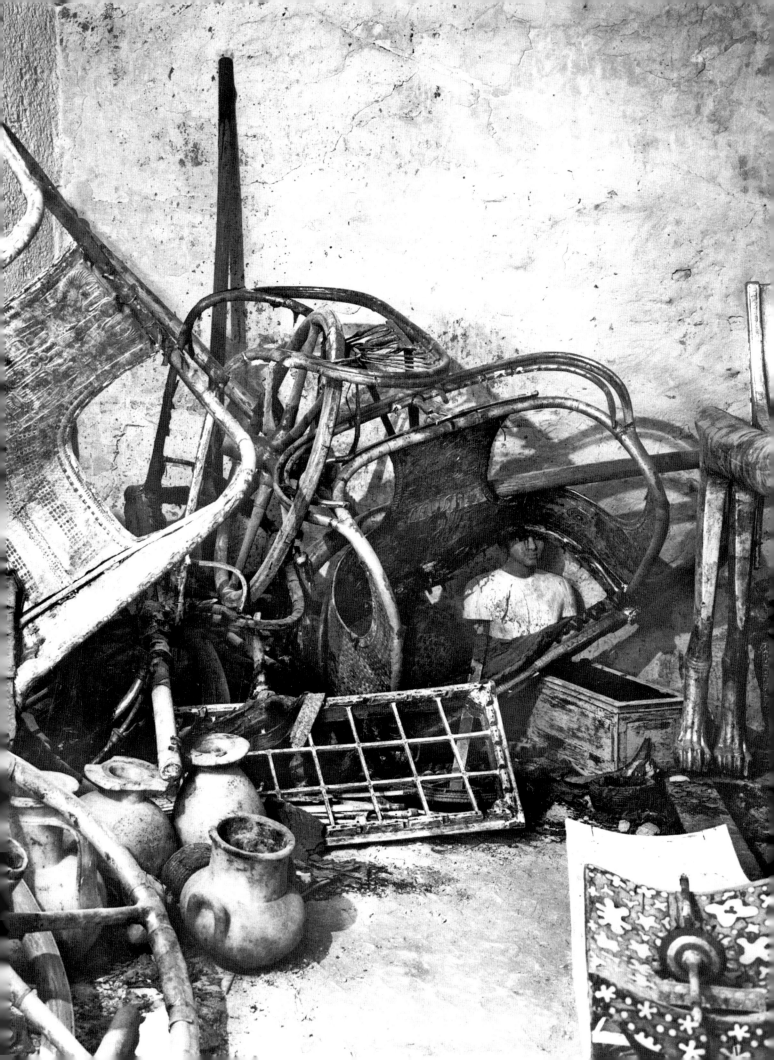

The KV62
ANTECHAMBER
Southwest Corner, *In Situ*

Dominating the long west wall of the Ante-chamber, the excavators found three massive zoomorphic ceremonial couches placed head to tail. The gilded one in the southwest corner, supporting a large black-&-white-painted linen chest, is an imaginary beast — combining hip-popotamus & lion features — which Carter called a "Thoueris" couch. Under this is situated the so-called Aten throne, gilded all over & inlaid with glass & semi-precious stones; on its seat rests a companion footstool. Also visible under the hippo-lion couch is a small gold-plated shrine, the doors wide open, its contents purloined by ancient robbers. Next to this, standing upright, is a large wooden ushabti figure of the king. Two stools are to be seen in the foreground; one, in imitation of a folding model, has its ebony seat inlaid with ivory, representing an animal skin; the stool's feet terminate in duck heads. Metropolitan Museum of Art

The KV62
ANTECHAMBER
West Wall, *In Situ*

The middle of the three animal couches in the Antechamber — placed directly opposite the entry door — represented the goddess Hathor in her bovine manifestation; gilded overall, its spots are indicated in blue glass-paste. Resting on the Hathor couch is a bed supporting a wicker chair & a small stool, another stool, an ovoid box & a pair of gilded-wood sistra. Most of the space under the couch is occupied by numerous white-painted variform wooden boxes containing food offerings. A carved cedarwood chair tilts askew between the Hathor & Thoueris couches. Two white-painted boxes, a low footstool & a dilapidated wicker stool occupy the foreground. Just visible ahead of the cow couch, partly obscured by a wooden box on a stand, are two ornate calcite vessels which proved to be perfume vases on tall pedestals; & next to these, under the third couch is a small ivory-inlaid child's chair. Metropolitan Museum of Art

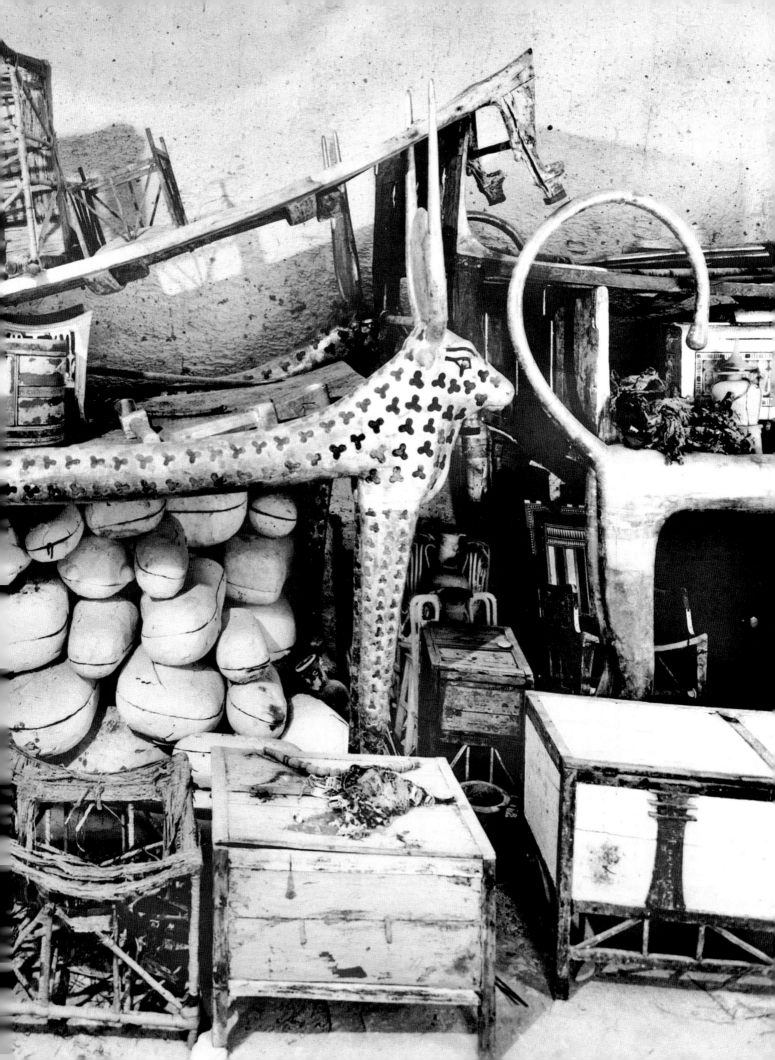

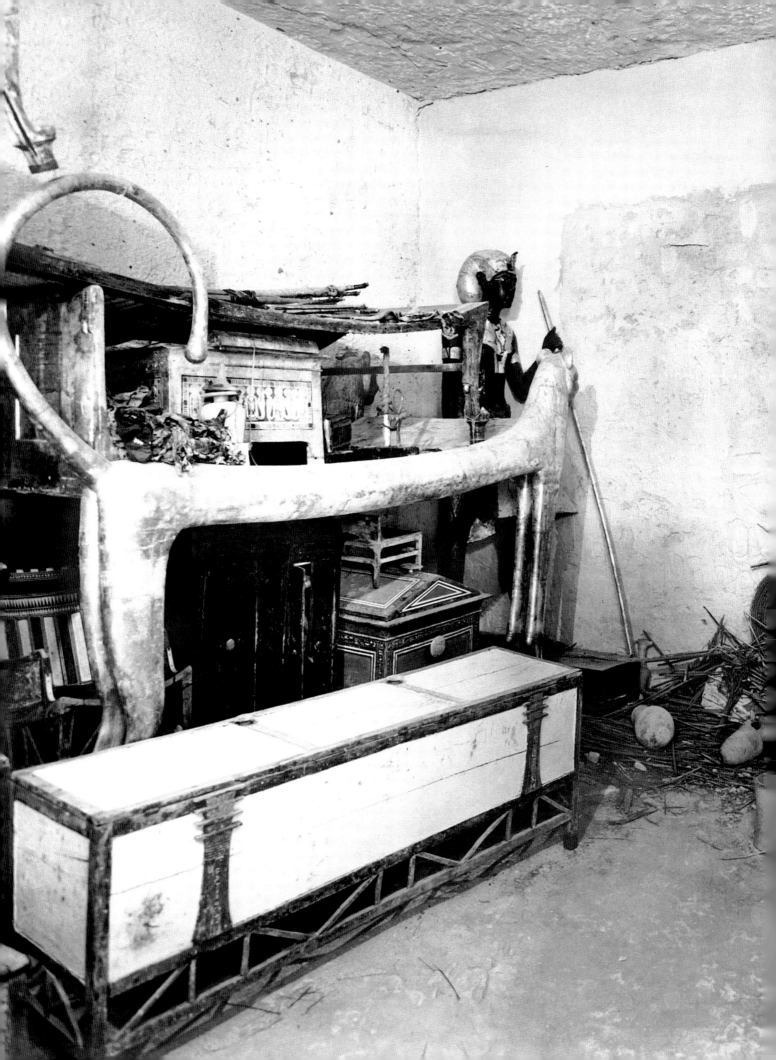

The KV62 ANTECHAMBER
North Wall, *In Situ*

The leonine couch occupying the northwest third of the Antechamber's long west wall is also completely gilded, with inlaid facial features. It supports another of the king's beds, under which rests: a shrine-shaped chest with side & lid panels of blue faience overlaid with gilt-gesso decoration; a small calcite lidded jar; & a wood-mounted bronze torch holder in the form of an ankh with human arms. Visible underneath the lion couch, in addition to the child's chair, are two tall bitumen-covered *naoi* on sleds (which would be found to hold gilded ritual figures), & a handsome cedarwood chest, veneered & inlaid with ebony & ivory, on top of which rests a small wooden stool. The long wooden chest with *djed* decorations in front of the couch was found to contain numerous articles of the king's clothing & other personal items. In each corner of the north wall stand life-sized wooden "guardian" statues of the king, the flesh parts covered in bitumen, the costume elements, staves & maces being gilded. The figure on the right had been partially draped in a linen shawl, clearly much decayed. The celebrated painted-wood casket stands angled apart from the rest of the chamber's contents; next to it, leaning into the east wall, is a large funerary bouquet, with a sizeable calcite urn in the foreground.

door's surface: impressions of the jackal-and-prisoners necropolis stamp covered the resealed portion, whereas the stamp with the king's name had been applied only to the untouched part of the doorway. Thus, it appeared that the tomb was almost certainly not intact, after all. Yet any violations had occurred not later than the reign of Rameses VI, when the huts covering the site were constructed; thus the tomb had not been subjected to the general dismantling of the royal burials which had occurred during the Twenty-first Dynasty. But there was something else which puzzled Carter. In the lowest strata of the rubble fill of the stairwell, in front of the doorway, he had found a quantity of potsherds and pieces of broken wooden boxes, the latter with the cartouches of not only Tutankhamen, but of his predecessors, Akhenaten and Smenkhkare, plus a scarab of Thutmose III and a fragment with Amenhotep III's name. Carter would write, *"Why this mixture of names? The balance of evidence so far would seem to indicate a cache rather than a tomb, and at this stage in the proceedings we inclined more and more to the opinion that we were about to find a miscellaneous collection of objects of the Eighteenth Dynasty kings, brought from Tell el Amarna by Tut·ankh·Amen and deposited here for safety."*[51]

Since Carter planned to remove the door blocking the next day, he had instructed his friend, Arthur Callender,[52] to have a heavy wooden grille built by local carpenters, which would be put in its place to secure the tomb. The morning of the 25th, the sealed doorway was photographed; and in the afternoon the tomb site was visited by Reginald Engelbach, chief inspector for the Antiquities Service in Upper Egypt, who witnessed final clearance of rubbish from the foot of the stairwell and the subsequent dismantlement of the door, which had been constructed from rough stones, thickly coated with plaster on its outer surface, in order to receive the seal impressions.

Beyond the open portal was another wall of sorts, consisting of the mass of rock rubble which filled the passageway beyond to its ceiling, as earlier had been observed by Carter through his *"peephole."* This passage appeared to be the same width as the stairwell (some six feet) and nearly seven feet high. The filling was for the most part composed of clean, white limestone chips; but the tomb robbers' irregular tunnel, in the upper-left-hand corner, had been plugged with larger, darker stones, which Carter described as *"flint."* The excavator instructed his workmen immediately to begin removing this mass of material.

He wrote: *"As we cleared the passage we found, mixed with the rubble of the lower levels, broken potsherds, jar sealings, alabaster jars, whole and broken, vases of painted pottery, numerous fragments of smaller articles, and water skins, these last having obviously been used to bring up water needed for the plastering of the doorways. These were clear evidence of plundering, and we eyed them askance."*[53] It now seemed to Carter that the tomb had been entered

The first "treasure" found in the Tomb of Tutankhamen — recovered from the debris blocking the entry passage — was the peculiar painted-wood sculpture, above & opposite, which depicts a shaved youthful human head atop a water-lily blossum. Although without an inscription, it generally has been thought to represent the youthful king as the god Nefertem emerging from a water lily floating on the primordial waters at the time of Creation. Because of its strong affinity in style with any number of sculptures in the round of the long-craniumed Amarna princesses, it might just as well be a contemporary portrait of one of the latter — most likely Tutankhamen's wife, Ankhesenamen, as a girl — in which case it would have been placed in the tomb as a family heirloom.

and robbed as many as three times in antiquity; the initial break-in occurring, perhaps with the connivance of the necropolis guards, shortly after the king's funeral, before the entrance passage was filled to its ceiling with quarried limestone chips — otherwise there would be no explanation for how a miscellany of things seemingly from the tomb had ended up on or near the floor of the passageway.

One object recovered during this excavation of the entry corridor went unremarked by Carter in his first account of the tomb's discovery, however, and indeed was not published by him until the third volume of his popular *The Tomb of Tut·Ankh·Amen*, after its existence had become known. This was a small painted-wood sculpture depicting the elongated shaven head of a child — arguably the king himself — emerging from an open water lily.

Clearance of the entry corridor continued throughout the morning of November 26th; by mid-afternoon, some thirty feet from the outer doorway, another blocked door was encountered, which like the first was plastered and stamped with the seal impressions of both Nebkheperure Tutankhamen and the officials of the royal necropolis. This blocking had also been breached and reclosed, in a manner identical to the upper doorway. Carter would write that he and Carnarvon were now certain that what they had found was not a tomb in the strictest sense, but rather a cache, like KV55 just across the wadi, barely a stone's throw away.

Finally the last of the passageway debris was removed and the entire doorway exposed. With the earl and Evelyn Herbert, and Callender standing by behind him, Carter moved to penetrate the mystery. *"With trembling hands,"* he wrote, *"I made a tiny breach in the upper left hand corner. Darkness and blank space, as far as an iron testing-rod could reach, showed that whatever lay beyond was empty, and not filled like the passage we had just cleared. Candle tests were applied as a precaution against possible foul gases, and then, widening the hole a little, I inserted the candle and peered in.... At first I could see nothing, the hot air escaping from the chamber causing the candle flame to flicker, but presently, as my eyes grew accustomed to the light, details of the room within emerged slowly from the mist, strange animals, statues and gold — everywhere the glint of gold. For the moment...I was struck dumb with amazement, and when Lord Carnarvon...inquired anxiously, 'Can you see anything?' it was all I could do to get out the words, 'Yes, wonderful things.'"* [54]

Carter moved away from the hole and allowed Evelyn to peer in. Then Carnarvon took his turn at the opening. This was further enlarged and Carter scrambled through, into the chamber, which he announced was some two feet lower than the bottom of the passageway. He moved about the long rectangular space, his flickering candle weakly illuminating the jumble of objects which seemed to fill up the undecorated low-ceilinged chamber, save for a generally open area in front of the sealed entry door. Immediately to the left of the latter was

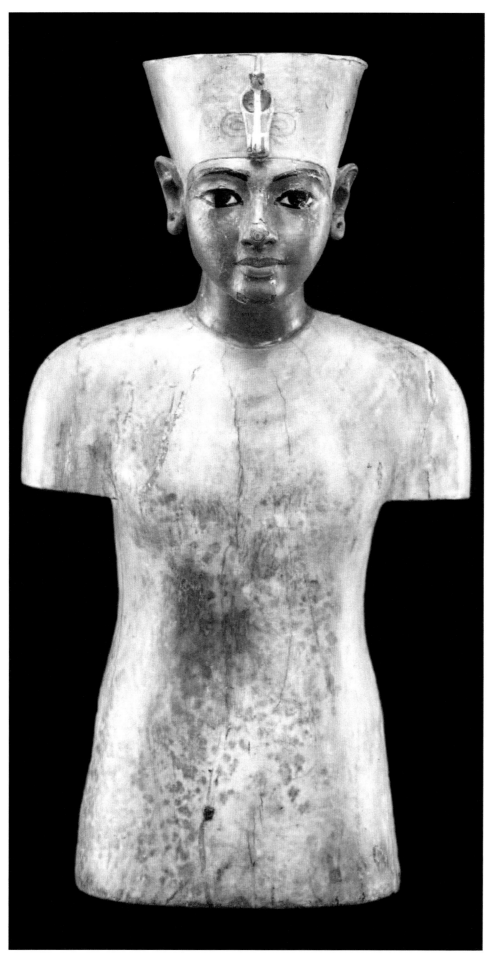

Among the truly unique things observed by those who first entered the Antechamber of KV62, sitting on the floor of the south wall, amid the jumble of objects there (above), was a realistically painted life-sized wooden effigy (left & detail opposite) which seems to be a portrait of the youthful king. Without arms or legs, its exact purpose is uncertain, although it has been speculated that it was intended for displaying the royal jewelry, perhaps while the king made choices regarding which items of same to wear on a particular occasion. The dark splotches on the torso are stains left by mold which grew after the closing of the tomb. The width of the figure's hips echoes the art style perpetuated during the Amarna period; it may also reflect Tutankhamen's actual physique, however.

a helter-skelter pile of large gilded spoked wheels, next to which, occupying a corner of one end of the room, rested a tangled heap of gold-plated chariot bodies, from which these wheels had been detached. Filling the entire length of the long wall opposite the entrance, placed head to tail, were three gilded, rather high, fantastic zoomorphic couches, underneath, atop and in front of which — stacked, piled, inserted, tossed or neatly arranged — was an astonishing array of miscellaneous storage chests, food boxes, *naoi*, stools, chairs, beds, ornate calcite vases and smaller motley items. Finally, in the corners of the other end of the chamber, facing each other, stood two life-sized striding, black-and-gold, nearly identical figures of a king, as well as a brilliantly painted lidded chest, large funerary bouquets and more calcite vessels.

By now Callender had brought down to the doorway an electric lamp — which was tapped into an outlet in KV9 up above — and, after slightly enlarging the entrance hole, Lady Evelyn, his lordship and Callender himself joined Carter in the crowded subterranean room which later would be dubbed the "Antechamber." With the far-brighter illumination of the lamp, the quartet was able to examine the overwhelming plethora of contents in greater detail. They remarked especially on a gilded throne with elaborate inlays, which was pushed against the wall under one gilded animal couch. Perhaps it was Carnarvon's daughter who pointed out a life-sized painted *"mannequin"* placidly peering at them from behind an up-ended chariot body. One at a time, each awed explorer squatted to study at close hand the painted chest standing apart from everything else, covered all over with jewel-like miniature scenes of a king hunting and fighting from his chariot. And the four gazed in turn at the serene handsome faces of a pair of *"guardian statues."* Perhaps Carter reminded the others that fragmentary ruins of similar figures had been found during Theodore Davis's clearance of the Tomb of Horemheb years before. Here these perfect images were separated from each other by a wide expanse of roughly plastered wall, stamped all over with yet-more seal impressions.

Another blocked doorway? Already Carter, on hands and knees, had spotted — under one of the ceremonial couches, next to the golden throne — a smallish rectangular opening gaping in the wall by the floor. Shining their electric lamp into the inky void, the genteel intruders beheld a smaller second chamber, also undecorated. As Carnarvon would recall, *"There the confusion was beyond conception. It was impossible to enter, as the room was packed with chairs, bed, boxes, statuettes, alabasters, and every other conceivable object to the height*

Over leaves: Left, A detailed view of the sealed & stamped doorway between the KV62 Antechamber & Burial Chamber. The heap of reeds & the propped-up basket lid hide the refilled breach in the blocking which had been discovered by Carter on the evening of November 26th, & enlarged to give him, Carnarvon & Evelyn Herbert unauthorized access to the spaces beyond. The numbers were later added by the excavators to facilitate their clearance of the Antechamber. Right, The view of the Treasury through the doorway leading from the Burial Chamber. In the foreground is an Anubis Shrine, & at the rear is a gilded baldachin which would be found to house Tutankhamen's canopic equipment. Several storage chests are also visible.

Both photos Metropolitan Museum of Art

of five feet."[55] This space would come to be called the "Annexe."

Where the wide sealed doorway between the king figures intersected with the chamber floor, near its middle, Carter apparently detected indications of another ancient breach. With Callender's assistance, unplastered loose stones were pried out, until there was an opening large enough to shine their lamp into the blackness — to reveal what appeared to be a wall of gold! Excitedly, they enlarged the hole even more, just enough so that it was possible for everyone, except the stout Callender, to squeeze through into the somewhat-lower adjoining space. This, Carter very well must have exclaimed, once he got his bearings, was undoubtedly the tomb's burial chamber, its "holy of holies," as it was all but filled with a huge, free-standing shrine-like structure, a tabernacle, which was decorated on all sides with blue-faience inlays and gilding. It reached almost to the ceiling and left only a very narrow walk space between it and the painted walls of the room. Yes, this was a *decorated* chamber, and in the cramped confines Carter could just make out a gaudily colored tableau of a funerary cortege and scenes of a king — the accompanying cartouches read "Neb-kheperure Tutankhamen" — in the presence of various deities of the ancient Egyptian pantheon.

Moving to his right around the tabernacle, careful not to step on small objects occupying the floor, Carter was surely torn between opening the unsealed door panels of the "shrine" structure itself and moving on to a large-but-low unblocked rectangular opening near the far corner of the cramped space. Because he never indicated which he did first, it may be assumed that the apparent portal to another room had the stronger attraction. Moving there and stooping to shine the electric lamp into the darkness beyond, Carter beheld yet a fourth chamber, filled with *"wonderful things"* to equal what he and his companions had already encountered. Carnarvon and Evelyn joined him at the low doorway and no doubt marveled aloud at what they saw: the startling image of an Anubis jackal, draped in linen and lying atop a gilded pylon-shaped chest with long carrying poles; and behind it, placed against the far wall of the low-ceilinged room, an elaborate gilded canopy-enclosed structure doubly crowned by friezes of rearing cobras, with large gilded free-standing small statues of female deities at the three visible sides of this amazing object, their delicate arms outspread as if to protect it from the intrusion taking place at just that moment. To the left of the Anubis shrine and the gilded baldachin — which Carter may have suggested to his companions was a canopic shrine, although nothing like it had ever been seen before — were positioned a row of various storage chests and against the chamber wall lay a jumble of chariot parts and miscellaneous other objects. Lined up along the right wall of the room were numerous tall *naoi* glossy black with bitumen, atop which sailed a small fleet of brightly painted model river-vessels of various sizes. Carter would dub this object-crowded chamber the "Treasury."

Perhaps lifting the lid on a storage chest or two, to see what might be inside, perhaps opening the doors to one of the myste-

50

rious black *naoi* (and discovering a pair of shrouded, gilded statuettes of a king striding atop panther figures), the trio eventually moved back into the burial chamber itself, to stand in front of the door panels of the huge tabernacle. After moving aside a calcite lamp sitting on the floor directly in front of the doors, Carter probably knelt to examine a long wooden bolt which secured the inlaid gilded panels near their bottom edge. Since there was no seal to break — and no doubt at Carnarvon's urging — Carter slowly slid this bolt and swung open both panels, to expose what at first must have been a puzzling sight: a large gilded open framework, on which were suspended remnants of a rotted, dark-brown cloth shroud decorated all over with gilded rosettes the size of medallions; a motley assortment of gilded staves, sticks and bows leaning into the opposite corners of the interior; two peculiar figurative calcite vessels; and, just beyond all of this, another gilded "shrine" decorated in sunk relief, its door panels closed and secured with a multiple twist of cording and a dab of mud stamped with the necropolis seal. Very likely Carter and Carnarvon congratulated each other at this point. Whoever had anciently violated Tutankhamen's tomb — and that certainly was what they had found — had apparently penetrated no further; and surely the king's coffined mummy lay within, surrounded by yet more of the shrine-like tabernacles, and a stone sarcophagus: *"a jewel within a series of golden safes,"* as Carter later would say.[56]

But the hour was very late; night had fallen since they had first entered the Antechamber; and Carter's workmen most certainly were growing increasingly restless, waiting up alone in the darkness and wondering about the occasional faint muffled English wafting up to them. Wriggling their way back through the small hole opening from the Antechamber, rejoining an anxious Callender there, Carter, Carnarvon and Lady Evelyn must certainly have paused and assessed the situation. Technically, they should not have entered even this first sealed room of the tomb, without the Antiquities Service inspector (Englebach, specifically) present; absolutely they should not have gone further, forcing their way through a reblocked breach into the anciently sealed burial chamber itself. Their impulsive exploring had very probably violated, in spirit at least, the conditions of their concession to excavate in the Royal Valley. If what they had done was to be discovered by the Service director-general, Pierre Lacau, the tomb might be, almost certainly would be, taken away from them by the difficult French bureaucrat. Or, barring that, at the very least their scientific work in the tomb would be prematurely interrupted by Egyptian officialdom. And, certainly, they would be subjected to the innuendo that they had had the opportunity illicitly to pocket and carry away small objects from the still unrevealed part of the tomb. That they had entered and explored throughout the sepulcher prior to its official opening must forever remain their secret alone. They agreed, and Callender assisted Carter in carefully replacing the few stones they had removed from the bottom of the sealed doorway to the *"holy of holies"* and beyond. To further disguise their handiwork, the pair heaped some loose reeds in

When the KV62 Treasury was officially entered on February 17, 1923, one of the several pitch-covered tall cabinets or naoi in the chamber was standing open (above), revealing the ritual statuettes inside. It can only be wondered whether the doors (removed in this photo) had been left open by the ancient tomb robbers, or by one of the secret visitors to the chamber on the evening of November 26, 1922.

51

When on the evening of November 26, 1922, Howard Carter slipped the bolt & swung open the unsealed doors of the huge gilt-&-faience veneered tabernacle that all but filled the Burial Chamber, what he & his companions saw by the light of their electric lamp was at first confusing (right & opposite). A second set of sealed *doors was visible, but an openwork frame of some sort intruded, on which was draped the tattered remains of a linen shroud sewn all over with innumerable gilded-bronze rosettes. Two figurative calcite vessels rested on the chamber floor, & leaning into the inner corners of the outer tabernacle were a quantity of staves, walking sticks & bows (above, left & right).*

The cording & mud sealing securing the doors to the Second Tabernacle.

front of the patched hole, and propped up the circular lid of a reed basket at hand. Luckily, no one soon enough would be the wiser as to the events of that night! For over fifty years their (understandable, if not wholly forgivable) surreptitious visit was, for the most part, a well-kept — if somewhat widely known — secret.[57]

Carter, of course, was completely disingenuous in his published account of the manner in which he, Carnarvon, Lady Evelyn and Arthur Callender had conducted what he called the *"preliminary investigation"* of the Antechamber, giving as he did in *The Tomb of Tut·Ankh·Amun*, Volume 1, a relatively detailed account of its contents — much of which certainly could not have been seen through the

initial small hole made in the sealed outer doorway, which is how they supposedly viewed the amazing space. Carter did back pedal: *"Such were some of the objects that lay before us. Whether we noted them all at the time I cannot say for certain, as our minds were in much too excited and confused a state to register accurately. ...We had seen enough, and our brains began to reel at the thought of the task in front of us. We re-closed the hole, locked the wooden grille that had been placed upon the first doorway, left our native staff on guard, mounted our donkeys and rode home down The Valley, strangely silent and subdued. ...I think we slept but little, all of us, that night."* [58] This concluding remark was certainly a considerable understatement!

According to the official record, Carter, Carnarvon, Lady

Evelyn and Callender all entered the tomb for the first time around noon of the next day, November 27th. That morning Callender had installed lights and the seal impressions on the inner doorway were carefully noted; the blocking was completely removed. Chief Inspector Engelbach was away from Luxor on official business, so he was represented at this opening of the tomb by an assistant inspector, one Abraham Effendi. With the benefit of Callender's electrical installation, a complete survey of the Antechamber was now possible. It was at this time that Carter — no doubt for Inspector Effendi's benefit — made the "discovery" that the sealed door between the king figures had been broken through at floor level and the breach refilled. He would write, ironically, *"We were then not to be the first. Here, too, the thieves had forestalled us, and it only remained to be seen how much damage they had had the opportunity or time to effect. ...Our natural impulse was to break down the door and get to the bottom of the matter at once, but to do so would have entailed serious risk to many of the objects in the Antechamber. ...Reluctantly we decided to abandon the opening of this inner sealed door until we had cleared the Antechamber of all of its contents."* [59]

For a second time, the robbers' opening into the "Annexe" side chamber was discovered by the excavators, but the total confusion of the jumbled contents therein — and the simple fact that there was no vacant floor space in which to stand — still precluded any entry at this time. If it had not been clear to them during their clandestine intrusion of the previous evening, it was now all too obvious to earl and archaeologist that they had a *"prodigious task"* (Carter's words) ahead of them. Carter again: *"This was no ordinary find, to be disposed of in a normal season's work; nor was there any precedent to show us how to handle it. The thing was outside all experience, bewildering, and for the moment it seemed as though there were more to be done than any human agency could accomplish."* [60]

The first task was to secure the tomb against modern robbers. In addition to the wooden grille already installed by Callender at the door to the entry corridor, something stronger would have to be put in the doorway to the Antechamber; Carter took the measurements of the latter, so that a *"gate made of thick steel bars"* could be ordered from Cairo. Until that was in place, it would be necessary to fill in the tomb's stairwell yet one more time.

But *"news of the discovery had spread like wildfire, and all sorts of extraordinary and fanciful reports were going abroad concerning it."* [61] One had great quantities of golden treasure being removed from the tomb and carried away by three airplanes, which had landed in the Valley of the Kings. *"To overtake these rumours as far as possible,"* Carter and Carnarvon therefore decided to have an "official" opening of the tomb two days later, on the 29th, at which several Luxor-area Egyptian notables and bureaucrats were present. The next day, the 30th of November, the director-general of the Antiquities Service, Pierre Lacau — Carnarvon's and Carter's once-and-future nemesis — paid his official visit to the tomb, in the company of Paul Tottenham, an adviser to the Minister of Public Works; neither had been able to attend the previous day.

December 3rd the tomb was again filled in to the surface level, after the entrance doorway had been sealed with heavy timbers. The next day Lord Carnarvon and his daughter departed Luxor for Cairo, en route to England to spend the holidays, but with plans to return to Egypt later in the season. With Callender left behind to watch over the tomb, Carter also departed for Cairo on December 6; there he intended to have the metal gate for the inner door constructed, and a quantity of supplies assembled, items which would be required for the clearance work that lay ahead. Using Carnarvon's money, he purchased an automobile (to facilitate travel to and from the Royal Valley), photographic materials, chemicals for conservation, packing boxes, thirty-two bales of calico, and a *"mile"* each of wadding and surgical bandages. Carter would write, *"Of these last two important items I was determined not to run short."* [62]

Also while in Cairo, the archaeologist began to consider what sort of expertise would be required to effect the task before him, and where he could turn for assistance. Foremost was his immediate need for a photographer to record the Antechamber contents *in situ*. The first person capable of this feat to come to mind was Harry Burton,[63] staff photographer for the Metropolitan Museum Egyptian Expedition, who was already in Luxor. Carter cabled Albert M. Lythgoe, curator of the Museum's Egyptian Department, inquiring if — *"for the immediate emergency"* — he could borrow Burton's services. Lythgoe cabled back, *"Only too delighted to assist in any possible way. Please call on Burton and any other members of our staff."* [64] Consequently, Carter requested and was granted the services of the MMAEE's draughtsmen, Lindsley F. Hall[65] and Walter Hauser.[66] Additionally available to him was Arthur C. Mace,[67] director of the Metropolitan's field activities at Lisht, who was noted for his accomplishments in artifact restoration. While he was in Cairo, Carter also learned that Alfred Lucas,[68] just then retiring as director of the Chemical Department of the Egyptian government, was willing to place his expert knowledge of chemistry at the archaeologist's disposal, an offer which Carter readily accepted. And philologists Alan Gardiner[69] and James Breasted[70] both communicated their eagerness to assist in dealing with the translation of any inscriptional material in the tomb. During his week in Cairo, Carter was thus able to assemble a team of specialists quite unequalled in the annals of Egyptian archaeology.

The steel gate was finished on December 13th and Carter returned to Luxor. Two days later the gate, automobile and the great quantity of other purchases arrived on an express train provided by the Egyptian State Railway. On the 16th the tomb was reexcavated and entered for the third time, with the gate being installed the next day. Harry Burton entered the tomb on the 18th and began his photography of the twelve-foot by twenty-six-foot Antechamber; Hall and Hauser likewise commenced working on their plan of the space and its many contents. Alfred Lucas arrived from Cairo on the 20th and immed-

The steel gate in place at the entry door to KV62's Antechamber. Carter had this specially constructed during his visit to Cairo in early December 1922, following the official first entry into the tomb on November 27th.

iately began chemical tests with the preservatives which Carter had purchased. Arthur Mace joined the team on Christmas Day; and on the 27th the first objects were removed from the tomb.

To accomplish the task of photographing the Antechamber, Harry Burton employed two electric lights on movable stands, which gave off 3,000 candlepower. Consequently the exposures were rather slow, although the light was very even. He took general panoramic views of the room as it appeared when first entered, and closer or more detailed views of smaller sections or groups of the contents. In order as quickly as possible to be able to determine the success of the exposure of a glass plate, the Antiquities Service allowed Burton to use KV55, the so-called "Amarna Cache" tomb, as a makeshift darkroom. This is only a few yards away from the Tutankhamen sepulcher, so the photographer could dash from one tomb to the other to develop

Howard Carter was quick to realize the importance of having the contents of KV62 photographed in situ, before any clearance began. He enlisted for that task fellow Englishman Harry Burton (seen at left, along with Carter), who was just then working for the Metropolitan Museum of Art Egyptian Expedition. Burton had originally gone to Egypt to photograph in the Valley of the Kings for its previous concession holder, Theodore M. Davis. Metropolitan Museum of Art

his plates, without moving his camera out of position.

Carter wrote in his and Mace's first volume of *The Tomb of Tut·Ankh·Amen*: *"Our next step...was to devise an efficient method of registering the contents of the* [Ante]*chamber, for it would be absolutely essential, later on, that we should have a ready means of ascertaining the exact part of the tomb from which any particular object might have come. Naturally, each object, or closely allied group of objects, would be given its own catalogue number, and would have that number securely attached to it when it was moved away from the chamber, but that was not enough, for the number might not indicate position. So far as possible, the numbers were to follow a definite order, beginning at the entrance doorway and working systematically around*

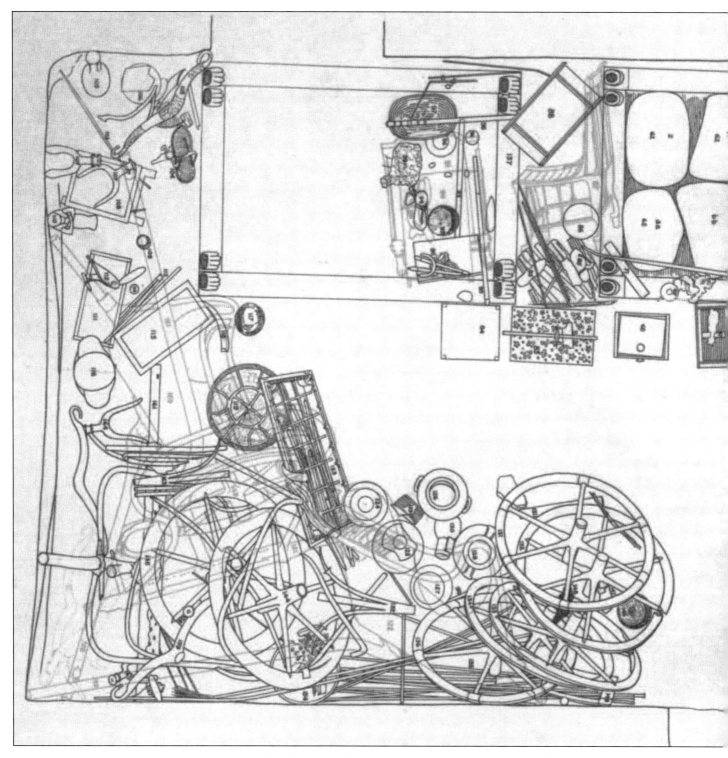

the chamber, but it was very certain that many objects now hidden would be found in the course of clearing, and have to be numbered out of turn. We got over the difficulty by placing printed numbers on every object and photographing them in small groups. Every number showed in at least one of the photographs, so that, by duplicating prints, we were able to place with notes of every single object in our filing cabinets a print which showed at a glance its actual position in the tomb." [71]

In order to conserve, store and ultimately pack the huge quantity of objects which would be removed from the tomb, Carter needed a space near at hand to use as both a laboratory/workroom and

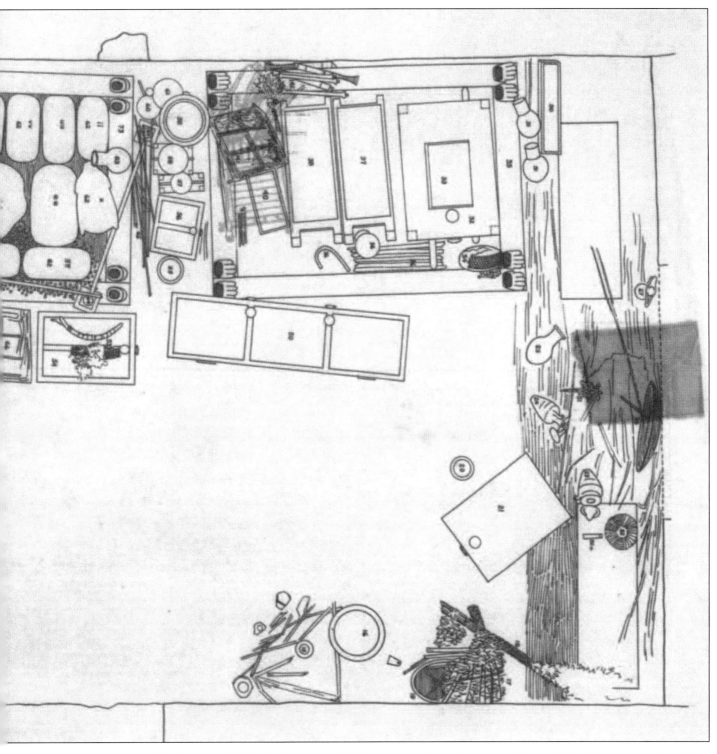

warehouse, which was relatively large, could be secured against potential thieves, and which also would allow him and his expert associates a degree of seclusion in which to undertake their labors. The Antiquities Service agreed to let the Carnarvon expedition have access to sizeable Tomb 15 in the Royal Valley, that of Seti II. This is a fair distance from the Tutankhamen site, but it had the advantage of being off the well-beaten tourist path, had a large space in front of it (which could be utilized as an open-air photo studio) and was situated at the base of overhanging cliffs, so that it never received any direct sun through its entrance, remaining relatively cool inside, even on the

The pencil-drawing-on-paper plan of the Antechamber of KV62, with objects in situ, produced for Howard Carter by the Metropolitan Museum of Art Egyptian Expedition draughtsmen, Lindsley Hall & Walter Hauser. The darkened area in the middle at the far right is a stain on the paper of the original drawing, which today is in the Carter archives of the Griffith Institute, Oxford, England.

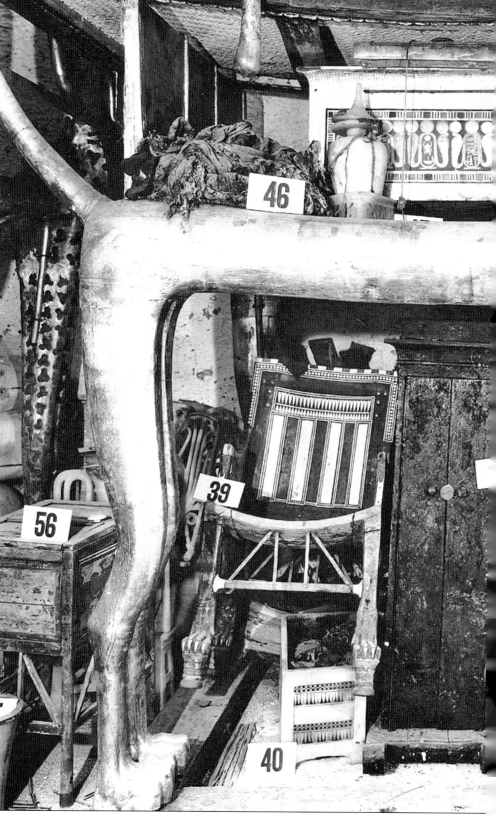

Burton's photograph of the objects on & under the lion couch in the KV62 Antechamber, showing the numbering system devised by Carter to carefully record each object & its position in the tomb, as found. In the case where a box or chest, as No. 32, held contents, these were individually indicated as 32a, 32b, etc.

hottest days of summer. It was decided to use the upper passages of KV15 as the workspaces and the lower reaches of the long corridor-tomb for storage of preservation and packing materials, as well as already packed objects awaiting ultimate shipment to Cairo. To insure the safety of the tomb, Carter installed a one-and-a-half ton steel gate with several padlocks.

The first object to be removed from the Antechamber on December 27th was the casket painted all over with miniature scenes of King Tutankhamen hunting and fighting from his chariot, which

when its lid was lifted was found to contain a great quantity of jumbled clothing items and accessories that apparently had been crammed without any rhyme or reason into the casket by the necropolis priests who attempted to reorder the tomb following one of the break-ins. Even a cursory examination of the readily visible top layers of the contents told Carter and his conservators (Mace and Lucas) that nearly everything was in a state of collapse and decay and would require a great deal of time and effort to extract, reorder, reconstruct and conserve. This casket was removed from the tomb — with its contents, un- *Narration continues p. 70*

The first object removed by Carter from the KV62 Antechamber was the elaborately painted wooden chest (No. 21), which sat apart from everything else at the northern end of the space. It is decorated on its two long sides & the halves of its domed (& warped) lid with similar scenes of Tutankhamen drawing a bow while riding in his chariot: he hunts desert fauna & lions on the lid & battles Nubian & Asiatic foes on the sides. In each miniature vignette the young ruler is followed by foot soldiers & courtiers in chariots, or by the latter only, with fan bearers running immedi-

ately behind him. The short end panels depict the king's cartouches, flanked by Tutankhamen as a sphinx trampling his foreign enemies. The battle scenes are among the very earliest showing an Egyptian king fighting from a chariot, a motif which would become standard royal iconography in the next dynasty. Although the chest held mostly items of clothing & footwear when found, whether that was its intended function is not known.

The sort of nightmare task confronting the KV62 conservators is illustrated at right in photographs of the contents of the painted chest (No. 21, opposite), as revealed, layer by layer. Altogether, there were 51 different items (mostly clothing & accessories, including sandals), many of these being composed of numerous parts & almost all of them in a state of collapse or decay. Griffith Institute

The second short side of painted chest No. 21, with another depcition of Tutankhamen as a sphinx trampling his enemies. Cairo Egyptian Museum

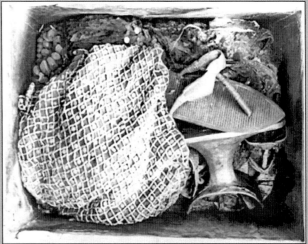

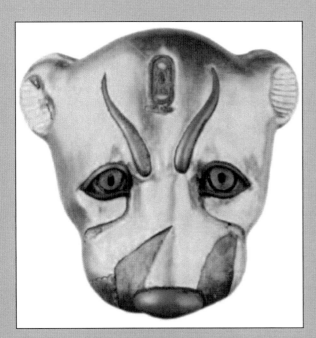

One of two similar feline-head appliqués found in chest No. 21. Both are made of gilded wood with crystal, glass & calcite inlays, & are are associated with priestly robes sewn with tiny gold stars, which the king may have worn while performing his sacerdotal duties. Cairo Egyptian Museum

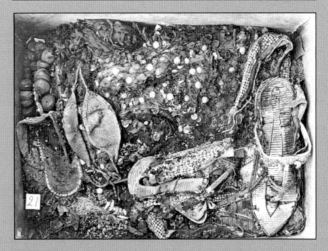

63

Above, Arthur Mace (standing, center) & Alfred Lucas are captured by Harry Burton's camera as they work in the open air in front of KV15 (Seti II) on the conservation of the body of the state chariot found in the KV62 Antechamber. Arthur Callender sits in the heavily secured doorway to the tomb used as both a laboratory & storeroom by the Carnarvon-Carter team. Griffith Institute

Opposite, Detail of the painted scene of King Tutankhamen in his chariot & attacking Nubian enemies of Egypt. In reality the youthful king would not have been driving the vehicle with the charging horses' reins around his hips, but rather would have been accompanied by a driver.

Left, Detail from one end-panel scene on the painted chest, depicting Tutankhamen as a sphinx wearing the Atef crown & trampling an Asiatic & Nubian emeny. Cairo Egyptian Museum

Strangely, the largest & arguably finest, of Tutankhamen's over 400 ushabtis — or Afterlife proxies (right & detail opposite) — was not found interred with the lot of others in the Treasury, but rather was isolated in the Antechamber, standing upright against the south wall, alongside the small golden shrine (two views right & below). Made of cedarwood with gildings, it depicts the king wearing the Nemes head-covering, a broad collar & wristbands; it is missing its Crook scepter.

Cairo Egyptian Museum &
Metropolitan Museum of Art

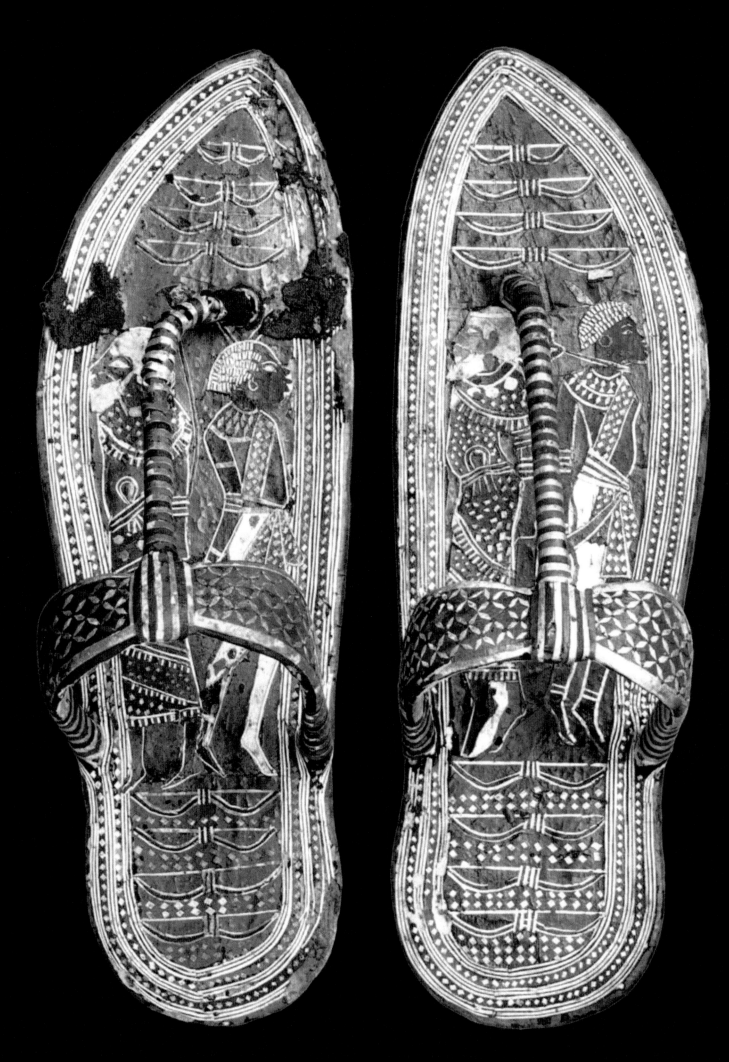

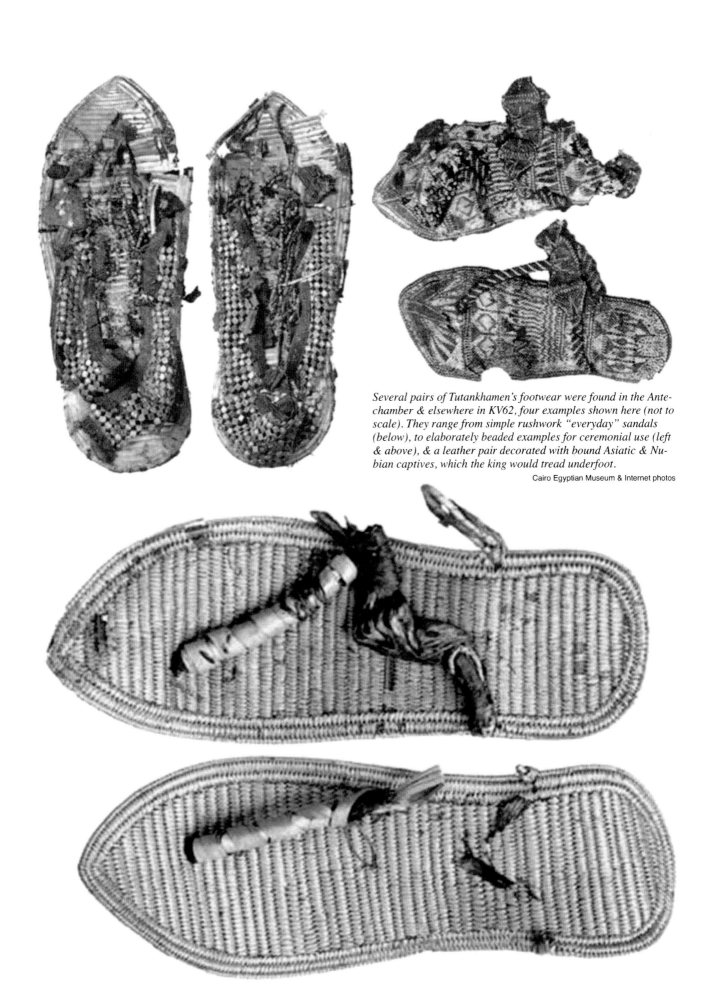

Several pairs of Tutankhamen's footwear were found in the Ante-chamber & elsewhere in KV62, four examples shown here (not to scale). They range from simple rushwork "everyday" sandals (below), to elaborately beaded examples for ceremonial use (left & above), & a leather pair decorated with bound Asiatic & Nubian captives, which the king would tread underfoot.

Cairo Egyptian Museum & Internet photos

touched, still inside — by placing it on a specially constructed padded wooden stretcher and then securing it with bandages. Carter would write: *"Enormous numbers of these stretchers were required, for, to avoid double handling, they were in almost every case left permanently with the object, and not re-used."* [72] When several of the stretchers had been loaded with their fragile cargo — usually towards the end of each workday — they would be taken up out of the tomb into the late-afternoon sunlight, and then under military guard were carried in a convoy through the main wadi and up to Tomb 15, where they were received by Mace and Lucas, and placed in the laboratory to await detailed noting, mending and preservation, then final packing for shipment to the Cairo Egyptian Museum

Starting with the painted casket, the excavators cleared the Antechamber by *"working from north to south, and thus putting off the evil day when* [they] *should have to tackle the complicated tangle of chariots,* [they] *gradually disencumbered the great animal couches of the objects which surrounded them."* [73] It was decided, however, to leave the so-called guardian statues in place, for the time being. As it turned out, the removal and transportation of the numerous chests,

The first zoomorphic couch of three from the Antechamber was dubbed the "Thoueris" couch by Carter, for its probable identification with the hippo goddess, Tauret, patroness of childbirth, that divinity having the head of a hippopotamus, the scaly back & tail of a crocodile, & the mane & legs of a lion. Perhaps by resting on this couch, the deceased king was assured of rebirth to eternal life. A piece of what must have been a nearly identical piece of funerary furniture was found in 1908 in the Tomb of Horemheb (KV57), as seen in the adzed wooden head at right. One head of the Tutankhamen couch is shown opposite, for comparison. Cairo Egyptian Museum

Davis, *Harmhabi*

The Hathor couch from the Antechamber, below, stands 188 cm. tall, is 128 cm. wide & 208 cm. long. It is made of gessoed wood which is gilded, with the trilobate spots on the bodies picked out with dark-blue paste inlays. The eyes (in the form of the Wadjet *eye) & brows are inlaid with stone & faience. Like KV62's other zoomorphic couches, this one is constructed of four parts: the bed with foot panel; the animal sides; & the open rectangular, black-painted base, into which the hooves of the cow forms are pinioned. The bed is attached to the sides by long bronze pins which slip into bronze staples on the inside of the legs. Although similar couches are known from tomb paintings & from fragments found in the Tomb of Horemheb, these from the Tomb*

of Tutankhamen are the only ones known to have survived from antiquity. Their exact function is uncertain, although it was most likely magical in nature & associated with the funerary rites & the Hereafter. It has been suggested that they may have served to magically transport the dead king during his nightly journey across the Abyss. Cairo Egyptian Museum

boxes, cases and smaller furniture items proved, in Carter's words, *"to be a relatively simple matter."*

The three large couches and the chariots were a greater challenge, however. Each of the former were composed of four sections: the two animal sides; the bed frame with footboard proper; and the open rectangular base to which the feet of the animals were attached. It was immediately apparent that they were far too large to be taken out of the tomb as assembled — and, in fact, anciently repaired gilding around the joins indicated that they had been brought into the tomb in parts and put together within the Antechamber following the king's funeral. But the disassembly proved to be no easy matter, as the bronze pins and staples holding each bed frame to the sides had somewhat bonded over three millennia, requiring that they be levered apart. This was a five-man operation (two holding the bed frame, one each supporting the animal sides, and the fifth working from underneath to ease up the hooks one after the other). Even so, the side animals, especially the Hathors with their tall horns, barely fit through the entry passage, and had to be maneuvered with great care. All of the couch parts were bandaged into the wooden carrying trays, which were waiting for them outside the entrance to the tomb.

But, as Carter had supposed would be the case, removing the various chariots was the greatest task in clearing the Antechamber. They had proven too wide to take into the tomb intact in the first place, so the burial party had removed the wheels of each vehicle, then sawed through all the axles. How these chariot parts had originally been positioned in the tomb is not clear, but they apparently were moved about subsequently by the looters; and, when the Antechamber was being tidied up by officials following the last break-in, the chariot bodies were simply stacked at odd angles loosely against one another in the southwest corner of the room, the wheels being leaned against the east wall next to the entry door. Because they had been roughly handled in antiquity, much of the embossed-and-inlaid gilding which decorated the chariot bodies proper was in a very fragile state, making them difficult

Opposite, Head of one side of the KV62 lion couch (below), which is surely to be identified with the goddess Sekhmet. The nose & tearing marks under the eyes are blue-glass inlays, the painted eyes being set in lids of black glass. That King Horemheb had a similar lion-couch as part of his burial apparatus is evidenced by the wooden lion-head fragment found in his tomb (KV57), seen at right. This had been stripped of its gilding in antiquity, more likely by those officials who dismantled the royal necropolis during the Twenty-first Dynasty, than by tomb robbers, who would not have gone to the effort to recover gold foil. It would appear in the Horemheb example that inlays had not been employed. Cairo Egyptian Museum

Davis, *Harmhabi*

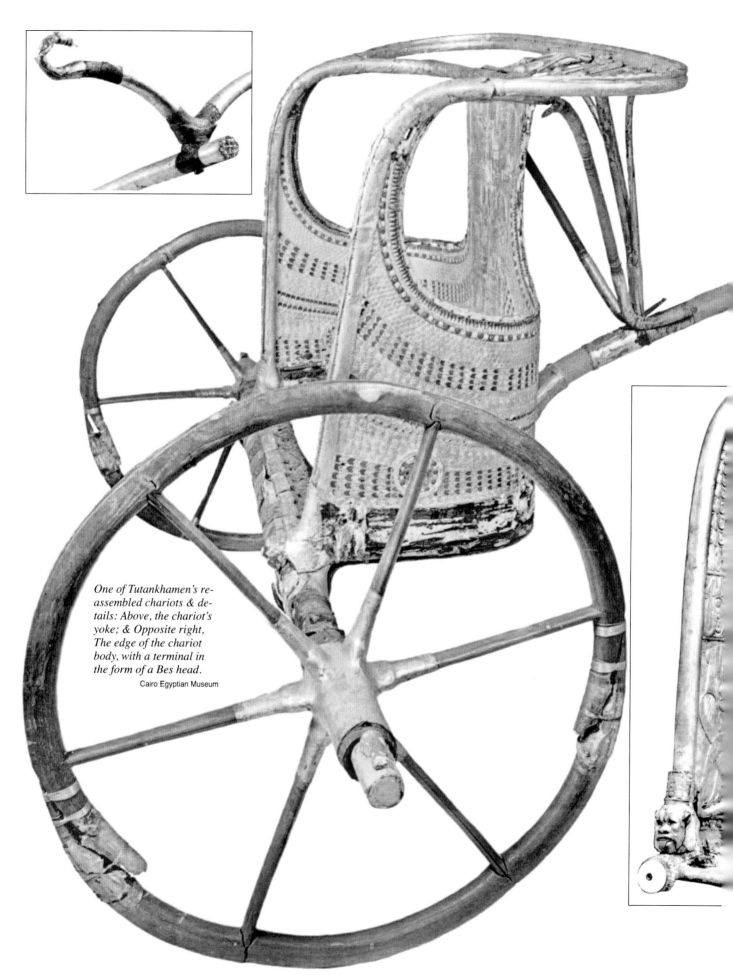

One of Tutankhamen's re-assembled chariots & details: Above, the chariot's yoke; & Opposite right, The edge of the chariot body, with a terminal in the form of a Bes head.

Cairo Egyptian Museum

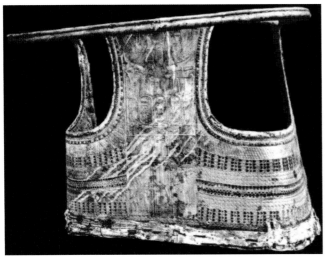

to handle. Complicating the situation was a quantity of other miscellaneous objects mixed in among the pile of dismantled vehicles, including the chariots' harnessing and related trappings. The latter had been made of undressed leather, which across the millennia had turned to a black, glue-like substance which had dripped and run down over the chariot bodies and everything else that lay on the floor under the latter. Although the leather itself had all but entirely vanished, the harnessing could be reconstructed later because of the gold ornamentation with which it had been covered.

According to Carter's inventory, some 170 numbered items were removed from the Antechamber during the course of the seven weeks it took to complete the clearance. Many of these objects, particularly the several chests, coffers and caskets, served as containers for yet further smaller things, sometimes numbering scores of individually identifiable pieces. For example, just in Box 54, inscribed and made of ebony and red-painted wood, were found crammed together: odd pieces of tapestry-woven cloth from a robe (54-a); a bronze snake with gold inlay (54-b); a model cutting knife of painted wood (-c); a

Above, The bodies of two additional state chariots from KV62, overlaid with embossed sheet gold & color-glass inlays.
Griffith Institute

Below, Details of the embossed & elaborate inlaid decorations of the interiors of the state chariots' sheet-gold bodies. The bottom image depicts bound captives of Egypt's Nubian & Asiatic enemies.
Cairo Egyptian Museum

Left, Another view of one of the restored state chariots. Cairo Egyptian Museum

Large inscribed cedarwood chest No. 32, inlaid & veneered with ebony & ivory, with carrying poles attached by bronze staples. Found under the KV62 Antechamber lion couch, it contained numerous pots & vases of calcite, faience, pottery & glass, plus a quantity of miscellaneous materials. Opposite, Detail of sunk-relief vignette on one end of the same chest, depicting Tutankhamen offering to Osiris.

Cairo Egyptian Museum

Above, Small incised-&-painted calcite casket with knobs of polished obsidian, found under the lion couch in the Antechamber. It contained an ivory pomegranate, gold caps, clay sealings & two mysterious balls of human hair wrapped in linen, which may have had a magical purpose.

Cairo Egyptian Museum

gilded-gesso-covered wooden throw stick (-d); another similar throw stick (-e); a tapestry-woven garment (-f); a dark-blue faience libation vase (-g); a green-faience bowl (-h); part of a linen glove [?](-i); an aragonite wine strainer (-j); a combined corselet, collar and pectoral (-k); another blue-faience libation vase (-l); a faience vase lid (-m); an inscribed blue-faience drinking cup (-n); remains of another linen glove (-o); a woven strip of tapestry (-p); a glass-and-gold scarab (-q); a collar of glazed pendants and beads (-r); an ivory dish in the shape of a swan (-s); two more inscribed blue-glazed cups (-t and -u); a glove-like garment (-v); a green-faience vase (-w); a blue-faience ewer; a sandal-shaped object of gilded leather [?] (-y); five more blue-faience ewers, these inscribed (-z, -aa, -bb, -cc and -dd); a statuette of hard crystalline limestone (-ee); a blue-glass statuette (-ff); a resin ring, possibly amber (-gg); an inscribed lid of a wooden box, with stone-and-glaze inlays (-hh); two more blue-faience ewers (-ii and -jj); a gilded-wood boss (-kk); five more blue-faience ewers (-ll, -mm, -nn, -oo and -pp); four blue-faience wine cups (-qq); two inscribed green-faience wine cups (-rr); two faience rings (-ss); a ring of aragonite (-tt); a harness bolt [?] of metal (-uu); a glazed-stone statuette (-vv); three green-faience game pieces (-ww); a blue-faience leg broken from? (-xx); a gold-plated scarab with carnelian-and-colored-glass inlays, forming the prenomen Nebkheperure (-yy); a blue-faience ewer stopper and two spouts from ewers (-zz); a five-pointed gold star (-aaa); an inscribed ewer of dark-blue faience (-bbb); an inscribed faience cosmetic vase (-ccc); and an inscribed small ivory casket (-ddd), containing: (54ddd-1) seven shells from a necklace; (-2) scraps of polychrome bead work; (-3) the ivory handle of a mirror [?]; (-4) a solid-bronze scarab with gilded details;

Above, Large ebony-wood storage chest, No. 101, with vaulted lid and white-painted side panels. The cartouches on the end are those of Tutankhamen & his wife, Ankhesenamen. This chest contained primarily the royal linen in great quantity & was found in the KV62 Antechamber sitting atop the hippo couch. Griffith Institute

An Antechamber small wood-veneered with gilding lidded box in the form of a half-oval (No. 79). Found on the Hathor couch, it held an assortment of loincloths, miscellaneous linen bandagings & other cloth oddments. Cairo Egyptian Museum

and (-5) a piece of jeweled ornamentation probably belonging to 54ddd4.[74]

Such a jumble of contents in this Box 54 and all the others from the Antechamber were clear indications to Carter and company that no single lot represented the original objects a receptacle contained when it was placed in the tomb at the time of Tutankhamen's funeral, but rather was the consequences of the post-looting reorderings by the necropolis officials, who simply had gathered off the floor the dumped-and-scattered objects thrown about by the robbers and returned these — without regarded to order or relationships — pell-mell to whatever box, chest or casket was nearest at hand.

Based upon the clearance of the tomb to this point, Carter was able to draw some conclusions regarding the activities of the robbers who had penetrated the King's burial in antiquity. Because of the sealings on the outer doorways (to the entry corridor and the Antechamber), it was apparent that the looting took place within a decade of the interment, and on at least two, possibly three different occasions. Because objects had been found by the excavators on or near the floor of the entry corridor, it was likely, Carter thought, that the tomb was first robbed immediately after the funeral, before the corridor was filled to its ceiling with protective rock debris. This subsequent fill had been tunneled through and all of the chambers of the tomb had been entered by a second group of thieves; and every room but the Burial Chamber had been ransacked in the search for easily portable objects of intrinsic worth, chiefly items made of solid gold. Certainly the thieves could not have carried off anything very sizeable, given the cramped dimensions of their crawlspace-tunnel through the corridor fill. The totally topsy-turvy state of the Annexe when first encountered by the excava-

tors is very likely how the Antechamber and, to a lesser degree, the Treasury also appeared to the necropolis officials, when they entered the tomb through the robbers' tunnel and began their thankless task of putting the spaces into some sort of order once again. Regarding the subsequent state of the Antechamber when found, Carter wrote, *"There was a certain amount of confusion, it was true, but it was orderly confusion, and had it not been for the evidence of plundering afforded by the tunnel and the re-sealed doorways, one might have imagined at first view that there never had been any plundering, and that the confusion was due to Oriental carelessness at the time of the funeral."*[75]

However, as the slow process of clearance got under way, it became apparent to Carter that this seeming orderliness was the result of a perfunctory tidying up following the last break-in. He continued, *"Parts of the same object were found in different parts of the* [Ante]*chamber; objects that should have been in boxes were lying on the floor or upon the couches; on the lid of one of the boxes there was a collar, intact but crumpled; behind the chariots, in an entirely inaccessible place, there was a box-lid, the box to which it belonged being far away, near the innermost door. Quite clearly the plunderers had scattered things here just as they had done in the Annexe, and someone had come after them and rearranged the chamber."*[76]

Additional circumstantial evidence of the robberies and clean ups was discovered when Carter, Mace and Lucas began to deal with the contents of boxes once these had been taken to the KV15 laboratory for unpacking. In only one instance did a box, chest or casket contain what specifically had been placed in it at the time of the interment of Tutankhamen. This could be determined because many of the boxes, etc., had dockets on their lids stating what the contents should

In the chest at top center, the excavators found a scarf (above) into which had been tied eight solid-gold rings. Carter presumed these had been plunderers' loot, left behind, then tossed into the chest by the necropolis officials who reordered the tomb.

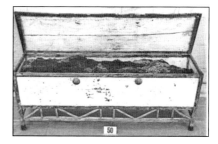

Large, long, painted-wood, undecorated box No. 50, with a hinged lid, was positioned prominently in front of the Antechamber lion couch; it was found to contain, along with considerable cloth items, a sizeable assortment of wooden sticks & staves belonging to the king, suggesting that he was possibly a collector of such.

have been.[77]

For example, in one chest — the one elaborately painted with scenes of the king hunting and fighting from his chariot (No. 21) — there were several decorated (beaded) robes which had been wadded up and stuffed in on top of numerous pairs of sandals; and the total contents of this box had been packed in so tightly that the metal

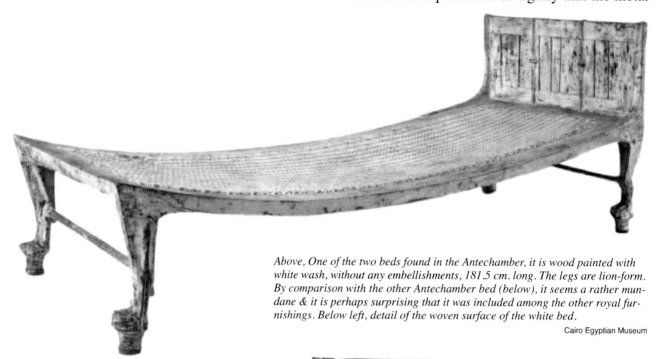

Above, One of the two beds found in the Antechamber, it is wood painted with white wash, without any embellishments, 181.5 cm. long. The legs are lion-form. By comparison with the other Antechamber bed (below), it seems a rather mundane & it is perhaps surprising that it was included among the other royal furnishings. Below left, detail of the woven surface of the white bed.

Cairo Egyptian Museum

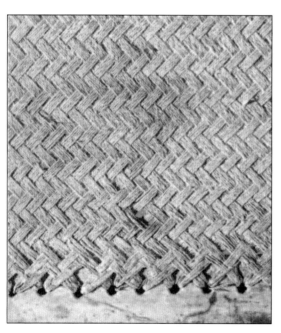

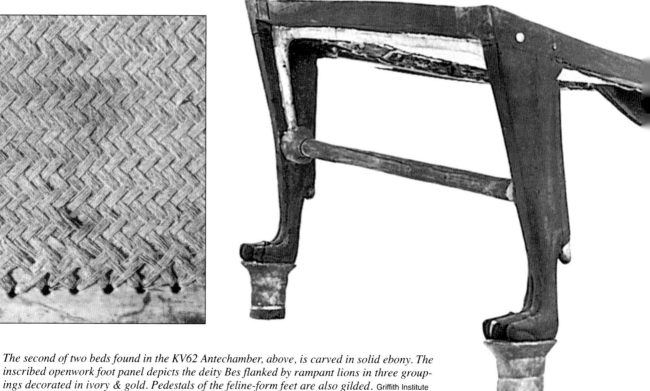

The second of two beds found in the KV62 Antechamber, above, is carved in solid ebony. The inscribed openwork foot panel depicts the deity Bes flanked by rampant lions in three groupings decorated in ivory & gold. Pedestals of the feline-form feet are also gilded. Griffith Institute

toe thong of one of the sandals had pierced its own leather sole and even penetrated the sole of the sandal which lay under it.

In the long hinged chest (No. 50) standing beside the lion couch, Carter found a mish-mash of the king's linen under garments and shawls stuffed on top of a quantity of sticks, staves, and bows and arrows — the metal points of the latter having been snapped off and presumably carried away. Scattered about the Antechamber were a number of other sticks, staves and bows which had no doubt originally been contained in the long chest, but had not been gathered up by those who reordered the tomb. While some of the boxes, etc., were over packed, others stood half empty or else contained only a few odds and ends of cloth.

The most obvious example of hasty and careless repacking of tossed-about objects was the situation of the king's complex inlaid-gold corselet/pectoral/collar garment. The largest porion of it was

Left, Detail of one of three openwork groupings of the dwarf-deity Bes flanked by rampant lions, all crowned by feathered headdresses; gilding on ebony. Cairo Egyptian Museum

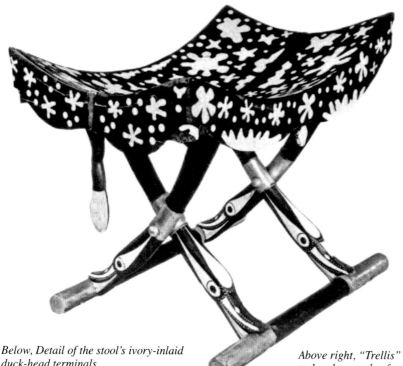

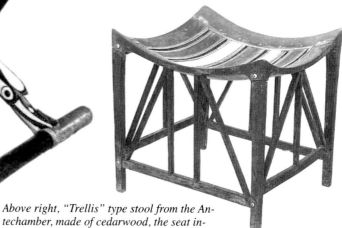

Left, Imitation folding stool of ebony wood inlaid with ivory & embellished with heavy gold mountings. The legs terminate in duck heads & the seat is meant to represent an animal skin, complete with tail. This stool, one of three of the type from KV62, was found in the Antechamber with a piece of harness equipment (a "cheek rowel") resting on its seat. An earlier example of the duck-legged folding stool is known from the Tomb of Kha & Merit, TT8. Cairo Egyptian Museum

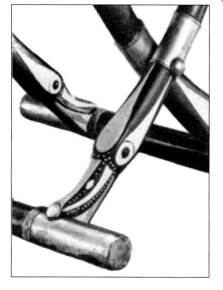

Below, Detail of the stool's ivory-inlaid duck-head terminals.

Above right, "Trellis" type stool from the Antechamber, made of cedarwood, the seat inlaid with ivory & ebony. Griffith Institute

Below, Stool from the Antechamber of white-painted wood with a concave seat, the legs terminating in lion paws. The openwork between the legs is the device symbolizing the unity of the Two Lands. Griffith Institute

found in a box with sixteen faience vases, while part of the collar element was stuffed into the small gilded shrine which rested on the floor behind the hippo couch. Other pieces of it were revealed in several other boxes, and even laying directly on the Antechamber floor. Clearly it had been intentionally pulled apart by a thief, who may have thought to steal it for its gold, then abandoned the idea and tossed it aside.

Based on the evidence offered by the condition of the Antechamber and the situation of its contents, it is possible to reconstruct the sequence of events regarding the tomb's second robbery:

1. The sealed outer doorway was breached in its upper left-hand corner, and tunneling began in the rubble fill of the corridor, making a crawlspace large enough to admit a single person, or several persons moving on hands and knees in single file. Passing baskets of rock debris and dirt back one to another, it would have taken about seven or eight hours' work (Carter's estimate) to reach the second sealed doorway, through which another breach was made, also in its upper left-hand corner. And the Antechamber was entered.

2. In the semi-darkness (at least one of the thieves doubtlessly would have been holding a torch of some sort, for the others' benefit), a mad scramble began in the search for easily portable objects of solid gold. Gold glittered everywhere, but most of it was merely gold leaf or thin sheeting on wooden objects too large to take away, in any case; and there was no time to strip the gleaming surfaces.

3. In the dim light it was difficult to distinguish what was solid gold and gilded wood. Objects first thought to be the real thing, on closer examination, proved otherwise and were contemptuously cast aside. The chests were carried or hauled one by one into the open space in the center of the Antechamber and their contents dumped on the

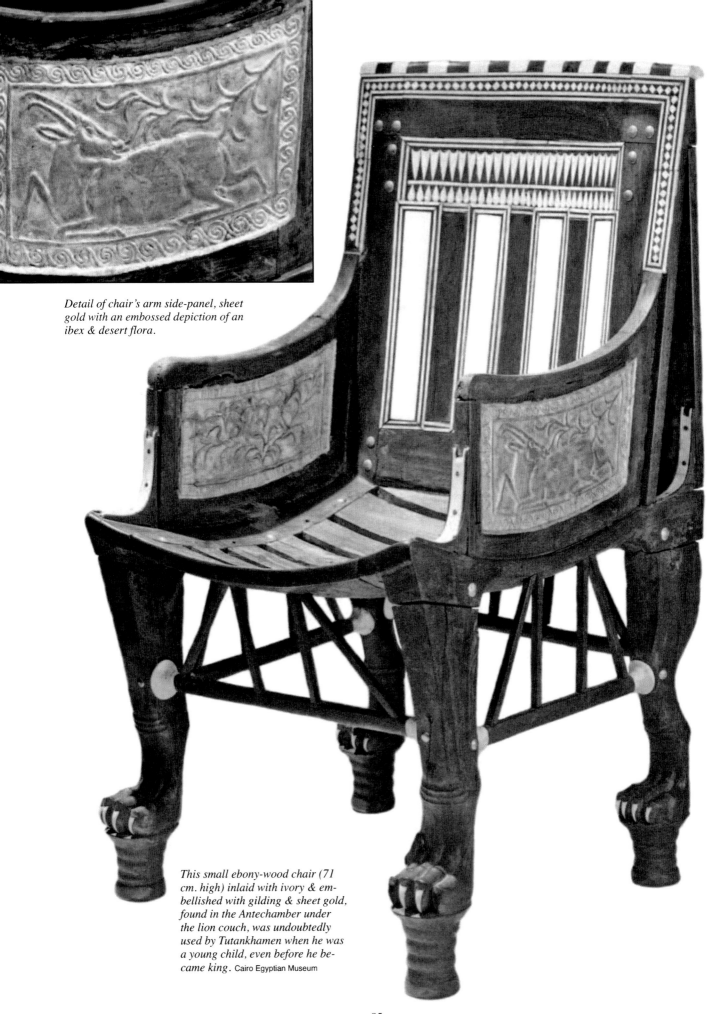

Detail of chair's arm side-panel, sheet gold with an embossed depiction of an ibex & desert flora.

This small ebony-wood chair (71 cm. high) inlaid with ivory & embellished with gilding & sheet gold, found in the Antechamber under the lion couch, was undoubtedly used by Tutankhamen when he was a young child, even before he became king. Cairo Egyptian Museum

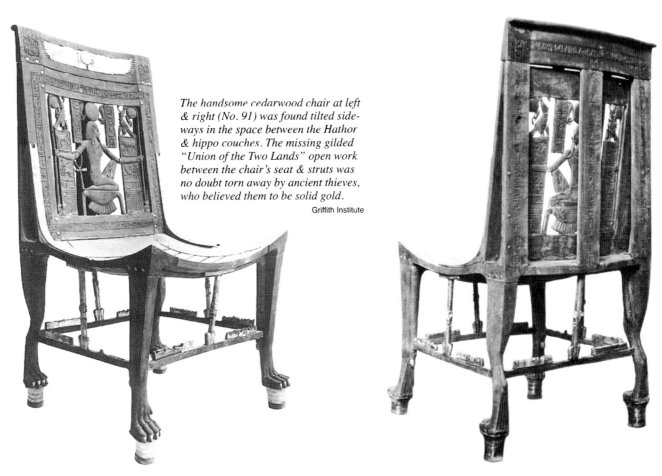

The handsome cedarwood chair at left & right (No. 91) was found tilted sideways in the space between the Hathor & hippo couches. The missing gilded "Union of the Two Lands" open work between the chair's seat & struts was no doubt torn away by ancient thieves, who believed them to be solid gold.
Griffith Institute

floor, then rummaged through in the search for heavy metal. The whole operation must have been done superficially in great haste, for numerous gold objects were overlooked. Only one thing which was taken is certain, a small statuette standing on a base inside the gold-plated small shrine. And one of the thieves apparently knotted a handful of solid-gold rings into a scarf; whether he subsequently dropped the small bundle, or merely set it aside and forgot to take it when exiting the tomb in haste can not be known; but it was apparently found subsequently by the necropolis officials who followed after the thieves, and was merely dumped, still tied up, into one of the boxes being refilled during the clean up.

4. Having done as much as was possible in the Antechamber — now totally in chaos as a result of their ransacking — the thieves broke through an already existing small hole in the plastered-over blocking of the doorway to the Annexe, which had been made by the first set of tomb robbers. The Annexe is a small space and, as a storeroom, was well filled with grave goods, so likely just one or two of the tomb robbers (one to hold a torch?) actually entered the chamber and went about rummaging through its contents, again searching for solid-gold objects, just as the Antechamber's containers had been dumped and their contents gone through. Here in the Annexe, several calcite jars already had been emptied of their valuable oils (poured into leather pouches carried by the earlier thief?), the perpetrator leaving his fingerprints on them as evidence of his deed. The new intruder left his dirty footprints on a large white-painted wooden bow box.

5. While the Annexe was being searched, others of the robbers broke a hole in the blocked wide doorway leading to the rest

The openwork carving of the back panel (opposite) depicts the god Heh kneeling on a nub-sign ("gold of eternity") between heraldic emblems & the Horus names of Tutankhamen. Embossed-gold decoration includes a winged solar disk at the top of the chair's back. Cairo Egyptian Museum

Cedarwood footstool (No. 92) belonging to the ceremonial chair (91); it is decorated with elegant relief carvings of the Nine Bows, Egypt's traditional enemies.
Cairo Egyptian Museum

Certainly the gem of the contents of KV62's Antechamber is Tutankhaten/ Tutankhamen's gold-plated & inlaid throne, right, found positioned under the hippo couch next to the robbers' hole into the Annexe. On the seat rested its footstool (below) with depictions of bound enemies. Originally the spaces between the seat & struts had been filled with openwork of the heraldic device representing the union of the Two Lands. Thieves apparently wrested these away, perhaps believing that they were solid gold rather than gilded wood. The lion-paw feet of the throne rest on spindles which in turn are shod with bronze.

Opposite, Detail of the inlaid-relief vignette decorating the inside back of the throne, depicting Tutankhamen & Ankhesenamen under the rays of the Aten Disk. The inlays are principally faience, colored glass & semi-translucent stone painted on the backside. The king's kilt & the queen's garment are silver foil. Tutankhamen's pose, sitting somewhat slouched on a cushioned chair, is pure Amarna style, as is the modeling of his & Ankhesenamen's hands & bodies. The diadem the king wears in combination with the elaborate **atef** crown is similar to the one which Carter would find encircling the royal mummy's head.
    Cairo Egyptian Museum

Above & left, Two views of the rear of the throne, with a marsh scene of papyri & flying ducks, plus six rearing uraei, *the four central ones supporting sun disks & the two flanking pair the White Crown of Upper Egypt.*

Side view of the throne. Griffith Institute

of the tomb chambers.[78] Entering the narrow walk space between the huge outermost tabernacle — which all but filled the Burial Chamber — the intruders easily enough made their way to the wide-open doorway of the Treasury. Their flickering torch light falling on the alert black-and-gold Anubis jackal resting atop the pylon-shaped chest immediately inside this entrance may have given them a momentary start; but these were not religious men, and they entered the small chamber with impunity. The doors on at least one of the tall pitch-covered *naoi* lining one wall may have been pulled open, its cord-and-mud seal broken, to reveal only gilded-wood cult statues inside. So the thieves would have turned their attention to a row of six smallish chests or caskets laying perpendicular to the Anubis Shrine. Throwing the lids off of these, they dumped the contents of each in turn on the floor. The boxes proved to contain a large quantity of the king's jewelry, the seemingly more valuable pieces being snatched up and stuffed into the cloth sacks which the robbers probably carried for stashing their loot. The polished (silver?) reflectors of two hand mirrors were also wrenched off their handles and taken. The docket of one compartmented casket listed sixteen identical gold or silver vessels for cosmetics, and all of these were, of course, pilfered.

6. Since a quantity of inlaid-gold jewelry was left behind in the so-called Treasury by the robbers, it is possible that a lookout's warning was sounded at this point in the nefarious operations. The gang of thieves would have made a hasty exit from the tomb, scrambling in panic back through their close tunnel and slinking off into the desert night, heavy bags of royal loot slung over their shoulders. It is not likely they were apprehended by the necropolis guards, but their break-in was no doubt discovered in due course by the former, who

then would have alerted the necropolis officials to the awful situation.

    7. A small inspection party of those responsible for the security of the royal necropolis would have entered the tomb via the robbers' tunnel, probably the following morning, to investigate what had been done by the intruders, and to make things right. They would have found the Antechamber in complete shambles: furniture and chariot bodies shoved about, empty boxes and chests tossed everywhere, and their miscellaneous contents in impossibly jumbled heaps on the floor. Working as hastily as the robbers before them, the officials uprighted those boxes closest at hand and began gathering the smaller objects and jamming them into the containers, without making any effort to sort the material or return things to the same boxes from which they had been dumped. Some chests were packed tight, others left almost empty, even though not all of the smaller objects were gathered up finally: sticks, staves and bows were left lying about; a bead collar was tossed, crumpled, onto the lid of a box; a harness trapping was dropped onto the seat of the duck-legged stool. The chariot bodies were carelessly piled together in one corner, atop an assortment of odds and ends; their wheels were leaned into the wall by the entry hole; and the large ceremonial couches were shoved back against the long wall, with

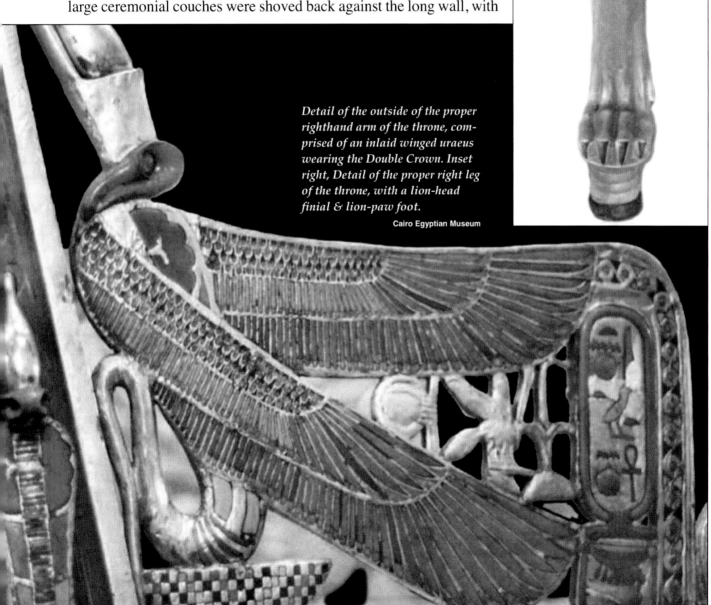

Detail of the outside of the proper righthand arm of the throne, comprised of an inlaid winged uraeus wearing the Double Crown. Inset right, Detail of the proper right leg of the throne, with a lion-head finial & lion-paw foot.

Cairo Egyptian Museum

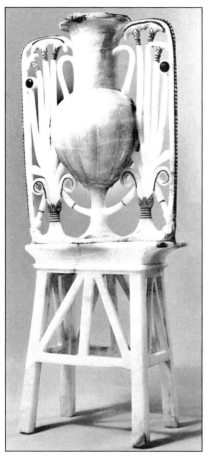

various chests, chairs and tall unguent vases being positioned under or piled on them, along with two of the king's beds.

8. In the course of arranging the tomb furnishings, the work party would have discovered the large gaping hole near one end of the long wall. Thrusting a torch into the blackness beyond, they no doubt viewed the thoroughly trashed Annexe and quickly concluded that reordering it would be next to impossible, inasmuch as there was not even any floor space in which to stand to do so. But two or three of them did wriggle through the small hole at floor level in the sealed doorway between the two *ka* statues of the king. Making their way to the open door of the Treasury, they entered this room and gathered up the jewelry which had been abandoned by the thieves in their hasty retreat from the tomb, and unceremoniously tossed this back into the various caskets standing empty, the latter being reclosed and arranged in an orderly row. Of the three chambers ransacked by the robbers, the Treasury had suffered the least disruption.

9. Returning to the Antechamber, the necropolis officials replaced the several stones which the robbers had pried out of the bottom of the doorway to the Burial Chamber, but they did not replaster these, nor did they make any effort whatsoever to fill the robbers' hole to the Annexe. Climbing back into the tunnel, they plugged the breach made through the Antechamber outer doorway, then plastered and stamped this with their jackal-and-prisoners official seal. Next the robbers' tunnel was filled in with rock debris, and the doorway of the corridor was likewise reblocked, plastered and stamped. Lastly, they had the rock-cut stairwell completely filled with rubble and sand — the tomb thus being buried out of sight, with Osiris Nebkheperure Tutankhamen's eternal rest hopefully secure from further disturbance. And it so remained until late November, 1922 AD.

By the middle of February of the next year, 1923, the modern-day work of clearing the Antechamber was completed, and the

subterranean rectangular room stood empty, swept bare save for the two *ka* statues, which had been left *in situ*, still standing guard, as it were, over the sealed door leading to the rest of the tomb. The next task before the excavators was penetration of that blocking and the revelation of what Carter and Lord Carnarvon secretly already knew lay beyond it. The earl and Lady Evelyn had returned to Luxor from England in late January, and so were present for the later stages of the Antechamber clearance. It was during this time that a series of press and public relations conflicts and crises began for "C. and C." over the tomb, which are detailed in an addendum to this chapter, "Chronology of the Tomb of Tutankhamen and Its Discovery," beginning p. 529.

The date set for the taking down of the Antechamber sealed door was February 17.[79] At 2:00 p.m. those privileged few who would be present for the operation[80] met above the tomb, and at 2:15 the assembly descended into the depths and took chairs arranged behind a barrier which had been put across the northern end of the cleared space. Beyond this stood the "guardian" statues — now fully screened with boarding to protect them — between which had been built a low plank platform, a sort of mini-stage for the drama about to unfold. Photographer Burton's two 3,000-candle-power electric lights affixed to their stands glared directly on the plastered doorway, stamped all over with its multitude of necropolis seals. Carter would write, *"There before us lay the sealed door, and with its opening we were to blot out the centuries and stand in the presence of a king who reigned three thousand years ago. My own feelings as I mounted the platform were a strange mixture, and it was with a trembling hand that I struck the first blow."*[81]

Carter carefully located the wooden lintel which framed the top of the door, chipped away the plaster covering it and the stones beneath. He then lifted out the latter which formed the topmost course of the door blocking. He wrote, somewhat disingenuously, *"The temptation to stop and peer inside was irresistible, and when, after about*

ten minutes' work, I had made a hole large enough to enable me to do so, I inserted an electric torch. An astonishing sight its light revealed, for there, within a yard of the doorway, stretching as far as one could see and blocking the entrance to the chamber, stood what to all appearance was a solid wall of gold. For the moment there was no clue as to its meaning...."[82] Carter very well knew, of course, that this *"wall of gold"* was the cornice and roof section of one long side of a faience-inlaid tabernacle, the outermost of a probable series, within which doubt-

The two striding life-sized jointed-wood figures of Tutankhamen which were positioned, guardian-like, on either side of the wide sealed doorway between the KV62 Antechamber & Burial Chamber were not unique discoveries; other greatly ruined or fragmentary examples of similar large ka-*figures were already known from the Tomb of Horemheb (one of two shown, Inset opposite* Davis, Harmhabi) & *Ramesside kings. The one on the right of the doorway (No., 22), wearing a* Nemes *headcover (opposite* in situ, J.A. Hammerton, Wonders of the Past, 1923, colorized Burton photo; *detail left & above,* Cairo Egyptian Museum) *had been draped with a linen cloth, which was found greatly decayed. The statues were conserved prior to shipment to Cairo by A.C. Mace & Alfred Lucas, seen inset opposite in the Tomb of Seti II, posing with the* Nemes *guardian figure.* Metropolitan Museum of Art

Two detail views of the second guardian figure (No. 29) wearing the Khat *covering. Both figures sport a uraeus of gilded bronze. The king's flesh is painted with black resin, as is each statue's base — black being the magical color of regeneration. Both five-foot six-inch figures (with bases, standing six-feet three-inches high) are attired in a girdled, pleated kilt with flaring triangular apron, & are adorned with arm- & wristbands, plus a broad collar over which a shrine-shaped pectoral is suspended. All of these elements of attire are gilded, as are the mace & long lotiform staff held by each statue. Sandals of sheet gold adorn the feet of both figures.* Cairo Egyptian Museum & Internet

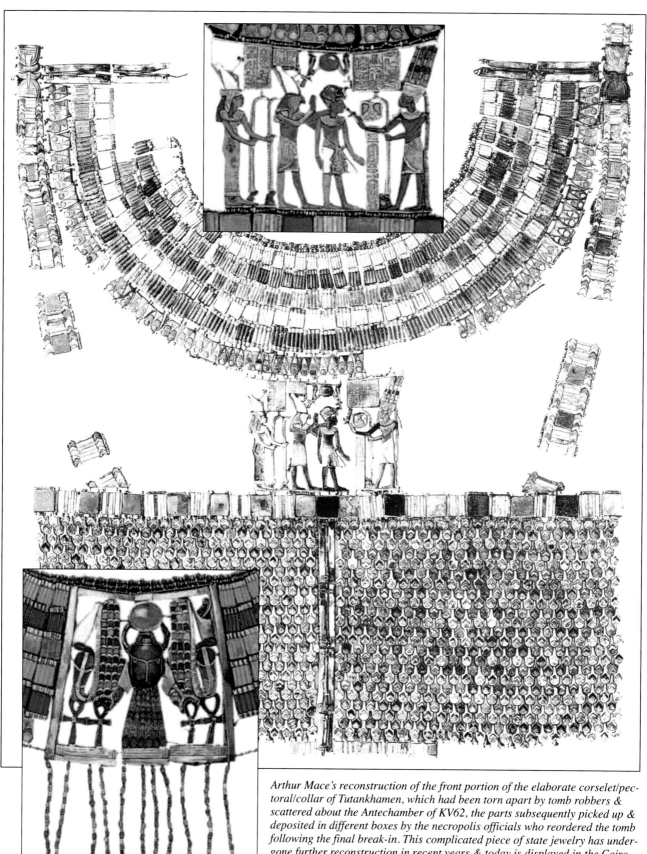

Arthur Mace's reconstruction of the front portion of the elaborate corselet/pectoral/collar of Tutankhamen, which had been torn apart by tomb robbers & scattered about the Antechamber of KV62, the parts subsequently picked up & deposited in different boxes by the necropolis officials who reordered the tomb following the final break-in. This complicated piece of state jewelry has undergone further reconstruction in recent years & today is displayed in the Cairo Egyptian Museum with the hinged elements in the center of Mace's reconstruction now serving to connect the front of the corselet to the rear portion, at each side. Nonetheless, several elements — chiefly plaques from the straps — are still missing, & must be presumed stolen — in antiquity or more recently. Insets, Details of the corselet's front (above) and back (left) pectoral-plaques.

lessly was nested the sarcophagus, coffins and mummy of King Tutankhamen.

Carter recorded that removal of the blocking stones was *"an operation of considerable difficulty,"* owing to the fact that these were not *"accurately squared,"* but rather were *"rough slabs of varying size"* and weight. Compounding the problem of removing the blocks one by one was Carter's effort to save as many as possible of the seal impressions stamped into the thick mortar with which the Antechamber side of the door blocking had been plastered. The archaeologist was assisted in the operation by Mace and Callender. The former would hold each block as Carter crowbarred it loose, to prevent it from falling into the *"wall of gold"*; Mace then helped him lift the freed block up and away and pass it back to Callender, who in turn handed it off to an awaiting Egyptian workman, to be carried from the tomb altogether.

As stone after stone was slowly wedged loose and removed, it soon enough became apparent to the assembly of spectators seated on their chairs arranged opposite the "staged" activity that what had at first appeared to be a *"wall of gold"* was, in fact, one side of a gigantic gilded structure heavily inlaid with blue faience, and that this in all probability housed the royal sarcophagus. So, it was the tomb's crypt itself that was about to be entered! But not for another two hours, which was the time it took to remove enough of the doorway blocking as was *"necessary for the moment,"* with several minutes further delay being required to recover the scattered beads of a necklace which had been dropped on the inner-chamber threshold by a departing plunderer.

Carter announced to his anxious audience that the floor level of the shrine-filled room beyond the now-exposed doorway was about four feet lower than that of the Antechamber, with somewhat less than a yard of space between the chamber wall and that of the

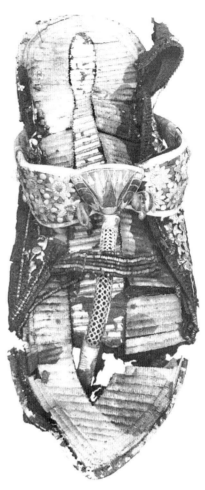

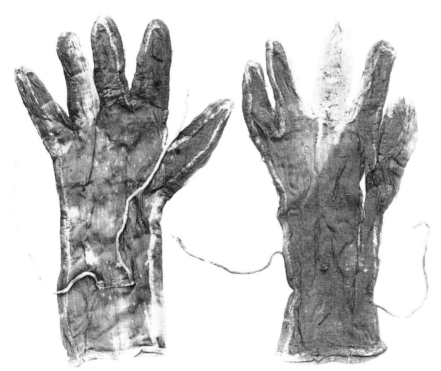

Among the clothing items belonging to Tutankhamen found in the Antechamber (Box 43) was a pair of linen gloves with strings attached for tying at the wrists, left. The painted chest with the chariot scenes (No. 21) contained several pairs of the king's sandals, including the especially elaborate one above, with the instep strap comprised of floral rosettes in gold, the buckle of inlaid gold & the toe thong of openwork gold. Griffith Institute

shrine The excavator carefully lowered himself into the chamber and requested one of Burton's portable lights on its stand. With this in hand, Carter moved to the corner of the shrine, where two *"graceful"* calcite vases stood in the walk space. He picked these up and passed them out to waiting hands (Callender's?) in the Antechamber, thus opening up a *"clear path."* He was now joined in the narrow space by Lord Carnarvon and Director-General Lacau, and the three of them played out the cord of Burton's lamp and began to explore the perimeters of the room. Coming to the unsealed doors of the tabernacle, they opened these to reveal a Second Tabernacle within, its doors closed with the necropolis seal intact. It was decided, by Lacau no doubt, to leave this unbroken for the present. Moving only a very little further on, the trio came to the open low doorway of the side chamber which would be dubbed the Treasury; and, as two of them had done once before, they each stooped, entered past the Anubis Shrine and together visually explored this space with its dazzling unique contents.

Carter would write, *"How much time we occupied in this first survey of the wonders of the tomb I cannot say, but it must have seemed endless to those anxiously waiting in the Antechamber. Not more than three at a time could be admitted with safety, so, when Lord Carnarvon and M. Lacau came out, the others went in in pairs: first Lady Evelyn Herbert, the only woman present, with Sir William Garstin, and then the rest in turn....It was an experience which, I am sure, none of us who were present is ever likely to forget...."*[83]

The next day, on February 18th,[84] the tomb was shown to Elisabeth, Queen of the Belgians, and her son, Prince Leopold,[85] plus Lord and Lady Allenby and several other distinguished visitors. One week later the winter 1922-1923 excavation season was declared over, and the Tomb of Tutankhamen was closed and once again reburied on February 26th. atory work continued for another day, however.

What ensued in the next weeks and months is well-known

105

In order to have full access to the Burial Chamber, it was necessary for the excavators to remove, finally, the two life-sized ka statues of the king from the Antechamber, one seen at left being "bandaged" by Carter & Callender to protect it during transport to the Tomb of Seti II laboratory/storehouse. It might be supposed that these figures were left in position after the rest of the Antechamber contents had been removed solely as an excuse to fully mask off — with protective wooden screens & a small elevated stage — the ancient robbers' hole at the bottom of the sealed doorway leading to the Burial Chamber, which had been used to access the latter space by Carter, Carnarvon & Evelyn Herbert their first night in the tomb. Note in the photo above that the doorway blocking has been completely removed to the floor on the right side, where the hole had been, effectively obliterating the very fact of its existence.

Metropolitan Museum of Art

generally, and need not be dealt with in depth for the present account (see the "Chronology" addendum, p. 283). Under a great deal of political and media pressure, Carter and Carnarvon quarreled and seemingly had a falling out by the closing week of February,[86] Carnarvon departing Luxor for Aswan on the last day of the month. At about this same time, the earl was bitten on the cheek by an insect (probably a mosquito), and he accidentally infected the raised welt while shaving with his straight razor. He was subsequently struck down with blood poisoning and a high fever (101°F), and, being already in frail health, was forced to bed. He seemed to rally and did not take his condition seriously, but then relapsed almost immediately. By now having returned to the cooler spring climate of Cairo with Lady Evelyn, he took accommodations at the Continental-Savoy Hotel on March 14th. However, further weakened by infection and still running a dangerously high temperature, he inevitably succumbed to pneumonia. Finally beyond recuperation, with his wife, son and daughter by his side, he expired at the Cairo hotel early in the morning of April 5, 1923, aged fifty-seven. His body was embalmed and returned to England, where he was buried on the grounds of Highclere Castle, the family estate. Because of inexplicably bizarre circumstances associated with the moment of Lord Carnarvon's death (the lights going out all over Cairo, his three-legged terrier purportedly howling and dropping dead far away in England), the press concocted and fed on the story of a "Pharaoh's Curse," to which the wealthy earl obviously had fallen victim for disturbing Tutankhamen's eternal rest (see Addendum Two, "Pharaoh's Curse," p. 306). Indeed, over the next several months — in fact, throughout most of 1923 and into the next year — it must have

Above left, View of the pall frame & Second Tabernacle within the First, the doors of the latter having been removed & the miscellaneous funerary goods stashed in the space between the portal & frame cleared away. Above right, The doors of the Second Tabernacle in full view after removal of the pall frame. On the left door, in incised relief, Tutankhamen is presented to Osiris by Isis; on the right door, Maat presents the king to Re-Horakhti. Griffith Institute

Above, Carter poses for Harry Burton's camera in a recreation of the act of opening the double doors of the Second Tabernacle. Metropolitan Museum of Art

seemed to Howard Carter and his team of associates that their enterprise of clearing the king's burial was every bit as ill fated as Carnarvon himself had been (see "Chronology" addendum).

Carnarvon's widow, Almina, assured Carter that her late husband's work in the Tomb of Tutankhamen would continue under her sponsorship, with the assistance of the earl's lawyer, Sir John Maxwell. Thus the excavator returned to Luxor to complete the final work of that winter season. This included finishing up documentation and conservation of the fragile objects removed from the Antechamber, and the careful packing of these, many of them cumbersome, in specially constructed wooden containers. The latter — thirty-four large packing cases accommodating eighty-nine boxes — were moved over the course of two days on portable rail tracks from the Valley of the Kings to Nileside, then onto a government steamer and thence to Cairo, for deposit in the Egyptian Museum — where they were unpacked and the Antechamber treasures put on display.

The death of Lord Carnarvon served to exacerbate the difficulties which had been festering between "C. and C." and the press and the Egyptian government since the very opening of the Antechamber, regarding: (1) access to the tomb site; (2) newspaper coverage (Carnarvon had granted the *Times* of London ongoing exclusive scoop-rights on the Tutankhamen find, much to the outrage of the world press generally — and of the Egyptian press, in particular); and, ultimately, (3) the unclear question of what sort of division of the tomb's objects there would be — if any — between Carnarvon and the Egyptian Museum. With the earl removed from the picture, it fell to his archaeologist to negotiate these touchy matters on behalf of the interests of the Carnarvon estate. The so-called "Sakkara Affair" of years before had proven that diplomatic skills and patience were not qualities attributable to Howard Carter, and it may be simply enough stated that he rather badly botched the job that summer and fall of 1923 (see "Chronology" addendum).

Over the summer a seeming accommodation had been reached between the Carnarvon estate and Director-General of the Antiquities Service Lacau; this amounted to the issuing of a new concession to Lady Carnarvon, in which the major difference between the original one held by the earl was the definition of future work in the Tomb of Tutankhamen as a "clearance" (*déblaiement*) rather than an "excavation" (*fouilles*). Because the issue of "division" (*partage*) of the tomb contents had not been raised again by Lacau in their negotiations through letter exchange, Carter returned to Egypt on October 8, 1923, confident that the Carnarvon family would, in the end, be duly rewarded with a selection of the king's treasures. He fully expected that his 1923-1924 winter season in the Valley of the Kings would be free of pressure from government quarters. In this he would be sadly mistaken.

The second season began with work in the Seti II laboratory. The chariots and ceremonial animal couches had not been among the Antechamber objects shipped to Cairo the previous spring, and Arthur Mace set about conserving these and packing them for future

Above, The yellow-quartzite sarcophagus of Tutankhamen revealed through the open doors of the in situ *Second, Third & Fourth tabernacles which nest it.* Griffith Institute

Opposite, Howard Carter & "Pecky" Callender (r.), assisted by two Egyptian workmen, raise a roof section of the First Tabernacle, for removal from the Burial Chamber to the Antechamber. Dismantling the total of 51 sections of the four structures required 84 days of the second season of the KV62 clearance. While the roof portions were stored in the Antechamber temporarily, the well-padded & wrapped side & end panels were leaned against the walls of the Burial Chamber for removal & conservation at a later time. Griffith Institute

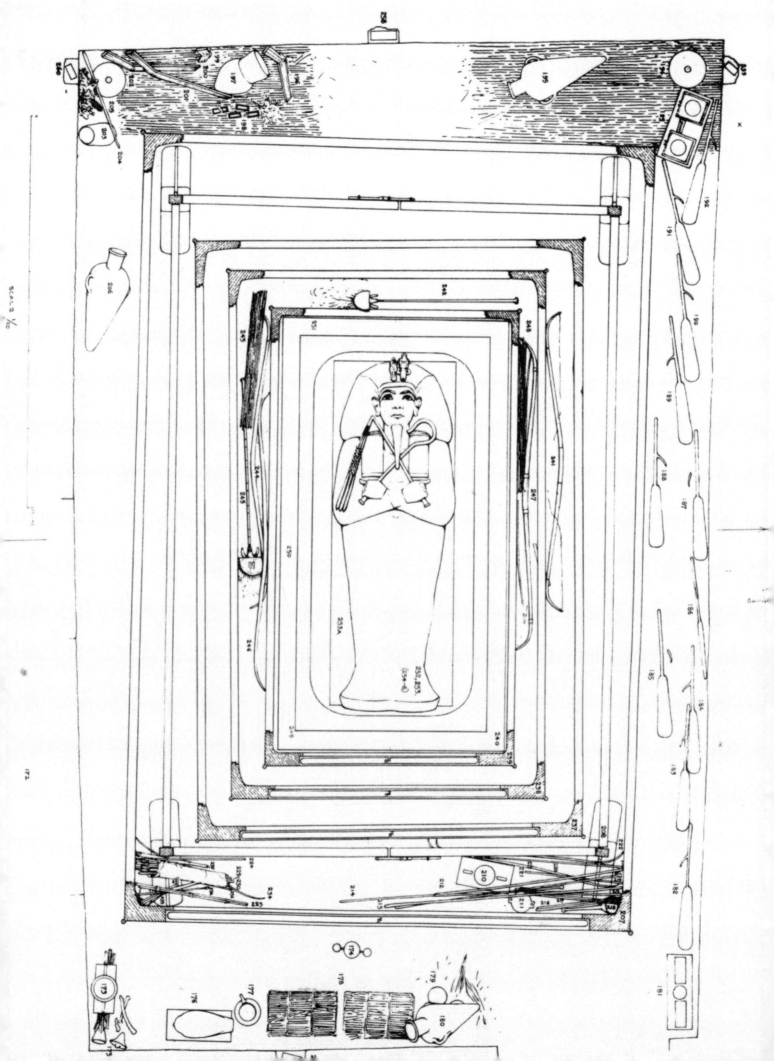

transport. Carter, meanwhile, turned his own attention to reopening the tomb itself and removing the so-called "guardian" statues which still graced the Antechamber. It is curious why these figures had been left *in situ* in the first place. It might be said that they added an element of drama as stage props for the opening of the Burial Chamber, except that both were completely hidden from the view of the invited spectators to this orchestrated event, each by a protective screen of wood planks. Rather, it may be that there was something a bit intentionally devious in the statues' presence, inasmuch as they conveniently served to frame the low wooden "stage" erected directly in front of the sealed door, on which Carter and Mace stood as the blocking stones were methodically removed. While comfortably elevating the dismantlers, this platform at the same time — and more importantly — completely disguised the fact that an ancient robbers' replugged hole existed in the door blocking at floor level — the very hole from which Carter and Callender had removed lose stones, thus permitting Carnarvon, his daughter and Carter himself to prematurely enter and secretly explore the Burial Chamber and Treasury that first night in the tomb.

Once the king's *ka* statues were safely in the laboratory, Carter's next task was to take down the thick masonry *"partitions"* which it was discovered walled off the Antechamber from the Burial Chamber, the open space between them creating the doorway to the latter. Demolishing these partitions was absolutely necessary in order to effect the removal of the funerary tabernacles, which had been introduced to the tomb's crypt before construction of the partitions. A problem was that the backside of the left-hand partition (as viewed from the Antechamber) contained part of the painted-plaster decoration of the south wall of the Burial Chamber: the standing figure of the goddess Isis and three squatting minor Underworld deities. Although the plaster was carefully pried away from the limestone which it veneered, inevitably pieces of the scene were destroyed in the process, as is evident in Harry Burton's photo of the removed wall section resting on a tray of sand. In taking down these dry-masonry partition walls, it was discovered that they had been bonded together with *"heavy logs of wood."*

Before dismantlement of the tabernacles could begin, however, it was necessary to label, photograph, remove and transport to the laboratory for conservation the several miscellaneous objects which had been placed on the Burial Chamber floor in the narrow space between the outermost tabernacle and the rock-cut walls. These included (moving counterclockwise around the tabernacle from the entry): a calcite lamp on a trellis stand; a silver trumpet and stopper; a bitumenized-wood statue of a goose shrouded in linen; a red-pottery libation vessel; the floriform calcite lamp which had originally stood in front of the doors of the First Shrine; a wooden *hes* emblem covered in resin; eleven small wooden oars; a pair of bitumenized-wood kiosks on a pedestal, each containing blue-faience cups; a gilded Anubis emblem on a pole and stand; four curious gilded-wood emblems shaped somewhat like a modern hockey stick; a second Anubis emblem iden-

Opposite, Howard Carter's sketch plan of the KV62 Burial Chamber, showing Tutankhamen's outer coffin within its sarcophagus & nest of funerary shrines. Note the miscellany of small objects placed on the chamber floor between the outermost tabernacle & the rock-cut walls, as well as the objects (mostly staves, sticks & bows) filling the space between the doors of the First & Second tabernacles. Griffith Institute

Life-size wooden goose found positioned in front of the doors to the First Tabernacle. Except for the gilded beak, it is thickly coated in bitumen & stands on its own bitumenized wooden base. Internet photo

Narration continues p. 127

Objects from the Burial Chamber, Associated with the Tabernacles

Left, The large (51.4 cm. high) chalice-shaped calcite lamp found in the southeast corner of the Burial Chamber. The vessel is flanked by openwork ornamentation bearing the king's nomen & prenomen & rests on a low trellis stand of typical Egyptian style. The chalice is undecorated on its inner & outer surfaces, but when lighted from within (in antiquity, with a wick floated in oil) a colored scene of the enthroned Tutankhamen & standing Ankhesenamen becomes visible. This effect was achieved by fitting a second calcite cup within the chalice proper, on the outside of which the royal-couple vignette had been painted in semi-translucent pigments.

Left, Bizarre fetish-emblem of Anubis, one of an identical pair found in each corner of the western end of the Burial Chamber. A calcite base with the king's cartouches supports a gilded upright pole representing a water-lily stem & bud, attached to which is a gilded plaster-&-wood form of a headless inflated animal skin, its entwined tail ending in a papyrus bloom.

Unique among the bows, maces, staves & sticks found in the space between the doors of the First & Second tabernacles were a pair of four-foot-long sticks which have as their finials small statuettes of King Tutankhamen as he must have appeared at the time of his ascension to the throne, at age nine or ten. One stick is gilded, the 3.5-inch figure being solid gold (seen at right in two views); the other is silvered, with a solid-silver figure. Due to their short length, it is unlikely that they would have functioned as walking sticks, even for the boy-king. It has been suggested that they may have served as wands or marking pegs in some ceremony connected with the coronation. Similar small king-figures are often shown adorning the royal barque & those of the god Amen & his family.

Left, From the space between the First & Second tabernacle doors is this highly intricate perfume vase belonging to Tutankhamen & his queen, made of four separate sections of calcite cemented together & embellished with gold & painted ivory. The central vase is flanked by an openwork emblem of the Union of the Two Lands, each of these supported by freestanding figures of the Nile god, Hapi. A delicately rendered figure of the goddess Mut, in vulture form with open wings, adorns the top of the vase, & is flanked by uraei with Red & White crowns. Panels of the low fretwork stand display solar hawks supporting the king's nomen & prenomen, the hawks & cartouches atop nub signs.

Below, Also found between the same tabernacle doors, was a cylindrical calcite cosmetic or ointment jar. It is flanked by two lotiform columns each with a Bes-head capital, the flat revolving lid being decorated with the recumbent figure of a lioness also sculpted of calcite. It rests on a base comprising four prisoners' heads in hard red & black stone. The knobs & lioness's tongue are ivory stained red. A hunting scene of lions & dogs attacking wild bulls & antelopes is etched on the sides of the cylinder & colored with different pigments. All Cairo Egyptian Museum

Objects not to scale.

View of the narrow space between the First Tabernacle & the Burial Chamber north wall, with numerous ritual oars as found & one of the Anubis fetishes visible in the northwest corner. Griffith Institute

Two views of the sides of the stock of one of two processional fans found situated on the floor between the Third Tabernacle & the Fourth. Because it was gilded all over, Carter labeled it the Golden Fan. It is decorated in incised relief with two scenes, the one above on the recto side depicting Tutankhamen in his chariot hunting ostriches with the assistance of his slughi hound.

The verso side, left, shows the king returning from the successful ostrich chase, with attendants carrying his bagged quarry — two birds.

Cairo Egyptian Museum

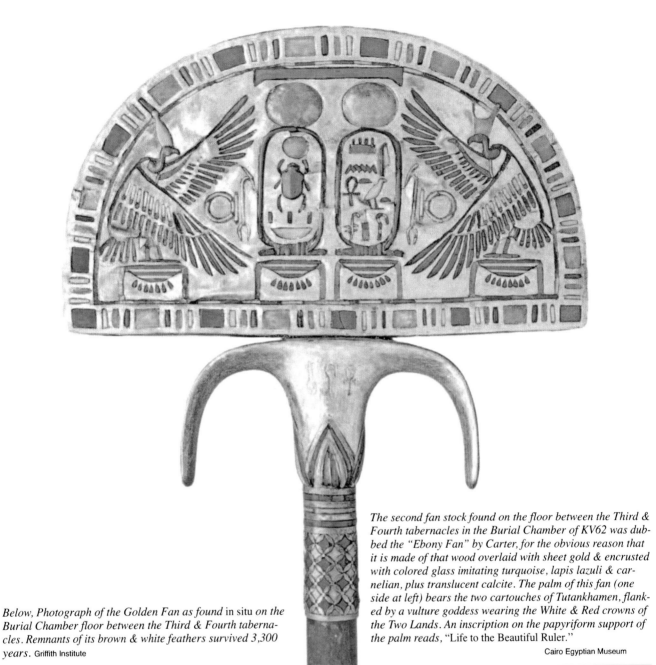

Below, Photograph of the Golden Fan as found in situ on the Burial Chamber floor between the Third & Fourth tabernacles. Remnants of its brown & white feathers survived 3,300 years. Griffith Institute

The second fan stock found on the floor between the Third & Fourth tabernacles in the Burial Chamber of KV62 was dubbed the "Ebony Fan" by Carter, for the obvious reason that it is made of that wood overlaid with sheet gold & encrusted with colored glass imitating turquoise, lapis lazuli & carnelian, plus translucent calcite. The palm of this fan (one side at left) bears the two cartouches of Tutankhamen, flanked by a vulture goddess wearing the White & Red crowns of the Two Lands. An inscription on the papyriform support of the palm reads, "Life to the Beautiful Ruler."

Cairo Egyptian Museum

I

The outermost **First Tabernacle** (above), resembling the sed-festival pavilion, measures 5.08 meters in length, 3.28 meters wide & 2.75 meters high. It is made of heavy planks of cedar (32 cm. thick) in 16 sections & is gessoed, gilded & inlaid on all its surfaces. The decoration of the exterior door panels & three side panels consists of a repeated pattern of incised pairs of tyet knots flanked by djed pillars, set against an inlaid background of brilliant-blue faience. The interior surfaces are incised with funerary texts. A curious, free-standing gilded-wood framework which supported a linen pall sewn all over with gilded-bronze rosettes is seen inside the structure.

III

The **Third Tabernacle**, left, is nearly identical in design to the Second, with the same sloping roof as the Per-wer. It is slightly smaller (3.40 m.long, 1.92 m. wide, 2.15 m.high) & is made of 10 separate sections. Funerary figures & texts cover the gilded-gesso exterior & interior surfaces.

The Nested Set of Great Gilded Tabernacles

II

*The **Second Tabernacle**, above, also of cedarwood in 16 sections, differs from the First in the shape of its roof, which, like the traditional Per-wer, "Palace of the South" of Upper Egypt, slopes from front to back. It is, of course, also smaller (3.74 m. long, 2.35 m. wide, 2.25 m. high.); & its gilded-gesso surfaces are decorated all over, in*side & out, with incised low reliefs of vignettes & passages from a variety of funerary texts, but without the faience inlays of Tabernacle One. The exterior of the doors depict King Tutankhamen being presented by Isis to Osiris (l.) & by Maat to Re-Horakhti (r.).

IV

*The innermost **Fourth Tabernacle** is constructed in five separate sections & measures 2.90 m. long, 1.49 m. wide & 1.90 m. high. Its roof style is distinctly different from the other three shrines & resembles the Predynastic Per-nu or "Palace of the North," being barrel vaulted with rectangular upright end sections. The gilded-gesso decoration of the exterior side panels consists of funerary texts & processions of Underworld deities, while both the rear panel & the exterior door halves depict the goddesses Isis & Nephthys with overlapping outspread wings. The goddess Nut — flanked by doubly depicted falcon-headed Horus — is represented on the ceiling of the interior.*

Colorized images adapted from
Piankoff, *The Shrines of Tut-Ankh-Amon*

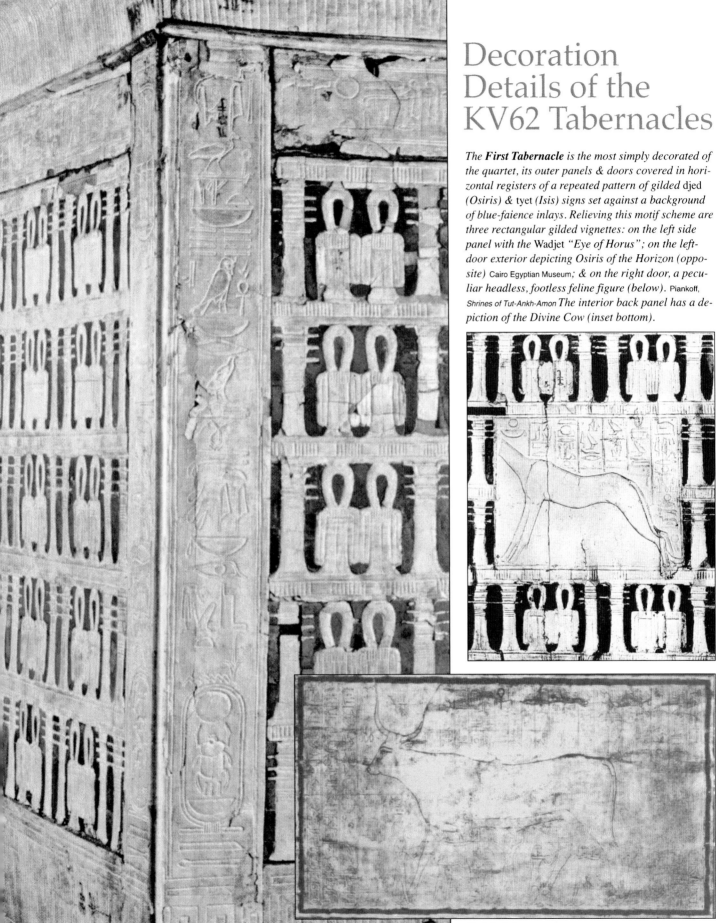

Decoration Details of the KV62 Tabernacles

The **First Tabernacle** is the most simply decorated of the quartet, its outer panels & doors covered in horizontal registers of a repeated pattern of gilded djed (Osiris) & tyet (Isis) signs set against a background of blue-faience inlays. Relieving this motif scheme are three rectangular gilded vignettes: on the left side panel with the Wadjet "Eye of Horus"; on the left-door exterior depicting Osiris of the Horizon (opposite) Cairo Egyptian Museum; & on the right door, a peculiar headless, footless feline figure (below). Piankoff, Shrines of Tut-Ankh-Amon The interior back panel has a depiction of the Divine Cow (inset bottom).

Piankoff, Shrines

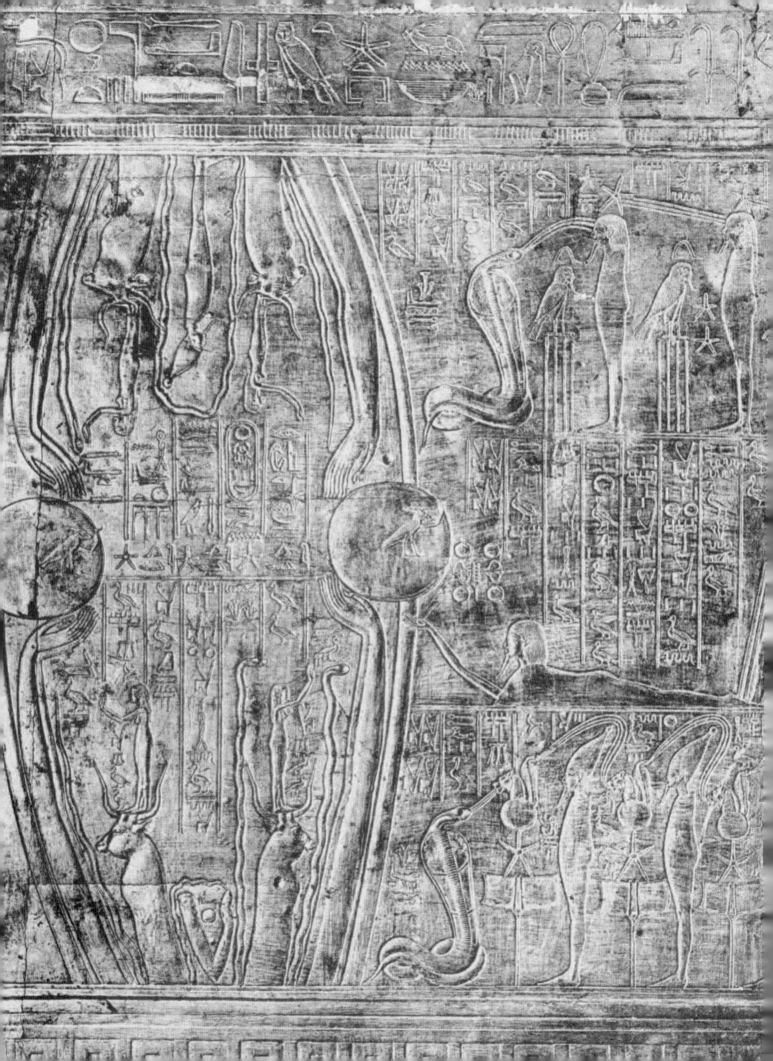

*The gilded **Second Tabernacle** is decorated both outside &
in with incised low-relief vignettes & texts from various funerary compositions, such as details at left & opposite from
the exterior right side panel, & the pairs of deities, above &
below, from the interior of the right door panel. The texts &
Underworld scenes on all of the KV62 tabernacles parallel
decoration painted on the walls of other New Kingdom royal tombs.* Adapted & colorized from Piankoff, *Shrines of Tut-Ankh-Amon*

The exterior door panels of the **Third Tabernacle**, Above, depict two ram-headed Underworld guardians & two heralds, one with a crocodile head, the other with a lion head sporting two uraei. The winged solar disk is to be seen on the lintel. The exterior side panels are decorated with funerary texts & figures, as in the detail at left.

Overleaves, The interior-rear panel of the **Third Tabernacle**, with winged depictions of the goddesses Isis (l.) & Nephthys.

Opposite, Left exterior door panel of the **Second Tabernacle** depicting King NebkheperureTutankhamen presented to Osiris by the goddess Isis. The companion righthand door-panel exterior has a similar vignette with the king being presented to Re-Horakhti by Maat.

Images adapted & colorized from Piankoff, *Shrines*

Decoration of the exterior rear panel of the **Fourth Tabernacle**, at left, is comprised of the winged goddesses Nephthys (l.) & Isis, only one of several such representations of these divinities on the quartet of tabernacles. The side panels of this 4th structure have processions of Underworld deities greeted by Thoth, as seen in the details below.

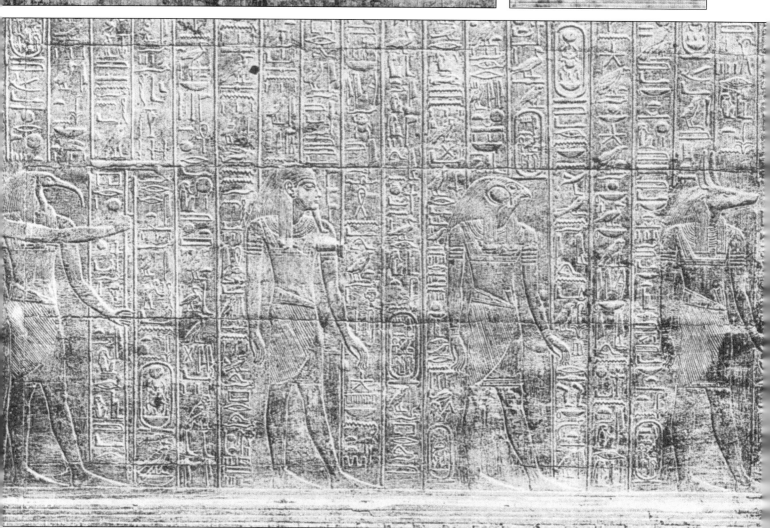

tical to the first; and a staff with glass inlay. Interspersed between these objects were: a diverse assortment of pottery and pottery fragments; various labels and seals; ox ribs and other bones; two reed baskets; four small clay troughs; and two funerary bouquets, one of persea twigs.

It was also necessary to extract another assortment of funerary miscellany from the narrow space between the door panels of the First Tabernacle and those of the the inner Second one, for a total of twenty-six different objects. These included: an elaborate calcite perfume vase with sculpted Hapi figures, all on an openwork low base; a cylindrical calcite ointment jar decorated with an engraved-and-pigmented hunting scene, a sculpted reclining lioness decorating its lid; and a quantity of decorated (gilded, silvered, inlaid, etc.) bows, maces, staves and sticks, two of the latter — one gilded, the other silvered — being unique for their finials: in each case a tiny statuette of the king in solid gold or silver respectively, showing him at the time of his coronation, aged nine or ten.

The reassembled gilded-wood framework which was positioned between the First & Second tabernacles & supported a massive linen pall decorated with large gilded rosettes or bosses.

Internet photo

Once the outermost tabernacle was freed of the funerary deposits which had surrounded it and cluttered the space behind its double doors, Carter and his team set about the challenging task of taking apart this imposing structure which in design was very much like the traditional *sed*-festival pavilion known from relief and painted representations, with battered walls and a double-sloping roof. It was determined that the 2.25-inch thick cedar-plank sections making up the shrine were held together *"by means of secret wooden tongues let into*

The sarcophagus as it stood fully exposed in early February 1924, surrounded by the sheet-wrapped end & side panels of the dismantled tabernacles leaning against the Burial Chamber walls. While the sarcophagus itself was carved from a solid block of the finest yellow quartzite, it was discovered that its lid (shaped like the roofs of the Second & Third tabernacles) was mismatched, being of rose granite tinted to look like the much harder yellow stone of the box. Additionally, the lid was cracked across its width, almost exactly in the center, undoubtedly the result of an accident when it was being lowered in place following Tutankhamen's funeral. Why the lid does not match the sarcophagus has never been satisfactorily explained. Carter proposed that it was substituted when the original yellow-quartzite cover was not finished in time. More likely the latter was itself accidentally broken in transit to the tomb & judged unusable, with the substitute hurriedly cut to replace it, perhaps from a slab of rose granite already at hand in a royal workshop. Metropolitan Museum of Art

the thickness of the woodplanking...." Carter recorded, *"It was only by slightly forcing open the cracks between those different sections, and by that means discovering the positions of the tongues that held them together, inserting a fine saw and severing them, that we were able to free them and take them apart."*[87] But the difficulty of disassembling the side panels, cornice sections and roof parts — aside from their great weight (a quarter to three-quarters of a ton apiece) — was compounded by the fact that the wood planks, while still perfectly sound, had shrunk over the thirty-three-plus centuries since being placed in the tomb, creating a slight void between the wood surface and the gilded gesso and faience inlays of the overall decoration. Touching the gilded surfaces with any pressure caused the gesso behind to crumble and fall away. *"Thus,"* Carter wrote, *"our problem was how to deal in that very limited space with those sections of the shrines ...when taking them apart and removing them, without causing them undue damage."*

The first step in the tabernacles' dismantlement was the introduction of scaffolding and hoisting tackle into the very cramped confines of the Burial Chamber, which, Carter reported, *"occupied practically all the available space, leaving little room for ourselves in which to work. When some of the parts were freed, there was insufficient room to remove them from the chamber. We bumped our heads, nipped our fingers, we had to squeeze in and out like weasels, and work in all kinds of embarrassing positions. ...Nevertheless, I am glad to say that in the conflict we did more harm to ourselves than to the shrines.*"[88]

The very heavy double-doors of the First Tabernacle were taken off by slightly raising the front part of the entablature (made up of the cornice molding and frieze beneath) and roof enough so that the copper pivots which hinged the doors could be freed from their sockets in the lintel and threshold. Next the three roof sections tongued into the entablature were hoisted by block and tackle, and removed. Then the four sections comprising the entablature itself were taken down. Without this molding to tie them together, the now-free-standing tabernacle side panels (supported only by their four corner uprights and the excavators' temporary struts), although very heavy, were relatively easy to manage. But there was no room to take them out of the Burial Chamber, so they were leaned against the corresponding walls — carefully padded and wrapped in great sheets of linen — to await removal at a future time. The corner uprights were freed from the rectangular floor frame, and the dismantling of the First Tabernacle was accomplished.

But before the Second Tabernacle could be dismantled, the strange wooden framework supporting the immense linen pall, and the decayed and very fragile pall itself, had to be dealt with. In addition to its great age — which had turned it dark brown — the drooping edges of the fabric were rent by the weight of the scores of gilded-bronze marguerites (floral rosettes) which had been sewn all over the pall. The linen material was first strengthened with duroprene (a chlorinated-rubber compound dissolved in an organic solvent), which enabled it to be rolled on a wooden rod so that it could be transported to the laboratory for further treatment and conservation. Freed of the pall which it supported, the peculiar gilded-wood framework was taken down, thus allowing the excavators full access to the Second Tabernacle.

Except for differing roofs (the Second having that of the archaic *Per-wer* shrine of Lower Egypt, rather than the double-sloping roof of the *sed*-festival pavilion), this structure was nearly identical in design to, if slightly smaller than, the First Tabernacle, except that its outer surface was decorated differently, being covered all over with incised funerary-themed reliefs and inscriptions on gilded gesso, without faience inlays. The double doors of this Second Tabernacle were bolted at their top and bottom, and secured with cording tied through metal staples, which bore a clay seal stamped with impressions of both the necropolis jackal-and-prisoners and the prenomen of the king, Neb-kheperure. This intact lump proved to Carter that the tomb robbers of antiquity had not penetrated any further into the king's funerary equipage, and that he could expect to find the mummy of Tutankhamen unviolated. As he wrote, *"Here was a great piece of luck, as manifestly behind those two seals we should be dealing with material unharmed since the burial of the king. It was with great care that the cords were severed, those folding doors opened, which, when swung back, re-*

Uncredited Internet graphic showing the KV62 tabernacles & sarcophagus to relative scale.

View of the Selket figure guarding the southeast corner of the KV62 sarcophagus. Visible is a large, painted-wood djed *amulet found positioned along the sarcophagus south side.* Internet photo

The sarcophagus of Tutankhamen contained his nest of three coffins & the lion bier on which these rested; but also found on its floor (along with some rags, floral fragments & a wooden lever) was an outstanding example of ancient jeweler's art, a six-inch-high gold perfume box on a silver base, seen above. It is in the shape of paired cartouches, each topped by a solar disk framed by double shu feathers. Rather than contain the prenomen & nomen of the king as is usual, the cartouches here are filled, front & back, with images of the youthful ruler, seated beneath the solar disk on the heb sign & holding the crook & flail regalia. On the side seen here Tutankhamen wears the the Khepresh helmet-crown, on the other the Horus lock of youth. The details are inlaid with opaque polychrome glass & translucent calcite. Cairo Egyptian Museum

Right, The west end of the yellow-quartzite sarcophagus of Tutankhamen in situ, with two of the four guardian goddesses visible, Isis on the right & Nephthys on the left. The concept of guardian goddesses at the corners of the royal sarcophagus dates at least to the reign of Akhenaten, when Queen Nefertiti was depicted in this capacity (the sarcophagus of Amenhotep III is missing, so it is not known whether this may have been an innovation of his reign). The style was continued on the sarcophagi of Ay & Horemheb, but neither example equals the workmanship of the KV62 sarcophagus. It has been proposed recently that the latter was actually made originally for Tutankhamen's immediate predecessor, Smenkhkare, the inscriptions being recut for the younger king. Metropolitan Museum of Art

Overleaves, Detail of the goddess Selket on the southeast corner of the sarcophagus. SCA photo

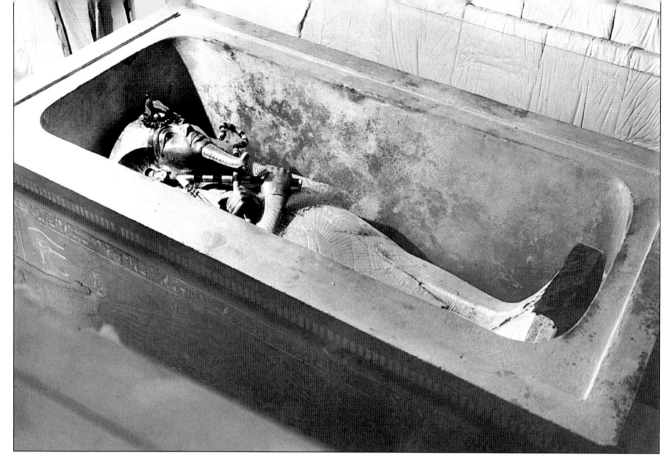

Above, The anthropoid First Coffin of Tutankhamen seen in situ, *resting in the king's sarcophagus. This is the sight which greeted Carter & his guests on February 12, 1924, when the sarcophagus lid was raised on pulleys & enveloping linen shrouds were rolled back to reveal the first totally intact king's coffin ever found in Egypt. Its great size (2.24 meters long) immediately suggested that it was but the outermost of a series of coffins housing the royal mummy. It was discovered to be resting on a low lion bier, & that the toe of the coffin lid had been adzed away in antiquity, to allow the sarcophagus lid to be lowered into place, a design miscalculation having caused the coffin to be too high at its foot end to be accommodated within the sarcophagus box. This alteration made it possible for Carter to determine that the coffin was made of cypress wood coated with gesso & overlaid with gold, ranging in thickness from sheet gold on the face to gold foil on the lid body & trough.* Griffith Institute

Opposite, Face of the First Coffin as seen today resting in the KV62 sarcophagus. Note the curious Khat-*like headgear worn by the king in this unique representation.* George B. Johnson photo

vealed yet a third shrine, also sealed and intact — the seal impressions upon this third shrine being identical to those on the second.

"At this point of our undertaking we realized that it would now be possible, by opening those further doors, to solve the secret the shrines had so jealously guarded throughout the centuries. I therefore decided before any other procedure to make the experiment. ...With suppressed excitement I carefully cut the cord, removed the precious seal, drew back the bolts, and opened the doors, when a fourth shrine was revealed, similar in design and even more brilliant in workmanship than the last. ...With intense excitement I drew back the bolts of the last and unsealed doors; they slowly swung open, and there, filling the entire area within, effectively barring any further progress, stood an immense yellow quartzite sarcophagus, intact, with the lid still firmly fixed in place...." [89]

The removal of the First Tabernacle had been something of a "figure-it-out-as-they-went" operation, and so it seemed from this experience that the dismantlement process of each of the remaining three tabernacles would follow the same steps: unhinging the door panels, taking off the roof sections, then the entablature, next lifting away the end and side panels (to be padded, wrapped and leaned against the First Tabernacle panels now lining the Burial Chamber walls), and, finally, taking down the uprights at each corner and lifting up the floor frame. But the Second Tabernacle presented a new problem: rather than wooden tongues holding the sections together, it was discovered that here these attachments were made of solid bronze. Carter wrote, *"These could not of course be sawn through as in the first case. We had therefore to find other methods. In fact, contrary to our expecta-*

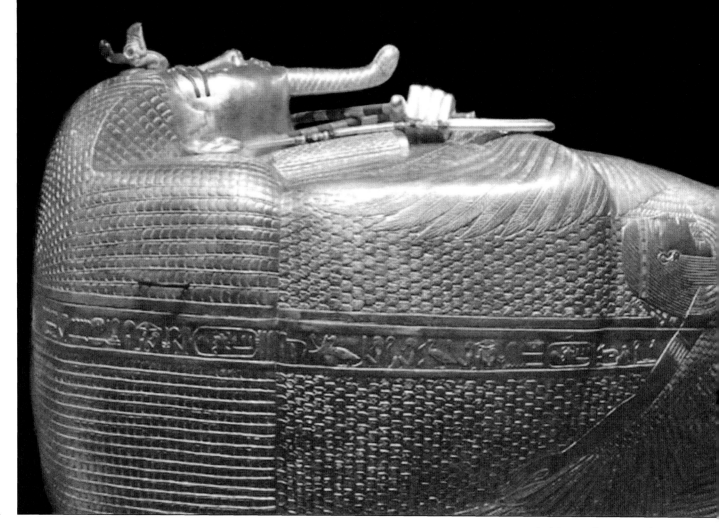

tions, the farther we proceeded, although the space in which we could work had been increased, new and unforeseen obstacles continually occurred," [90] such as how to raise and turn in the narrow space the very heavy roof of the Fourth Tabernacle, which it was discovered was constructed in one piece instead of in sections as with the other shrine roofs. It took another month of intensive labor to accomplish the task of fully exposing the sarcophagus.

Between the Third and Fourth tabernacles additional small objects were discovered placed on the floor, mostly ceremonial bows and arrows, but also two processional fans, such as are frequently depicted being carried by attendants accompanying a king. One of these was gilded all over and thus dubbed the "Golden Fan" by Carter; it was decorated on the two sides of the semi-oval stock with incised scenes of Tutankhamen hunting ostriches and returning from this hunt with two bagged birds, apparently an actual event which took place, according to the inscription on the fan's handle, in the eastern desert near Iunu (Heliopolis). The second fan was made of ebony, the stock gilded and inlaid in colored glass with the king's cartouches.

With removal of the Fourth Tabernacle (at least as far as the Burial Chamber walls, where its end and side panels were leaned against the same sections from the outer three tabernacles), the sarcophagus itself was finally fully revealed on February 3, 1925. As Carter wrote, *"We were more than repaid. For there, free standing from all surrounding structure, stood, as if in state, a magnificent sarcoph-*

Opposite, Detail of the cornflowers-&-olive leaves wreath found adorning the vulture & uraeus insignia on the brow of the peculiar headcovering. The coffin itself is in the rishi-*(or feathered) style employed on royal mummy cases of the Eighteenth Dynasty, depicting the king as Osiris, his mummiform body being embraced by the winged goddesses Isis & Nephthys. Inexplicably this outermost coffin does not seem to have been photographed in full length by Harry Burton, as neither the Griffith Institute nor the Metropolitan Museum of Art has a negative of the First Coffin other than for the view opposite.* Metropolitan Museum of Art

Above, The upper half of the outermost First Coffin in profile. Internet photo

254, A. B.

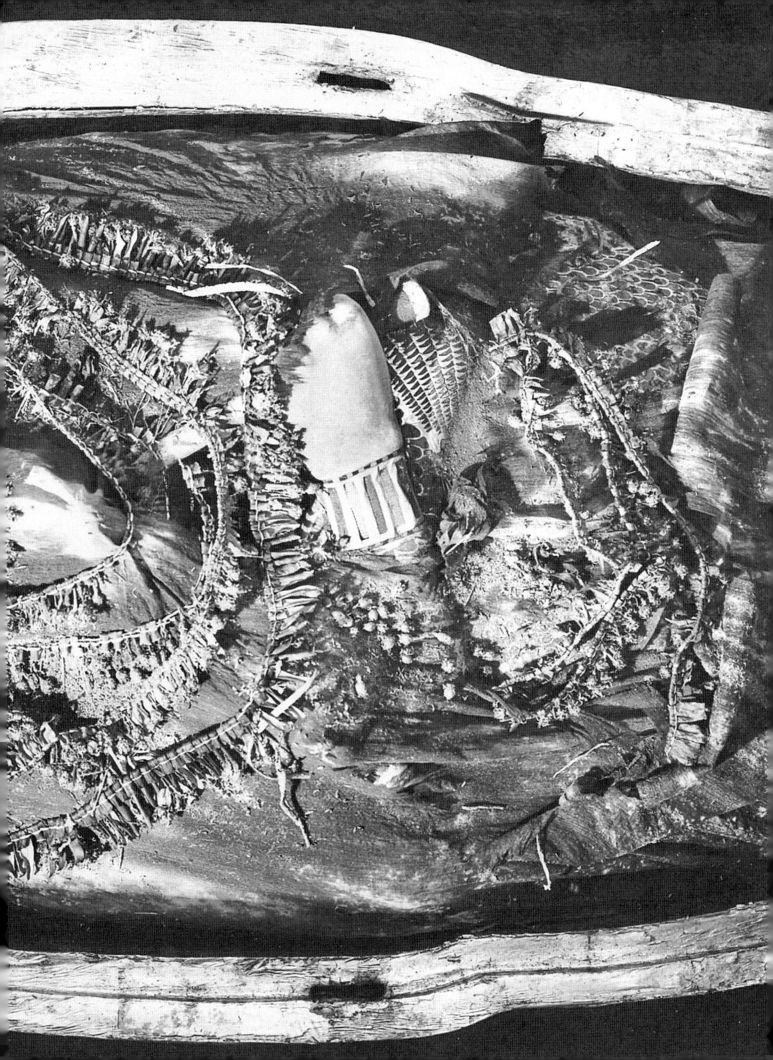

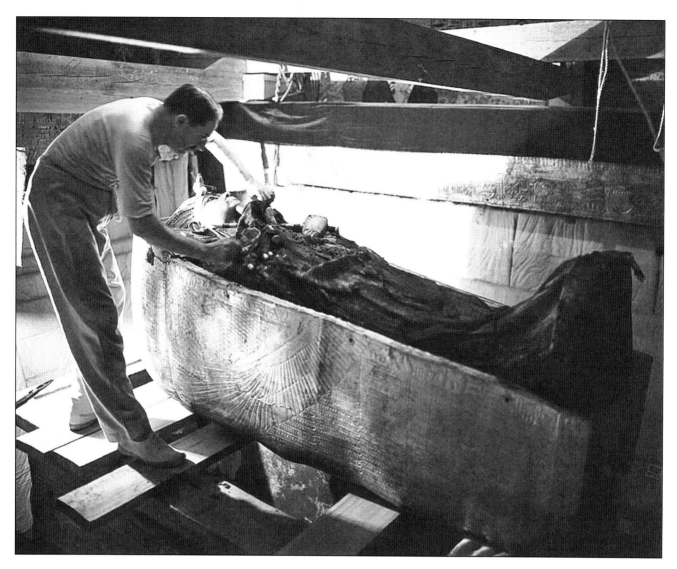

Above & opposite, Howard Carter poses for Harry Burton's camera, removing the shroud from the Second (middle) Coffin of Tutankhamen & cleaning the face piece with a brush, as it rests in the basin of the First Coffin, which has been elevated out of the sarcophagus & rests on planks laid across the latter. Metrolopitan Museum of Art

Previous overleaves, The Second Coffin as revealed, shrouded with a linen pall & adorned with multiple floral garlands.
Metropolitan Museum of Art

agus of wonderful workmanship, carved out of a solid block of finest yellow quartzite, measuring 9 feet in length [2.74 m.], 4 feet 10 inches in width [1.47 m.], and 4 feet 10 inches high. ...It has a rich entablature consisting of a cavetto-cornice, taurus moulding and frieze of inscription. But the outstanding features of the sarcophagus are the guardian goddesses Isis, Nephthys, Neith and Selket, carved in high relief on each of the four corners, so placed that their full spread wings and outstretched arms encircle it with their protective embrace. Around the base is a dado of protective symbols Ded [djed] and Thet [tyet]." [91]

Two things were immediately apparent about the lid of the great box: it was somewhat crudely cut from a different stone than the yellow quartzite of the finely carved basin — later determined to be rose granite tinted yellow — and it was cracked completely through, across its width almost exactly in the middle of its length. This break had been disguised with gypsum and the latter painted to match the rest of the pseudo-quartzite surface. Carter proposed that this lid was, in fact, a hasty substitute for an original lid of yellow quartzite, which had not been finished in time for the king's interment. More probably, the original had been damaged in transit to the tomb in such a way that it could not be salvaged, and another lid of more easily worked granite

was quickly prepared instead. Ironically, this would seem to have been accidentally dropped while being lowered into place. Supporting the sides with angle irons permitted its raising in one piece by differential pulleys. This was effected on February 12, in the presence of a rather large audience of invited dignitaries and Egyptologists.[92] Carter wrote of the event, *"The tackle for the raising of the lid was in position. I gave the word. Amid intense silence the huge slab, broken in two, weighing over a ton and quarter, rose from its bed. The light shown in the sarcophagus. A sight met our eyes that at first puzzled us. It was a little disappointing. The contents were completely covered by fine linen shrouds. The lid being suspended in mid-air, we rolled back those covering shrouds, one by one, and as the last was removed a gasp of wonderment escaped our lips, so gorgeous was the sight that met our eyes: a golden effigy of the young boy king, of the most magnificent workmanship, filled the whole of the interior of the sarcophagus."* [93]

The Second Coffin freed from the basin of the First Coffin & resting atop the sarcophagus. Internet photo

   Satisfied that the mummy of Tutankhamen in all certainty was to be found within this previously unequaled example of funerary art, Burton's floodlights were turned off and Carter and his guests slowly mounted the sixteen steps of the tomb back into the harsh light of reality. Little did the English archaeologist guess just then that it

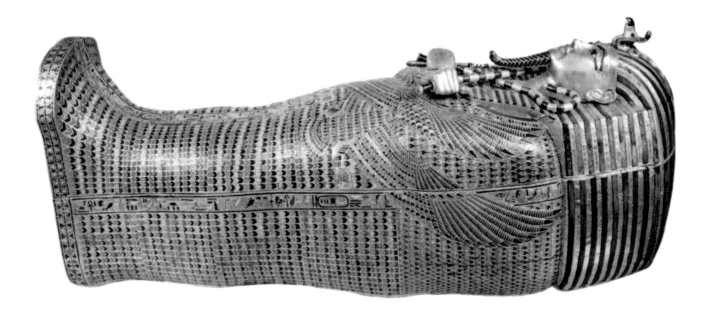

would be some twenty months before he would be permitted to raise the coffin's lid to proceed with revealing the mortal remains of the long-forgotten third-to-last ruler of Egypt's glorious Eighteenth Dynasty. Over a relatively petty matter in dispute with the Antiquities Service, Carter and his team went on "strike" the next day. And two days later, February 15, 1924, they found themselves locked out of Tutankhamen's tomb by the Egyptian government, the sarcophagus lid still suspended precariously by its block-and-tackle rigging over the great gilded coffin of the boy-king (see "Chronology" addendum for the details of the events precipitating the strike and lockout, beginning p. 283).

It was not until October 10, 1925, that Howard Carter was again allowed access to the Tomb of Tutankhamen, his disputes with the Egyptian Antiquities Service having been finally resolved more or less to mutual satisfactions. Clearance of the entry stairwell to the re-buried tomb was begun on that day (in temperatures ranging from 97° to 105° F.) and completed the next. Timbers blocking the outer door-way were removed, and the wooden gate unlocked. At the end of the descending passageway, the steel door securing the Antechamber was likewise unlocked; and Carter conducted an inspection tour of the inner chambers, determining that everything was in satisfactory condition after twenty months of abandonment. Antiquities Service personnel had removed the precariously suspended sarcophagus lid, and the king's great gilded anthropoid coffin was found to be undisturbed beneath the sheet of plate glass which had been placed over the top of the sarcophagus by the Service for protection of its contents.

Carter decided to remove the lid of the coffin while it still rested in the sarcophagus, using four protruding silver handles (two per side) which appeared designed for that very purpose. The effigy on this lid could readily enough be seen to depict the king as bearded Osiris, wearing a peculiar (unique?) headdress reminiscent of the *khat* wig bag seen on one of the tomb's pair of *ka* statues, but with thickly

Opposite, Detail of the upper portion of the Second Coffin lid, depicting the deceased bearded king wearing the striped Nemes *head covering, with an unusual cobra-vulture combination adorning the forehead. The arms are crossed in the Osiride fashion, the hands clasping the Crook & Flail scepters. As with the First Coffin, the decoration here is the* rishi *pattern, although the protective goddesses, Isis & Nephthys, have been replaced with the Nekhbet vulture & a winged cobra. While the outermost coffin is gilded all over & the decoration incised, the Second is elaborately inlaid with colored glass imitating jasper, lapis & turquoise.* Internet photo

The Second Coffin of Tutankhamen's set of three, above, measures 2.04 meters in length. Its elaborate decoration of glass inlays — in a feathered pattern set in gold foil covering an unidentified wood — had suffered from dampness & tended to fall out when the coffin was handled during its removal from the tomb. Details such as the Nemes *stripes, the eyebrows, cosmetic lines & braided beard are inlaid with lapis-blue glass, while the crook & flail combine blue faience & glass — imitating lapis & turquoise. It has been remarked that the facial features of this coffin are somewhat dissimilar to those of the First & Third coffins (which are quite alike), leaving open the possibility that this piece of funerary equipment was made originally for another king (Smenkhkare? Ankhkheperure?), & later appropriated by those responsible for burying Tutankhamen. The overall decoration here recalls the recycled coffin containing the anonymous skeletal mummy found in KV55.*

Cairo Egyptian Museum

Narration continues p. 150

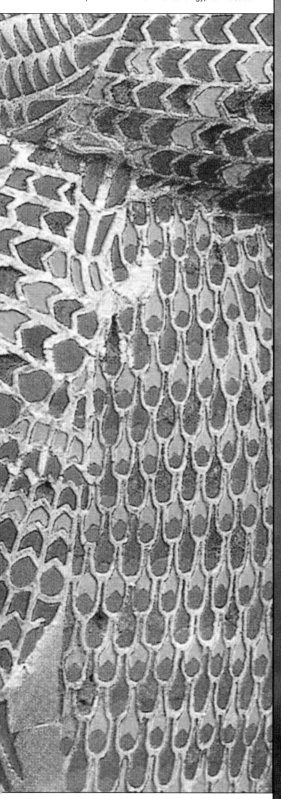

Right, Harry Burton's full-length "portrait" of the Second Coffin; Below & opposite, Details of the chevron rishi-*pattern of inlays within a gold matrix, including the inscription band on the coffin lid's lower half, with Tutankhamen's nomen, Tutankhamen.*

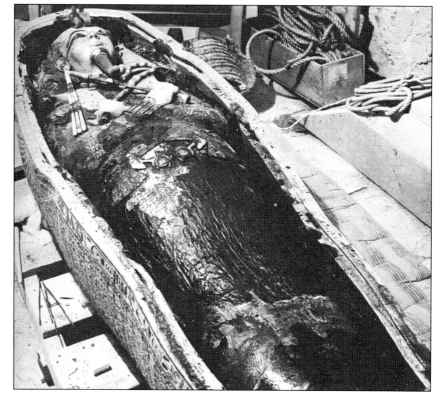

Previous overleaves, View of the head portion of the Third (innermost) Coffin of Tutankhamen, as it appeared when the lid of the Second Coffin was raised. The innermost coffin was all but completely shrouded by a red-linen sheet, with the face having been left bare, & an elaborate floral-&-bead collar covering the throat. Note the encrustation of the stone inlays forming the eyes. The latter could not be saved, which accounts for the empty-eyed aspect of the Third Coffin in subsequent photographs (opposite), & today. Right & below, The Third Coffin still in situ *within the shell of the Second, but with the shrouding removed. Note the black unguent which had been poured in great quantity over the innermost coffin, "cementing" it to the interior of the Second Coffin trough. When the innermost coffin was finally exposed, Carter at last was able to determine the cause of the great weight of the nested set of coffins: rather than being of gilded wood like the outer two, the Third Coffin proved to be formed of solid gold, varying from 0.25 to 0.30 centimeters in thickness & weighing 296 lbs.* Metropolitan Museum of Art

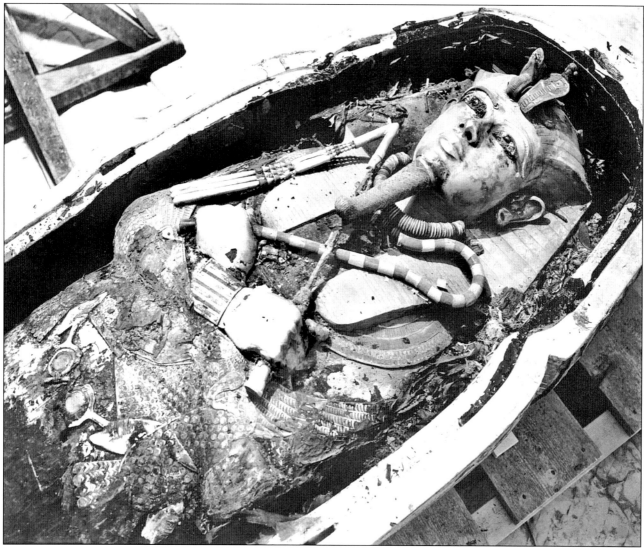

plaited shoulder "lappets," as well. From the brow of this headdress rear both the vulture (l.) and *uraeus* (r.), symbols of the protective goddesses of Upper and Lower Egypt[94] — rather than the *uraeus* only, universally worn by kings since earliest dynastic times. The king's arms cross in the Osiride fashion on his chest and his hands grip the standard regalia of Egyptian kingship, the crook and flail scepters. The mummiform lower body of the king is decorated in the all-over feathered pattern known as *rishi*-style, with the addition of figures in low relief of the funerary goddesses Isis and Nephthys, who embrace the king's mummiform, literally wrapping it in the feathers of their winged arms. The forehead emblems, the king's eyebrows, cosmetic lines, eyes and

Previous page, The gleaming solid-gold Third Coffin of Tutankhamen, following cleaning & restoration. Note that the stone-inlaid eyes — which were badly corroded — could not be salvaged, giving the king's beautifully modeled visage a somewhat impersonal aspect. The Osiride figure again wears the Nemes head covering with the paired vulture & cobra on the brow The separately fashioned beard is inlaid with lapis-colored glass. The ears are likewise cast separately & attached, as is the broad collar on the chest, which is inlaid with eleven rows of colored glass simulating lapis, quartz, carnelian, feldspar & turquoise. A double shebyu *collar of separate construction covers the neck. The mummiform body is once again decorated with a* rishi *pattern & wrapped with the protective wings of both bird-headed & cobra-headed vultures & the goddesses Isis & Nephthys.* Cairo Egyptian Museum

Right, The foot end of the Third Coffin, with an incised figure of the kneeling goddess Isis. Both the prenomen nomen & nomen cartouches of the king are present.
Cairo Egyptian Museum

Opposite, Detail of the inlaid cobra-headed vulture on right side of the Third Coffin.
Cairo Egyptian Museum

Overleaves, Full-length profile & frontal views of the KV62 Third Coffin.
Cairo Egyptian Museum

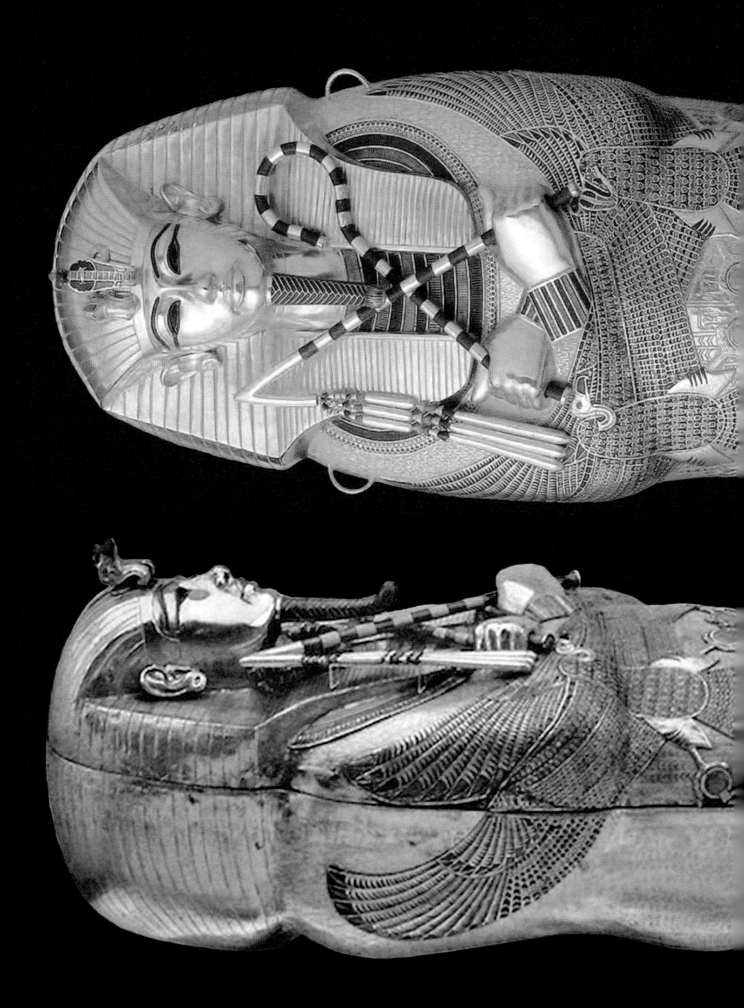

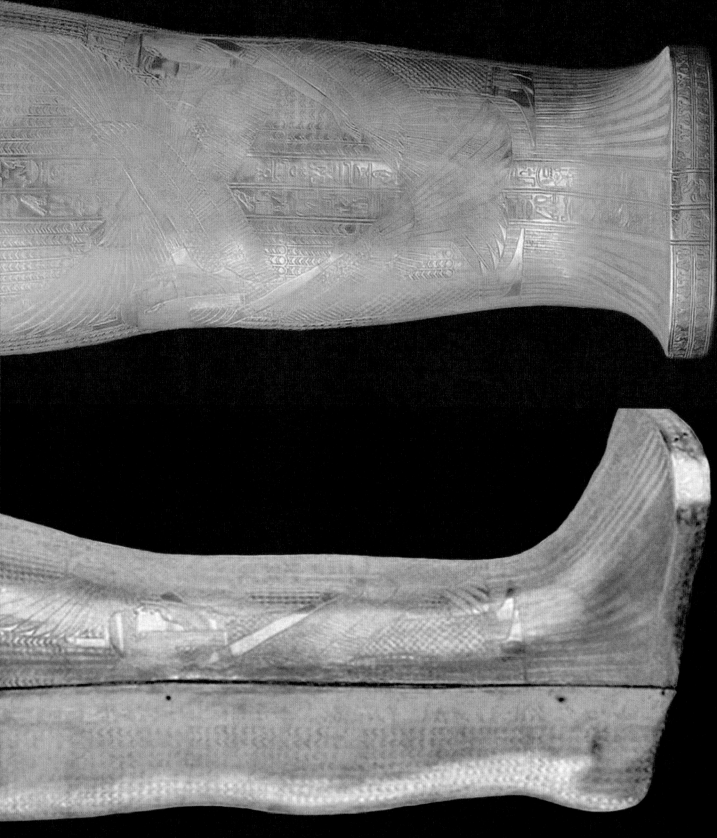

the scepters are all inlaid with colored glass and semi-precious stones.

When the outermost coffin had been placed in the sarcophagus — or, more correctly, when it came time to secure the lid on this coffin once the inner coffins had been deposited in its basin already resting in the sarcophagus — it was found by the necropolis officials, no doubt to their great consternation, that the foot end of the lid was too high to permit the lowering of the sarcophagus cover — a miscalculation in design by someone in the royal workshops! — and so the "toes" of the mummiform feet had to be adzed off, exposing the raw cypress wood from which the First Coffin was carved. Carter later discovered the adzed-off pieces on the floor of the sarcophagus box.

The excavator determined that the lid was attached to the coffin trough by ten solid-silver tongues fitted into corresponding sockets in the thickness of the shell (four to a side, and one at the head and foot ends). He wrote, *"By careful manipulation...it was found possible to withdraw them, with the exception of the pin at the head-end where there was only space enough to pull it half out. It had therefore to be filed through before the inner half could be withdrawn."* [95]

Using the hoisting tackle still in place which had been used to raise the sarcophagus lid twenty months earlier, Carter succeeded in lifting the coffin lid without incident. *"It was a moment as anxious as exciting,"* he wrote. *"The lid came up fairly readily, revealing a second magnificent anthropoid coffin, covered with a thin gossamer linen sheet, darkened and much decayed. Upon this linen shroud were lying floral garlands, composed of olive and willow leaves, petals of blue lotus and cornflowers, whilst a small wreath of similar kind had been placed, also over the shroud, on the emblems of the forehead. Underneath this covering, in places, glimpses could be obtained of rich multi-colored glass decoration encrusted upon the fine gold-work of the coffin."* [96]

At this point Carter closed the tomb to await the arrival of Harry Burton, so that the latter's photographic record of the Second Coffin *in situ* with its shroud and floral accoutrements could be made. Burton was in Luxor three days later, and on the 17th of October he took his photographs. With this accomplished, Carter turned his attention to how to best deal with extracting the Second coffin from the basin of the First. Because of the depth of the sarcophagus box, it was decided that it would be most productive to raise the First Coffin basin and its contents out of the sarcophagus altogether, to allow greater access to the coffins themselves. This was accomplished using the pulley system previously employed, although the coffins proved far heavier than anyone had imagined. Planks were slipped under them once they had been elevated above the sarcophagus rim, so that they could rest on this improvised trestle, thus suspended over the now empty stone box. Carter wrote, *"In the confined space, and with the restricted headroom available, the task proved one of no little difficulty. It was much increased by the necessity of avoiding damage to the fragile gesso-gilt*

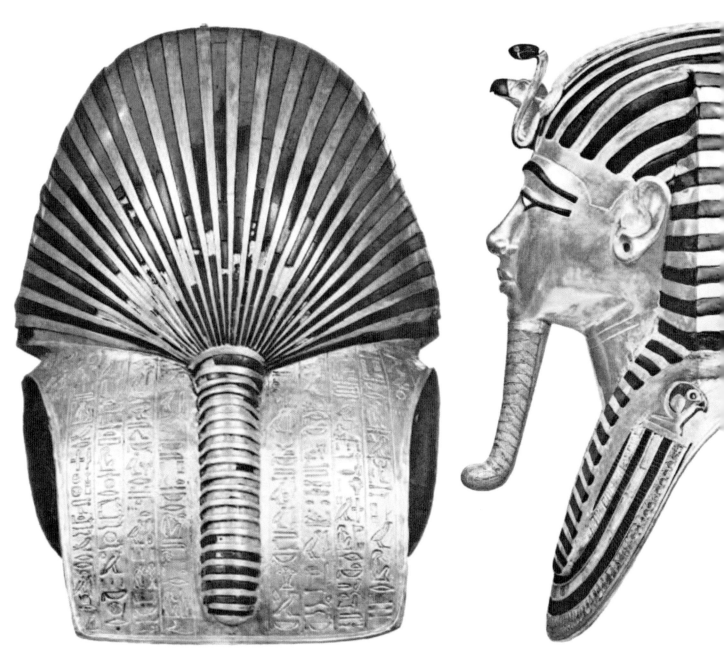

surface of the outermost coffin." [97]

More photographs were taken by Burton, and Carter removed the intimate floral wreath and the garlands and rolled back the fragile shroud, to reveal fully the gilded and inlaid lid of the six-foot, eight-inch-long Second Coffin, like the First depicting the king in Osiride form gripping the crook and flail regalia, but different in its details. Here the deceased wears the *Nemes* head covering — stripes indicated in blue glass imitating lapis lazuli — also surmounted on the forehead by a paired vulture head and uraeus. In this instance the braiding of the Osiride beard is indicated by pseudo-lapis inlays. But the chief difference is that the fully gilded Second Coffin (made of an undetermined wood) is inlaid all over in a feather (*rishi*) pattern with small chevrons of colored glass (simulating jasper, lapis and turquoise in color); and the winged protective goddesses Isis and Nephthys have been replaced with the Nekhbet vulture and a vulture with a cobra

Opposite & above, The solid-gold 54.0 centimeters-high funerary mask of Tutankhamen is formed from two sheets of gold, joined by hammering, chasing & burnishing, then inlaid The idealized portrait of the young king depicts him wearing the striped Nemes *head covering & false beard. As with all three of the king's coffin portraits, the* Nemes *is surmounted on the forehead by the cobra of the goddess Wadjet, & the vulture head of the goddess Nekhbet. The inlays of the headcloth stripes & pigtail are blue glass, as are the eyebrows & cosmetic lines; the eyes are quartz & obsidian. The broad collar is inlaid with colored glass simulating lapis lazuli, jasper, carnelian & obsidian, in twelve rows. On the back of the mask, as seen above left, are vertical registers of text from the* Book of the Dead *(Spell 151b).*

Cairo Egyptian Museum

159

head, their spread wings serving to enfold the torso in a protective manner similar to the goddesses on the First Coffin. Carter was puzzled and disturbed that humidity had apparently invaded the outer coffin and loosened the colored-glass inlays, making the surface extremely fragile and difficult to handle. Still it was deemed absolutely necessary to extract the Second Coffin from the basin of the First, or else the metal pins which Carter had determined fixed its lid in place could not be reached for full manipulation.

But how? Unlike the First Coffin, the Second was not equipped with metal handles. In fact, the fit between the two was so tight that it was not possible to pass even one's little finger between them. Finally, it was decided to make use of the metal pins which attached the Second Coffin's lid to its basin. Carter wrote, *"...although the space between the shell of the outer coffin and second coffin was insufficient to enable us to withdraw these pins entirely, they could still be pulled out about a quarter of an inch, so as to permit stout copper wire attachments to be fixed to them and to the overhead scaffold. This we did successfully. Strong metal eyelets were then screwed into the thickness of the top edge of the shell of the outer coffin, so as to enable it to be lowered from the second coffin by means of ropes working on the pulleys. ...The process adopted was the reverse of that which might at first appear to be the natural order of things. We lowered the outer shell from the second coffin, instead of lifting the second coffin out of the first. The reason for this was that head-room was insufficient, and the weight being stationary, there would be less risk of undue stress upon those ancient silver pins. The operation was successful. The shell of the outer coffin was lowered once more into the sarcophagus, leaving for a moment, the second coffin suspended in mid-air by means of ten stout wire attachments. A wooden tray sufficiently large to span the opening of the sarcophagus was then passed under it, and thus the second coffin strongly supported, stood before us free and accessible. The wire attachments having been severed, the overhead gear removed, Mr. Burton made his records, and we were able to turn our energies to the raising of its lid."* [98]

To accomplish this, four metal eyelets were screwed into the lid (at points where there would be no permanent damage, and these were used to hoist it high enough so that the gold-headed silver nails attaching it to the basin could be pried out. Although it stuck at first, the lid was slowly raised high enough to clear the contents of the basin, then was lowered onto a wooden tray ready to receive it.

As expected, the coffin within was also Osiride shaped, evident despite the fact that it was shrouded by a reddish sheet of linen, although the golden face had been left uncovered. A large, elaborate floral-and-bead collar was laid over the neck and breast, behind the beard of divinity; and a linen sheet was tucked around the top of the *Nemes* head covering. Humidity had evidently penetrated here as well, since the white-quartz and obsidian eyes of the coffin face-piece were heavily corroded, as were the faience inlays of the beard. It would later

The mummy of Tutankhamen, as first revealed when the lid of the Third Coffin & a shroud were removed by Carter, after he decided to leave the basin of the latter within the shell of the middle coffin, "cemented" there by the liquid unguents which had been poured over it & hardened in antiquity. The humidity resulting from this ancient anointing had also damaged the mumy wrappings & accoutrements.

Griffith Institute

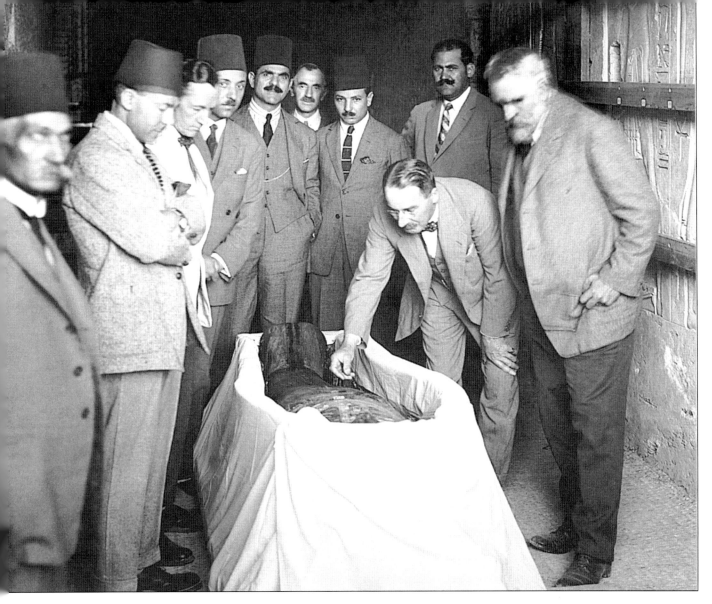

prove impossible to save the eyes. Likewise, the floral collar and shroud — which at first appeared in perfect condition — proved to be so brittle that they literally crumbled when touched.

Harry Burton exposed his photographs, then Carter took away the collar and shroud — in pieces, it would seem. Finally the secret of the Third Coffin's great weight was revealed: six-feet, three-quarter-inches long, it proved to be made of solid gold; which, as Carter wrote, *"explained also why the weight had diminished so slightly after the first coffin, and the lid of the second coffin, had been removed. Its weight was still as much as eight strong men could lift."* [99]

The face of the Third Coffin closely resembles that of the First, except that the king appears even more idealized and youthful. The design of the coffin is again *rishi*, although it is doubly protected by the widespread wings of both the goddesses Isis and Nephthys (engraved over the legs of the mummiform); and by the emblems of Upper and Lower Egypt, the Nekhbet vulture and the cobra-headed vulture, Buto (indicated in a massive cloisonnéed separate piece of solid gold superimposed at the king's waist and enfolding his crossed arms). Like the outer and middle coffins, the paired vulture and uraeus rear on the king's forehead, and the crook and flail are gripped in his hands, cross-

Examination of the mummy of Tutankhamen commenced on the morning of November 11, 1925, in the outer corridor of the Tomb of Seti II. In addition to a group of Egyptian officials, those in attendance included Dr. Douglas Derry (third from the left), who would perform the "autopsy"; Alfred Lucas (sixth from the left), Howard Carter (leaning over the sheet-draped coffin); & Pierre Lacau, director-general of the Egyptian Antiquities Service (far right). The external trappings of the mummy had been removed, except for the golden mask, which was stuck to the bottom of the innermost coffin by the unguents poured over the coffins & mummy during the funerary ritual.

Items Found on the Mummy of Tutankhamen
(Object-Group 256)

256a-Golden mask of king
b-External mummy trappings
  1-Hands of burnished gold
  2-Gold *ba*-bird pectoral
  3-Two longitudinal & transverse
     inlaid-gold bands
  4-Ornamental side strap
c-Y-shaped amulet of gold
d-Oval plaque of gold
e-Gold vulture-collar
f-Gold collar with vulture &
     cobra
g-Gold cobra-collar
h-Gold hawk-collar
i-Two hawk-collars
j-Inlaid-gold apron
k-Iron dagger & sheath
l-Girdle of sheet gold
m-T-shaped amulet of gold
n-Gold wristlet
o-Faience-beadwork collar
p-Gold hawk-collar
q-Black-resin scarab suspended on
     beaten-gold wire
r-Uraeus insignia (of diadem)
s-Vulture insignia (of diadem)
t-Gold hawk-collar
u-Gold circlet
v-Gold circlet
w-Gold Circlet
x-Bracelet
y-Beads
z-Cloisonné hawk-collar
aa 1 & 2-Hawk-collars
bb-Beadwork
cc-Gold circlet
dd-Gold dagger & sheath
ee-Sheet-gold girdle

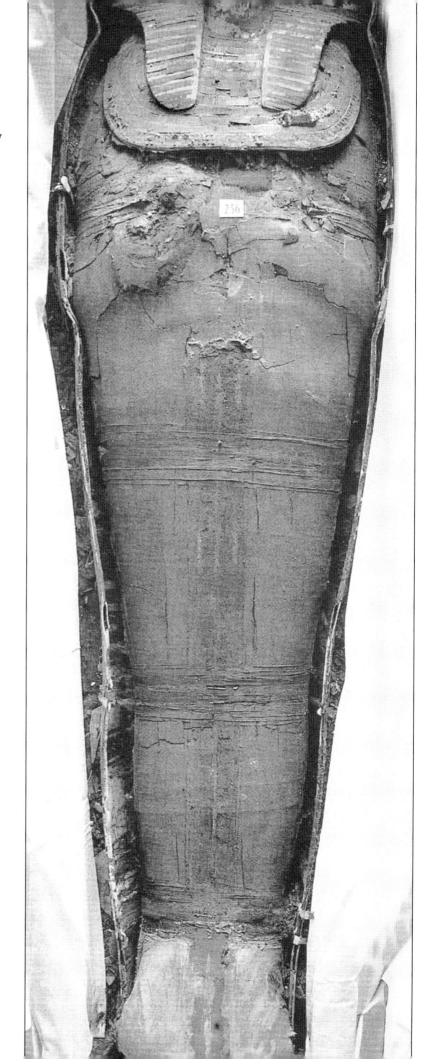

ff-Group of five finger-rings

gg-Gold hawk-collar

hh1-Amuletic bracelet with lapis
    barrel-bead

  2-Amuletic bracelet with iron
    Wadjet eye

  3-Amuletic bracelet with carnel-
    ian barrel-bead

ii-No object for this number

jj-Four gold-circlets

kk-*Djed* amulet

ll-Gold sandals & gold toe & finger
    sheaths

mm-Gold-wire bangle

nn-Beadwork of tail appendage (eee)

oo-*Wadjet*-eye bracelet

pp-*Wadjet*-eye bracelet

qq-Scarab/uraeus bracelet

rr- Barrel-bead bracelet

ss-Scarab bracelet

tt-Gold amuletic knot

uu-Gold bangle with carnelian *ment*
    bird

vv-Group of finger rings

ww-Barrel-bead bracelet

xx-Beaded bracelet

yy-Beaded bracelet

zz-Beaded bracelet

aaa-*Wadjet*-eye bracelet

bbb-Finger ring

ccc-Gold finger ring

ddd-Lapis-&-gold bracelet

eee-Ritual bull-tail

fff-*Tyet* amulet

ggg-*Wadj* amulet

hhh-*Djed* amulct

iii-Double-leaf amulet

jjj-Leaf amulet

kkk-Gold amuletic knot

lll-Gold cobra-collar

mmm-Cloisonné Nekhbet-collar

nnn-Cloisonné Nebti-collar

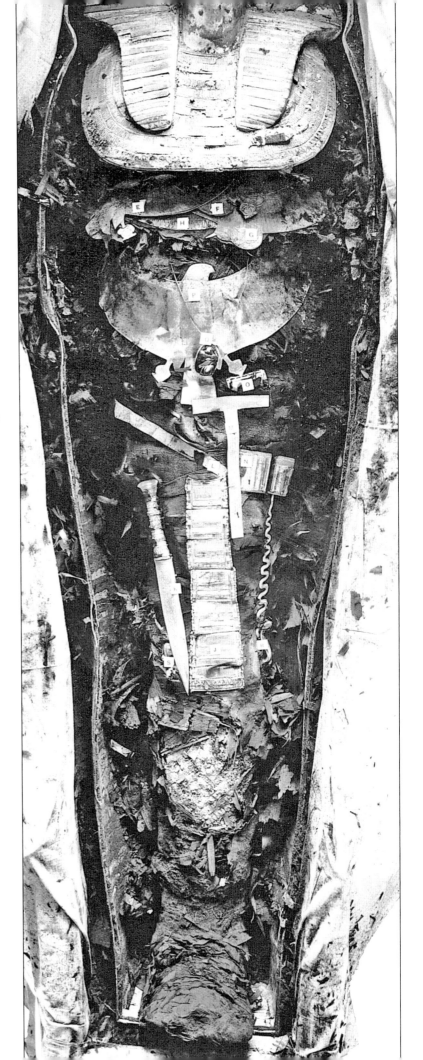

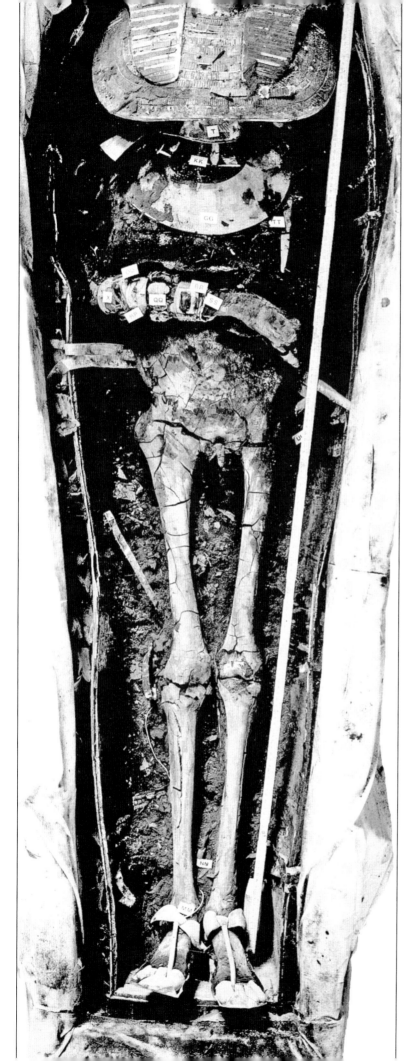

Items Found on the Mummy of Tutankhamen
concluded

ooo-Inlaid-gold pectoral
ppp-Inlaid-gold pectoral
qqq-Inlaid-gold pectoral
rrr-Blue-faience *Wadjet* eye
sss-String of cylindrical & disk-
    beads
ttt-Bead collar with hawk-headed
    clasps
uuu-Inlaid-gold pectoral
www-Small amuletic bracelet
xxx-Anubis bracelet
zzz-Serpent-headed amulet
4a-Thoth amulet
b-*Wadj* amulet
c-Large bead
d-Gold chain
e-Group of five pectoral clasps &
    pendants
f-Human-headed winged uraeus
g-Double uraeus
h-Vulture amulet
i-Vulture amulet
j-Vulture amulet
k-*Uraeus* amulet
l-Vulture amulet
m-Collar of four strings of beads
n-Two fibrous fillets bound with
    string
o-Diadem of inlaid gold
p-Gold temple-band
p-*bis* Linen headdress
q-Uraeus insignia of headdress
r-Vulture insignia of headdress
s-Sheet-gold temple-band
t-Skullcap of fine linen beaded with
    uraeus design
u-Linen pad of conical shape
v-Amuletic headrest of iron

ing on his breast. In addition to a broad collar of colored-glass inlays, a detachable *shebiyu* collar formed from disk beads of gold and blue faience rests on the king's throat, enhancing, as Carter wrote, *"the richness of the whole effect."*

"But," he continued, *"the ultimate details of the ornamentation were hidden by a black lustrous coating due to liquid unguents that had evidently been profusely poured over the coffin. As a result this unparalleled monument was not only disfigured — as it afterwards proved, only temporarily — but was stuck fast to the interior of the second coffin, the consolidated liquid filling up the space between the second and third coffins almost to the level of the lid of the third."* [100] He concluded that *"these consecration unguents...were doubtless the cause of the disintegration observed when dealing with the outer coffins which, as they were in a practically hermetically sealed quartzite sarcophagus, cannot have been affected by outside influences."* [101]

So that the problem of the "cemented" coffins could be dealt with more effectively, the Second Coffin basin and its weighty contents were lowered off the improvised trestle over the sarcophagus and taken into the Antechamber. Carter's first concern was consolidation of the inlays decorating the trough of the Second Coffin. The surfaced was lightly brushed free of dust, then sponged with warm water and ammonia. When dry it was covered all over with a thick coating of hot paraffin applied with a brush, which upon solidifying held the chevron-shaped inlays in place so that the basin could be handled with less risk of damage.

Next came the matter of the hardened unguents which coated the Third Coffin lid and entirely filled the space between the two basins. Carter's chemist, Alfred Lucas, made an analysis of the substance, which in appearance, Carter recorded, *"was black and resembled pitch; in those places where the layer was thin, as on the lid of the coffin, the material was hard and brittle, but where a thicker layer had accumulated, as was the case under and between the coffins, the interior of the material was soft and plastic. Its smell when warm was penetrating, somewhat fragrant, not unpleasant, and suggestive of wood pitch* [and] *was found to contain fatty matter and resin* [although] *there was no mineral pitch or bitumen present, and even the presence of wood-pitch, which was suggested by the smell, could not then be proved. There can be,"* Carter continued, *"little doubt from the manner in which this material had run down the sides of the third coffin and collected underneath, that it was in a liquid or semi-liquid condition when employed."* [102]

Although the substance could have been melted by the application of heat, the circumstances made that not practicable. Thus Carter decided to leave the separation of the coffins until later and to proceed with revealing the mummy of Tutankhamen by raising the lid of the Third Coffin.

This proved to be attached to the basin by eight gold tenons (four per side), which were held in their sockets by solid-gold

Overleaf, The head of the mummy of Tutankhamen, full face & in profile, as it appeared when first freed of its wrappings & most accoutrements (diadem, decayed Khat headdress, etc.). Note that it still wears a sheet-gold temple band, & the beaded-linen cap which covered the shaven skull (with one of the uraei being held in place with modern pieces of tape). These are the only "portraits" of the mummy's head published by Carter in his popular report on the discovery of KV62 & its clearance (The Tomb of Tut·Ankh·Amen, volume II, plate XXXI) & it is not apparent from these views that the head itself is completely detached from the body, which fact is disguised in Harry Burton's photographs by the cotton batting surrounding the head & creating the effect of a shroud. For a full discussion of the mummy of Tutankhamen & its treatment in 1926, & subsequently, see Tombs.Treasures.Mummies, Book 5, Addendum Two, "Abusing Pharaoh."

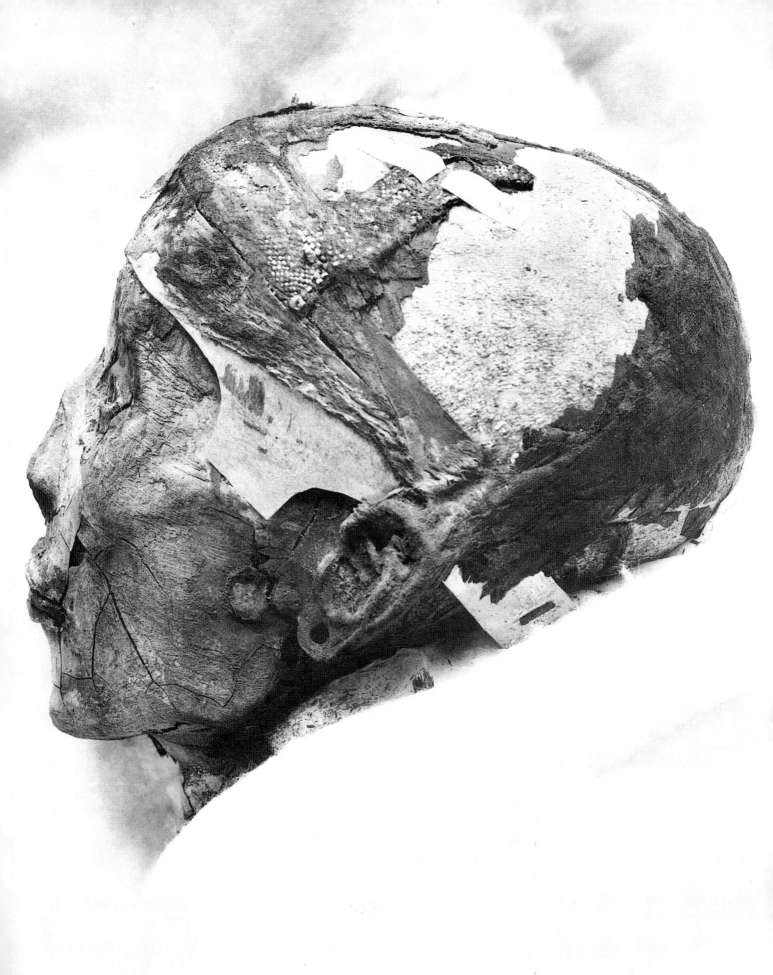

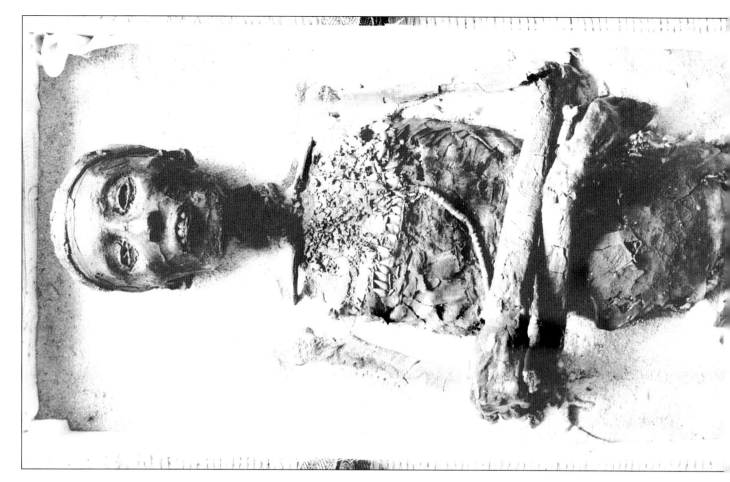

Above, The fully exposed mummy of Tut-ankhamen photographed by Harry Burton prior to its reinterment in the First (outer-most) Coffin, which was returned by Ho-ward Carter to the in situ sarcophagus of KV62. The king's rather pitiful remains rest supine on a low sand-filled tray which Carter had constructed for the purpose, & which conveniently serves to disguise (except on close inspection) the fact that the mummy was decapitated & fully dis-membered by Carter & Dr. Douglas Derry in the process of removing it from the solid-gold Third (innermost) Coffin — to the basin of which it was adhered by the consolidated unguents which had been poured over the wrapped remains as part of an anointing ritual at the time of bur-ial. Tutankhamen was denuded by Carter of all of his personal funerary accoutre-ments, except for the beaded-linen skull-cap covering the totally shaved scalp, & the beads of a broad collar embedded in a thick layer of resin covering the chest of the mummy. Griffith Institute

nails or pins. Using specially contrived screwdrivers enabling him to work in the cramped space between the two coffins, Carter removed the pins one by one, *"sacrificing"* them in the process. Then the Third Coffin's lid was lifted by its golden handles, exposing, as Carter later wrote, *"an impressive, neat and carefully made mummy, over which had been poured anointing unguents as in the case of the outside of its coffin — again in great quantity — consolidated and blackened by age. In contradistinction to the general dark and sombre effect, due to these unguents, was a brilliant...burnished gold mask or similitude of the king, covering his head and shoulders, which like the feet, had been intentionally avoided when using the unguents."*

Carter thought that this beaten-gold and inlaid portrait mask bore *"a sad but calm expression suggestive of youth overtaken prematurely by death."*[103] Like the face piece of each of the three coffins, the mask sported the Nekhbet vulture and Buto serpent em-blems on the forehead of, once again, the *Nemes* head covering, its stripes being indicated in lapis-colored glass inlays, as on the Second Coffin. The Osiride beard of faience-inlaid gold was attached to the king's chin; and at the throat, separate from the mask itself, were three strands of a *shebiyu* collar composed of disk beads of red and yellow gold, and blue-faience. Beneath this was the same broad collar seen on each of the coffins, inlaid with colored glass imitating semi-precious stones, but in this instance having hawk-headed plaques (indicating clasps?) at each shoulder. Moisture resulting from the unguent anoint-

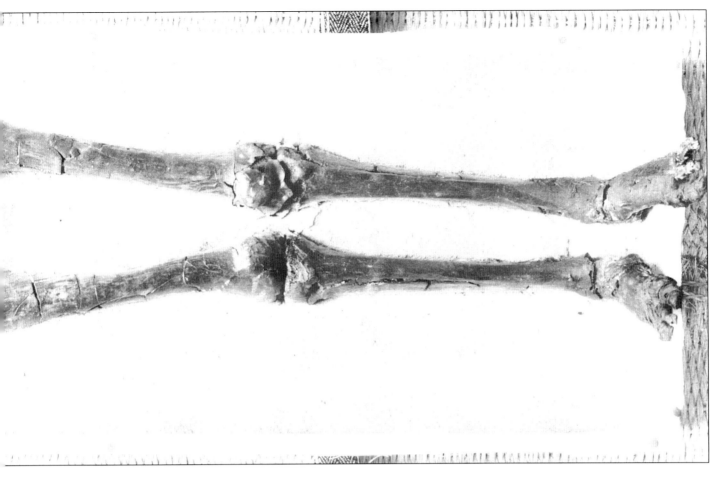

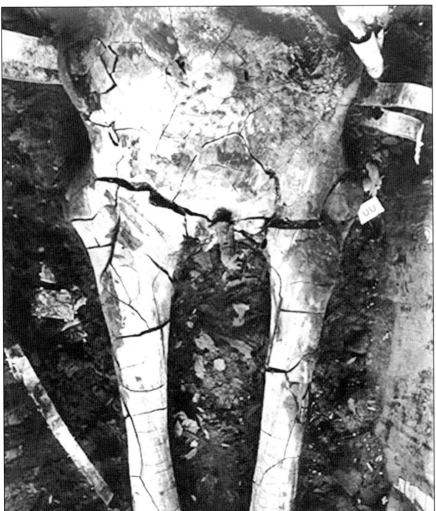

Left, Detail view of the pubic area of the mummy of Tutankhamen, as it still lay in the Third Coffin. The highly brittle, cracked state of the mummified tissue is clearly evident on the abdomen & thighs; & it is apparent that both femurs, as well as the penis & immediately surrounding area, have not yet been detached from the mummy's trunk during Carter & Derry's dismemberment of the king's remains.

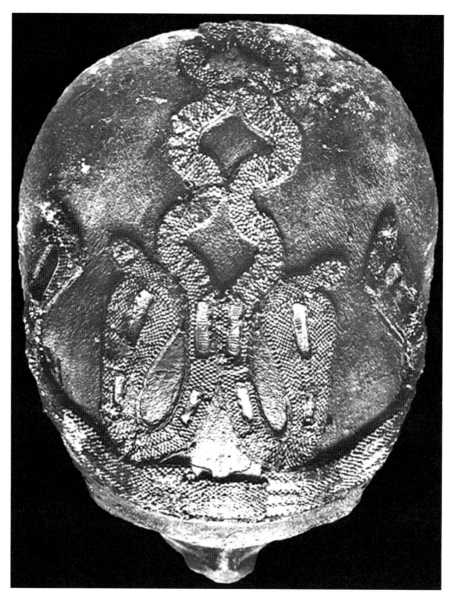

Right, The top of the head of the mummy of Tutankhamen, showing the beadwork of the linen skullcap which was found covering the shaved scalp of the king. The fabric of the cap was so carbonized that it could not be salvaged, & has been brushed away in Harry Burton's photograph. Each of the four uraei *formed by the beadwork carries incised-gold cartouches (two in detail, below) which display a previously unrecorded form of the didactic name of the Aten, deity of the Amarna heresy. The shaved royal head had apparently been smeared with a fatty substance prior to the placement of the skullcap.* Griffith Institute

ments had greatly corroded much of the mask surface, and when Carter first gazed upon it — save for the face proper — it was far from the pristine gleaming masterpiece of ancient portraiture seen on display today in the Cairo Egyptian Museum.

Separately fashioned beaten-gold crossed hands had been sewn onto the breast of the mummy bundle below the mask (although the threads were now totally decayed), and these clasped what remained of inlaid crook and flail scepters, both having almost completely corroded away. Resting between the hands, pendent from the neck of the mask on flexible straps of inlaid gold, was a large black-resin scarab (covered by minute fissures probably caused by contraction). Below the hands, also originally sewn onto the outermost linen covering of the mummy, was a large pectoral-like inlaid-gold figure of the *ba* bird, its widespread wings of cloisonné work, the tiny face a portrait of the dead king, whose soul this emblem represented.

The additional outer trappings of the mummy consisted of a pair of longitudinal bands running down its center front and over the feet, composed of heavy inlaid-gold plaques held together by threads of beads and bearing funerary texts. Transversing the mummy at three points along the longitudinal bands were pairs of similar bands, also with texts. Running down both sides of the mummy from shoulders to feet, and attached to the transverse bands, were further straps made up of small, bead-strung inlaid-gold plaques decorated with *djed* and *tyet* emblems, solar uraei and the king's cartouches. Interestingly, when these bands were cleaned, it was discovered that some of the plaques — on their reverse sides — bore the purposely erased name of Tutankhamen's immediate predecessor, Smenkhkare, suggesting that they were made for the latter's burial originally, and subsequently appropriated and altered for Tutankhamen.

Carter wrote, *"The farther we proceeded the more evident it became that the covering wrappings and the mummy were both in a parlous state. They were completely carbonized by the action that had been set up by the fatty acids of the unguents with which they had been saturated."* [104] In fact, it was discovered that both the gold mask and mummy itself were firmly stuck by the consolidated unguents to the bot-

Above, Left hand from the mummy of Tutankhamen, which had been detached by Carter & Derry, was photographed by Burton resting in a cardboard box, on a cushion of cotton batting. The separately wrapped digits are each encased in a gold sheath reproducing the shape, joint lines & nail of the finger within. Rings (objects 256 BBB & CCC) also adorn two of the finger sheaths.

Left, The feet of Tutankhamen's mummy, with their sheet-gold sandals, a gold-wire ankle bangle & gold toe sheaths still in position. Like the head, the feet of the mummy had not been saturated with anointing unguents at the time of the king's interment, but had suffered from indirect oxidation; & some of the soft tissue disintegrated when the sandals & sheaths subsequently were removed.

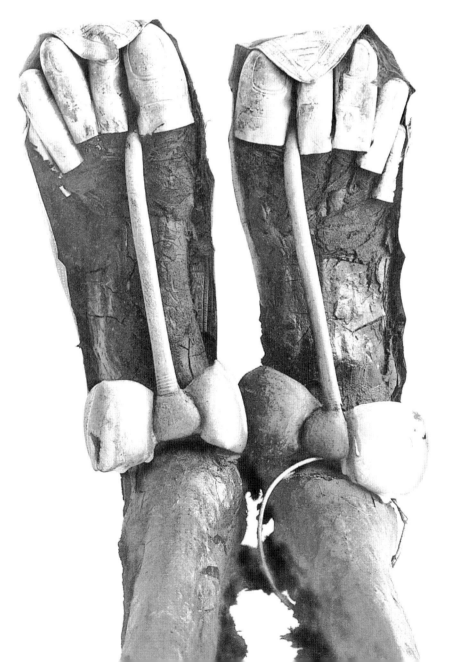

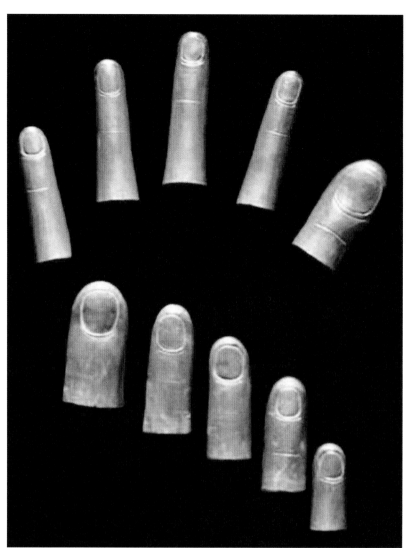

*Above, Sheet-gold amulets found on the Tut-
ankhamen mummy.* Colorized Griffith Institute photo

*Left-hand & right-foot gold finger & toe sheaths
from the Tutankhamen mummy.* Adapted Internet photo

*Below, Sheet-gold sandals worn by the king's
mummy.* Cairo Egyptian Museum

tom of the Third Coffin trough and could not be budged, let alone removed. Carter continued, *"Since it was known that this adhesive material could be softened by heat, it was hoped that an exposure to the midday sun would melt it sufficiently to allow the mummy to be raised. A trial was made for several hours in sun temperature reaching as high as 149° Fahrenheit (65° C.) without any success and, as other means were not practicable, it became evident that we should have to make all further examination of the king's remains as they lay within the two coffins."* [105]

It was on November 11, 1925, that this *"examination"* commenced, with a group of Egyptian officials in attendance, as well as Pierre Lacau of the Antiquities Service, chemist Alfred Lucas, photographer Harry Burton and Dr. Douglas Derry, a professor of anatomy at the Egyptian University in Cairo, who would conduct what amounted to an autopsy of the royal remains. The two coffin basins containing the mummy had been removed from Tutankhamen's tomb to the outer passageway of the Tomb of Seti II, which it will be remembered was serving as the Carter team's laboratory and temporary warehouse. The external ornaments of the mummy had already been removed and only the highly carbonized outermost wrappings (a large linen sheet held in place by longitudinal and transverse linen bands) and the gold mask covered the mummiform bundle, which Carter noted, *"lay at a slight angle, suggesting that it had been subjected to some shock when lowered into the sarcophagus."* He also observed that there was *"similar evidence to imply that the unguents had been poured over the mummy and coffin before they were lowered into the sarcophagus — the liquid*

Above, An amuletic apron found resting on the thighs of the mummy of Tutankhamen, made of seven gold plaques inlaid with polychrome glass & threaded together with a border of beads.
Griffith Institute

Below, Three chased sheet-gold amuletic collars from the neck & chest of the king's mummy. Colorized Griffith Institute photo

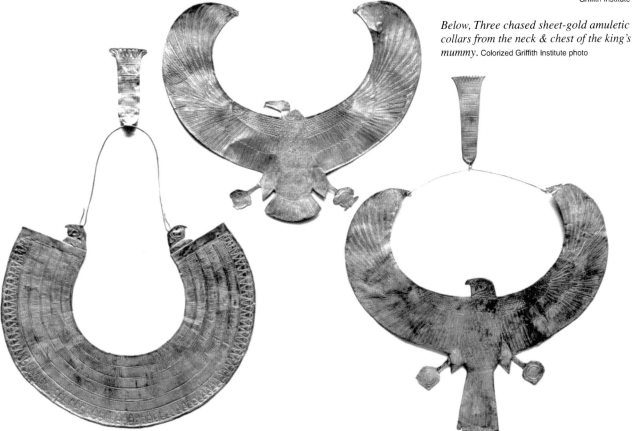

Large ba-*bird amulet with effigy of Tut-ankhamen (above & detail opposite) found on the exterior of the king's mummy, resting at the midsection (seen* in situ *at right). It is gold inlaid with polychrome glass & cloisonné work.* Griffith Institute photos & adapted Cairo Egyptian Museum image

Right, The inlaid sheet-gold mummy bands & accompanying Ba bird & Crook & Flail regalia (full view of the latter, opposite, including heart scarab), plus detail (below) of a section of the bands with the prenomen & nomen catouches of Tut-ankhamen.

Cairo Egyptian Museum & George B. Johnson photos

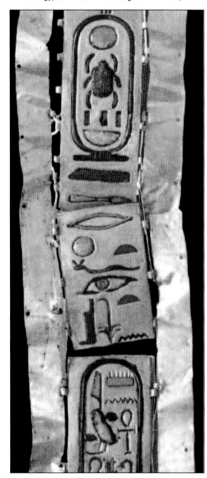

176

being at different levels on the two sides, suggesting the tilting of the coffin." [106]

With the spectators standing about the coffin basin — which had been draped with sheets and slightly elevated on wood planks — it was Dr. Derry who made a longitudinal incision down the front of the outer wrappings (which earlier had been painted with melted paraffin to consolidate the carbonized fabric), and these subsequently were removed in large sections, to reveal that the interior bandages were in an even more carbonized and decayed state than was feared. Removing the outer bandages did not serve to free up the mummy, as had been hoped it would; the linen at the back of the body (and the body itself) proved to have been so saturated with the pitch-like mass at the bottom of the gold coffin that the royal remains were embedded firmly in place. So, indeed, the "unwrapping" would have to take place with the body *in situ*.

Despite their disintegrated state, it was possible for Carter to determine that the *"general system of bandaging...was of normal character: it comprised a series of bandages, sheets and pads of linen, where the latter were required to complete the anthropoid form, the*

Opposite, Two sheathed daggers were found on the mummy of Tutankhamen, one with a blade of hardened gold (on the right), the other with an iron blade. Tucked into a sheet-gold girdle at the king's waist, the gold dagger has a haft of alternating geometric bands of granulated goldwork & cloisonné. One side of the sheath is cloisonné inlay in a feathered pattern, with the chased-gold reverse depicting a scene of wild animals terminating in an ornate floral device.

Adapted Internet photo

Below, Seventeen elaborate pectoral necklaces were suspended from the neck of Tutankhamen's mummy; three are shown below.

Cairo Egyptian Museum & Metropolitan Museum of Art

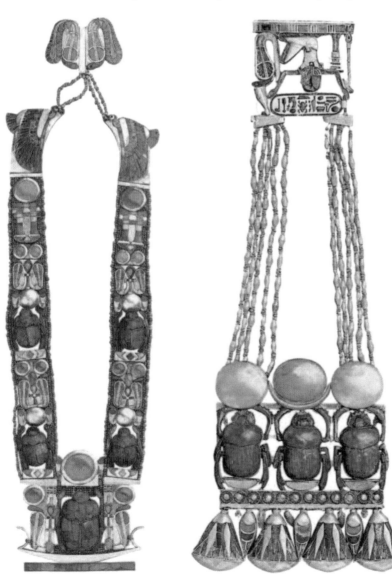

179

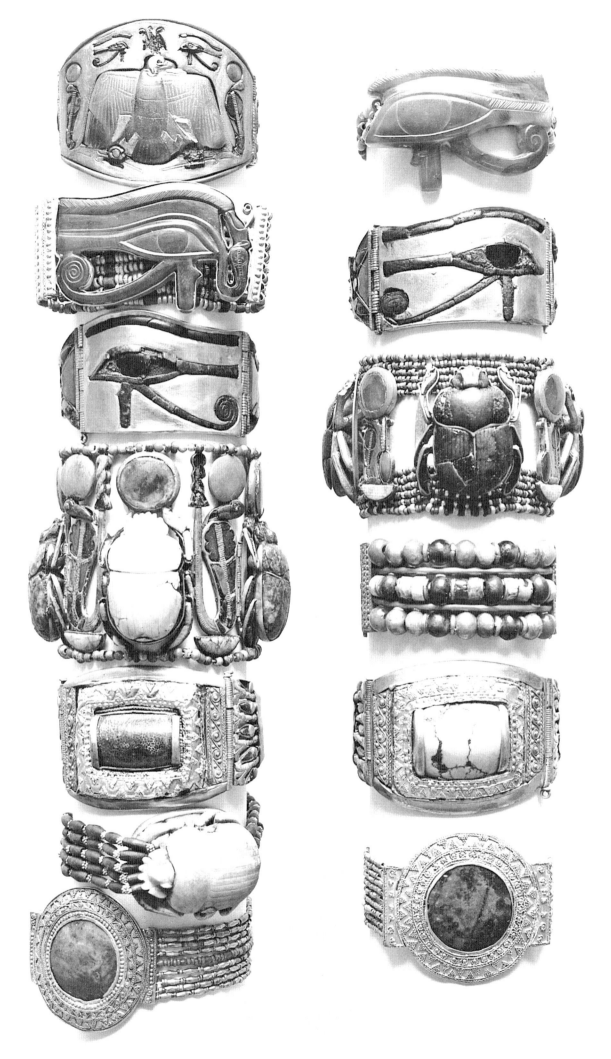

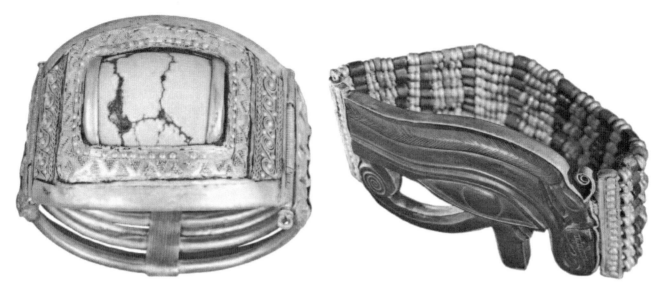

whole showing evidence of considerable care. The linen was evidently of a very fine cambric-like nature. The numerous objects found upon the mummy were enclosed in alternate layers of the voluminous wrappings, and literally covered the king from head to foot; some of the larger objects were caught up in many different layers of bindings which were wound crosswise and transversely." [107]

The revealing of the mummy began at the feet and worked upward towards the head — which, of course, along with the upper torso, was totally concealed by the gold mask. The feet proved to be shod with sheet-gold sandals embossed to imitate rushwork, and each digit was covered with a hollow sheath of gold engraved with the details of joint and toenail. Deposited in the wrappings over the legs were seven gold circlets inlaid with polychrome glass and four "hawk" collarettes of cloisonné work which had been folded and then literally crushed over the knees and shins. An eighth inlaid-gold circlet was found on the mummy's abdomen. A gold dagger in its sheath was placed along the king's right thigh, and along the left lay the cobra insignia of the diadem which would be found encircling the head within the mummy mask (the vulture insignia of the diadem was positioned above the right knee). A long rectangular amuletic apron composed of gold plaques inlaid with polychrome glass and strung together with beads covered the king's pubic area, extending downward to the knees; and a glass-inlaid gold clasp bracelet was found in its open position on the royal left hip. Several plain sheet-gold amulets were revealed in the area of the midsection, and an iron dagger in its gold sheath was tucked into one of two sheet-gold girdles which encircled the waist.

Once the lower portion of the king's remains was denuded of its wrappings and the layers of objects deposited therein, it was discovered that the forearms of the mummy had been positioned so that each crossed over the upper abdomen — the left higher than the right, with the right hand over the left hip, the left hand reaching the lower right side of the thorax — with both arms being covered from midpoint to elbow with several elaborate bracelets (seven on the right, six on

Opposite, Thirteen bracelets recovered from the forearms of Tutankhamen's mummy — seven from the right, six from the left — after these had been detached at the elbows & the hands likewise removed, so that the jewelry could be slipped off. They are made of gold & silver inlaid with semi-precious stones & polychrome glass. At least three pairs of matched bracelets can be recognized. Wadjet-eye & kheper-beetle motifs predominate. Griffith Institute

Above, Two of the mummy bracelets in color. Cairo Egyptian Museum

Harry Burton's photographic record of Tutankhamen's bracelets in situ *on the mummy's forearms crossed over the mid-torso.* Internet photo

Above, The conical pad of linen wrappings which was found on top of the head of Tutankhamen's mummy. Howard Carter thought it bore a resemblance to the atef *crown, but speculated that its practical purpose was to fill the void within the curve of the Ne-*mes *head covering of the gold funerary mask.* Griffith Institute

Above, Two cord-wrapped fiber circlets on the mummy's head. No other examples of these are known & Carter thought they might have served to cushion the head from the weight of a crown. Note the (modern) straight pins which hold them in place, and that cotton batting masks the fact that the head has been decapitated.

Griffith Institute

Above, The mummy's head in the first stages of the unwrapping, with a sheet-gold vulture amulet revealed resting atop it.

Griffith Institute

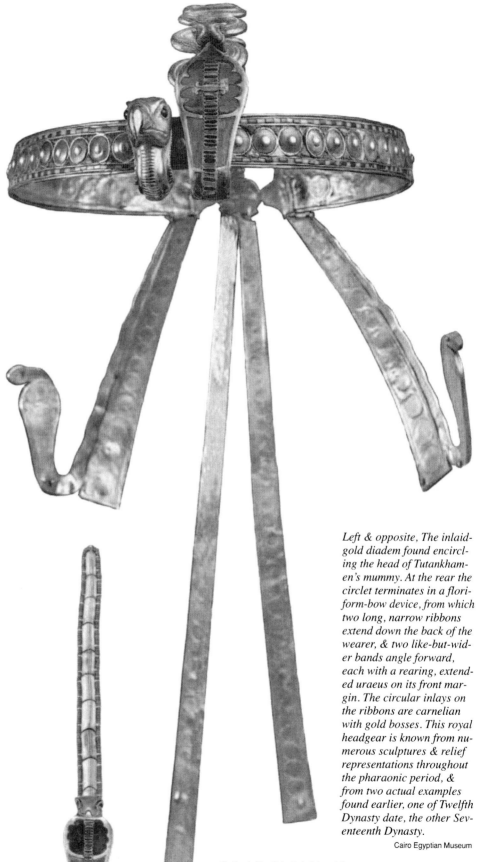

Left & opposite, The inlaid-gold diadem found encircling the head of Tutankhamen's mummy. At the rear the circlet terminates in a floriform-bow device, from which two long, narrow ribbons extend down the back of the wearer, & two like-but-wider bands angle forward, each with a rearing, extended uraeus on its front margin. The circular inlays on the ribbons are carnelian with gold bosses. This royal headgear is known from numerous sculptures & relief representations throughout the pharaonic period, & from two actual examples found earlier, one of Twelfth Dynasty date, the other Seventeenth Dynasty.

Cairo Egyptian Museum

Left, A flexible inlaid-gold uraeus was sewn atop the decayed head dress of the mummy. It was perhaps a wig attachment in actual use.

the left), which had been slipped on while the mummy's hands and arms were still flexible. As were the arms, the hands and fingers proved to have been wrapped separately, and each finger was encased in a sheet-gold sheath imitating the digit it covered, with incised nail and joint lines.

In his popular account of the discovery and clearance of the Tomb of Tutankhamen, Howard Carter is silent about the procedures decided upon for the rest of the *"examination"* of the king's mummy. Because the bracelet-laden royal arms were totally rigid, the only way that could be thought of to remove this invaluable jewelry was to literally remove the forearms themselves, detaching them from the mummy at the elbows; and then to separate the hands from the forearms in order that the bracelets could be slipped off. Thus began the total dismantlement of the mortal remains of Tutankhamen! (For a full discussion of the postmortem treatment of the king's mummy, in antiquity and following its discovery, see Book Five this series, Addendum Two, "Abusing Pharaoh," beginning p. 162.)

Because the uppermost part of the mummy's torso was covered by the gold portrait-mask (the back of which, it will be remembered, was firmly stuck to the bottom of the inner-coffin basin) — and it was apparent that numerous pieces of funerary jewelry in several layers rested under the collar portion of the mask — it was next decided

Above, The inlaid-gold diadem as found encircling the head of Tutankhamen's mummy. The uraeus & vulture emblems have been detached, to accommodate the wrappings & space within the funerary mask. Also visible is a sheet-gold head-band which is to be seen in Burton's formal photos of the king's head. Griffith Institute

Opening the coffins & examining the royal mummy occupied the whole of the fall-winter 1925 season in KV62. When Howard Carter returned to the tomb in early October of 1926, the task before him & his colleagues was the clearance of the small room off the Burial Chamber, which had been dubbed the "Treasury" by Carter & the press because of its rich contents. As seen through its low doorway, above, the space housed a quantity of model boats & other magical equipment — not to mention the king's canopic chest enclosed in an elaborate gilded baldachin. There were also numerous naoi *(& gilded ritual figures within these), plus a variety of storage chests, & even two dismantled chariots. This room had been entered by thieves in antiquity & at least its storage chests rifled & looted; although it was re-ordered by the necropolis officials immediately following discovery of the break-in.*

by Carter and Derry to extract the trunk of the mummy from the coffin, in order that these objects could be reached, recorded and removed. So the thorax was sawed through above the iliac crest (top of the pelvis), and heated knives were used to slowly loosen and ultimately free it from the bottom of the coffin trough. But the head, as had been supposed, was indeed firmly cemented by the congealed unguents to the inside back of the mask, so there seemed no choice but to severe it from the trunk at the neck; and Tutankhamen was thus decapitated, his head being left within the mask, the problem of finally extracting it to be dealt with later.

Returning to the severed torso — which, from Harry Burton's photograph, appears to have been left in the coffin still, but shifted to rest on a large sheet of heavy paper placed over the legs of the mummy — Carter found thirty-five different objects deposited in seventeen groups within thirteen layers of the complicated bandaging of the body. First came a series of four large amuletic collars of sheet gold, which had been suspended from the mummy's neck on gold wires, each with a counterpoise at the back. Below these was Tutankhamen's equivalent of the heart scarab, in his case made of black resin on a gold mounting, inlaid colored glass over the wings depicting a *Bennu* bird (heron), which was associated with the sun god, Re. Beneath this was another large sheet-gold funerary amulet in the form of a *"hawk collar."* This covered a very similar but far-superior pectoral of inlaid-gold plaques, which was very probably the personal jewelry of the king. A sheet of plain papyrus separated this from yet another sheet-gold hawk collar, on either side of which, parallel with the left and right arms, were positioned a pair of sheet-gold "knots" of amuletic nature. On the right and left of the lower part of the thorax were three amuletic "bangles," one of which was an iron *Wadjet* ("Eye of Horus").

After several more layers of carbonized bandages were lifted away, the eighth layer of objects was reached, which included yet another large chased-gold pectoral collar, this one representing the serpent goddess, Buto. It covered (with a slip of plain papyrus separating them), one on top of the other, two elaborate inlaid-gold (cloisonné) pectoral collars, the first representing the vulture goddess Nekhbet, the other a combination of the latter and Buto (called by Carter the *"Collar of Nebti"*). Each proved to be composed of scores of separate gold plaques, engraved on the reverse and minutely inlaid on the front with opaque colored glass, imitating turquoise, red jasper and lapis lazuli. Like the similar cloisonné "hawk collar," both include a *menat* plaque (counterpoise) of glass-inlaid gold, attached by gold

Along the south wall of KV62's Treasury (below), those who buried King Tutankhamen placed a large bitumen-coated flat box containing a ritual "Osiris bed," as well as a quantity of bitumenized tall naoi *on sledges housing gilded ritual figures, & several model boats of varying sizes. The doors of one shrine stand open in Burton's* in situ *photographs, perhaps evidence of the ancient robbers' presence which had not been corrected by the necropolis officials reordering the royal burial — or else inadvertently left that way by the curious Carter, Carnarvon & Lady Herbert that evening of November 26, 1922, when they explored the tomb unofficially.* Metropolitan Museum of Art

The most elaborate of the ritual objects found in the Treasury of KV62 — after the protective canopy of the canopic chest — was the so-called Anubis Shrine (bottom & detail opposite Adapted Internet photos)*, which greeted both ancient tomb robbers & Carter/Carnarvon at the entrance to the small storage room off the Burial Chamber. This sizeable piece of funerary furniture is constructed of wood & comprises a sledged pylon-shaped shrine with cavetto cornice, covered on its surfaces with embossed gilding on gesso, the sides decorated with two registers of* djed & tyet *glyphs framed at the top & sides by horizontal & vertical bands of text, & at the bottom by a palace-facade dado. The top of the shrine serves as a sliding lid onto which is attached the elegant figure of a crouching Anubis jackal (57 cm. high) of bitumenized wood detailed in gilt. The compartments inside the shrine (which measures 95.0 by 37.0 by 53.4 centimeters) were found to contain a quantity of assorted objects possibly associated with the mummification ritual (over which Anubis presided), as well as eight large pectoral-ornaments wrapped in linen.*

Above, A bitumen-coated wooden Anubis figure — its gilt-gesso collar fallen away — was found in the rubbish of the Tomb of Horemheb (KV57). It is fragmentary: one front leg, part of one ear & the tail are missing; but it is nearly the same size as the KV62 Anubis & almost certainly once adorned a shrine like that of KV62. Davis, Harmhabi

Above, Detail of the Anubis figure as found, wrapped with a shawl of decayed linen. Placed between the image's forelegs is painting palette inscribed with the name of Meritaten, eldest daughter of Akhenaten & Nefertiti.
Metropolitan Museum of Art

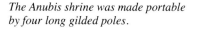

The Anubis shrine was made portable by four long gilded poles.

wire. These very complex (but highly flexible) collars were almost certainly worn by Tutankhamen in his lifetime.

Carter had now come to the eleventh and twelfth layers of objects, which were comprised of personal jewelry of the king. These included an exquisitely fashioned gold vulture-pendant inlaid with green glass, lapis and carnelian, suspended from two straps of

Second guardian of the KV62 Treasury was a large gilded & bitumenized wooden head of Hathor, depicted as a long-horned cow emerging from a papyrus swamp, her guise as goddess of the Wasetan necropolis (right). Ninety-one-plus centimeters tall, it was positioned facing west between the Anubis & canopic shrines, & was partially shrouded in linen (right Griffith Institute)*. The graceful tall horns are wood covered with thin copper & varnished black with resin. The inlaid eyes of crystalline limestone & obsidian are accented by cosmetic lines & brows in blue-black glass.* Adapted Internet photo

188

gold and lapis-lazuli plaques, fastened by an inlaid-gold clasp in the form of a pair of hawks. Interestingly, the under or reverse side of the Nekhbet pendant is chased in great detail, with obsidian eye and lapis beak, and depicts the vulture goddess herself wearing a miniature pendant necklace showing the king's prenomen flanked by *uraei* and surmounted by a plumed sun disk. Carter remarked that this particular masterpiece of the ancient goldsmith's art was *"perhaps the finest of all found upon the king."* [108] Just lower on the chest at the same level rested a second elaborate inlaid-gold pendant, this depicting a row of three lapis-lazuli *kheper* beetles supporting gold and gold/silver-alloy (electrum) disks of the sun, moon and crescent moon. Pendant from a marguerite-decorated bar beneath the beetles are inlaid lotus flowers and buds. Two straps, each composed of five strands of gold beads, attach the scarabs pendant to a *menat* of gold openwork, the device of which depicts the king's titulary and prenomen held aloft by a kneeling deity flanked by a crowned uraeus at one side and a *was/djed* combination at the other.

Immediately below the last described pieces of Tutankhamen's personal jewelry rested three more ornate inlaid-gold pendants, all evidencing actual wear of the sort that would place them in the category of real rather than funerary jewelry. Under these was a collection of some twenty smaller amulets of various types and materials (sheet gold and inlaid gold), all suspended around the mummy's neck on thin gold wires. And closest to the surface of the latter, but separated from the desiccated flesh by several thicknesses of gossamer linen charred almost to powder, rested a collarette formed from small blue-glass and gold beads threaded together in four stands. Also recovered from the thorax and abdomen wrappings were two groups of finger rings, five from over the wrist of the right hand, and next to the left wrist another group of eight. These rings — plus the two found on one hand of the mummy — were variously fashioned of solid gold, lapis lazuli, cloudy-white and green chalcedony, turquoise and black resin.

Having thus denuded the dismembered, severed through and decapitated corpse of Tutankhamen of its ornamentation, Carter next turned his attention to the still-bandaged royal head left within the gold funerary mask. In employing the same hot-knife technique used on the thorax to extract the cranium from the congealed unguents in which it was embedded, the carbonized flesh at the back of the neck was pulled away, revealing the cervical vertebrae there. Generally speaking, the bandages of the head were far better preserved than those on the rest of the body (save the feet), not having been saturated with the anointing unguents and consequently suffering only indirectly from oxidation. On top of the head those who wrapped the king's mummy had placed a large cone-shaped pad of wads of linen bandaged together. While Carter thought this bore some resemblance to the *Atef* crown, he believed it more practically served to fill out the space between the crown of the king's head and the hollow of the *Nemes* of the gold mask. A small amulet in the form of a headrest made of iron was recovered from the back of the head bundle, the third object in that "foreign" ma-

Wooden Hathor-cow heads are known from the tombs of Thutmose IV (below) & Amenhotep II (bottom). Neither of these earlier examples had ever been gilded, however; rather they were painted yellow & the Amenhotep II example with details painted in black. Archival & Cairo Egyptian Museum photos

Overleaves, The four guardian gilded-wood goddess statues – details of the one depicting Selket — have often been suggested to have the facial features of Tutankhamen's consort, Ankhesenamen. Author's photo & Cairo Egyptian Museum

terial found on the mummy (the others being the second dagger and a *Wadjet*-eye amulet).

      Under the conical pad on top of the head bundle were two cord-wrapped fiber circlets with loops at their ends for threading cloth tapes, so that they could be tied in back. Nothing like them had been found previously, and Carter posited that they may have functioned to provide relief to the head from the pressure of a crown. Removing a few more layers of wrapping revealed a magnificent fillet-type inlaid-gold diadem, which completely encircled the king's head. It consists of a heavy gold ribbon decorated in a continuous band of carnelian circles with gold bosses in their centers, terminating at the back with a floral-shaped bow, from which are suspended two long, narrower ribbons of like decoration. On both sides of the fillet are a pair of similar-but-wider appendages, along the front edges of which are attached pendant *uraei*, their fully extended bodies parallel to these secondary

ribbons. It will be remembered that the detachable cobra and vulture insignias from this diadem had been found earlier, positioned on the mummy's legs. This particular kind of diadem is known from numerous representations throughout the Dynastic Period, and is always shown being worn over a short, tightly curled wig. Two similar actual diadems had been discovered previously in royal burials, one of Middle Kingdom date and the other from the Seventeenth Dynasty.[109]

Removing a few more layers of wrappings, Carter next found a wide sheet-gold temple band with short lappets, which terminated behind the ears and was perforated so that tapes for tying it at the back of the head could be attached. This band had served to hold in place a *Khat* (or wig bag) head covering of finest-quality linen; but this had so deteriorated that only its characteristic "pig tail" could be salvaged. Sewn onto the front and top of the *khat* were the royal insignia (an inlaid-gold uraeus with flexible tail and a spread-winged vulture in chased sheet-gold). Pads of linen had been stuffed into the *Khat* to give it its conventional shape.

More bandaging was removed to expose an elaborately beaded linen skullcap resting directly on the scalp of the mummy's head — which proved to have been shaved completely smooth and smeared with a coating of a fatty substance. The fabric of the skullcap had deteriorated to the extent that it fell apart at the slightest touch; but the multiple-uraeus device of the beaded decoration, in almost perfect condition, still adhered to the king's head. It was decided that to remove this would be disastrous, so it was brushed with a thin coating of paraffin and left in place.

A delicate sable brush was employed to remove the carbonized final (or first, more correctly) wrappings from the face of Tutankhamen, the latter proving to be in only a little better state of preservation than the rest of the body, having suffered from the same effects of carbonization, if less directly. Carter was struck with what he thought was a strong resemblance between the features of the youthful king (and the *"uncommon"* shape of his skull) and those later portraits of Akhenaten which depict that king in a more flattering (and realistic) way than the caricaturing style of the early years of the Heretic's reign. He concluded, therefore, that they were related by blood, very likely father and son.

Carter had photographer Harry Burton record the king's head in profile and full face surrounded by a wide masking of cotton batting, with the second sheet-gold head band still in place; these two views were used as the mummy's portraits in Carter's popular account of the tomb clearance. But Burton also photographed the severed head from several other angles, in these views placed like a scientific specimen on a raw-wood plank and held in place by a wooden-dowel prop and carpenter's nails. These disturbing images record the fact of Tutankhamen's decapitation by his discoverer all too clearly, as well as the unfortunate damage done to the back of the neck during the head's forced extraction from the gold mummy mask (the cervical vertebrae

When the canopic baldachin-&-shrine unit was dismantled, it was found to contain, as expected, the king's linen-shrouded calcite Canopic Chest (below Internet photos*), which likewise rests on a wooded sledge which is gilded. The* djed/tyet-*patterned dado of the shrine-shaped chest itself is gilded as well. Repeating the iconography seen on the sarcophagus, four guardian goddesses executed in high relief are positioned at the corners of the chest, their outstretched arms in a protective embrace of the contents therein. When the cavetto-corniced lid was removed (opposite* Metropolitan Museum of Art*) four calcite portrait stoppers — in a king's likeness wearing the* Nemes & Buto/Nekhbet *insignia — were covering cylinders cut into the solid block forming the chest.*

The features of the all-but-identical portraits on the Canopic Chest stoppers (one seen full frontal, opposite Cairo Egyptian Museum*) are somewhat different from those of Tutankhamen, suggesting the KV62 canopic equipment may have been made originally for another king, with Smenkhkare the most likely candidate.*

Above, The four stoppers nose-to-nose in the chest (Author's photo) *& these removed (below), revealing the receptacles holding linen-swathed miniature coffins of inlaid gold which contained the royal viscera.*

Internet photo

exposed). And on close inspection, it is evident that the top portion of the king's left ear was broken away between the time of the first "glamour" photos for publication and Burton's subsequent, more clinical ones.[110] But Carter did not mean for these "record shots" to be seen by the public at large; and they were not until 1972, when the series was included in the Griffith Institute's "Tutankhamun Tomb Series," Volume V, *The Human Remains from the Tomb of Tutankhamun* by F. Filce Leek.

In his diary entry for November 18, 1925, Howard Carter wrote, *"After photographic records are made of the King's remains, these will be reverently re-wrapped and returned to the sarcophagus."*[111] But before this was done, the body parts were re-assembled on a tray of sand especially constructed for the purpose, with the body in a supine position, the hands and feet (the latter also having been severed by Dr. Derry during his "autopsy") reattached with resin. The sand in which the remains were partially submerged served to disguise the fact that the head and limbs were no longer attached to the trunk of the body, while the rearranged crossed arms hid any indication that the torso had been sawed in half above the pelvis. Thus seemingly intact, the sorry denuded mummy of Tutankhamen was photographed in full length from overhead by Burton, and this image was subsequently published in various later accounts of the KV62 discovery and clearance (although not by Carter himself in his own account). But reinterment did not follow until nearly a year later, when on October 23, 1926, Carter wrote in his dairy, *"The first outermost coffin containing the King's Mummy, finally rewrapped, was lowered into the sarcophagus this morning. We are now ready to begin upon the investigation of the Store Room."*[112] Where Tutankhamen had resided in the interim is not remarked upon, but presumably he was "stored" in the Tomb of Seti II

warehouse. (For further discussion of the mummy of Tutankhamen, see Addendum Five, beginning page 326).

Between November 20th and December 31st of the 1925 season, Carter focused all of his efforts on cleaning and restoring the coffins and funerary mask, and the objects found on the mummy. The greatest effort was expended on separating the basins of the Second and Third coffins. It had been determined that the unguents cementing them together could be melted by the application of sufficient heat. Thus, the innermost (Third) coffin was completely lined with zinc plates to protect it, the two coffin basins were turned upside down on trestles, and the middle (Second) coffin was covered with heavy wet blankets. Then primus paraffin lamps were set burning *"full blast"* under the hollow of the Third Coffin, for some three hours before movement could be detected, when the lamps were turned off and the two basins very slowly came apart, the gold coffin's trough falling out of the other. Carter remarked that when the unguent material melted it *"was of an exceedingly plastic nature and of the consistency of thick treacle, which even when the coffins came apart was very difficult to remove — even with quantities of various solvents — among which the final cleaning*

Full-frontal, back & interior (of lid & basin) views of one of the four solid-gold coffinettes which contained the mummified viscera of Tutankhamen. Detail opposite. Cairo Egyptian Museum *These were found within the cylindrical receptacles of the interior of the Canopic Chest, each wrapped in linen. In design they imitate the Second Coffin. The set of four miniature viscera coffins — like the Second Coffin & the portrait stoppers of the Canopic Chest — would seem to represent some other king than Tutankhamen. It has been suggested by various scholars that they were made originally for the interment of King Smenkhkare, & later were appropriated for his successor's use. Evident alterations to incised cartouches on the interior of the coffinettes would seem to support this argument. The design relationship between the coffinettes & Second Coffin is obvious as well.*

199

Discovered when Tutankhamen's canopic equipment was dismantled & removed from the Treasury, & clearance of five large chests found in a row there was completed, Carter turned his attention to a white-washed large wood chest (right Cairo Egyptian Museum) *the tossed off (by ancient robbers?) lid revealed two miniature black-&-gilt anthropoid coffins resting head-to-foot within (below,* Internet photo). *Each would prove to hold a second gilded-all-over coffin which housed a fetal mummy, one of these with a minature gilded-cartonnage mask.*

was done by means of acetone." [113] The funerary mask ultimately was unstuck from the coffin basin using a similar application of heat.

On December 31st, 1925, Carter and Lucas left Luxor bound for Cairo, taking with them three packing cases containing the gold coffin and funerary mask. They would not return to continue clearance work in the Tomb of Tutankhamen for nine months, unlocking the Seti II tomb/laboratory on October 9th, 1926. Lucas immediately set himself to the task of cleaning and repairing the outermost (First) coffin for its return to the lidless sarcophagus standing empty in the KV62 Burial Chamber; and Carter completed *"the final touches"* to the royal mummy, which was then reinterred within the coffin when the tomb itself was finally reopened on October 26th.

The next task which lay before Carter and his colleagues was the dismantling of the contents of the Treasury. It will be remembered that the low entry into this space from the adjacent Burial Chamber was the only one in the tomb which had not been blocked up and sealed in antiquity. In order to protect the plethora of almost certainly fragile objects within — and, also, to avoid the temptation to examine any of these prematurely — Carter had the Treasury doorway closed off with wooden boarding throughout the lengthy clearance of the Burial Chamber. This was now removed and, four years after the tomb's discovery, the work of revealing exactly what "treasures" the Treasury held began.

The room itself is relatively small, some fifteen feet eight inches by twelve feet six inches, and only seven feet eight inches from floor to ceiling. The first of its partially ransacked then reordered contents to be dealt with was the large Anubis Shrine which was situated in the doorway — in fact all but blocking access to the chamber beyond. This peculiar object was comprised of a squat rectangular gilt-wood pylon resting on a gilded-wood sledge, atop which — draped in a gossamer-thin linen shawl over which was tied a linen shirt dating to Year 7 of Akhenaten — crouched a life-sized statue of the god of embalming in his full-jackal manifestation. The wooden figure, when relieved of its shroudings and a leash-like linen scarf tied about its neck, was found to be painted all over with glistening bitumen, details of the ears and a collar with pendant ribbons being set off in gold leaf, the toenails picked out in silver, and the eyes and brow lines inlaid with calcite, obsidian and gold. When the lid of the pylon chest that supported the jackal figure was slid back, the interior was discovered to be made up of five compartments holding a number of linen-wrapped small amuletic objects perhaps related to the mummification ritual, plus eight large pectoral ornaments, also originally wrapped in linen that had been disturbed by the ancient thieves in their search for solid-gold loot. While nothing quite like this Anubis Shrine had been discovered previously, an almost identical couchant bitumenized-wood jackal sculpture was recovered a few years earlier (1908) in the funerary debris of the Tomb of Horemheb (KV57); and it almost certainly originally adorned a similar shrine belonging to the burial equipment of Tutankhamen's second successor.

Interestingly, placed between the forefeet of the Tomb 62

Below, The smaller of the anthropoid coffin sets found in the Treasury of KV-62. Of the two coffins comprising the set, the outermost (bottom left) is decorated in the fashion favored by high-status individuals during the second half of the Eighteenth Dynasty: painted all over in black pitch, with longitudinal & lateral gilded bands of inscription, the wig-cover stripes, face & hands gilded as well. The interior second coffin (bottom middle) is gilded all over, with brows & eyes indicated in black pigment. The younger of the two fetal mummies was covered with a some-what-too-large gilded-cartonnage mask (bottom right), & was considerably smaller than the interior of the second coffin. Griffith Institute

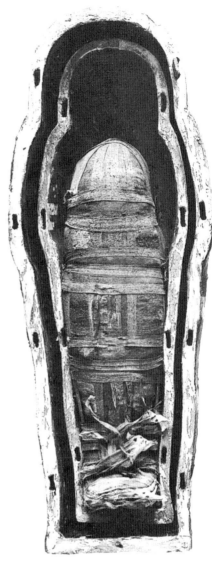

*Above, The Treasury's second, larger bitu-
menized & gilded-wood coffin set also was
found to contain a mummified fetus — the
latter, however, not having been supplied
with a cartonnage mask (unless this was
the miniature mask found in KV54, see p.
10). The brief inscription on this pair of
coffins & the two housing the other fetus
do not contain any names, so the two female still-born infants are anonymous. It
was supposed by Howard Carter that they
were the children of Tutankhamen & Great
Royal Wife Ankhesenamen, a conclusion
seconded by most scholars. A minority view
holds that their presence in KV62 had a ritual significance connected with the young
king's rebirth in the Hereafter.* Griffith Institute

Anubis figure, Carter found an ivory writing palette inscribed for Meritaten, eldest daughter of Akhenaten and Nefertiti, and older sister-in-
law of Tutankhamen. What this memento was doing in his tomb will
be speculated on below.

Sitting on the Treasury floor directly behind the Anubis
Shrine, facing to the west, was the sculpted head of a long-horned cow
resting on a low rectangular base, a linen scarf knotted at its throat.
Made of wood that had been gilded (except for the lower portion and
base, which were covered with the ubiquitous bitumen), this near-life-
sized sculpture was identified by Carter as representing the Mehurit
cow, a manifestation of the goddess Hathor as *"Mistress of the Moun-
tain of the West."* The wooden cores of the horns were found to be
sheathed in copper, which had been painted black with pitch. The eyes
lines (in the form of the *Wadjet*) and brows are indicated in lapis-colored glass, the eyes themselves inlaid with calcite and obsidian. Similar
cow heads were known previously from the tombs of Amenhotep II
and Thutmose IV (see p. 188), although these earlier examples show
no evidence of ever having been gilded.

Behind the Hathor cow, positioned directly on the floor in

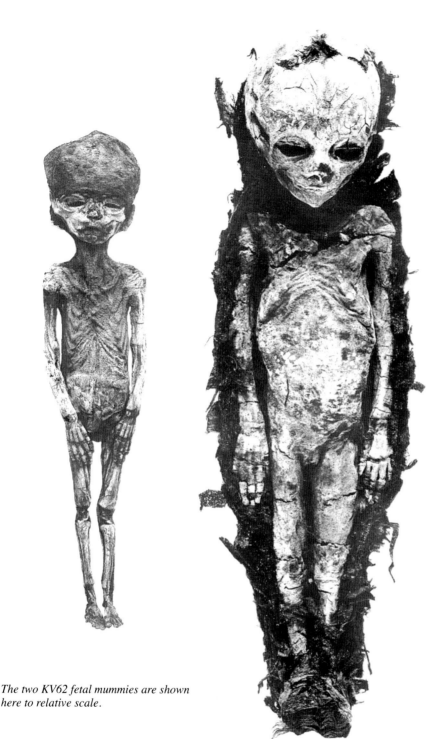

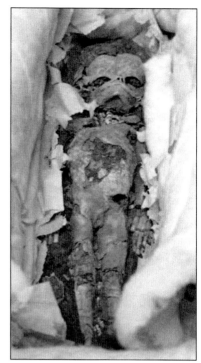

Above & below, The KV62 fetal mummies as they appear today (the smaller at top). Both are regrettably badly deteriorated, really beyond the point of reconstruction. Internet photos

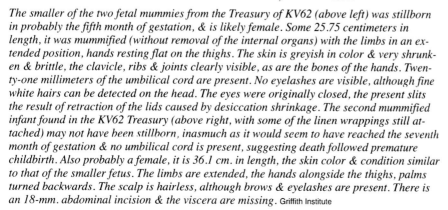

The two KV62 fetal mummies are shown here to relative scale.

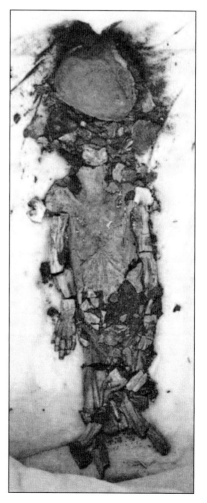

The smaller of the two fetal mummies from the Treasury of KV62 (above left) was stillborn in probably the fifth month of gestation, & is likely female. Some 25.75 centimeters in length, it was mummified (without removal of the internal organs) with the limbs in an extended position, hands resting flat on the thighs. The skin is greyish in color & very shrunken & brittle, the clavicle, ribs & joints clearly visible, as are the bones of the hands. Twenty-one millimeters of the umbilical cord are present. No eyelashes are visible, although fine white hairs can be detected on the head. The eyes were originally closed, the present slits the result of retraction of the lids caused by desiccation shrinkage. The second mummified infant found in the KV62 Treasury (above right, with some of the linen wrappings still attached) may not have been stillborn, inasmuch as it would seem to have reached the seventh month of gestation & no umbilical cord is present, suggesting death followed premature childbirth. Also probably a female, it is 36.1 cm. in length, the skin color & condition similar to that of the smaller fetus. The limbs are extended, the hands alongside the thighs, palms turned backwards. The scalp is hairless, although brows & eyelashes are present. There is an 18-mm. abdominal incision & the viscera are missing. Griffith Institute

a row, were three small calcite stands (*tazzas*) which supported shallow calcite dishes. Two of these, to the right and left, were covered by inverted bowls of the same material and contained what Alfred Lucas analyzed as natron, common salt and sulphate of soda. He thought the middle bowl once held water, long evaporated. Carter suggested these peculiar objects may have had a mummification-ritual context.

Clearly dominating the contents of the Treasury was the Canopic Shrine within its baldachin canopy which reached nearly to the ceiling of the chamber. This unique monument was centered on the Treasury's east wall, and aligned with the row of funerary ritual objects beginning with the Anubis Shrine. Although it was not dismantled until everything else had been removed from the Treasury (in order to have full access to it), the Canopic Shrine and its contents will be discussed here because of their direct relationship to the rest of Tutankhamen's funerary equipage.

Standing some six feet six inches in height, the gilded-wood canopy of the Shrine rests on a massive sledge, also gilded, which occupied some four by five feet of floor space. The roof of the canopy is formed from a cavetto cornice, atop which, on all four sides, is a free-standing frieze of rearing inlaid uraei, each crowned by a gilded sun disk. This elaborate roof is supported at its four corners by two-sided posts affixed into the sledge base. On each of the sledge's side, centered between these corner posts, stands a small gilded-wood figure of a goddess (Isis, Nephthys, Neith and Selket), facing inward but with head slightly turned, her arms outspread in a protective gesture. These four goddess figures are modeled in the best post-Amarna

Above & inset, Miniature solid-gold pendant figure of a squatting king wearing the Khepresh *& holding the Crook & Flail in one hand. It was in a small coffin-set found in the KV62 Treasury (right* Cairo Egyptian Museum*) & has been identified (although uninscribed) as representing Amenhotep III, thus possibly linking that king's paternity to Tutankhamen. It is suspended on a woven gold-wire chain tied with a tasseled cord. A bead* shebiyu *(shown detached) adorned the tiny statuette's neck.* Metropolitan Museum of Art

style, and it has been suggested that the identical facial features of each are those of youthful Queen Ankhesenamen. Each figure is adorned in a tight-fitting pleated gown typical of the end of the Eighteenth Dynasty and wears a *Khat* head covering, perched on which is the appropriate symbol of the goddess represented. Eyes and brows have been indicated in black paint.

The outspread arms of these guardian goddesses in effect encircle the Canopic Shrine itself, which is a tall rectangular chest, covered in gilded gesso with incised inscriptions and a scene on each side panel depicting the tutelary goddess represented in the accompanying statue facing one of the four canopic *genii*.[114] Like the canopy the Shrine has a cavetto cornice, which is also surmounted by a *uraei* frieze identical to that of the canopy, except smaller in scale.

When this Shrine was taken apart, its contents — as Carter had suspected all along — proved to be a linen-shrouded shrine-shaped canopic chest carved from a single block of veined, semi-translucent calcite. Its dado (with a design of alternating paired *djed* and *tyet* glyphs) is covered with thin sheet-gold, as is the silver-handled sledge on which it rests. The massive lid — comprised of an entablature with incised, pigment-filled inscriptions, topped by a cavetto cornice and a shrine-type roof — is also carved in calcite (a separate block from the chest?), and was bound to the chest itself by cords threaded through four gold staples. Incised on the sloping top of the lid is a jackal recumbent over nine prisoners: the motif of the royal necropolis seal.

Once the lid was removed, four royal *Nemes*-adorned portrait heads — also carved from calcite, with details picked out in black and red pigments — were found to be functioning as stoppers to the openings of the *faux* jars holding the king's viscera.[115] The interior of the chest is carved out only to a depth of about five inches, giving the appearance of four separate squared compartments, each containing what appears to be the uppermost portion of a separate canopic jar, but which in fact is only a cylindrical hole drilled into the solid block of calcite. Removing the human-headed lids revealed that each of these compartments held an upright bundle wrapped in linen, which had been liberally anointed with the same unguent substance poured over the inner coffin and king's mummy, thus sticking the mummiform package to the bottom of the cylindrical hole. When extracted these four bundles proved to be identical exquisite miniature solid-gold coffins, elaborately inlaid with colored glass and closely resembling the king's Second Coffin. Besides an inscribed funerary formula running in a text band down the front of the coffinette lid, the interiors of each lid and trough are engraved with texts pertaining to the preservation of the royal viscera. It is in these latter texts that alterations to the cartouches can be detected: the prenomen Ankhkheperure (Akhenaten's first successor, Smenkhkare) has been mostly rubbed out and replaced by that of Tutankhamen. This erasure and over writing has led to the speculation that the coffinettes were originally commissioned for Tutankhamen's immediate predecessor, and then later appropriated for his own use.

While not discovered until clearance of the Treasury was

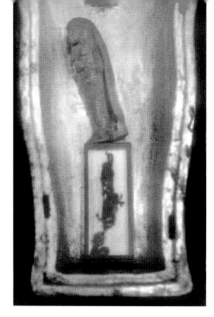

Also housed within the bitumenized-&-gilded coffin set found in the KV62 Treasury, along with the linen-wrapped solid-gold pendant statuette of a squatting king figure, was another plain-wood miniature coffin (below left Griffith Institute*) which held a small mummiform bundle that had been heavily anointed with unguents (below right* Griffith Institute*). This proved to be yet another wooden coffin inscribed with the titulary & name of Great Royal Wife Tiye, & within it was a linen-wrapped plaited lock of human hair, presumably from the head of the royal lady herself, & kept as a royal memento (above, as displayed today* Author's photo*).*

Overleaves, Harry Burton's in situ views of the many pitch-coated naoi found grouped together in the Treasury supporting several model boats. These small shrines held gilded "ritual" figures & images of a king (perhaps not Tutankhamen, in a few cases).
Metropolitan Museum of Art

Narration continues p. 215

Left, one of the two falcon-standards from the Treasury, this depicting Sopdu, the other Gemehsu. It is 65.5 cm. high, with blue pigment & glass eyes enhancing the gilding. Below, The cobra figure of Netjer-Ankh was housed in a naos also contianing the two falcon-standards. It has inlaid glass eyes & is 56.5 cm. high. Cairo Egyptian Museum

There was a total of 27 deity statues housed in the bitumen-coated naoi found in the KV-62 Treasury, both anthropomorphic & zoomorphic in type. They are all carved of wood & gilded overall, many with inlaid eyes & additional painted details. Each is mounted on a flat wooden base coated with bitumen, many inscribed with the name of the deity depicted. Cairo Egyptian Museum

Harry Burton's "record shot" of five of the KV62 ritual figures from the Treasury, but for one with their shrouds in place, as found. Internet photo

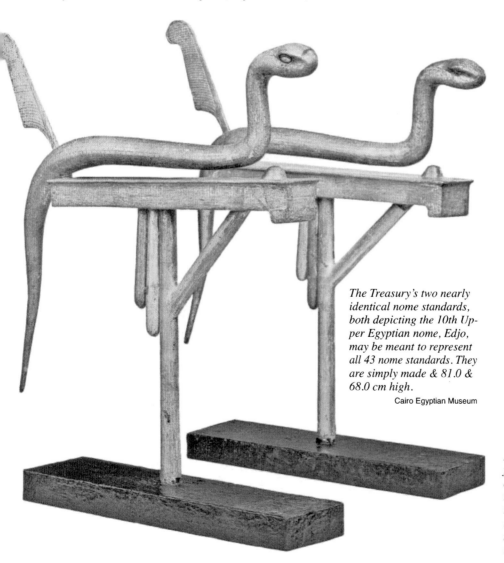

The Treasury's two nearly identical nome standards, both depicting the 10th Upper Egyptian nome, Edjo, may be meant to represent all 43 nome standards. They are simply made & 81.0 & 68.0 cm high.

Cairo Egyptian Museum

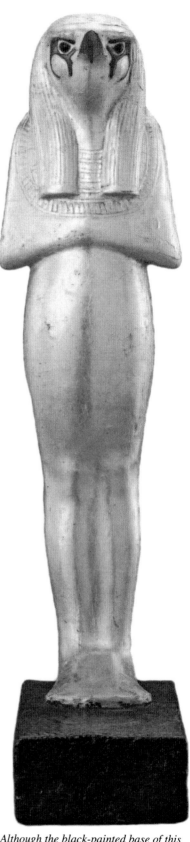

Although the black-painted base of this flacon-headed deity is uninscribed, it is almost certainly meant to depict one of the Sons of Horus, Qebhesnuef, who was responsible for protecting the deceased's intestines. The beak is black glass & eye markings in inlaid blue glass. The figure is 55.5 cm tall. Cairo Egyptian Museum

Among the Treasury's deity statues were two figures of the child-god Ihy, depicted as a nude boy holding a sistrum (one at left). They are coated all over with bitumen, with a gilded sistrum & gold details around the inlaid eyes. They are each 60.5 cm tall. Another of the Sons of Horus is represented by the jackal-headed Duamutef (one of two below). The eyes & brows are painted in black. They are 58.0 cm. tall. Arguably the most attractive of the deity statues is the elegant depiction of the god Ptah (right & detail opposite). His skull cap is a shiny blue faience, the eyes & brows inlaid, the feathered garment rendered with great detail; the mummiform god holds a long copper scepter combining was, ankh & djed *elements. It is 60.2 cm. tall.* Cairo Egyptian Museum

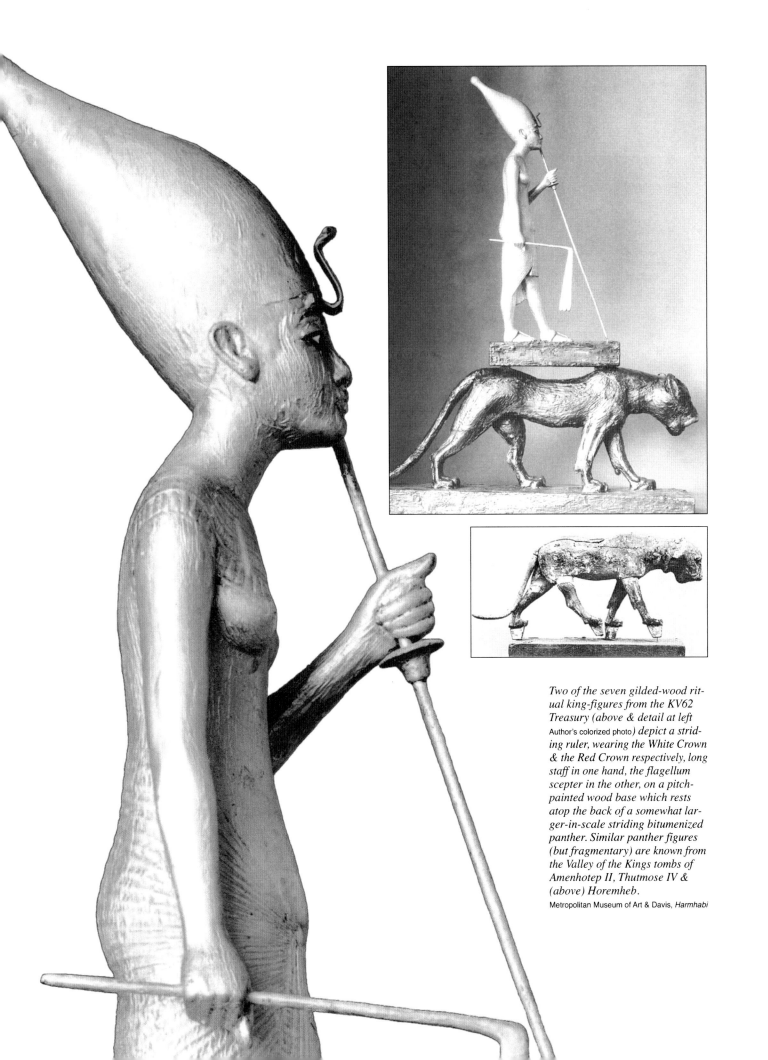

Two of the seven gilded-wood ritual king-figures from the KV62 Treasury (above & detail at left Author's colorized photo*) depict a striding ruler, wearing the White Crown & the Red Crown respectively, long staff in one hand, the flagellum scepter in the other, on a pitch-painted wood base which rests atop the back of a somewhat larger-in-scale striding bitumenized panther. Similar panther figures (but fragmentary) are known from the Valley of the Kings tombs of Amenhotep II, Thutmose IV & (above) Horemheb.*
Metropolitan Museum of Art & Davis, *Harmhabi*

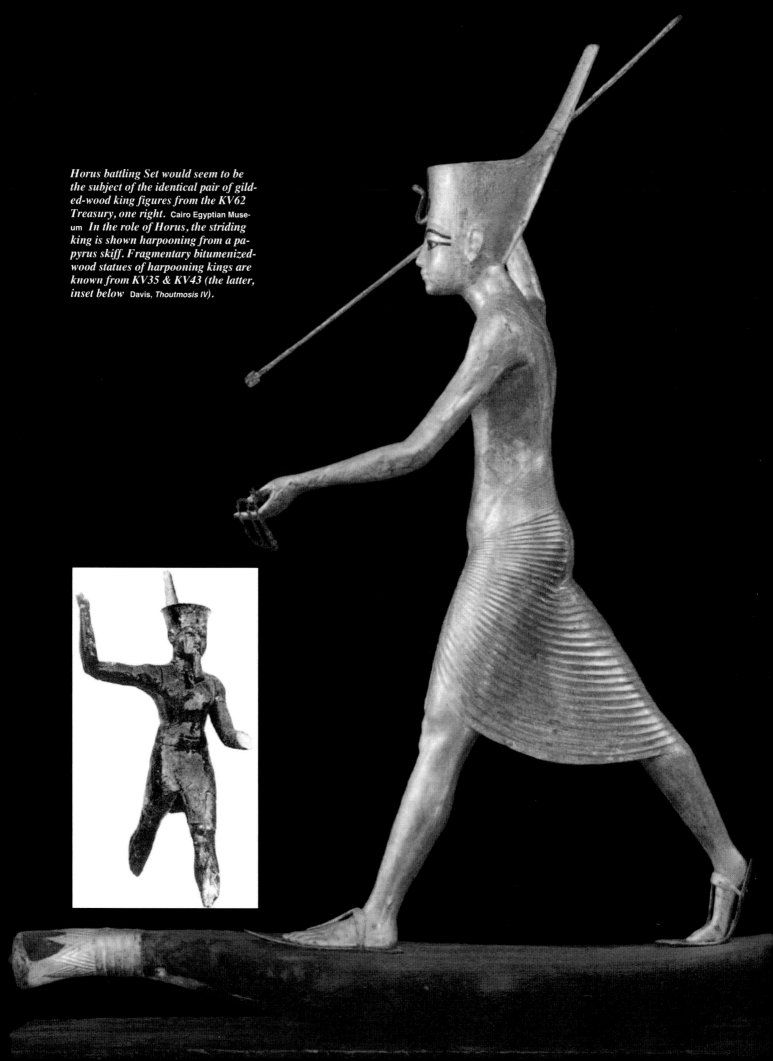

Horus battling Set would seem to be the subject of the identical pair of gilded-wood king figures from the KV62 Treasury, one right. Cairo Egyptian Museum *In the role of Horus, the striding king is shown harpooning from a papyrus skiff. Fragmentary bitumenized-wood statues of harpooning kings are known from KV35 & KV43 (the latter, inset below* Davis, Thoutmosis IV)*.*

well under way, it seems appropriate to discuss at this point the other human remains which had been interred with Tutankhamen's own. Within a plain white-painted wooden chest (the lid of which had been removed in antiquity), situated in the northeast corner of the chamber — along with the pitch-painted kiosks holding the king's ushabtis — were found two small wooden anthropoid coffins, placed side by side, head to foot, the toe end of the larger of the pair having been hacked away to enable the lid of the box to be closed (recalling the same treatment to Tutankhamen's own outermost coffin, in order to facilitate lowering of the sarcophagus lid).

These two coffins were fashioned in the manner employed for high-status individuals of the latter half of the Eighteenth Dynasty: painted with black pitch and ornamented with vertical and horizontal gilded bands of funerary inscriptions on the lids and basins, the alternating stripes of the wig covering and the face and hands gilded as well. Within each black-and-gold coffin, Carter found a second anthropoid one of wood gilded all over, thus also following the fashion of the day for high-status burials. These two inner coffins also bear longitudinal and transverse bands of funerary texts; but as in the case of the outer coffins, no name appears in either set of inscriptions — each being dedicated merely to an "Osiris," i.e. the deceased — rendering the tiny occupants of both coffin sets intriguingly anonymous.[116]

The smaller of the pair, when its inner lid was removed, was found to contain a neatly bandaged miniature mummiform bundle, over which had been placed a small gilded-cartonnage funerary mask — several sizes too large, however. The second, larger inner-coffin held its own similarly well-wrapped mummy bundle, this half again longer than the other, but without a cartonnage mask present.[117]

Both infant mummies were eventually fully exposed, the smaller by Carter without Dr. Derry present. The bandaging in each case had been very carefully applied and included transverse and crisscross linen strips and sheeting, plus numerous linen pads to help fill out the infant body to the desired anthropoid shape. The smaller (and therefore more premature) of the two fetuses measured 25.75 centimeters (ten-plus inches) in length, and appeared to be that of a female child, almost certainly still-born, probably in the fifth month of gestation (judging from its size and the fact that a portion of the umbilical cord was present). The body had been mummified without removal of the internal organs, as no abdominal incision was to be seen. Its state when unwrapped was very fragile: the shriveled skin greyish, with white patches of natron, and very brittle, the clavicles, ribs and limb-joints being clearly visible. A few white hairs could be detected on the scalp, but no brows or eyelashes were present; and the just-open slits of the eyes themselves were the consequence of the desiccation process. The tiny body had been laid out with the limbs fully extended, palms flat on the front of the thighs. No jewelry or amulets were found among the wrappings.

The second infant mummy, also almost certainly female,

It would seem that the Treasury king-figures represent someone other than Tutankhamen, possibly even a female pharaoh, judging from the feminine physiques depicted, especially the full breasts on one of the king-on-panther pair (seen in detail above Author's colorized photo*). However, it is possible that the individual represented is Amenhotep IV, these ritual figures having been commissioned prior to his name change (to Akhenaten) & abandonment of the Wasetan (Theban) necropolis.*

Opposite, Two of three striding king-figure statues of gilded hardwood found housed in pitch-painted naoi *in the Treasury of KV62. It is debated whether these decidedly feminized images represent Tutankhamen, with whom they were interred; or Akhenaten at the outset of his reign— for whom they may have been commissioned but never employed; or even one of the ephemeral royal females who seem to have reigned in the guise of king between Akhenaten & Tutankhamen. Apparently there was a fourth figure originally, inasmuch as two of the statues depict the king wearing the Red Crown of Lower Egypt, but only one (above) sporting the White Crown of Upper Egypt.*
Cairo Egyptian Museum

Narration continues p. 221

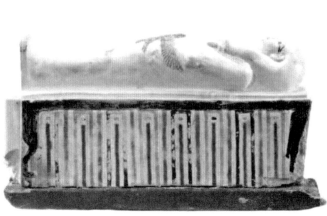

Among the interesting objects found in the KV62 Treasury was a small bitumen-covered sarcophagus chest containing a carved-wood figure of a mummiform Osiris/Tutankhamen recumbent on a lion bier, flanked by a ba bird & a falcon-figure (below & detail right Metropolitan Museum of Art, Cairo Egyptian Museum), the latter perhaps representing the king's ka. This ritual/magical sculpture apparently was a gift to the funerary furnishings of the deceased ruler by Maya, chief treasurer of the king & one of the highest ranking nobles in the Two Lands. A non-royal precedent for this object is a similar limestone Osiride figure recumbent on a lion bier accompanied by a ba bird, which was found in the Tomb of Yuya & Thuyu (KV-46), seen at top. Cairo Egyptian Museum

Of Tutankhamen's 413 ushabtis, those executed in wood & then gilded & painted in part (examples this & the following page) are the finest of the lot, especially six large (averaging some 50 centimeters tall) effigies presented to the deceased king by two of his highest officials, such as the one at right, gift of a General Nakhtmin, who may have been the son of Tutankhamen's successor, Ay. The ushabti at left (52 cm. high) — with painted details, gold-foil brow band & gilded-bronze uraeus & Flail scepter— is another of five presented to the deceased king by General Nakhtmin. This gift is indicated by the inscription under the figure's feet which reads: "Made by the Royal Scribe & General of the Army, Nakhtmin, for his lord, Osiris Nebkheperure, justified." Cairo Egyptian Museum

217

The KV62 ushabtis — found housed in 24 pitch-painted kiosks distributed between the Treasury & Annexe — are represented in a variety of headgear — crowns, wigs & headcloths — with & without the Crook & Flail scepters of kingship; in a few cases only one scepter is present, or both are missing altogether, as in the two examples at left. The ushabtis also clasp an assortment of implements in their crossed hands — including ankhs, djeds & hoes & baskets — or else are empty handed, presumably to employ as necessary in the Afterlife any of the 1,866 model implements interred with the king's worker-substitutes.

Internet photos

Figures these two pages not shown to relative scale

While the wooden Tutankhamen ushab-tis tend to range from 63.0 cm to 48.0 cm in height, those of other materials are smaller scale, such as the above painted-quartzite example in a Nemes headcloth, which is 25.7 cm. high. As with the latter category of figures, the facial features here are more generically "king" than specifically Tutankhamen.

Cairo Egyptian Museum

Cairo Egyptian Museum

This page, *A selection of Tutankhamen ushabtis, illustrating the disparate variety of styles, sizes and materials in which they are executed. Numerous ones of the effigies with kingly insignia & regalia bear no facial resemblance to their owner & many of those wearing the "archaic" tripartite wig without a uraeus are of poorer design & workmanship than might be expected in even non-royal funerary furnishings of the period. These might very well be described as "generic" king's ushabtis, & — except for the inscription with the Nebkheperure cartouche — might easily enough have come from the tombs of Thutmose III or Amenhotep II. Were it not for their absolute provenance, many of the crudely crafted KV62 worker-substitutes could understandably enough be suspected as forgeries, in fact.* Cairo Egyptian Museum

Figures not shown to relative scale

220

measured 36.1 centimeters long (fourteen-plus inches), and thus was judged by Carter and Dr. Derry to have been born in its seventh month. Because no umbilical cord was evident (having been cut off close to the navel), it may have been that the child survived birth, only to die very soon afterwards, due to its premature condition. Like that of its companion, the small body had been laid out with the limbs fully extended, in this instance with the open hands positioned alongside the thighs, palms down. Unlike the other, it had been mummified in the traditional manner, with the brain extracted through the nose and internal organs removed via a very short (18-mm. long) incision in the left abdominal wall, the resulting cavity then being filled with natron-impregnated linen rags (the skull cavity was likewise stuffed with linen, inserted through the nose).

The condition of this mummy when unwrapped was similar, if not inferior, to that of the smaller one: skin greyish with patches of natron, and so brittle that not all of the oxidized bandaging adhering to the backside could be removed. Both eyebrows and lashes were present, although the scalp was mostly free of hair (except for some down-like fine strands in the occipital region, although other hair may have come away with removal of the bandaging). The eyes themselves were wide open, the eyeballs mostly having shrunken away, but without any packing being applied by the embalmers. Fingernails were visible, although their presence may have been due to the shrinking of the finger soft tissues during the desiccation process. As in the case of its companion, the larger infant mummy was unadorned by jewelry or protective amulets, although animal tissue of some sort had been applied to the abdominal incision to seal it (in lieu of a gold plate typical

The magical "Osiris bed" found in KV62 (right) had been carefully bandaged in the manner of a mummy & was contained in a large, shallow, lidded wooden case painted inside & out with pitch (below). This "coffin" occupied the entire floor space of the Treasury's southwest corner. Griffith Institute

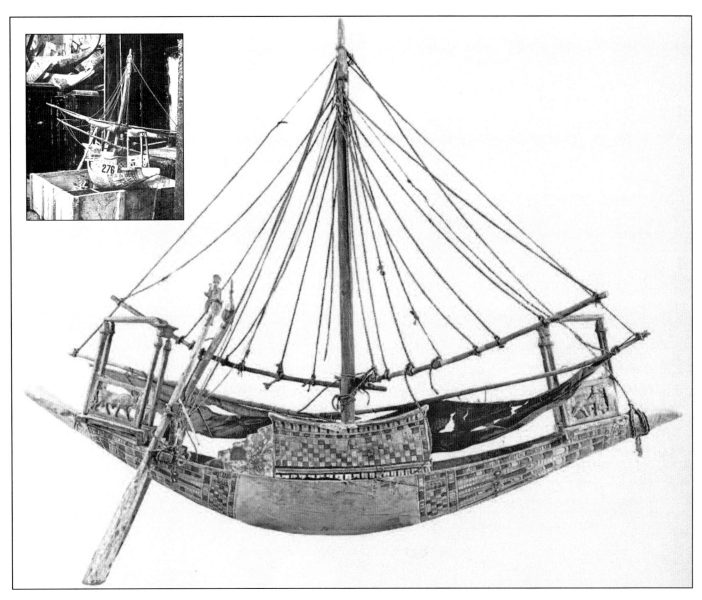

Inset above, One of the large model sailing vessels found in the KV62 Treasury, in situ atop a model granary resting on the chamber floor in front of the bitumenized naoi containing the gilded ritual statues of deities & a king Metropolitan Museum of Art; *& (above) a very similar model which was found on the floor against the west wall of the Treasury, where it probably had been placed by necropolis officials straightening the chamber following ransacking by thieves. Both boats have a tall mast amidships, emerging from a large cabin which is elaborately painted in a checkerboard motif, with stairs to the roof; & gilded pavilions (for Tutankhamen's throne?) are positioned on the bow & stern of both models. The pair of long steering oars in each case have finials with tiny heads of the king.* Cairo Egyptian Museum

of the period).

The above discussion of the KV62 fetal mummies' appearance has been in the past tense, since the modern-day history of the two remains is somewhat confused. When permission was given to a British medical team to examine and x-ray these mummies in 1971, they could not be located in the Cairo Egyptian Museum, nor were they apparently ever logged into that institution's collections, inasmuch as there is no listing of them in the *Journal d'Entrée* of same. Likewise they could not be located at that time among Dr. Derry's collection of mummy specimens housed in the Kasr El Ainy Hospital, Cairo. Recently they have been shown to be in the conservation laboratory of the Grand Egyptian Museum (GEM).[118] Why they were separated from the rest of the KV62 contents is not known, and was not commented on by Carter in any of his records of the tomb.

Another, larger (about thirty inches long) anthropoid coffin set of wood was found resting near the chest with the coffins containing the fetal mummies. The outer of the pair is of the black (resin)-and-gold type, bearing longitudinal and transverse bands of funerary inscriptions, but with the *Khat* headdress represented rather than a striped wig-cover. The inner coffin, gilded all over, is decorated in a royal *rishi* pattern quite like Tutankhamen's First and Third coffins; while the *Nemes* head covering is represented, it does not have the Nekhbet and Buto insignia, nor do the crossed, clasped hands on the lid hold the Crook-and-Flail regalia. Tutankhamen's name, however, is included in the funerary formulae inscribed on both coffins.

The second coffin of this set contained a very much smaller plain-wood anthropoid coffinette, and beside it, wrapped in a piece of linen rag, was a solid-gold pendant figure depicting a squatting king wearing the *Khepresh*, with the Crook-and-Flail scepters casually clasped in one hand, while resting on the tiny figure's shoulder. This peculiar pendant is suspended on a woven gold-wire chain, tied with tasseled cords at it ends. Although the statuette is uninscribed, it has been thought (by Carter and scholars) to probably represent Amenhotep III, this mostly because of its association with the content of yet another coffinette found within the plain-wood one just mentioned.

This fourth tiny coffin (only about five inches long) was also of plain wood in anthropoid form. It was separately wrapped in linen and heavily anointed with the same unguents used on the king's Third Coffin and mummy. It was found to bear the titulary and name of Tiye, Great Royal Wife of Amenhotep III and mother of the Heretic, Akhenaten. Within this last coffin Carter revealed a plaited lock of hair, carefully wrapped in linen. Because of the coffinette inscription, it was

Below, One of two elaborately inlaid wooden "treasure" chests found in the Treasury of KV62 (No. 267), positioned in the row of boxes & chests aligned between the Anubis & Canopic shrines. The marquetry inlay consists of more than 45,000 individual minute pieces of ivory & ebony. Bottom, The interior of the same chest with its jumbled contents of about a dozen pieces of jewelry, as found. A note inked on the lid of the chest indicated that its original contents were "golden jewelry of the funerary procession made in the bed chamber of Nebkheperure," *but whether the inlaid-gold pectoral necklaces, etc., it contained were those mentioned cannot be certain, as the chest had been emptied by the tomb robbers & subsequently refilled by the necropolis officials.*

Cairo Egyptian & Metropolitan museums

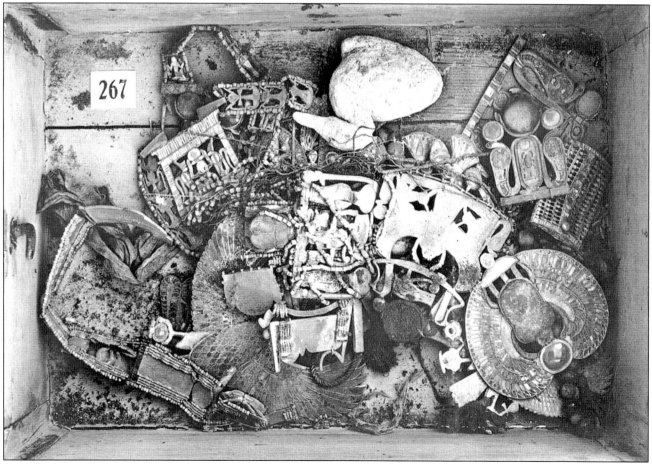

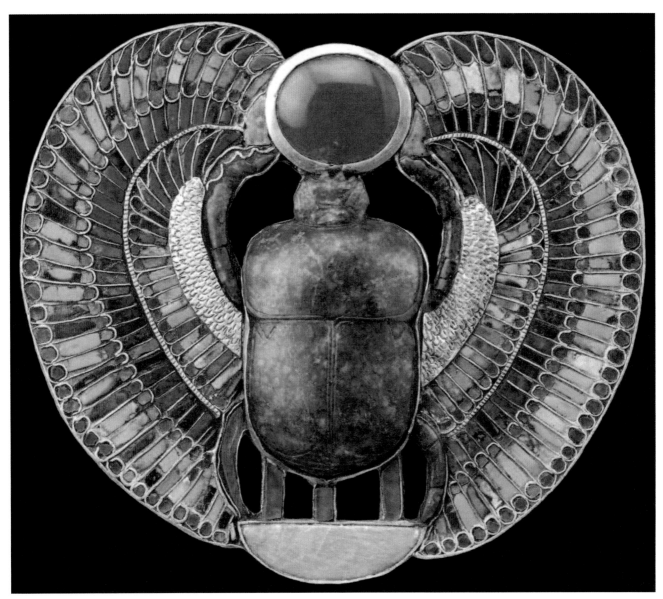

Above, Solid-gold pectoral element inlaid with semi-precious stones, found in Treasury chest No. 267 (see previous page). The winged Kheper beetle forms a rebus of the prenomen or throne name of Tutankhamen (Nebkheperure). Cairo Egyptian Museum

automatically assumed by Carter that the hair was that of the dowager-queen, an "heirloom" retained by Tutankhamen in remembrance of the great lady to whom he was doubtlessly directly related (whether as son or grandson is disputed by Amarna-period scholars, who likewise argue over whether Amenhotep III was the young king's actual father, or only his grandfather, at best).

After the canopics and human remains, the most important objects found in the Treasury (from an Afterlife-requirement point of view) were the numerous ritual figures housed in the pitch-coated tall (most nearly three-feet high) wooden *naoi* or shrine-shaped cabinets, which were grouped together along the chamber's south wall, filling the space between the southeast corner and the Canopic Shrine. There were twenty-two of these all totaled, and the swinging double doors of all but one were securely fastened with cording and a dab of Nile mud stamped with the royal necropolis seal. The shrine cabinet standing open had either been investigated by the tomb robbers in antiquity, or else by the modern intruders who explored the tomb that same evening the blocked doorway to the Antechamber was breached by Carter

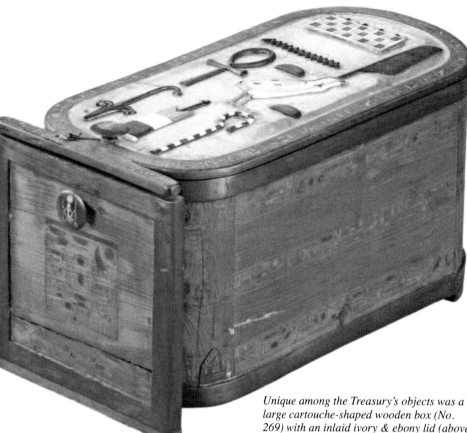

Unique among the Treasury's objects was a large cartouche-shaped wooden box (No. 269) with an inlaid ivory & ebony lid (above Cairo Egyptian Museum*) depicting Tutankhamen's nomen, seen* in situ *in the middle of Burton's photo at top left* (Griffith Institute)*. Its contents (seen in Burton's photo at bottom left* Griffith Institute*) included a jumble of various elaborate jewelry pieces, two sets of Crook & Flail scepters (see next page) & an inscribed gilded mirror in the form of an* ankh.

and company.

As each *naos* was opened in turn for the purpose of Harry Burton's continuing photographic record of the tomb contents *in situ*, it was found to house one or two small statues made of hardwood and gilded, except for their bases, which are coated with the ubiquitous bitumen. Two figures — depicting nude Ihy musicians — were exceptional, in that they were pitch painted all over, with gilded details. There proved to be a total of thirty-four of these statues, twenty-seven of them depicting various deities associated with the Hereafter, and seven representing a king in the crowns of Upper and Lower Egypt: three shown striding, two on a papyrus skiff in the act of harpooning and two striding atop leopard figures. Each of the statues was enveloped (shrouded) in a section of linen, these all bearing marks dating them to the reign of Akhenaten, one as early as Year 3 of that king. The faces of the statues were left uncovered, however, and many of the small figures had been decorated with tiny fillets of real flowers and sprouting seeds placed around their heads.

The eyes of all but two of these figures are inlaid with bronze frames inset with calcite and obsidian; the emblems on the crowns of the king figures, their sandals and the regalia carried by same are gilded bronze. One of the divinities, mummiform Ptah, has his traditional skullcap rendered in bright-blue faience, and he holds the usual gilded-bronze *was/ankh/djed* scepter. The names of the gods and goddesses (along with the king's prenomen, Nebkheperure) are painted in yellow pigment on their black-varnished stands. One deity, Menkeret,

The ankh-*shaped mirror case is made of wood covered with sheet gold. It is decorated with a rebus of the king's prenomen.*
Cairo Egyptian Museum

Right, The two sets of Osiride scepters found in Chest 269 in the Treasury. These are the He-ka (Crook) & Nekheka (Flail), & the only functioning examples (as opposed to coffin accessories) to have survived from Egyptian antiquity. The smaller pair, top, are inscribed on their butt ends with the nomen Tut-ankhaten ("Living Image of At-en"), which suggests they were used by the young king before his name change to Tutankh-amen in Year 2 or so of his reign, & thus may have been associated with his coronation. Both Crooks & Flails have bronze cores supporting alter-nating sections of gold & blue glass or obsidian. The beaded portions of the flails are paint-ed & gilded wood. Internet photo

Found in Treasury Box 271 was an elaborately inlaid gilded holder for reed pens inscribed with the king's prenomen, seen above. Internet photo

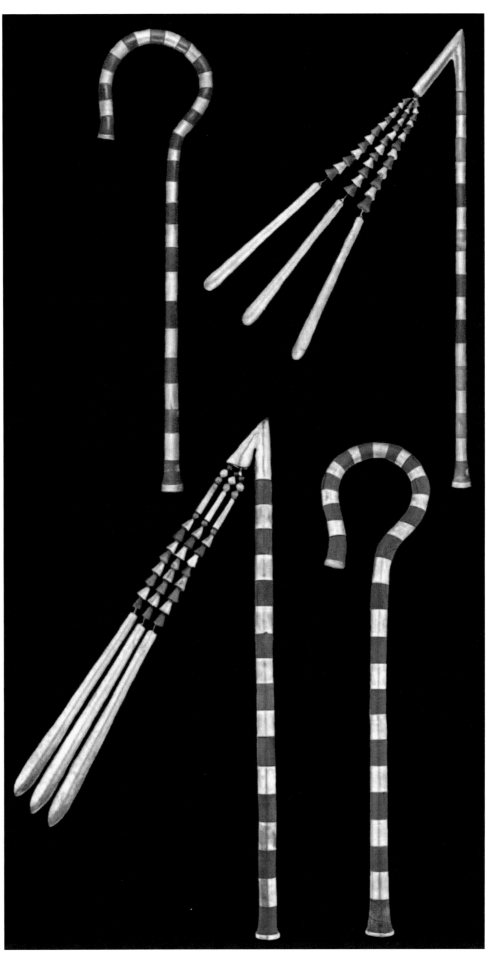

The fourth chest (No. 271) in the row of such containers which Carter found in the Treasury (above Cairo Egyptian Museum *) is highly ornamental, made of a coniferous wood which is veneered on its rails & stiles in ivory, this engraved in hieroglyphic script filled with black pigment. The panels formed by the rails & stiles are filled with an openwork of gilded* ankh, was *& neb signs, these standing out against the dark-brown of the basic wood. The four feet of the legs are capped in silver. The chest interior is divided into sixteen rectangular compartments & among the contents were a gilded-wood Heh mirror case (above left* Cairo Egyptian Museum*) & a gold-embellished ivory papyrus burnisher (below* Cairo Egyptian Museum*).*

carries on his head a small seated mummiform (Osiride) king figure wearing the Red Crown. Three deities (Duamutef, Seshet and the aforementioned Ihy) are each represented by a pair of statues. The three figures of a striding king would seem to be an incomplete set, with a fourth statue required to make two pairs wearing the Red and White crowns of Lower and Upper Egypt.

Although close correspondences to these ritual figures were already well-known in Howard Carter's time (he, himself having recovered fragmented examples of similar wooden statues from the refuse of the Tomb of Thutmose IV)[119] — in actuality as well as from two-dimensional representations (paintings of them in the Tomb of Seti II) — the excavator seemed uncertain as to the statues' purpose in KV62. He wrote, *"The exact meaning as well as the presence of this series of figures in the tomb is not clear to us. It may be that some, if not all, of the divinities comprise 'the Divine Ennead which is in Duat' (the Nether World), or it may be that they represent the Ennead — the divine tribunal or synod of gods — associated with the struggle between Horus and Seth, for two of the statuettes of the king obviously pertain to that myth, while the others seem to represent him in various forms of his future existence, to show that he 'die not a second time in the Nether World.'"*[120]

Perhaps more interesting than the exact purpose of the KV62 figures is the speculation regarding which king may have commissioned them originally. Iconographically, the deity figures could easily enough have been carved towards the end of the reign of Amenhotep III — or else during the post-Amarna period of Tutankhamen, when there was somewhat of a return to the highly refined art style of the third Amenhotep's last decade, but with distinct Amarnaesque influences. The seven king figures (not including the Menkeret/Osiride king pair-statue) present a different sort of problem. They would not

Detail of the central embossed gold-foil panel of one side of Tutankhamen's marquetry-decorated wooden bow case found associated with two dismantled hunting chariots in the KV62 Treasury (Griffith Institute). *Approximately five feet in length, it would seem to have been meant to be attached to a chariot by means of bronze staples, one seen here. The idealized hunting scene depicts the young king in his vehicle, racing across the desert & shooting arrows at fleeing antelopes, accompanied by two hounds which harass the quarry. The elaborate marquetry decorating the case's borders is composed of different tree barks, tinted leather, gold foil & even the iridescent wings of beetles.*

seem to represent Tutankhamen at all (the faces are different from his other KV62 portraits); and it has been argued that they do not even portray a male ruler, but rather a female one in the guise of a king, *à la* Hatshepsut.[121] This judgment is based on the fact that all seven of the figures in question have somewhat feminine physiques, in one case (the White-Crowned striding figure atop a panther) the breasts being undeniably female rather than just another representation of feminized pectorals seen in the many depictions (both relief and in the round, exaggerated and moderated) of Akhenaten. The scholarly consensus seems to be that these ritual figures were, in fact, made for Amenhotep IV in the very first years of his reign (during a coregency with his father, Amenhotep III?) and were intended for eventual deployment in his Wasetan royal tomb. According to this interpretation, when the fourth Amenhotep ultimately changed his name to Akhenaten and abandoned Waset (Thebes) for his newly founded capital in Middle Egypt — with its own royal necropolis — these figures (intimately identified with the pantheon which Akhenaten eventually proscribed) would have remained behind in storage, later to be recovered and employed in Tutankhamen's behalf (the prematurely deceased young king not yet having commissioned a set of his own). This seems more logically to have been the case than an alternate theory that these images depict an ephemeral female successor to Akhenaten, who briefly preceded Tutankhamen on the throne (Nefertiti or Meritaten in the guise of Nefer-

Left, below & overleaves, Views through the low doorway from the Antechamber into the Annex & the topsy-turvy contents of that small storeroom. The last space to be cleared in KV62, it had been thoroughly ransacked by the tomb robbers of antiquity, who left such total dis- order in their wake that the necropolis officials — who other- wise cleaned up after them — abandoned any effort to reorder what Carter called "a jumble of every kind of funerary chattels." His clearance began in late November of 1927 & continued through the next spring. In the photo below are visible — on the white-painted wooden bow box in the up- per-middle portion of Burton's image — the footprints left by one of the ancient tomb robbers who thoroughly ransacked the small storeroom on two different occasions, in search of solid metals & precious oils & unguents. In the overleaves photograph, the cham- ber has been partially cleared &visi- ble on the left is a modern wooden stake use to prop up items yet be removed. The bow box is repositioned in the foreground.

Right, Detail of the embossed central panel of the footboard of gold-plated bed No. 466 found in the Annexe. Depicted is the sma-tawy *motif, representing the "Union of the Two Lands." Because of its elaborate floral ornamentation, Carter was inclined to believe that that this bed had originated in Akhetaten.* Colorized Griffith Institute

Certainly among the more interesting objects found in KV62 (from a modern-technology point of view) is Tutankhamen's folding bed, above (& fully extended, below Griffith Institute*), which he probably used either on board the royal barge while sailing the Nile, or else while overnighting on the hunt (or military campaigns). Constructed of lightweight wood painted white, it has string webbing & is supported on eight short legs of leonine form. The three sections are fastened together by heavy bronze hinges. This was one of four beds recovered from the Annexe. Two others were found in the Antechamber.*

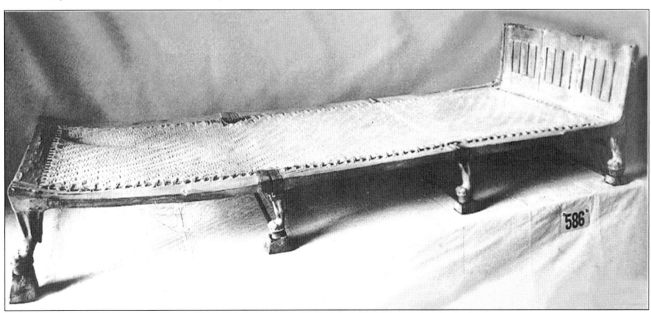

neferuaten Ankhkheperure?).[121]

Another sort of ritual effigy of the king found in the Treasury by Carter was unquestionably made specifically for Tutankhamen's interment, commissioned as a gift to the dead young king by chief treasurer of the Two Lands, a nobleman named Maya, whose own private chapel tomb was found at Sakkara in recent years.[122] This object rested in a small wooden chest shaped like a sarcophagus and heavily coated with black pitch. It is finely carved of cedarwood and depicts *"the justified Nebkheperure,"* mummiform in a *Nemes* headdress and holding the Crook and Flail scepters, recumbent on a lion bier. The figure, seemingly related to the king's ushabtis in its Afterlife function, was provided with a set of miniature tools, such as accompanied the latter as well.

Tutankhamen was provided with a grand total of 413 ushabtis and 1,866 model implements. One hundred seventy-six of the ushabti complement were found in the Treasury, with the balance later discovered in the Annexe — one of the latter, a stray, having been relocated to the Antechamber in antiquity, and positioned near the small golden shrine that had been robbed of its contents. These ushabtis and their miniature agricultural implements — the latter made of copper, wood and faience — were housed in twenty-four pitch-coated shrine-shaped tall (averaging some two-feet high) boxes on sledges, ten of which were recovered from the northeast corner of the Treasury, the balance from the Annexe. An additional white-washed rectangular box in the Treasury also held a quantity of ushabtis and model tools. The vaulted roofs of the shrine boxes served as their lids, and were held in place with cording tied around knobs protruding from the lid top and box side, and sealed by a dab of Nile mud impressed with the jackal-and-prisoners necropolis seal.[123]

Tutankhamen's plethora of ushabtis are made from a wide variety of materials: wood; calcite; gray and black granite; quartzite; indurated, white and yellow limestone; and blue, turquoise, violet and white faience. Those of wood are painted; linen-covered, gessoed and painted; gesso-covered and gilded in part; and gilded and painted in combination.[124] The small figures are depicted in eight different sorts of headdresses: *Nemes* and *Khat*, the Blue, White, Red and Double crowns, and the Nubian and tripartite wigs (some 286 of the worker figures wearing the latter "archaic" wig). The crowns and other head-gear are adorned in many instances with the uraeus (and sometimes the Nekhbet vultures, as well), but many of the Tutankhamen ushabtis — including all of those in the tripartite wig — are without the cobra insignia of kingship. The Crook and Flail scepters — most made of gilded metal — are held in the crossed hands of numerous (seventy-two) specimens; two hold double Flails; many clasp two *ankhs*; ten have an *ankh* and Flail; some a Flail and a ribbon; others a *djed*, Flail and ribbon; a total of seventy-nine are equipped with hoes and a basket; and the hands of 162 ushabtis are altogether empty. Pre-

Associated with the beds found in the Annexe are four headrests (three shown above), discovered together in a cabinet & comprising half of the number of headrests recovered from KV62. Two of the Annexe four are unique in design. The one numbered 403d (top), made of tinted ivory, is in the form of a miniature folding stool, of the duck-headed legs variety. The "pillow-rest" portion is formed from flexible strands of threaded beads in ivory stained red, green & black. The terminals of the rest are Bes masks, stained in the same colors. The second unique headrest (No. 403c, middle), also carved in ivory, represents the god Shu kneeling between lions of the eastern & western horizons. The pillow portion here symbolizes the heavens, which Shu bears on his shoulders. Headrest No. 403b (bottom) is of deep-blue faience of typical form, with an inlaid-gold band & the king's nomen in turquoise glaze. Internet photos

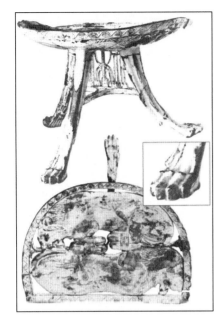

One of the "extraneous" furniture pieces found among the jumbled contents of the Annexe was a three-legged white-painted wooden stool, its semi-circular concave seat with a depiction of two lions bound head to tail. A spiral pattern decorates the seat rim. This stool is in a way unique, inasmuch as the legs terminate in canine feet (detail, above) rather than the usual leonine or bovine feet seen on most furniture of pharaonic Egypt. Griffith Institute

sumably those effigies without their own implements could, in the Afterlife, draw as necessary upon any of the nearly 2,000 model tools interred with Tutankhamen's worker-substitute contingent. These miniatures represent hoes, picks, yokes and baskets.

While several of the KV62 ushabtis are very well-carved with careful attention to details and inscriptions — particularly those made of wood — and have facial features generally recognizable as Tutankhamen's, many more are rather summarily executed and bear no resemblance whatsoever to the king with whose name they are inscribed — this being particularly true of the great quantity of smaller figures represented in the tripartite wig (over half of the total lot).[125] And at least one largish gilded-wood effigy (No. 458) may not have been meant by its maker to represent Tutankhamen at all, inasmuch as the facial features and shape of the mummiform body are somewhat feminine, suggesting this particular ushabti was originally commissioned for the pre-Akhenaten Amenhotep IV, or else was intended for the funerary furnishings of the elusive Ankhkheperure.

Several of the ushabti kiosks arranged along the Treasury's south wall rested on top of a very large, shallow rectangular wooden box thickly coated with bitumen, which took up the entire floor space of the southwest corner of the chamber. When this was finally freed up and the lid removed, it was found to contain yet-nother important ritual object already known from previously discovered examples: a so-called "Osiris bed."[126] Very much like the empty one

One of three hassocks found in the KV62 Annexe. It is constructed of a rushwork frame covered with linen onto which is attached an extremely elaborate design in minute polychrome beadwork, all badly decayed in this example. Each hassock depicts bound & prone foreign captives (here a Nubian & a Western Asiatic) arranged to encircle a central rosette motif. Carter thought that if footstools (of which there were several in the tomb) were intendd for the royal foot, perhaps these hassocks were "intended for the royal knee." Griffith Institute

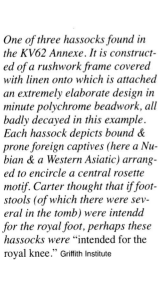

found in the Tomb of Horemheb a few years earlier, that of Tutankhamen is the silhouetted image of the Lord of the Underworld, hollowed out of planks of wood so that a tray with raised sides was created. The resulting depression, linen lined, was filled with Nile soil and sown with grain seed. When this germinated, became green and had grown an inch or two, the resulting "bed" was carefully bandaged in linen, mummy-like, and — in the KV62 example, at least — was placed in the tomb in an appropriate "coffin" of sorts, where the grain sprouts would presumably continue to grow and thereby, through sympathetic magic, impart regeneration and new life to the deceased Tutankhamen, now likewise an Osiris.

       Also magical/symbolic in nature was the flotilla of thirty-five model river craft which Carter cleared first from the Treasury and later the Annexe. Ranging in length between approximately one meter and more than 2.5 meters, fourteen of these painted and gilded wooden vessels complete with riggings had been placed atop the twenty-two black-varnished *naoi* that contained the gilded ritual statues; one rested on a miniature granary in front of the *naoi*; another was in the northwest corner of the chamber perched atop the small coffin containing the Queen Tiye "heirloom" and squatting-king pendant; and two others were situated on the north and west sides of the room on the floor, among the parts of two dismantled hunting chariots. The balance of the lot — unfortunately most of them badly damaged by ransacking thieves in antiquity — were found among the disorder in the Annexe.

Above & below, A small white-painted wooden chair from the Annexe, which Carter thought might have come from the royal nursery. Its legs & feet are leonine, the spaces between the stretchers filled by the heraldic plants of Upper & Lower Egypt forming the sema-tawy *"Union of the Two Lands" motif. An openwork Horus falcon with widespread wings fills the back-rest panel.*

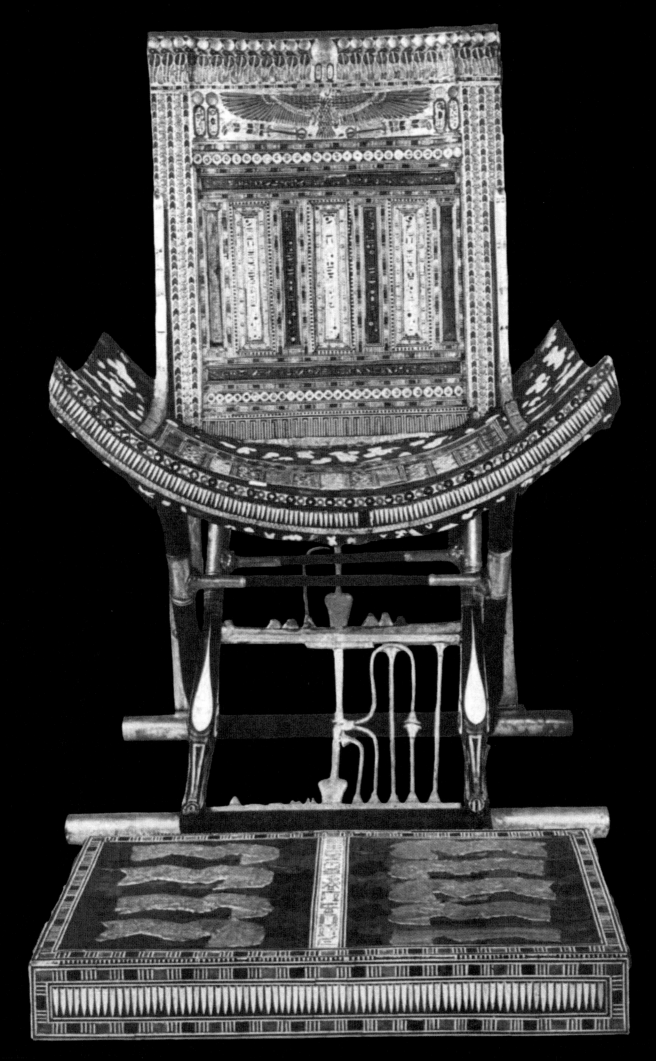

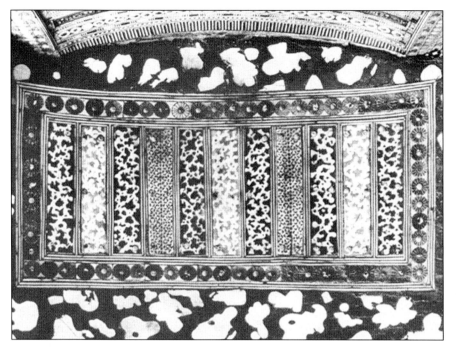

Each model craft on the south side of the Treasury had its bow pointing west; those on the north side had been disoriented from handling by the ancient thieves or the necropolis officials who came after them.

Each model craft on the south side of the Treasury had its bow pointing west; those on the north side had been disoriented from handling by the ancient thieves or the necropolis officials who came after them.

Miniaturized river vessels (symbolizing full-scale originals) became a feature of upper-status Egyptian burials beginning in the Middle Kingdom,[127] with numerous examples having been discovered in tombs of that period through those of the New Kingdom; and they appear to have been a standard part of Eighteenth Dynasty royal burials, as well, judging from the fragmentary boat models found in the Tomb of Amenhotep II and Tutankhamen's complete fleet.

The KV62 models fall into two categories: those which are strictly ritualistic, four "solar" and two "lunar" barques associated with the deceased king's voyage through the Cosmos; and those which are purely practical in nature, river-going transportation, including pleasure, cargo and fishing/hunting craft. Depending upon their type, some of the vessels have full masting and long steering oars, others simply steering oars; almost all of the "practical" craft are equipped with an elaborately decorated cabin amidships (some two storied), and a few have kiosks or throne pavilions fore and aft.

All of these models are similar in construction, the hulls having been carved from either a single block of soft wood (acacia?) or from joined sections of same, with the addition of separately fashioned papyriform bows and sterns, cabins, kiosks/ pavilions, masts, oar posts, etc., all likewise carved in wood and pegged onto the hulls. The models were then gessoed and painted — in many cases, somewhat crudely — and, as appropriate, sails of dyed linen and riggings of twisted cording were added. Judging from their slap-dash craftsmanship, it may be assumed that this flotilla of magical and symbolic models was hastily made in the period between Tutankhamen's demise and interment.

Also included among the Treasury's symbolic equip-

Opposite, The so-called "Ecclesiastical Throne" found by Carter in KV62's Annexe. The "throne" itself is one of the most unique pieces from the Tutankhamen funerary assemblage. Quite clearly it was not a "chair" intended for mere everyday use — its elaborateness & hybrid nature belie that. It is actually a faux folding-stool of the familiar duck-head-legged type that is rigid, combined with an upright sheet-gold-covered back panel minutely inlaid (in faience, glass & semi-precious stones) with inscriptions including both the Aten & Amen forms of Tutankhaten/amen's nomen. The concave seat (detail left) is ebony, inlaid with irregularly shaped pieces of ivory in imitation of a piebald animal skin; yet the rectangular central portion depicts, in parallel rows, other types of hide patterns, in dyed ivory. An openwork ornament in gilded wood of the "Union of the Two Lands" originally filled the space between the leg stretchers & foot bars; much of this was torn away by the thieves in antiquity who were seeking solid gold. The throne's footstool, equally rich in its detailing, depicts Egypt's traditional nine alien foes, on which the king's feet rested while he was enthroned. Carter concluded that this unique seat was used by Tutankhamen when he was functioning as Egypt's "highest spiritual authority." Cairo Egyptian Museum & Griffith Institute

Among the several furniture pieces found in the Annexe were two very similar cedarwood cabinets on long legs (one shown above). The open fretwork between the legs is partially gilded, as are the incised inscription bands & two knobs. Carter thought the cabinets orginally held the king's linen garments. Cairo Egyptian Museum

One of the genuine treasures found in the Annexe is the ivory-veneered wooden casket (No. 551, lid No. 540) seen in two views, left & opposite. It is one of only five objects discovered in KV62 which depict King Tutankhamen in the company of his Great Royal Wife, Ankhesenamen (the other three being the small golden shrine, the golden throne, both from the Antechamber, a calcite urn & a game-board detail). When discovered, the chest proper was empty & the lid rested several feet away, where it had been tossed aside by the thieves. Besides the ivory veneer, both chest & lid are also decorated with elaborate inlays of painted calcite, faience & ebony, plus gilding. The feet are capped with ferrules of bronze or copper. Above, Detail of the foot-end panel with hunting scenes.

ment — in addition to the aforementioned model granary that supported one of the boat models, the sixteen compartments of which were found filled with grains and seeds — were objects which seemingly had some Afterlife function for the Osiris Tutankhamen, but which otherwise are mundane utensils that seem out of place in a royal burial. These include two wood (gessoed)-and-copper strainers (for beer?) and a model hand-mill of the sort used for grinding corn. Carter guessed that they may have been connected with the deceased king's role as *"triturator"* to the gods, preparing for the latter their bread and beverage.

Although they were among the first objects removed from the Treasury by Carter — in order to have clear access to the Canopic Shrine, etc. — the row of *"treasure"* caskets and white-painted storage chests which had been aligned parallel to the Anubis Shrine and the Hathor-head sculpture will be dealt with next, along with their contents. As Carter wrote in his third volume on the tomb, *"Unfortunately this group had been attacked by the dynastic tomb-plunderers for the more valuable gold and silver articles that the caskets and boxes had contained. Their seals were broken, their contents ransacked, their pieces of greater value stolen; moreover, the remainder of their contents was left in utter disorder."* [128]

Of these containers, the closest to the doorway of the chamber was a largish wooden casket (No. 267) veneered with ivory and inlaid with a marquetry of some 45,000 minute pieces of ivory and ebony. Inked on its vaulted lid was an enigmatic notation reading, *"Golden jewelry of the funerary procession made in the bed chamber*

Above & opposite bottom, Two views of Annexe box No. 547 (the lid cleared separately was numbered 615), which Carter identified as made to contain the king's headdress. Constructed of plain rectangular wooden panels bordered in a simple inlaid pattern of blue & yellow faience & semi-translucent calcite, it has a flat hinged lid & stands on short rectangular legs which are extensions of the corner uprights. (Caption continues opposite bottom.)

238

Both long sides of the casket with a caveto cornice are decorated with inlaid floral groupings & repeated hunting scenes similar to the detail obove left. Internet photos

of Nebkheperure," which Carter thought might have been a reference to the king's "bier chamber," (i.e., the tomb). Whatever exactly this chest's original contents, these had doubtlessly been dumped on the Treasury floor by the tomb thieves in their search for portable solid gold. When they were reordering the chamber following the discovery of the break-in, the necropolis officials had unceremoniously deposited in the empty container a jumble of some dozen inlaid-gold pectoral necklaces and related necklace parts, plus the openwork lid of a small inlaid-gold casket and a small, summarily modeled wax figure of a bird (a heron?). It took Carter and Lucas considerable effort to extract the tangled and corroded jewelry, even before restoration and cleaning of these objects could begin.

To one side of casket 267 stood another smaller one, likewise inlaid with a marquetry of ivory and ebony (No. 268). It was lidless (the lid resting on top of chest No. 269) and its four-compartmented interior was empty of whatever it had held originally. A hieratic docket on the chest reads, "[lacuna] *of gold in* [?] *the place of the funeral possession*," which may explain why the chest was found empty, the gold vessels it originally contained having been taken by the tomb thieves.

Next in the row of chests was a wholly unique wooden container (cedar and ebony) in the shape of a *"three-dimensional"* cartouche, the gilded and ivory-and-ebony-inlaid lid forming the king's nomen (Tutankhamen, *"Living Image of Amen, Ruler of Waset"*). Contained within this chest (No. 269) were five pairs of elaborate inlaid-gold earrings; three ornate bracelets of inlaid gold, two scarabform,

Inside Box No. 547 (above), in its middle, is a round block of wood raised on a dowel, which once supported a fine-linen cap embroidered all over in elaborate beadwork, the fabric of which had decayed beyond recovery. Strangely, a docket on the lid said that the box contained ushabtis, which Carter thought might have been an excess which would not fit into the other kiosks & boxes more properly housing these funerary statuettes. No ushabtis were found in No. 547, however. In addition to the cap fragments, it did contain a headrest, a double circlet & a bracelet. Griffith Institute

one with a large amethyst setting; a scarab of hard green stone; a gilded mirror case in the shape of an *ankh* and lined with silver foil; the counterpoise and chains of a pectoral ornament found in box 267; a pectoral necklace in the motif of a lunar orb; a peculiar bead-work *"scarf"*-like neck (?) ornament, terminating at each end in a row of *ankhs*, perhaps some sort of ecclesiastical accoutrement; three linen shawls, plus a pad of cloth; and, most importantly, two pairs of Crook (*Heka*) and Flail (*Nekheka*) scepters, composed of alternating sections of gold, dark-blue glass and obsidian on bronze cores, the flail beads being gilded wood. One set of these Osirian regalia is smaller than the other, and is inscribed on the gold-capped butt ends with the nomen "Tutankh*aten*," causing Carter to surmise that it had been used by the child-king between his coronation and subsequent conversion to the Amen cult, when he underwent a name change. The larger set bears his *"Living Image of Amen"* nomen. Despite the scores and scores of depictions of these regalia in dynastic sculpture and reliefs, Tutankhamen's two sets (plus the uninscribed Crook discovered in the KV62 Antechamber) are the only actual examples to have survived to the present day — not counting those which are integral parts of his coffins and mummy embellishments.

A white-washed wooden chest with a vaulted lid (No. 270) was next in line, and stood all but empty, containing only a pair of leather sandal-like slippers embellished with gold and beadwork; the lid of a small box also found in chest 269; and a stone anklet, probably made of schist.

The box which occupied the fourth position in the row (No. 271) is truly regal in appearance: rectangular — with a flat lid

Opposite, Detail of the central panel of the lid of the ornate inlaid-ivory chest recovered from the KV62 Annexe. It depicts Tutankhamen & Ankhesenamen standing in a garlanded bower, the queen offering two large bouquets of papyrus & water lilies to the young king, who leans on a walking staff & raises his hand in greeting or anticipation. In a register below the royal couple, two female servants gather additional flowers. This scene of domestic bliss is reminiscent of joint depictions of Akhenaten & Nefertiti, albeit rendered in a more formal style than is seen in the art of the Amarna period.

Cairo Egyptian Museum

Below, Detail of the head-end panel of the same chest, in which Tutankhamen & his consort are shown hunting fish & fowl in a marsh setting, accompanied by a servant who retrieves the king's catch. Interestingly, in this instance the queen is depicted on a smaller scale than Tutankhamen, although the servant's smaller size is typical.

Griffith Institute

and short, silver-capped legs flush at the corners — its core of cedar-wood is veneered all around and on the lid surface with a fretwork of ivory-covered stiles and braces between which are two horizontal registers of alternating, gilded *ankh* and *was* glyphs resting on *neb* baskets. Black-pigment-filled engraved inscriptions on the ivory stiles and braces give all five of the names of Nebkheperure Tutankhamen — and the titles and cartouche of Ankhesenamen as well, along with a wish that the Great Royal Wife *"may live forever."* The interior of this chest is divided into sixteen rectangular deep compartments, which probably originally had held a like number of gold or silver vessels, of a ceremonial or cosmetic nature. These were all missing, stolen for their bullion by the tomb robbers no doubt; and in their place the necropolis priests had deposited a finger ring, a small rushwork square basket, a red-stained ivory bowl, two scribal palettes (one ivory, the other gold), an ivory-and-gold burnisher, an ornamental tube-case for writing reeds, and an empty gilded mirror-case. All of these objects had originally been interred in (an)other container(s), but which it is impossible to know.

Fifth and last box in the row (No. 272) is also of white-washed plain wood, similar to if a little larger than the third one described, likewise with a vaulted lid. Surprisingly it was found by Carter to be all but empty, containing only three persea fruits and an ivory hand fan, its dark-brown and white ostrich feathers still intact, if extremely fragile after 3,300 years. The handle is in the form of a bent papyrus stalk and umbel, and this attaches to a semi-circular mount for the feathers, which bears the king's cartouches within a border of repeated rectangles.

After clearing the six caskets and boxes of their collective contents, Carter estimated that at least sixty percent of what they originally contained was missing and presumably stolen. He wrote, *"The exact amount of jewellery taken is of course impossible to tell, although the remaining parts of some of the stolen ornaments enable us to conjecture that it must have been considerable, but we can tell that two mirrors, at least twenty vessels from two of the caskets, four of which are stated to have been of gold, were stolen."* [129] In remarking on the huge quantity of jewelry, personal and amuletic, which had been recovered by the excavators from the tomb and mummy (143 pieces on the untouched mummy alone), Carter concluded, *"...the greater mass, probably those of more intrinsic value, had been stolen from the caskets. Thus we have only a portion of what was originally placed there."* [130]

Other than two dismantled light-weight hunting chariots positioned along the chamber's north wall[131] and a whip which might be regarded as another heirloom,[132] the last major piece of equipment found in the Treasury was the king's bow case — probably to be associated with one of the chariots, to which it had been fastened by means of copper attachments. About five feet long, it was standing on one end, leaning into the northwest corner of the room and had contained three composite bows, which unfortunately had become viscous, leaked out

Above, A pair of tapestry-woven linen gloves with a brightly colored scale pattern, found neatly folded in a box in the Annexe. Carter thought that these were intended to go with the two "gala robes" which were also recovered from the same chamber, wadded up & crushed into a different box. Both robes are made of linen & richly ornamented with tapestry-woven & needlework decoration — around the neck opening & down the sides & across the bottom, as well as, in one of the pair, throughout the entire front & back panels of the garment. The robe opposite, with plain front & back panels, also has narrow sleeves, detached & placed above the garment in Burton's photograph. The excavator likened these robes to dalmatics worn by officiants in the Christian church, & proposed that they were vestments donned by King Tutankhamen for certain religious rites or special ceremonial occasions.

Internet photo & Griffith Institute

Detail views of the Annexe in different stage of clearance, reflecting the challenge the excavators faced. Internet photos

onto the Treasury floor and then dried into a solid black mass.

The bow case itself is made of wood covered with an elaborate marquetry of different barks, tinted leather strips, iridescent beetles' wings and gold foil, with inset panels on both the *recto* and *verso* of embossed gold-foil, each with a scene of the king hunting fleeing antelopes from his chariot. In the triangular panels at both ends of the overall acute-triangle-shaped case are depictions of several other arrow-pierced antelopes (and hyenas), which are accurately enough portrayed to be identified by species. The tapering ends of the case have finials of cheetah heads in violet faience with gilded manes.

With the Treasury's clearance completed, Carter was able to turn his attention, during the last days of November, 1927, to the remaining part of the tomb still housing Tutankhamen's funerary furnishings, the small storeroom off the Antechamber, which had been dubbed the Annexe. It will be remembered that this space, when first viewed through the hole made in its blocked doorway by the tomb robbers, proved to be totally inaccessible, due to the confused state of its contents. As Carter wrote, *"In contrast to the comparative order and harmony of the contents of the...Treasury, we* [found] *in this last chamber...a jumble of every kind of funerary chattels, tumbled any way one upon the other, almost defying description. Bedsteads, chairs, stools, footstools, hassocks, game-boards, baskets of fruits, every kind of alabaster vessel and pottery wine-jars, boxes of funerary figures, toys, shields, bows and arrows, and other missiles, all turned topsy-turvy. Caskets thrown over, their contents spilled; in fact, everything in confusion. ...To exaggerate the confusion that existed would be difficult; it was but an illustration of both drama and tragedy. While contemplating its picture of mingled rapacity and destruction, one felt that one could visualize the robbers' hurried scramble for loot — gold and other metals being their natural quarry; everything else they seem to have treated in the most brutal fashion. There was hardly an object that did not bear the marks of depredation, and before us — upon one of the large boxes — were the very foot-prints of the last intruder."* [133]

In order to gain access to the Annexe, it was necessary for Carter to do some shifting about of objects which had been temporarily stored in the Antechamber, particularly a number of the large roof sections of the dismantled tabernacles of the Burial Chamber. These were moved from the southern end of the Antechamber, where the Annexe doorway is located, to the northern end. This doorway, only fifty-one inches high by thirty-seven wide, had been blocked with large splinters of limestone which were plastered over on the Antechamber side, then stamped repeatedly with Tutankhamen's prenomen seal and the jackal-and-prisoners necropolis seal. The ancient thieves had breached the plastered blocking in its lower portion, and this hole was not filled in during the reordering of the tomb following the second robbery (or following the first, either, most likely).

The Annexe — like the Burial Chamber and Treasury — is on a lower level than the floor of the Antechamber, a deep step-down of more than three feet. A smallish space — some fourteen feet long by eight feet six inches wide and eight feet five inches high — it is only roughly cut without any attempt at finishing the squared-off walls, ceiling and floor, which were discovered to be discolored from intermittent dampness over the millennia.

Carter's own words best describe the *"prosaic"* method adopted *"to remove those three-hundred-odd pieces of antiquity"*: *"To begin with, sufficient floor-space had to be made for our feet, and that had to be done as best we could, head downwards, bending over the sill.... Whilst carrying out this uncomfortable operation, every precaution had to be taken lest a hasty movement should cause an avalanche of antiquities precariously piled up and beyond our reach. More than often, to save an object of heavy nature, so situated that the slightest disturbance would cause it to fall, we were obliged to lean over and reach far out, supported by a rope-sling under our arm-pits which was held by three or four men standing in the Antechamber. In that manner, by always removing one by one the uppermost object in reach, we gained ingress and gradually collected the treasures. Each object, or group of objects, had first to be photographed, numbered and recorded, before they were moved. It was by means of those records that we were eventually able to reconstruct to a certain degree what had previously occurred in the chamber."* [134]

Carter's initial impression that the positions of the plethora of tossed-about objects in the Annexe were without rhyme or reason was revised as individual pieces were removed one by one. While it was impossible to be absolutely certain about the original order of the room, certain deductions were possible. First, it was probably mistakenly decided that the *"little apartment"* — as Carter characterized it — had undergone two separate thefts: the first (second, actually) being by metal robbers, who had ransacked three of the tomb's four chambers for portable solid gold, silver and bronze; and the second (first) by thieves who were looking only for costly oils and unguents, which were stored in the numerous stone vessels found in the space. Carter also concluded that the Annexe had been intended simply as a storeroom for funerary food offerings — the oils and unguents, as well as preserved meats, dried fruit and wine. But an overabundance of furniture, storage chests and their contents, ushabtis in kiosks and boxes, model boats and other miscellaneous materials belonging to the burial equipment necessitated that a fair quantity of these items finally be placed in the Annexe by the necropolis agents who stocked the tomb — which was, after all, unusually small for a royal interment. But Carter also noted a certain inconsistency in the deposition of objects, as well. For example, the large stack of whitewashed ovoid wooden cases holding preserved meats, found under the Hathor couch in the Antechamber, should by rights have gone into the Annexe with the other food-offerings. Were they somehow overlooked, or else not brought into the tomb until after the doorway to the Annexe was already sealed, then had to be left in the Antechamber, logically the last space to be provisioned before the tomb was closed? Carter could

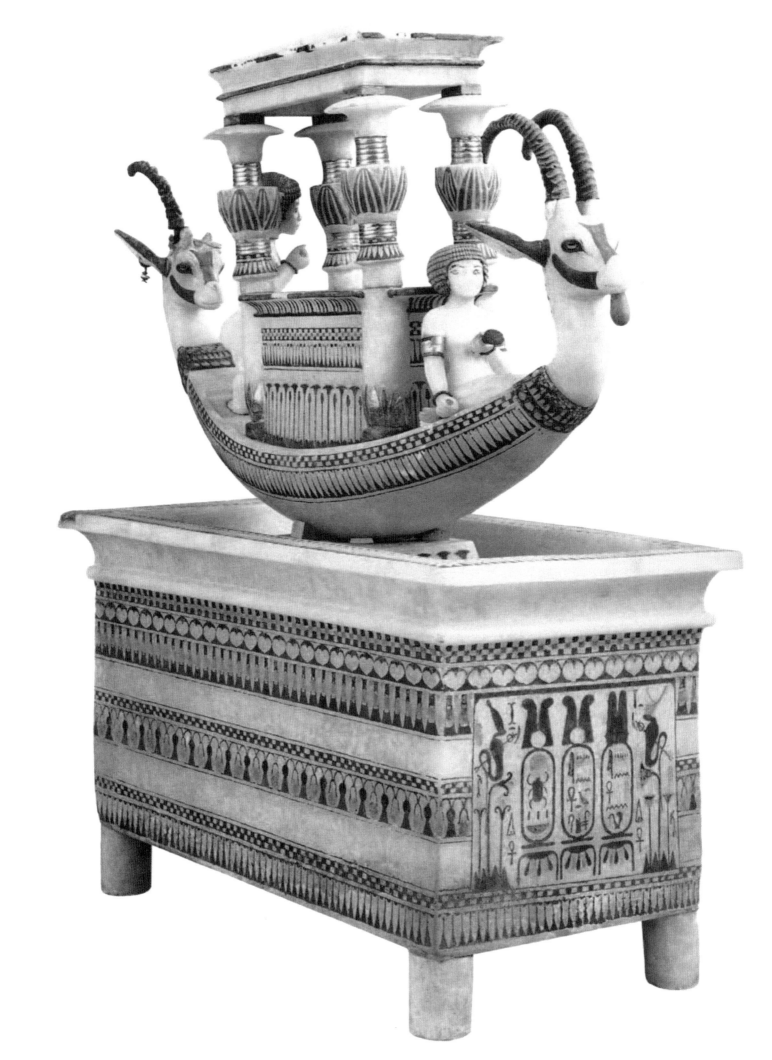

Opposite, Semi-translucent calcite "center-piece" from the KV62 Annexe, 27 inches (68.58 cm.) in height. Appearing to float in a rectangular four-footed "tank" (within which water lily blossoms were no doubt arranged in water when the vessel was in use) is a small barque with forward-facing ibex heads on its stem & stern. It carries amidships what appears to be an open sarcophagus resting under a canopy supported on four elaborate papyriform columns. On the foredeck, also facing forward, kneels a young female — attired only in a short curled wig, armlets & bracelets — holding a water-lily blossom between her breasts. At the stern, facing to the side & grasping a steering pole, stands a likewise nude female achondroplasic dwarf, almost certainly a slave. Both pedestal-tank & the barque are incised with detailed floral decorations filled with colored pigment & have touches of gilding. Tutankhamen's cartouches & that of Ankhesenamen are contained in panels on the short sides of the tank. One of the ebony horns of the ibex head at the stern was missing when this whimsical palace furnishing was found in otherwise perfect condition, despite the chaos within which it rested on the Annexe floor. Cairo Egyptian Museum

Above, Also from the Annexe, a calcite vessel in the form of a bleating ibex at rest, one of a pair. The absent real horn & vase neck (on the figure's back), & both horns & neck on the companion vessel were missing when found, so probably had been accidentally broken off prior to interment in KV62. Cairo Egyptian Museum

only wonder.

Once enough of the *"extraneous"* objects were cleared from the Annexe, it was possible to see the order, such as it was, that had originally existed in the space. The first items introduced by the necropolis workers were nearly forty wine jars made of pottery (bearing dockets in hieratic indicating their contents came from vineyards in the Delta domains of the Aten, Amen and Tutankhamen), which were positioned on the floor at the north end of the room. Next to these were placed some thirty-five vessels of heavy calcite containing oils and unguents. Stacked beside and on top of these were 116 baskets (oval, round and bottle shaped) of dried fruits, seeds and *dom* nuts. The remaining floor space was then used for the *"excess"* furniture, chests and ritual objects (model boats, ushabtis in their kiosks, etc.) that would not fit conveniently in the Treasury. These were no doubt stacked on top of one another, in as orderly a fashion as their disparate shapes permitted. Then the doorway was blocked up with rough limestone splinters and plastered over.

In his account of the clearance of the Annexe, Carter expressed some dismay at how slipshod the original introduction of objects into the tomb was overall, there having been an *"absence of system."* He wrote, *"Tradition holds that in burial custom each article belonging to tomb equipment had its prescribed place in the tomb.*

247

One of the decorative calcite vessels from the KV62 Annexe, in the form of an upright-standing lion (60 cm. h.), Carved from several separate pieces & fitted together, its right front paw is raised in either a salute or threatening gesture, the left resting atop a sa glyph, meaning "protection." On the beast's head sits a coronated water-lily blossom, which forms the neck-piece & opening of the vase. The figure itself is on a four-legged stand with a trellis openwork all around. Teeth & tongue of the lion are ivory, the latter tinted pink. The incised decoration of the figure & stand is filled in with pigmentation. Cairo Egyptian Museum

However, experience has shown that no matter how true the governing conventions may be, seldom have they been strictly carried out. Either the want of forethought with regard to requisite space, or the want of system when placing the elaborate paraphernalia in the tomb-chambers, overcame tradition. We have never found any strict order, we have found only approximate order." [135]

Of the so-called *"extraneous"* objects removed from the Annexe, the chief furniture pieces were four beds, bringing to a total of six — not counting the three large zoomorphic ritual couches — the number of beds found in KV62 (including the two from the Antechamber). These were all of the type familiar from tomb representations and actual examples found in earlier discoveries (e.g., Yuya and Thuyu, Kha and Merit), with the exception of one of those from the Annexe, which is a unique example of a folding bed which was in all probability used by King Tutankhamen when traveling (on the hunt or campaign, or perhaps sailing the Nile). Constructed of lightweight wood painted white, it is similar in design to the typical pharaonic-period bed — consisting of cord webbing strung between a rectangular wooden framework, a footboard and legs terminating in lion feet resting on truncated conical bases — except that the legs in this instance are somewhat short and there are eight of them rather than the usual number, the middle four of these supporting the center third of the frame, which folds back on itself into three sections by means of heavy bronze hinges.

One of the Annexe beds had been so roughly handled by the thieves in antiquity that it was regarded by Carter as *"of not much account."* Another, of gilded ebony, he described as *"not very fine work."* The fourth bed, however, was both in good condition and was assessed by the excavator as *"perhaps finer than any of the others found in... [the] tomb."* This is also constructed of ebony and overlaid entirely in heavy sheet gold with embossed and chased floral ornamentation, which prompted Carter to think that it was *"of El Amarna make."*

Of the chairs and stools recovered from the Annexe, the most important by far is what Carter dubbed a *"faldstool,"* being a hybrid combination of a *faux* folding-tool and a rigid chair with an upright back panel. About it Carter wrote, *"There is nothing to tell us definitely its use, but its extremely elaborate detail, and its austere appearance, suggest that it is of an entirely different order from the rest of the chairs [found in the tomb]. Indeed, in character, it seems appropriate only to a 'Chair of State,' like the specimen named the 'secular throne,' which is far too rich and ornate for any ordinary house use. In point of fact, it would appear to have been the king's ecclesiastical throne when presiding as the highest spiritual authority...."* [136]

The seat is indeed a hybrid composed of an overly large version of the familiar folding stool — with concave seat covered by *faux* animal hide and legs terminating in the heads of ducks or geese — joined to an upright back panel, with vertical rails affixed to this back, the seat and the rear foot bar. Between the stretchers and the foot bars there originally had been openwork gilded ornamentation of the "Un-

248

Left, From the Annexe is a small (10.8 cm. d.) silver vessel in the form of a pomegranite with incised petal & leaf decoration. Internet photo

A calcite vase lid from the Annexe. in the form of a nest containing four eggs & a young hatchling (which is made of painted wood with a red-stained ivory tongue). Internet photo

ion of the Two Lands" motif, although much of this was torn away by the ancient metal thieves.

Simulating flexible leather, the curved seat is fabricated from ebony and inlaid with irregularly fashioned pieces of ivory, imitating a piebald hide, and is similar in this respect to the seat of the somewhat smaller imitation folding "duck stool" found in the Antechamber. In this case, however, the central portion of the seat is further ornamented with eleven parallel small rectangular ivory panels stained to suggest various other spotted animal hides. These are framed within a border of rosettes.

The upright back is subtly curved in its center portion and is covered all over with sheet gold, this being elaborately inlaid with faience, colored glass and semi-precious stones. Of particular interest is the inclusion of two paired sets of the young king's nomen and prenomen cartouches, the former being both forms of his personal name: Tutankh*aten* and Tutankh*amen*. This led Carter to conclude that transition from heretical Aten worship back to the traditional supremacy of Amen had been *"gradual"* rather than *"spontaneous."*

Two other chairs were removed from the Annexe, a small white-painted wooden one that the excavator thought might have originated in the royal nursery, and a badly decayed *"garden"* chair made of rushwork covered with strips of painted papyrus, its decoration consisting of lotus petals on the back and the Nine Bows bound foreign prisoners on the seat. Its state of deterioration was so advanced, only a few fragments of this chair could be salvaged.

Related to the chairs were two stools extracted from the Annexe clutter. One, wood and painted white, was thought by Carter to be a companion to the "nursery" chair, both because of its small scale and because it had the same "Union of the Two Lands" openwork decoration between its seat and rails. The other, also of white-painted wood, is three legged with a semi-circular concave seat. The legs terminate, peculiarly, in canine feet (rather than the usual leonine or bovine feet seen on most Egyptian furniture of the pharaonic era). The carved openwork of the seat depicts two lions bound head to tail.

Additional furniture from the Annexe included several miniature rectangular footstools that Carter thought were only *"appropriate for a child"* because of their small dimensions. Although not furniture per se, three rather decayed hassocks were also recovered

Elegantly simple long-necked vase (62 cm. h.) is carved from a single block of calcite. Discovered among the jumble of objects in the Annex, it is decorated with three bands of inlaid turquoise & dark-green faience imitating garlands of water-lily leaves. Cairo Egyptian Museum

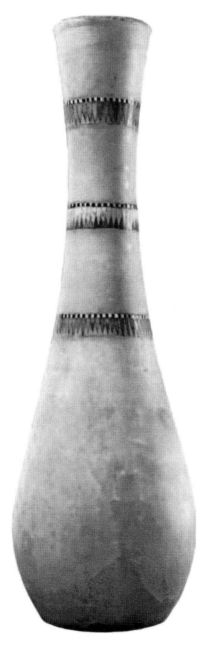

Two calcite vessels from the KV62 Annexe. Left, Lidded bell-shaped krater on a tall stand (58.5 cm. h.), with bands of painted & incised floral decoration & a central panel presenting the names of Nebkheperure Tutankhamen & King's Great Wife Ankhesenamen. Although found laying on its side, the lid some distance away, it still contained some of the unguent it was made to hold. Above, A second vase in the form of a situla or bucket used in religious rituals (25.8 cm. h.). The decoration, including two incised bands, consists of deeply carved openwork of winged cobras presenting the cartouches of the king, separated by nefer & ankh glyphs. Enough reside remained inside to indicate that it had also originally held an oily unguent. Cairo Egyptian Museum (another one, it will be remembered had been found in the Antechamber). These are all circular and constructed on a frame of rushwork overlaid with linen, to which are sewn thousands of minute polychrome beads forming a design of bound foreign prisoners around a central rosette. Carter thought they *"doubtless figured in some ceremony"* and were *"intended for the royal knee."*[137]

The rest of the "extraneous" furniture pieces in the Annexe consisted of chests or cabinets, boxes and an exquisite casket made of tinted ivory. Two of what Carter called table-shaped cabinets were of similar design and size; he likewise thought them of *"modern"* workmanship. Both are made of cedarwood with rails and uprights of ebony, and are squarish in shape, with flat lids hinged along the back edge for raising. These could have been secured with cording wrapped around gilded knobs of the lid and front panel. Each cabinet stands on long slender ebony legs positioned at the four corners. Between rails joining the four legs, both cabinets have an openwork frieze all around of pairs of alternating *djed* and "knot of Isis" emblems resting on *neb* baskets, with the first and last elements being gilded and the knots made of ebony. The more elaborate of the pair has encrusted titulary and other hieroglyphic inscriptions on all of its rails and uprights. It was apparently discovered to be empty.

The simpler of these cabinets, found broken, nonetheless contained the four headrests discussed earlier, although Carter thought, because of a hieratic docket written on one of its panels, that it origi-

Three of four game boxes belonging to Tutankhamen found in the KV62 Annexe. Although there was apparently a funerary context for including games among one's burial furnishings (as evidenced by Chapter 17 of the Book of the Dead*), the number & variety interred with the young king sug- gest that he was an avid game player in life, as well. The largest of the four boxes (right), veneered in ebony, rests on its own stand, also ebony, in form like a bed with leonine legs, these attached to an ebony sledge. Two of the medium-sized game boxes (below & bottom right) have two playing surfaces, top & bottom. A drawer in both of the narrow ends of each box held 10 ivory gaming pieces, as well as a pair of ivory knuckle bones, which functioned as dice.*

Cairo Egyptian Museum

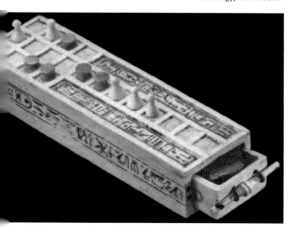

251

Above, Two of the four so-called ceremonial shields found in the KV62 Annexe. Made of lightweight wood which is gilded overall, each is about a meter high & is decorated with an openwork image of the king contesting with traditional foes: in one case, on the right, represented collectively as a lion which Tutankhamen grasps by its tail, a scimitar raised to strike a fatal blow; in the other, at left, by an Asiatic & Nubian being trampled by the king in the form of a human-headed sphinx wearing the Double Crown atop a Nemes head covering. Internet photos

Opposite, One of four "real" shields from the Annexe. Also made of light wood, it is covered (as was one other) with the skin of a cheetah & is emblazoned with the king's gilded nomen & prenomen car- touches. Two of these defensive shields were covered with antelope hides. Griffith Institute

nally was intended for the king's *"fine linen raiments."* He suggested these had been scattered or stolen and that the headrests *"had evidently been put there after the robbery."* [138] How this would have been accomplished is not explained, and contradicts the archaeologist's earlier contention that the necropolis priests had made no effort to straighten up the Annexe following its two burglaries.

At the northern end of the chamber, one of the tomb's genuine masterpieces was recovered, albeit in two parts. This is a medium-sized wooden chest, which itself was found empty amid the room's jumbled contents, the humped lid (shaped like a shrine roof) tossed aside by the robbers in antiquity. Both chest and lid are veneered in colored-ivory inlays carved in raised low relief, with additional inlays of colored calcite, faience and ebony, plus touches of gilding. The chest stands on four square legs, which are extensions of the corner uprights. Each foot is capped with a ferrule of bronze or copper. The rim or entablature of the chest is in the form of a cavetto cornice (gessoed and gilded, with ebony trim). While the uprights and rails are plain-ivory veneer, the panels on the two long sides and one short side have borders

252

of banded decoration surrounding elaborately inlaid friezes of fauna and flora imagery in tinted ivory.

The second end panel — interrupted at its top by a gilded-wood knob corresponding to another on one end of the separate lid — is a highly detailed low-relief scene in stained ivory of King Tutankhamen and Queen Ankhesenamen (plus a diminutive servant) depicted shooting fowl and fish in a lush marsh setting. The young king, wearing K*hepresh* crown, sits on a leonine stool draped in garlands and draws his bow, while his smaller-scaled consort — in a diademed Nubian-style wig topped by a modius of uraei and a perfume cone decorated with a floral circlet — sits gazing up at him from on a cushion at his feet, holding an arrow in one hand and a water-lily blossom in the other. The tiny servant figure approaches the royal couple, having retrieved two of the king's arrows, one piercing a fish, the other a duck.

But it is the scene on the large central panel of the chest lid that particularly distinguishes this object, and which Carter described as *"certainly the unsigned work of a master."* [139] This depicts the royal couple standing facing one another in a flower-festooned pavilion, the young king with one hand resting on the finial of a long staff or walking stick, the other raised in greeting to the queen, who offers her husband two large, ornate bouquets of bound papyrus and water-lily umbels. In the narrow register beneath the scene of the royal couple, two kneeling female servants gather garlands of flowers and fruits of the mandrake plant.

The king is attired in an elaborate beaded collar which covers his shoulders, and wears a pleated kilt with a wide belt or waistband, this fronted by an ornate apron from which pairs of long streamers extend at each side. On his head is the tiered Nubian wig favored at this time, fronted by a uraeus. Ankhesenamen, likewise sporting a large beaded collar, wears a pleated flowing white gown, transparent enough that the ripe contours of her lower body are visible. It is belted just below her bosom (with one breast seemingly bared), double pairs of cloth streamers falling almost to the ground on either side of her full hips. The queen wears a tightly curled, close-fitting wig to which is appended a heavy, multi-braided and doubly clasped side lock falling well below one shoulder, a hair style peculiar to the Amarna period and immediately following reigns. Atop this rests a modius supporting a garlanded perfume cone flanked by a pair of uraei with sun disks. The wig is fronted by double uraei, each with horned sun disks.

Three additional cedarwood-and-ebony chests were recovered from the Annexe, each originally containing what Carter described as *"interesting mementoes of the king's youth."* [140] These, found strewn on the chamber's floor, included: a quantity of bracelets and anklets in ivory, horn, wood, leather and crystalline limestone (plus two pairs in faience bearing the names of Tutankhamen's two immediate predecessors, Akhenaten and Smenkhkare, and thus of some historical importance); miniature game-boards of ivory; slings for hurling stones; leather gloves, and linen and leather wrist braces for archery;

Among the genuine treasures found in the KV62 Annexe is Tutankhamen's Kherp *scepter of sheet gold & cloisonné inlay. It is made of five separate pieces on a wooden core. The "blade" is decorated on one side with a band of inlaid inscription, & on the other (detail below) it is embossed with a depiction of five slaughtered bulls. Inlays include carnelian, green feldspar, faience, colored glass simulating lapis lazuli, turquoise & malachite. The scepter is 54.0 cm. long.* Cairo Egyptian Museum & Griffith Institute

a fire-starting device, described by Carter as a *"lighter"* and consisting of a stock and drill; mechanical toys; mineral samples; paint pots and pigments; and two blue-glass mandragora fruits, one with the cartouche of Thutmose III — obviously another heirloom.

Six other boxes were cleared from the Annexe, but these were of rough construction and found broken apart and empty of their original contents. Another box, crudely made and painted red, although broken, was found to contain a large number of delicate vessels of pale-blue faience; and Carter thought it was probably a companion to a similar box found in the Antechamber, which contained like vessels in lapis-lazuli-colored faience. Another rough, painted box cleared from just in front of the doorway to the Annexe was found to hold — in addition to a quantity of miniature amuletic bovine forelegs in light- and dark-blue faience, a pair of rush sandals, a pair of gloves and a ritualistic turquoise-glass palette — two of the king's garments, which Carter thought were *"gala robes,"* inasmuch as they reminded him of dalmatic vestments worn by officiants in the Christian church, or by kings during their coronation. These were wadded up and crushed into the box with the ill-sorted lot of objects[141] and their preservation had suffered consequently, due not only to their rough handling, but also from moisture in the tomb over the millennia.

Both garments are in the form of simple linen tunics of the sort known from the Tomb of Kha and Merit, a long rectangle of fabric folded in the middle horizontally with a neck opening at the fold (quite like a modern *serape*). One of the robes additionally has narrow tubular sleeves, although these were apparently found detached. Both garments are richly ornamented with tapestry-woven and needlework decoration around the neck opening, down both sides and across the bottom front and back. In one case these broad bottom hems are comprised of a palmette pattern and desert flora and fauna imagery, with the front and back panels being plain. In the other both panels are completely woven with colored rosettes and floral designs, as well as the king's cartouches; and the collar of this robe is in the design of a falcon with spread wings, the royal titulary running down the front.

Carter was of the opinion that these vestments were customary apparel of Pharaoh, worn for special religious rites or other highly ceremonial occasions (such as possibly the king's coronation), even though they are not depicted in any known artistic representations of the Dynastic Period. As proof that Tutankhamen's garments were not peculiar to his reign, Carter noted that he himself had found the fragment of a similarly embroidered robe in the Tomb of Thutmose IV — although it bore the cartouche of Amenhotep II, and so was something of an heirloom in the context of his successor's interment.

Related to the *"gala robes"* — and perhaps worn with them, as the archaeologist suggested — are a pair of long linen gloves with a tapestry weave in a brightly colored scale pattern. These were found neatly folded in another box in the Annexe, and their fabric was in a far better state of preservation than that of the robes. Both gloves

Representative examples of the mundane objects found in the KV62 Annexe, for which it was originally intended: Above, a small rushwork basket woven in the shape of a bottle, which contained dried food offerings; &, Below, one of some three-dozen pottery amphorae which had once held vintage wines from the Delta vineyards of the Aten, Amen & King Tutankhamen, as indicated by hieratic dockets inscribed on their shoulders. The wine evaporated long ago. Griffith Institute

have two long linen tapes for tying them around their wearer's forearms.

Last of the wooden cases recovered from the Annexe included a small, plain, white-painted wooden one shaped like an attenuated shrine, empty when discovered but which Carter thought once held a standard cubit-measure, no doubt of solid metal and carried off by the robbers during the first (actually second) break-in. The other chest — also of plain wood, roughly made and painted white — is quite large and its bow shape and contents when opened make it clear that it was intended to hold a quantity of the king's archery equipment. Several boomerangs were found in it along with the bows and arrows, although Carter thought these had possibly been placed originally in the tomb in another box or chest.

Decorative objects of calcite also were discovered among the clutter of the Annexe. The most ornate of these, found sitting on the floor and remarkably undamaged, was what Carter dubbed as a *"centerpiece,"* even though he admitted that he had no clear explanation for the *"true nature of this little monument."* It consists of a rectangular *"tank"* resting on four short cylindrical legs at each corner, in which appears to float (although it is supported by a rectangular pedestal) a skiff with large forward-facing ibex heads terminating its bow and prow. Amidships is an open rectangular box with a cavetto cornice, looking very much like a sarcophagus. This is covered with a canopy (shaped like a shrine roof) supported by four very ornate two-tiered papyriform columns. Forward, with her back to the chest and canopy, kneels the figure of a young woman, naked except for a tightly curled short wig and arm and wrist bands, who clutches a water-lily blossom to her bosom. At the stern, facing sideways, is the standing figure of a similarly "attired" female achondroplasic dwarf, who holds a steering pole. The tank, skiff and its pedestal, and chest are all elaborately decorated with pigment-filled incised floral and checkered designs in horizontal bands; one end panel displays the cartouches of Nebkheperure Tutankhamen and Ankhesenamen. The horns of the ibex finials are ebony (one of these is missing, the only damage to the piece) and there are embellishments of gilding on the columns and figures.

Carter speculated that it was either a ritualistic object in some obscure way connected to the model funerary barques found in the Treasury, or else a *"purely fanciful"* *"palace ornament"* used to display lotus or other flowers floated in water filling the tank. The latter seems more likely, inasmuch as nothing else remotely like this object was found in the tomb, and its only parallel with Tutankhamen's fleet of model boats is that a water-going vessel is its central element.

Two other calcite vessels from the Annexe are zoomorphic in form and were used to hold unguents. One depicts a bleating ibex at rest (with details in black pigment and a red-stained ivory tongue), the horns and neck portion of which are missing and may have been of gilded metal which caught the attention of the tomb robbers. The other is a lion striding erect on it hind legs, one foreleg awkwardly raised in a salute or threatening gesture, the other resting on the *sa* glyph meaning "protection." It is crowned by an open water-lily blossom rising from a modius — which serves as the vessel's opening — and an ivory tongue stained pink protrudes from the beast's open mouth baring ivory fangs. This figure is supported by a four-legged stand with trellis open-work all around. Crown, lion and stand are incised with pigment-filled decoration, and the royal couple's cartouches and titles are emblazoned on the lion's chest. It will be recalled that another unguent vessel found in the Burial Chamber has a recumbent lion decorating its lid.

While most of the thirty-four calcite vessels which had been placed in the Annexe containing oils, fats and unguents were of a utilitarian form, several were somewhat ornate in shape or decoration. Two in particular deserve to be singled out for mention. Both might be described as round-bottomed urns or situlae resting on separate stands, in one instance also of calcite, in the other of metal. The first of these vessels is subtly fluted, with alternating lotus flowers and buds in raised relief decorating its flared rim, the latter supporting a lid shaped like an inverted dish. Lid and urn are further decorated with pigmented incised bands of floral motifs, and the king's and queen's incised cartouches and titles fill a panel on one side of the vessel. The second urn, lidless, has its base delicately carved to represent overlapping lotus petals, above which is a narrow band of incised inscription. And above this is a wide panel of openwork depicting two back-to-back rearing winged cobras (a large *ankh* separating them), which protect or present Tutankhamen's cartouches. Another register of incised petals decorates the unflared rim of the vessel. The lid of a third calcite vessel is particularly unique, being in the form of a dish holding four eggs, situated among which is a wing-flapping, squawking hatchling of painted wood with a tongue of red-stained ivory.

A final vessel from the Annexe to be noted here is made of silver in the form of a pomegranate fruit. About 13.5 centimeters high, it is chased on the neck, shoulders and bowl with bands of flowers and olive leaves. Despite being of precious metal, it was either over-looked by the thieves or else dropped by them in their haste. Carter wrote of this object, *"In aspect, the vase is modern enough to resemble the work of the silversmiths of the Queen Anne period, and, did we not know its provenance, none of us would dare to date it as belonging to the fourteenth century B.C."*[142]

Another category of *"extraneous"* objects removed from the Annexe was the king's game boards (or boxes, more accurately), of which there were four in sizes from two small plain-ivory portable ones to a large (46.0 centimeters long) ebony-veneered specimen which rests on its own bed-like ebony stand with leonine legs attached to an ebony sledge. Its playing pieces were missing, and Carter suggested that they may have been of gold and thus were carried away by the tomb's metal thieves. The most elaborate of the four (27.5 centimeters long) is made of wood overlaid along its long sides with carefully carved floral motifs of ivory stained red and black, the playing squares being gilded. It has two drawers, one on each end, and these both held ten ivory playing-pieces, plus a pair of ivory knuckle-bones, which functioned as the dice. All four of the game boxes had two playing surfaces. Also found in the Annexe and probably to be associated with the boxes, were four ebony and ivory throwing sticks which apparently were used to determine the moves in the board games.

It will be remembered that two fan stocks were found between the Third and Fourth tabernacles surrounding Tutankhamen's sarcophagus. To this number were added three additional such ostrich-feather "flabella" fans recovered from the Annexe confusion. These are made of solid ivory (carved, stained and gilded); of ebony veneered with decorative barks; and of embossed and engraved sheet gold on a wooden core. The latter specimen bears the prenomen, nomen and epithets of Akhenaten, as well as the cartouches of the Aten sun disk — which puts it into the category of an heirloom. The papyrus-umbel stock of the stained-ivory fan is particularly ornately carved. All of the ostrich feathers had so deteriorated that they could not be saved, but Carter was able to determine that each fan once held forty-eight, in two parallel rows of twenty-four feathers.

One of the Annexe's genuine treasures is a scepter belonging to King Tutankhamen, of the type called a *Kherp* scepter. About this unique piece of royal regalia, Carter wrote, *"It is difficult to comprehend why such a sacred object should be in a store-room of this kind, and not where one would have expected it to be, among similar insignia* [e.g., the two sets of Crook and Flail scepters] *in the Innermost Treasury. The only explanation that I can suggest is that, either the plunderers cast it there owing to some misgivings in stealing it, or that it belonged to a complete outfit which included the garments pertaining to religious ceremonies* [i.e., the embroidered robes and gloves]...*that were originally deposited in one of the ornate caskets found in this chamber."* [143] Some fifty-three centimeters long, it is composed of five separate pieces made of sheet gold on wooden cores, with cloisonné work embellishments. The "blade" or tip of the scepter extends from a "capitulum" in the form of a papyrus umbel, on one side displaying a band of inlaid inscription, on the other depicting slaughtered bulls in five embossed registers. The inscription reads: *"The Beautiful God, beloved, dazzling of face like the Aten when it shines, The Son of Amen, Tutankhamen."* Carter thought that this was *"of interest, as it suggests a compromise between the Aten and Amen creeds."* [144]

In addition to a great quantity of walking sticks and staves (of a variety of types, some ritualistic, others for daily use — so many of these, in fact, that Carter thought the young king must have been an *"amateur collector"* of same) — the KV62 Annexe yielded up numerous bows (both "self" and "composite" types) and arrows (278 of the latter), a variety of throw sticks, clubs and boomerangs, plus two sickle-shaped bronze falchions or scimitars. Related to these weapons of offense were what Carter called *"arms of defense,"* including a cuirass — in the form of a bodice without sleeves, made up of thick overlapping tinted-leather scales attached to a linen basis, all unfortunately too decayed to be preserved — and eight shields, four of which were possibly for actual employment in battle, the remaining being purely ceremonial in nature.

Two of the so-called *"real"* shields are made of light-weight wood covered with antelope hide and emblazoned in their centers with the gilded cartouches of the king. The other two are similarly constructed and embellished, but covered with cheetah hides. These four shields had a maximum measurement of 73.5 by 52.0 centimeters. The four *"ceremonial"* shields are slightly larger, also made of light wood, but in an openwork design that is gilded. Two of these heraldic emblems depict the king enthroned, in this life and in the Hereafter, respectively. The third shows Tutankhamen as a human-headed sphinx, wearing the Double Crown atop the *Nemes,* and trampling his Asiatic and Nubian foes. The fourth has the young king (in a short wig worn with a diadem, horns, sun-disk and feathers) raising a scimitar to strike his foes, collectively represented as a lion grasped by the base of its tail.

Thus, such were the major so-called extraneous objects which Howard Carter cleared from the KV62 Annexe between October 30 and December 15, 1927. Additionally of interest were: a pair of sandals made of wood and veneered with a marquetry of bark, green leather and gold foil on a stucco base (the inner soles of which bear two bound figures each of Egypt's traditional enemies, plus depictions of the Nine Bows); thirty-two pairs of basket-work sandals; a small bronze statuette of a dog; an ivory monkey or ape figure; a pair of ivory castanets or clappers terminating in hands and inscribed with the cartouche of Queen Tiye (thus another heirloom); a bronze razor and spatula; a number of bracelets and anklets in inlaid ivory, and other armlets, bracelets, circlets, ear studs and finger rings of various materials (faience, crystalline limestone, lapis lazuli and beadwork); any number of miscellaneous amulets in a variety of materials (largely faience, stone and wood); numerous libation and other small vases in blue faience; plus the disassembled (mostly hinged) parts of a portable pavilion, other sections of which had been found in the Antechamber amid the heap of chariots. In fact, there were so many bits and odd pieces of things, as well as particular objects found laying on the floor that could not be related to any larger container which once may have held them, that Carter simply gave these the collective inventory number 620, with 123 sublistings, one of which — 620 (66), a group of finger rings bearing either royal names or various devices — itself numbered twenty-three individual items.

In fact, there was a total of 283 groups of objects removed from the Annexe, consisting of over 2,000 separate items and constituting well over half of the entire contents of Tutankhamen's tomb — all of this contained in a space only fourteen by eight feet square and some eight feet high! It was the hands-on experience gained by Carter and his remaining colleagues (chiefly Lucas, Callender and Burton) in the earlier clearance of the Antechamber, Burial Chamber and Treasury which enabled them to dispose of the Annexe's difficult jumble in such relatively short order.

Of course, the emptying of KV62's final chamber did not mark the end of Carter's work involving the Tomb of Tutankhamen.

As had been the case since 1923, the focus of his and his associates' efforts shifted from sepulcher to laboratory, where the plethora of Annexe objects had to be photographed (individually or in small groups of related objects), to be measured and special features drawn and noted (including methods of construction), to be cleaned and restored as necessary, to be conserved and, finally, to be carefully crated for shipment to Cairo's Egyptian Museum. This *"scientific"* endeavor continued, in fact, for two more seasons, 1928 and 1929, and it was not until the 10th of November, 1930, that the very last objects were removed from KV62, these being the many quite sizable elements of the four Burial Chamber tabernacles, which earlier had been stored in the Antechamber. And so, just a few days more than eight years after its discovery, the dismantling of Tutankhamen's last resting place was finally complete, with the sarcophagus, outermost coffin and the king's own mortal remains being all that was left in place of the assemblage of royal funerary "treasure" with which the last male of the Thutmosid line of warrior kings had been provisioned for the Afterlife, following his premature demise in the last quarter of the Fourteenth Century BC.

In due time the greater part of Tutankhamen's treasure was put on display at the Cairo Egyptian Museum, where today it takes up most of one long side of the entire second floor (galleries 8, 9, 10, 15, 20, 25, 30, 35, 40 and 45, and room 4), with many of the multiple and more mundane objects being in storage (the *naoi* for the ritual figures, the ushabti boxes, the pottery vessels and food-offering cases and baskets, the plain storage boxes and chests, etc.). Certain select objects (the gilded Hathor cow head, two model boats, two pairs of sandals, several gilded-bronze pall rosettes and a few arrows) were returned to Luxor and are presently displayed in the antiquities museum there. The botanical material from the tomb now is in the Agricultural Museum at Dokki; and the two fetal mummies apparently rest in the conservation laboratory of the Grand Egyptian Museum, where all of the treasures from KV62 will be displayed in the near future. Tutankhamen himself today rests on view in a glass display-case positioned in the Antechamber of his tomb.

Howard Carter, the man whose name will forever be linked with that of the boy-king of antiquity, who was arguably the most famous individual in the world during the decade of the 1920s, was himself all but consumed by the exhausting and often tedious work which totally occupied him for nearly a decade following the happy accident of his discovery, finally, of Tutankhamen's tomb and its amazing contents. By the time the clearance of the Annexe was completed, the international spotlight on Carter had dimmed and all but flickered out, as the public's prolonged interest in the tomb's vast and remarkable contents inevitably waned. Everything that followed was anticlimactic.

After a life of romantic adventure (he became, after all, in the eyes of the world, the consummate archaeologist) and considerable professional achievement (securing for him his place in history), the decade of the 1930s saw Carter reduced from an overnight celebrity to a gloomy and increasingly ill recluse. His Egyptological activities

Howard Carter towards the end of his life, perhaps sitting on a veranda of the Winter Palace Hotel, Luxor. Internet photo

became limited, finally, to dealing in antiquities as an agent for collectors and institutions, and occasionally guiding important dignitaries around the archaeological sites of Luxor, where he maintained his home on the west bank. He was often to be spotted sitting alone in the reception area or on a veranda of the Winter Palace Hotel, lost in his own secret thoughts and ignoring the curious stares and exchanged whispers of passerby tourists who recognized him. Carter never married and, while he could claim a wide circle of acquaintances, he had few close friends. His fleeting great fame gone, he was in his last years a lonely old man plagued by regrets.

As the clock ran down, what no doubt troubled Carter most was the realization that he would never fully complete his involvement with the Tomb of Tutankhamen and thereby fulfill his obligation to Egyptology: he would never write his planned six-volume fully scientific report on the boy-king's sepulcher and its contents. To be sure, there were the three volumes of his "popular" account of the discovery, *The Tomb of Tut·Ankh·Amen*, published between 1923 and 1933, which he co-authored in part with archaeological colleague Arthur Mace (volume one) and English professor and novelist Percy White (volumes two and three). But these did not meet the scholarly expectations of the professional Egyptological community, nor were they what his discovery of discoveries deserved. He did manage to produce the bare-bones outline for his projected *A Report Upon the Tomb of Tut·Ankh·Amun*; but Howard Carter — not a university-trained scholar — just could not bring himself to commit the countless deskbound hours — ultimately adding up to years — that would be required to see such a project through, from field notes, sketches and diaries to full-blown formal publication. As the decade of the 1930s wore on and he suffered increasingly frequent bouts of ill health, the prospect of undertaking this prodigious task and marshalling it to its full completion faded and disappeared altogether.

The Tomb of Tutankhamen has never been fully published, subsequently. The Griffith Institute of Oxford University in England — where Howard Carter's papers, including his field notes, diaries and drawings from the Tutankhamen tomb-clearance years are preserved — has undertaken, however, to publish the tomb in a fascicle form as the *Tut'ankhamun's Tomb Series*, which consists to date of nine slender volumes authored by specialist scholars who deal in formal detail with individual categories of items from the tomb (e.g., model boats, the chariots and related equipment, musical instruments, the human remains, etc.). This series promises to be ongoing, with additional volumes in press and projected.[145] In 1990 publisher Thames and Hudson Ltd. released British Egyptologist Nicholas Reeves's *The Complete Tutankhamun*, which, while intended for a lay audience, is the fullest account of the tomb and its contents to date — save for the present work.

Howard Carter succumbed to Hodgkin's Disease at his home in London on March 2, 1939. He was sixty-five. His last resting place is a simple grave at Putney Vale Cemetery in London. One of

Howard Carter's modest gravesite in Putney Vale Cemetery, London. Below, His house on the Luxor west bank, now restored & a tourist attraction. Internet photos

American edition of the first volume of the popular account of the discovery & clearance of the Tomb of Tutankhamen. All three volumes were republished in the U.S. in 1963.

the executors of his estate was a long-time colleague in the Tutankhamen tomb clearance, British photographer Harry Burton. Carter bequeathed his land, house and its contents at Qurna on the west bank, Luxor, to the Metropolitan Museum. He left the sum of 150 Egyptian pounds to his servant in Luxor, Abd-el-asl Ahmed Saide. Except for £250 for each of his executors, the balance of Carter's estate, property both real and personal, went to his niece (daughter of his sister), Phyllis Walker. To the latter's embarrassment, Carter's fairly extensive personal collection of Egyptian antiquities included some objects that had come from the Tomb of Tutankhamen, which Burton identified as a blue-glass headrest, three faience ushabtis, cups of glass and faience, an *ankh* amulet, three gold harness ornaments and a metal tenon from one of the outer coffins. Miss Walker was advised to return these objects to Egypt. They were sent in short order to the Egyptian Museum via King Farouk himself, and in due course were merged with the rest of the boy-king's treasures.

As said above, Howard Carter's locating the forgotten burial place of the last Thutmosid king, the third to last ruler of ancient Egypt's glorious Eighteenth Dynasty, after years of searching for it, was the "discovery of discoveries," and has never been surpassed in subsequent Egyptian archaeology. In many ways the tomb itself is an anomaly. In the first place, it is unorthodox in plan and scale for a royal tomb of the New Kingdom. Secondly, KV62's extensive contents are a mixture of the truly magnificent and the most mundane — there being some question as to whether Tutankhamen's solid-gold innermost coffin and funerary mask were unique to this particular interment of a short-reigned juvenile king, the last of his illustrious line, or, in fact, were standard burial equipment for monarchs of the later Empire. Thirdly, the only mummy of an Egyptian ruler found undisturbed in its original funerary equipage, Tutankhamen's, ironically, is the least well-preserved of the numerous Egyptian royal remains which have survived from antiquity. Lastly — except for sealings, dockets, and titulary and other standard inscriptions on furnishings and the funerary equipage and Burial Chamber wall decoration — there was, disappointingly, nothing found in the tomb in the way of written information throwing light on the history of this much-debated period or on the full identity of its somewhat enigmatic occupant.

What KV62 did reveal, circumstantially, is that the background of Tutankhamen's nine-year reign was one of confusion regarding the abandonment of the Aten cult and the reestablishment of the ancient pantheon under Amen's supremacy. The transition from heresy to orthodoxy did not occur overnight. It was already known at the time of Tomb 62's discovery that its owner had come to the throne with an Atenist nomen, Tutankh*aten*. But the presence in the Antechamber of the golden throne — which bore not only the sun-disk emblem of the Aten, but the king's nomen in both its Aten and Amen forms — indicates that even at the time there was some uncertainty during the transition back to normalcy. This is further reinforced by the inclusion in Tutankhamen's food provisions of amphorae of wine which had come from the Delta vineyards of both Amen and the Aten. That items were found in the tomb bearing the names of Akhenaten and Smenkhkare would likewise suggest that these two immediate Atenist predecessors of the boy-king had not yet become non-persons at the time of his early demise.

But who was Nebkheperure Tutankhamen? And how did he happen to be buried in an appropriated private tomb in the necropolis of his Thutmosid predecessors?

From his many depictions found in KV62, young Tutankhamen seems quite familiar to us today. Judging from these he was apparently a rather handsome youth, despite the obvious idealizations of his various portraits — all of which, nonetheless, even with their variations, are easily recognizable as depicting Tutankhamen and no one else. His mummy suggests that he was a slightly built young man of medium height, whose skull was of the broad-oblong type, large but not excessively so, and that his facial features in life were as refined as his portraits suggest, even though he had the pronounced overbite which was characteristic of his Thutmosid ancestors.

That he was a scion of that ruling house is not really questioned; but exactly who Tutankhamen's parents were is a matter of contention among those Egyptologists who like to debate such matters. An inscription from a monument which had originally stood at Akhetaten — the capital of the Aten Heresy — indicates he was a *"King's bodily son, his beloved."* But which king? Those scholars who are persuaded that there was a long coregency (up to twelve years) between Amenhotep III and Amenhotep IV/Akhenaten would like to see the former king as Tutankhamen's parent. Had the "Magnificent" Amenhotep lived into the twelfth year of Akhenaten's seventeen-year reign, and had he fathered a son during the last year of his life, the chronology would work for a nine- or ten-year-old Tutankhaten to have come to the throne following Akhenaten's demise (allowing that Smenkhkare did not rule on his own for two years post-Akhenaten, but rather shared the throne in a coregency from Years 15 to 17 of Akhenaten's reign).

But if Nebmaatre Amenhotep III was the boy-king's father, who would his mother have been? Romantics have offered the shadowy Sitamen, Amenhotep III's daughter who was also his Great Royal Wife, married to him towards the end of his reign, during the period of his three *sed*-festivals. There is no evidence for this, however, nothing inscriptional or otherwise to link Tutankhamen with Sitamen.

The other candidate most often proposed as the boy-king's mother by Amenhotep III is none other than the Great Royal Wife Tiye, a lock of whose hair was found among the KV62 burial goods, housed in a set of coffins, obviously a memento signifying some sort of relationship, probably familial, between Tiye and Tutankhamen. But would she have been too old to have mothered a son in the last year of her royal spouse's life? Amenhotep III himself came to the throne as a minor only ten or twelve years old. In his Year 2 he married Tiye, the daughter of non-royal courtiers. Presumably she was his junior by a year or two at the time, making Tiye a bride of ten or twelve. Amenhotep reigned into Year 39,

In 1963 the Griffith Institute at Oxford University began to publish in fascicle form a series of slender volumes dealing with select categories of items from KV62, under the general title Tut'ankhamun's Tomb Series. These are written by specialist authors and now number nine volumes, with additional titles planned. The Institute has also published other volumes dealing with Tutankhamen objects (one above) in the same format as the Tomb Series, but for some reason these are not considered part of the latter.

An imaginary portrait of King Nebkheperure Tutankhamen painted by the South African artist/Egyptologist Winifred Brunton in the 1920s, depicting the teenage ruler attired in some of the pieces of jewelry found in his tomb, & holding the dagger with a blade of iron which was found on his mummy.

Brunton, *Great Ones of Ancient Egypt*, 1929

Uninscribed limestone head in the Luxor Museum depicting the god Amen-Re with the unmistakable features of the youthful Tutankhamen, indicating it was carved early in his reign. Author's photo

dying at between his forty-ninth and fifty-first year of age, when Tiye herself would have been in her mid-to-late forties. Too old to bear a child? Probably, but not necessarily. There is no way of knowing; and that lock of hair is attractive circumstantial evidence.

Those Egyptologists who reject the possibility of a coregency of any length between Amenhotep III and his successor, the majority view, offer Akhenaten himself as Tutankhamen's father, even though the Heretic never claimed paternity for a son, despite his obvious public pride in having produced a brood of six daughters by his Great Royal Wife Nefertiti. The latter is seldom proposed as Tutankhamen's mother, however. Instead, the candidate most often put forth is Wife of the King Kiya, an enigmatic second spouse of Akhenaten, who appears on the monuments of Akhetaten before Years 9 or 10 of Akhenaten's reign. She disappears from the record in Year 11, about the time of Tutankhamen's birth, possibly dying during his delivery — an event which may be depicted in a very badly damaged relief in the Royal Tomb at El Amarna. Who exactly Kiya herself was is unknown. Some have seen her as the Mitannian princess-bride Tadukepa, known to have been sent to Egypt for a diplomatic marriage at the beginning of Akhenaten's reign. Kiya's name, however, might suggest some affiliation with the courtier family of Akhmin (Ipu), which seems to have paralleled the Thutmosid royal house for two or more generations and counted among its members possibly Great Royal Wife Mutemwiya (Amenhotep III's mother) and certainly royal in-laws Yuya and Thuyu, their daughter, Great Royal Wife Tiye, and their putative son, Ay, who would succeed Tutankhamen on the throne. *If* Akhenaten was the father of his (second) successor, then Kiya is very likely Tutankhamen's mother.

But, consider two other candidates for the boy-king's parents, who — as far as this writer is aware — have rarely been proposed for those roles: King Ankhkheperure Smenkhkare Djoserkheperru and his Great Royal Wife, Meritaten!

Who Meritaten was is not disputed. As the eldest daughter of Akhenaten and Nefertiti, the only thing that is uncertain about her is when she would have been born. She is represented as a child on the Aten monuments raised by her father and mother at Waset (Thebes/Luxor) during the first eight years of Akhenaten's reign (prior to the removal of the Aten court to the new capital at Akhetaten in Year 8). Thus, Meritaten almost certainly was born while her father was still crown-prince. By Akhenaten's Year 11 or 12, she could, therefore, have been as old as fourteen or fifteen, certainly capable of bearing children. From the monuments it is known that she was Great Royal Wife to both Ankhkheperure Neferneferuaten and Ankhkheperure Smenkhkare Djoserkheperru (who most probably were one and the same).

But who was Smenkhkare? He either succeeded Akhenaten with an independent reign of one-to-three years, or shared a short coregency with him during the elder king's last years — or was both Akhenaten's coregent and successor, but only wearer of the Double Crown for a maximum total of four years. The skeletal remains from

Kings' Valley Tomb 55, which are almost certainly his, suggest that Smenkhkare was in his early twenties when he died — although some have estimated the age of death of the individual in question as high as forty-five years. Even if he was as young as twenty at death, it is unlikely that Smenkhkare was a son of Akhenaten (but chronologically not impossible). More probably he was a son of Amenhotep III (by Tiye or Sitamen?) and, thus, Akhenaten's younger brother or half-brother. As such, he would have been in line to succeed Akhenaten only if the latter had no son (i.e., Tutankhaten). Thus, since he did succeed his brother, it may be presumed that Tutankhaten/amen was the son of someone other than Akhenaten (allowing that Smenkhkare was not, in fact, a son of the latter, born when he was still crown-prince).

It has been commented on by some experts that the cranial morphologies of Tutankhamen and the individual found in KV55 are so similar that they were probably brothers. If both Smenkhkare and Tutankhamen were the sons of Amenhotep III, by the same or different mothers (Tiye or Sitamen), this similarity would be explained: they *were* brothers. Likewise, if Smenkhkare (unlikely) and Tutankh-

Another Winifred Brunton imaginary portrait, with the subjects being Amenhotep III & his King's Great Wife Tiye, as they may have appeared towards the end of the king's 39-year reign. A minority of scholars of the period hold the view that there was a coregency of up to a dozen years between the third Amenhotep & his successor Amenhotep IV/Akhenaten. If so it would have been possible for the elder king to have fathered Prince Tutankhaten in Year 10 or 11 of his coregent's reign. But who would the prince's mother have been in such an instance? The most logical choice is Queen Tiye, a lock of whose hair was found in Tutankhamen's tomb. This memento has been seen as indicating a special relationship between the boy-king & Amenhotep III's highly influential consort. But would Tiye, in her mid/late forties, have been too old to bear a fourth son to her husband?

Brunton, *Great Ones of Ancient Egypt*, 1929

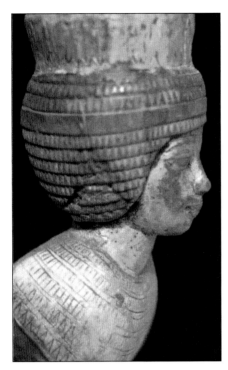

Might Amenhotep III's daughter/wife, Princess-Queen Sitamen, have been the mother of Tutankhamen in an incestuous union with her father/husband? There is no inscriptional or other evidence to link the boy-king to Sitamen — seen above in one of the pair of gilded wood busts of her decorating the throne-like chair she donated to the grave goods of her maternal grandparents, Yuya & Thuyu. Author's photo

amen (more possibly) were the sons of Akhenaten, they *were* brothers (although, it is never postulated *who* Smenkhkare's mother might have been in such a relationship). But, what if Tutankhamen was the "bodily son" of *King* Smenkhkare? Would the similar cranial morphology between two brothers (with likely different mothers) be any greater than that between a father and his son?

Aside from cranial morphology correspondences between Smenkhkare and Tutankhamen, what else might be cited to relate them as father and son? The name of Akhenaten's coregent appears on several minor objects found in KV62. But, more importantly, there is the matter of the the tomb's major pieces of funerary equipage which seem to have once belonged to Smenkhkare and were appropriated and reinscribed for his successor: the quartzite sarcophagus, the gilded and inlaid Second Coffin, possibly the calcite canopic chest and its portrait-head stoppers, and certainly the solid-gold coffinettes which held Tutankhamen's viscera. When Smenkhkare's burial in the Royal Wadi at Akhetaten was dismantled early in Tutankhamen's reign, for removal to Waset and semi-anonymous reinterment in Kings' Valley Tomb 55, it seems evident that his kingly Osiride equipage was placed in storage — perhaps with the full intent that it would be re-inscribed for his son's eventual use. That Tutankhamen's own demise was premature and unanticipated made it certain that the Smenkhkare equipment, ready at hand, was required for that purpose.

Back to Meritaten. While there is no inscriptional evidence (known to date) to link her in a mother-son relationship with Tutankhamen, there certainly exists a piece of circumstantial evidence which suggests some sort of special affinity between the boy-king and Akhenaten's eldest daughter. It will be remembered that an ivory paintinging palette inscribed for Meritaten was found in the Treasury

Yellow-quartzite portrait thought to depict Ahkenaten in the modified style of his late reign. Musée du Louvre

Scholars who do not allow for a long coregency between Amenhotep III & Akhenaten, assign the latter as Tutankhamen's father. Great Royal Wife Nefertiti is never offered as the boy-king's mother; rather Akhenaten's shadowy second wife, Kiya, is put forth for that role. A badly damaged relief in the Royal Tomb at El Amarna (drawing, right) depicts what may be Tutankhamen's birth & Kiya's death, representing as it does an infant being carried by a nurse from a chamber where Akhenaten & Nefertiti seemingly mourn over a prostrate female lying on a bed (not seen here). Kiya's disappearance from the monuments at Akhetaten in Year 10 or 11 of Akhenaten's reign coincides with when Tutankhamen would have been born. Author's graphic

of Tutankhamen's tomb. Since palettes belonging to the king, and other writing equipment as well, also were found among his grave goods, it would seem that Tutankhamen was not only literate but, in fact, something of a writer himself. It would have been appropriate, then, to have kept the palette belonging to his mother as a memento — a token of the woman who had, perhaps, encouraged his own scribal skills in the first place. Certainly this possession of Meritaten's was left in the tomb in a manner indicating that it was regarded as something special, having been placed between the paws of the Anubis figure atop the portable shrine-chest found positioned just inside the open doorway of the Treasury.

  Tutankhamen's parentage probably never will be determined to Egyptologists' satisfaction, and the boy-king will always remain an individual from antiquity about which so much is known, and yet so little. That he found himself suddenly Lord of the Two Lands at the tender age of nine or ten would seem to be confirmed by the depictions of him in his tomb as a juvenile ruler (particularly the two tiny gold and silver statuettes of him atop gilded staves). Other non-tomb images of Tutankhamen (or of him in the guise of Amen-Re) likewise show him to have been a young juvenile when he began to wear the Double Crown.

  When Tutankhamen married his Great Royal Wife (the only woman whom he seems to have wed) is not known, but presumably it was before or soon after his coronation. Her identification is undebated: Ankhesenpaaten, the third eldest daughter of Akhenaten and Nefertiti. Depending on who his father was, she was Tutankhamen's niece (Amenhotep III), half-sister (Akhenaten) or aunt (Smenkhkare). Whichever, in all probability she was her young husband's senior by as many as six or eight years, likely having been born soon after her father's accession as king. When Tutankhaten changed his nomen to Tutankhamen, she also abandoned the Aten element in her own name and became Ankhesenamen. Unless the depictions of the couple interacting together on objects from the tomb are pure fabrication — or artistic convention left over from the preceding Amarna period — there seems to have been genuine affection between the boy-king and his older-woman wife. Their efforts at beginning a family were futile, if the two fetal mummies in the tomb are to be identified as their daughters. Howard Carter suggested that the small floral wreaths found encircling the cobra/vulture emblems of Tutankhamen's

No certain portrait of Kiya in the round exists, but she may be represent-ed in two very similar plaster studies (one seen above) found by German excavators in the sculptor Thutmose's workshop at El Amarna. Both depict a pleasant-featured young woman wearing large earrings, who does not have the facial features associated with the other royal women of Akhetaten.

Berlin Ägyptisches Museum

To the several candidates put forth as Tutankhamen's parents should be added two who are seldom considered for those roles: King Ankhkheperure Smenkhkare Djoserkheperure and his queen, Meritaten, eldest daughter of Akhenaten & Nefertiti. Seen at right in the famous uninscribed relief plaque now in Berlin, this royal couple would have been mature enough in Year 10 or 11 of Akhenaten's reign to have parented Prince Tutankhaten — Meritaten being in her early teens & Smenkhkare only a little older.

Berlin Ägyptisches Museum

267

Tutankhamen claimed to be a "king's bodily son," & Smenkhkare — probably to be seen above left in a plaster study from El Amarna — was king of Egypt for up to four years, part of which time he was co-regent with Akhenaten, a position he would not have held if the latter king had had a son to associate himself with on the throne. Because of his apparent age, it seems more likely that Smenkhkare was Akhenaten's brother than his offspring.

Meritaten — above right, in another plaster sculptor's study from El Amarna — is linked circumstantially to Tutankhamen by the fact that her ivory painting palette was found in his tomb, conspicuously placed between the outstretched front paws of the Anubis figure resting on the shrine-like chest just inside the entry to the Treasury. This could very well have been a memento the boy-king kept of the mother who encouraged his writing skills, but whose name was no doubt proscribed by the time he reached his teenage years.

Both Berlin Ägyptisches Museum

First and Second coffins were the farewell gifts of his grieving still-young widow.

A few things about Tutankhamen beyond familial relationships can be gleaned from the contents of his tomb. It would appear that he was not averse to wearing elaborate gold jewelry, including large ornate earrings, baroque pectorals and bracelets encrusted with inlays of semi-precious stones. He apparently enjoyed playing board games and may have collected walking sticks and staves. Perhaps taking after his ancestor Amenhotep III, Tutankhamen was something of a sportsman, judging from the extensive archery equipment, throw sticks and boomerangs interred with him, and scenes of him fishing and fowling depicted on the small golden shrine and the ivory chest. And he apparently loved racing the several lightweight chariots he took to the Afterlife, as seen in the representations of him hunting lions and other desert fauna from such a vehicle — on the painted chest, a fan stock and his bow case. Whether Tutankhamen personally ever went into full-scale battle is problematic, but he did own a leather cuirass, bronze scimitars and defensive shields, plus numerous self and composite bows. And he is shown fighting his Nubian and Asiatic enemies from his chariot — again, on the painted chest from the Antechamber.

How or why Tutankhamen died young is not known. There has been speculation that he was murdered through the agency of one of his non-royal successors, Ay or Horemheb.[146] But the slim circumstantial evidence put forth for this is not convincing to the present writer. Instead, it seems very possible that one of his beloved char-

268

iots very likely was the instrument of his demise. In short, a chariot accident may have taken teenage Tutankhamen's life. The large lesion on his mummy's left cheek (which seems to have begun to scab over prior to death) could have been sustained in a fall from his speeding chariot; so too, the possible trauma that may possibly exist at the back of his mummy's skull.

Whatever the exact circumstances of Tutankhamen's death, the fact is that his demise was premature and his tomb and full funerary equipage were not ready. It is generally agreed by Egyptologists with an opinion on the matter that a royal-scale sepulcher was being prepared for the young king in the western branch of the Royal Valley, where Amenhotep III had chosen to situate his tomb (WV22), breaking from the tradition of his Thutmosid predecessors, all of whom were buried in the eastern or main branch. This tomb, today numbered Western Valley 23 (WV23), originally may have been begun for Amenhotep IV, with early work on it being terminated when the latter changed his name to Akhenaten and moved his court to Middle Egypt, where a new capital was under construction and a joint tomb for the king and his immediate family was being excavated.

Work on WV23 resumed when Tutankhamen came to the throne and the royal necropolis at Akhetaten was abandoned, along with the "Horizon of the Sun Disk" itself. But the new king was a minor and apparently there seemed to be no rush to complete his sepulcher. In fact, when Tutankhamen died in Year 9 of his reign, probably little more than the long entry corridor had been hewn. Thus those re-

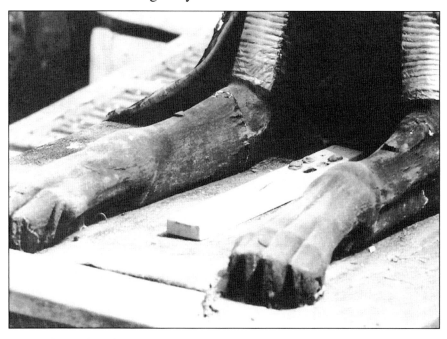

The peculiarly placed in situ *ivory painting palette of Meritaten, found resting neatly aligned between the forelegs of the jackal figure atop the Anubis Shrine situated just inside the doorway to the KV62 Treasury (Above* Griffith Institute*). While this certainly might have been placed there by the necropolis officials reordering the tomb following the second break-in, it seems more probable that this object was originally so prominently positioned, instead of having been deposited in one of the chests found in the Treasury — where Tutankhamen's personal writing gear was discovered. Is it possible, then, that those who buried the young king meant to acknowledge a special relationship between him and the Heretic's eldest daughter?* Cairo Egyptian Museum

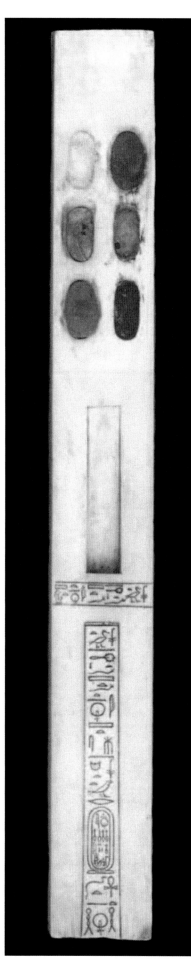

269

sponsible for interring the dead king had to decide whether to bury Nebkheperure in a wholly inappropriate passageway, or to find some substitute site.

Tomb 55 in the Royal Valley — which had been made available to receive the transferred burial of King Smenkhkare — very likely was in the process of being hewn for the God's Father Ay, so that he could lie in proximity to his (putative) parents, Yuya and Thuyu. When he gave up this unfinished sepulcher for the reinterment of his royal relation, he in all probability began a new burial place for himself, only a few yards away from KV55: the tomb today known as KV62. The latter two-chambered site was clearly nearing completion when, suddenly, Tutankhamen was dead and required a "mansion of eternity" in only seventy days time.

Through court intrigues that can only be guessed at, Ay himself was declared the new Horus, and thus he became responsible for burying his predecessor, the Osiris Nebkheperure Tutankhamen. As Lord of the Two Lands now, Ay no longer had personal use for the modest non-kingly tomb he had all but finished in the Royal Valley; so it was obvious that Tutankhamen's immediate need for a suitable (if not exactly royal scale) "mansion of eternity" could be satisfied if Ay once again gave up his own tomb (the third he had begun for himself) for its employment by of one of his royal relatives. It need not be thought that he was substituting his non-royal tomb for Tutankhamen's regal one because he deviously coveted the latter for himself; rather the decision to inter the dead boy-king in KV62 was a purely practical one: WV23 was totally inadequate in its preliminary state of execution for Tutankhamen's final resting place. Ironically, though he would indeed be buried in WV23, Ay's short reign of only some four years did not permit this last of his tombs to be finished on the grand scale which had been established by the earlier rulers of his dynasty. In fact, despite its long entry corridor, WV23 is comprised of just three chambers: a truly modest anteroom and an only slightly larger, low-ceilinged storeroom opening off the burial chamber — which, had the tomb been finished, itself would have been only one of the antechambers.

Even more ironically, Ay's repose in WV23 was apparently brief. It appears that his burial was dismantled and desecrated soon after his interment, no doubt at the order of his successor, Horemheb. His likenesses and titularies painted on the walls of the burial chamber were purposely mutilated (along with those of his Great Royal Wife, Tiy) and his mummy apparently destroyed — all in an attempt to wipe out his eternal existence. Ay's association with the "Criminal of Akhetaten" had been too imtimate and he became one of Amenhotep III's four successors (Akhenaten, Smenkhkare, Tutankhamen and Ay) whose names were removed from the kings lists and their memories officially damned.

Even though Tutankhamen's very existence was thus proscribed, his tomb and mummy somehow escaped desecration. Although it had been partially robbed twice and reordered in turn by

Winifred Brunton's imaginary portrait of King's Great Wife Ankhesenpaaten/Ankhesenamen, the only known spouse of boy-king Tutankhamen. The third daughter of Akhenaten & Nefertiti, she would have been a few years older than her husband, who also would have been either her uncle, half-brother or nephew, depending on who his parents were. She is known to have survived Tutankhamen & possibly to have married his successor, Ay — who also would have been a relative, likely her great-uncle. Ankhesenamen disappears from the historical record following Tutankhamen's funeral.

Brunton, *Great Ones of Ancient Egypt*, 1929

270

necropolis officials (almost certainly during the reign of Horemheb), Tutankhamen's burial nonetheless was never officially dismantled and the young king's mummy destroyed — despite all of the recyclable bullion the tomb contained. Its entry stairwell filled in, its location was apparently forgotten; and when, several generations later, rock debris from the cutting of the Tomb of Rameses VI was deposited on top of the hidden entrance, Tutankhamen's final resting place remained safe from the official dismantling of the Valley of the Kings burials during the Twenty-first Dynasty.

For thirty-three centuries the royal youth reposed undisturbed, cocooned in his golden mask, three coffins, sarcophagus and four tabernacles, and surrounded by a multitude of *"wonderful things,"* official and personal, that had marked his brief existence, waiting for the advent of two foreign "barbarians," a lord and his steadfast liege, who would tear down the blocked doorway and enter the silent, darkened chambers of this obscure boy-king's modest "mansion of eternity," thereby assuring that his name and fame would be known and celebrated throughout a vast world that Nebkheperure Tutankhamen could not have dreamed would exist one day; and the young *"Ruler of Waset"* would truly "live again" for the rest of recorded time.

In a detail of one of the vignettes from the painted wooden chest found in the Antechamber of KV62 (Internet photo), King Tutankhamen is seen charging Asiatics in his chariot. That he is shown steering the vehicle with reins wrapped around his hips has been suggested by some Egyptologists to be purely an artistic convention: in reality there would have been a driver in the chariot with the king, but to depict him would have cluttered the scene & diminished Pharaoh's own superhumanity.

Might Tutankhamen have been accidentally thrown from a speeding chariot, sustaining injuries which ultimately proved fatal? Such an explanation for his premature death & antemortem injuries to his body makes more sense than scenarios of his murder by conspirators at his court. Internet photo

NOTES

1. The elderly and ailing Davis's personal involvement with the Valley ended in 1912, although his expedition completed one additional season of work in 1913.
2. This is catalogued by Georges Daressy in Davis's *The Tombs of Harmhabi and Toutânkhamanou* (London, 1912), 125-135, as follows: (1) Uninscribed funerary statuette of a high-status male, in calcite, 23.5 cm. high; (2) Piece of gold leaf en-

The ka *of Ay, the only image of the king in his tomb, WV23, which was not defaced when it was dismantled & desecrated, & Ay's mummy in all likelihood destroyed, very probably on the orders of his successor, Horemheb. Almost certainly WV23 had originally belonged to Tutankhamen.*

George B. Johnson photo

Opposite, A life-size granite statue of a mature Nebkheperure Tutankhamen, as he must have appeared towards the end of his life, at about age 18. This is one of a pair found in the Karnak Cachette during the early 1900s. Author's photo

graved with two bound captives, an Asiatic and a Nubian; (3) Piece of gold leaf engraved with scene of Ay in his chariot drawing his bow, and includes his prenomen and nomen cartouches; (4) Piece of gold leaf engraved with a depiction of Tutankhamen smiting a Libyan captive between saluting figures of *"the Divine Father Ay"* and Great Royal Wife Ankhesenamen, with cartouches of both king and queen; (5) Piece of gold leaf engraved with scene of three foreigners saluting the prenomen and nomen cartouches of Ay; (6) Piece of gold leaf engraved with scene of a seated king in *khepresh*, drawing a bow; (7) Piece of gold leaf engraved with human-headed lion trampling a fallen enemy; (8) Piece of gold leaf engraved with cartouches of Tutankhamen and Ankhesenamen; (9) Piece of gold leaf engraved with prenomen and nomen cartouches of Tutankhamen, flanked by crowned *uraei*; (10-14) Pieces of gold leaf engraved with floral designs; (15) Various small scraps of gold leaf engraved with the pre-royal name and titles of Ay, and with his cartouches; (16) Eighteen miniature gilded-bronze *uraei*; (17) Four calcite knobs, probably from clothes chests; (18) Two faience furniture knobs, one with Ay's prenomen; (19) Faience furniture knob; and (20) Piece of linen with ink inscription written in Year 6 of Tutankhamen's reign. Daressy remarks that the gold leaf when found had been *"torn into small pieces, crushed or made into pellets"* (125). In his *Valley of the Kings* (London, 1990), Nicholas Reeves proposes that much of this gold leaf had originally served as veneer decoration for two chariots and associated harnessing (73). He believes Daressy's knobs (no. 17) were yoke-saddle finials and knob no. 19 was the finial from a whip. Reeves speculates that the KV58 materials may be *"workshop debris"* resulting from a reburial of Ay, perhaps in the nearby Tomb of Horemheb (KV57) — which was found to contain several anonymous skeletons (75).

3. This was the view of Daressy (*Harmhabi and Touatânkhamanou*, 125); but since the statuette was found directly on the floor of KV58, under some three feet of flood debris, it might be argued that it belonged to the original owner of the pit tomb (who was not likely Citizen Ay).

4. This precise date is given by Reeves in his *Valley of the Kings* (69), although Davis wrote in *Harmhabi and Touatânkhamanou* (3) that the pit cache (KV54) was found *"a few days after"* the discovery of KV58, the date for which is given by Reeves as *"early January 1909."* Davis, writing from memory in February 1912, clearly confused the dates and order of the discoveries of KV54 and 58. John Romer in his *Valley of the Kings* (New York, 1981) narrates the sequence of these discoveries according to Davis (219-224).

5. Which became KV54 in the Valley numbering scheme.

6. Such as those found with the viscera of Thuyu in KV46; see Chapter Four, p. 144; also Chapter Seven, p. 322.

7. Romer, *Valley of the Kings* (221), relates that Davis had used the jars to entertain the new British consul-general in Egypt, Sir Eldon Gorst, when the latter paid a visit to the Valley of the Kings and then lunched at Davis House. At least one of the large vessels had previously been opened by Davis, to reveal the small gilded-cartonnage mask; apparently the American therefore presumed that similar small treasures in the other jars would sufficiently impress the British bureaucrat (in addition to the jewelry from the so-called "Gold Tomb"). Jar after jar was opened for Gorst's benefit, all producing nothing but funerary rubbish; when Gorst left that afternoon, Davis purportedly turned his disappointment on Ayrton, blaming the young assistant for the jar-opening demonstration's failure to suitably impress his departed guest. Subsequently Davis is reported — by Romer (222) — to have used several of the floral funerary wreaths from the KV54 cache to entertain guests at Davis House dinner parties, by personally tearing them apart with his bare hands — solely to demonstrate how strong they still were some thirty-three centuries after their fabrication.

8. Winlock, however, did not formally publish the KV54 miscellany until nearly two decades later, in H.E. Winlock, *Materials Used at the Embalming of King Tut-ankh-Amun* (New York, 1941). According to his inventory, the cached KV54 materials included: (1) Twelve to fifteen identical whitewashed ovoid ceramic pots — averaging 71.0 centimeters in height, with mouths 35.0 cm. in diameter — six of which are preserved in the Metropolitan Museum collection;(2) Six mud impressions of ring or scarab seals, broken from tomb furniture, and five pats of dried mud, probably

Above, below & opposite, Details of the Antechamber clearance.

left over from sealings which had gone into Tutankhamen's tomb; (3) Numerous miscellaneous pieces of linen cloth, ranging from sizeable fringed sheets (one 32.0 by 94.0 cm., another 61.0 cm. by 2.44 m.) to bandage fragments and odd rags used to wipe up the embalming shop; (4) Three linen kerchiefs (two white, one blue), which would have been worn as wig covers; (5) Four dozen small linen bags (of a greater original number by at least double), which contained chopped straw and natron, and were used in the mummification/desiccation process; (6) Five cloth cylinders (100.0, 85.0 and 75.0 cm. long), sewn on one end and side and tied at the other end, each filled with natron, and their use unknown; (7) Two curious small cloth bags filled with natron, having pairs of tapes at each end; (8) A string of miniature linen sacks filled with chaff, perhaps some sort of charm: (9) Between forty and fifty (judging from the number of fragments found) unbaked gray earthenware, roughly rectangular trays, averaging 15.0 cm. long, 7.0 cm. wide and 3.0 cm. high; (10) A miniature mummy mask of cartonnage (15.0 cm. high) painted yellow all over, with details in blue, red, black and white pigment, of the sort associated with canopic viscera bundles during the New Kingdom; (11) A score of odd sticks of reed, papyrus and wood, all perhaps used as probes, five wrapped with linen, two coated with papyrus pith, and several charred from burning; (12) A wooden tenon, a couple of pieces of limestone and a number of square, fairly well-polished limestone blocks (all of which remained in Egypt and were not part of Davis's gift to the Museum); (13) Twenty-five jar lids of different sorts and materials, from food containers and embalming vessels, both of the latter now missing; (14) Seven small cups of reddish-brown pottery labeled in hieratic in black ink; (15) Sixty-five similar cups which are uninscribed, the lot probably *"token offering pots"*; (16) A flat-bottomed, spherical, double-handled ceramic wine jar, with cylindrical neck and flared lip; (17) Four wine bottles with oval bodies and long, thin necks and flared mouths, three plain red, one decorated with painted floral patterns on the shoulder and neck in black, blue and red; (18) A set of four ovoid ceramic bottles, with wide, straight-walled necks, decorated on the exteriors with a dark-red hematite slip; (19) Eight drinking cups made of light-brown clay, rounded on the bottoms with flared mouths, covered on the exteriors with dark-red, highly polished hematite slip; (20) Eight identical jars and drinking vessels of red or light-brown clay, slipped with red hematite, six decorated around their shoulders with a garland design in blue pigment; (21) Four fragmentary whitewashed tall, almost shoulderless pottery jars; (22) Two undecorated clay vessels similar in shape to the drinking cups [no. 19], but much larger; (23) Three small pottery jars of various shapes; (24) A few chips from a painted bowl, decorated with a band of garlands and a large rosette on its interior; (25) A dish-shaped plate covered inside and out with a thick whitewash; (26) Sixty-one pottery dishes of varying shape, size (ranging from 9.0 to 46.5 cm. in diameter) and color, which also may be described as bowls, plates or saucers, most of which have a fine dark-red, polished hematite wash; (27) The shoulder and connecting bones of a cow, four ribs of a sheep or goat, and bones of nine ducks and four geese, which were the remnants of a funerary feast; (28) The surviving three of an original half dozen or more floral-and-leaf collars which had been worn by the funeral banqueters, the others wilfully destroyed by Theodore Davis; (29) and Two brooms (one of reeds, the other of grasses) that had been used to sweep the sand in order to remove the footprints of the funeral guests.

Winlock remarked in *Materials* (18) that — while the embalming leftovers from KV54 were similar to like stuff known from Theban caches dating *"at least as early as the Eleventh Dynasty and as late as the end of the pagan period"* — the remnants of a last funerary banquet had not been found before those discovered in the Tutankhamen cache. He surmised that this meal had been partaken of by at least eight persons, and *"consisted of meat and fowl, and probably bread and cakes, and that it was washed down with copious draughts of wine or beer and water."* Winlock concluded, *"at the end, as the eight people...withdrew from the room, their footprints were swept away and the door was closed. Whether or not this gathering up of the remains of such a meal is to be considered an innovation of the period of the heresy, I know of no other trace of it. But then we must always remember that this is probably the only known cache of its kind belonging to a king"* (18).

It should be remarked that the yellow-painted miniature cartonnage mask which was given with the embalming/banquet materials by Davis to the Metropolitan (no. 10 in Winlock's inventory) was apparently the American's substitution for the one actually found in KV54. This was gilded cartonnage and is today in the Egyptian Museum, Cairo, erroneously displayed in a wall vitrine with the miscellany of small objects found in the so-called "Amarna Cache" (KV55); see p. 310. Nicholas Reeves in his *Complete Tutankhamun* proposes that this is the "missing" mask which should have accompanied the mummified remains of the more developed fetus found in the KV62 Treasury.

9. See note 7 above.

10. For a detailed account of this turning point in Carter's professional career — indeed, in his life — see T.G.H. James, *Howard Carter: The Path to Tutankhamun* (London, 1992).

11. Despite the sincere urgings to do so by his Service superior, Maspero, and his former employer, Theodore Davis.

12. E.g., for F.W. von Bissing's *Ein thebanischer Grabfund aus dem Anfang des Neuen Reiches*; the Marquis of Northampton's *Report on Some Excavations in the Theban Necropolis*; and J.R. Buttles's *The Queen of Egypt*.

13. Davis paid Carter £15 each for the fourteen watercolor images (total £210) he commissioned as illustrations for *The Tomb of Youiyou and Thouiyou*. The artist was ultimately most unhappy with how his paintings were reproduced in the Davis volume, and he complained bitterly to his friend, Percy E. Newberry, in a letter of September 29, 1907. For this see Nicholas Reeves and John H. Taylor, *Howard Carter Before Tutankhamun* (New York, 1992), 85.

14. Albeit not your run-of-the-mill tourists: T.G.H. James in his Carter biography (see note 10 above) offers a list of the persons Carter accompanied to Deir el Bahari on February 5, 1906, which includes the American financier Frank Jay Gould of New York and his wife, as well as French princes Louis and Antoine de Orleans, and members of their entourage (*Carter*, 129-130).

15. As recounted in an extract of an autobiographical sketch by Carnarvon. Reeves and Taylor, *Before Tutankhamun*, 86.

16. For a full account of Lord Carnarvon's 1907 excavation season, see the Earl of Carnarvon and Howard Carter, *Five Years' Exploration at Thebes* (London, 1912; reprinted Brockton, MA, 1996), 12-21, 34-37.

17. As if in anticipation of Carter's Egyptological resurrection, in the early spring of 1908 Maspero allowed the financially destitute watercolorist and tour guide to move back into the unoccupied old Antiquities Service house at Medinet Habu, which had been Carter's "castle" during his years as chief inspector at Luxor (James, *Carter*, 142).

18. From Lady Burghclere's introduction to Howard Carter and A.C. Mace, *The Tomb of Tut·Ankh·Amen*, Vol. 1 (New York, 1963), 30.

19. Carter photographed the painted wall decorations of the Tomb of Tetiky for the volume. T.G.H. James suggested that this may have been done even before Carter was finally engaged by Carnarvon (*Path to Tutankhamun*, 147).

20. As remembered by Percy E. Newberry some thirty-four years later (1947) in a letter to philologist Alan H. Gardiner (Reeves and Taylor, *Before Tutankhamun*, 105).

21. Carter thought it was Diospolis Parva, ancient Paiwenamen, the capital of the Seventeenth Nome in Lower Egypt, Smabehdet (ibid., 105-106).

22. Later (1992) reassessment by a British Museum expedition has identified this structure as a Twenty-sixth Dynasty fort (ibid., 106).

23. Ibid., 110.

24. As reported by the sixth Earl of Carnarvon, who once said in a speech, *"Carter proved very apt at this business and I have heard* [my father and him] *talk of many good deals that they brought off in this fashion...."* Ibid., 114.

25. For Carter's full report on this tomb (numbered AN-B) and its excavation, see his article, "Report on the tomb of Zeser-Ka-Ra Amen-Hetep I, discovered by the Earl of Carnarvon in 1914," *Journal of Egyptian Archaeology* 3 (1916), 147-154.

Above, below & opposite, Details of the Treasury clearance. Griffith Institute/Internet photos

26. Plus the problematic "Amarna Cache," KV55, which had contained the mud sealings of Tutankhamen.

27. Carter and Mace, *Tut·Ankh·Amen* I, 78-79.

28. Ibid., 79.

29. Carter's interest in the Amenhotep III site seems to have been sparked by the purchase he had made for Carnarvon in 1912 of three bracelet plaques believed to have come from that tomb, as a result of Harry Burton's investigations around WV22 for Theodore Davis the same year.

30. In fact, Carnarvon's official permit to dig in the Valley of the Kings was not signed until April 18, 1915, by Georges Daressy, who was operating on behalf of the newly appointed director-general of the Antiquities Service, Pierre Lacau (Carter's mentor and benefactor, Gaston Maspero, having retired the previous year for health reasons, and returned to France). James, *Path to Tutankhamun*, 174.

31. Indicating that WV22 was begun for Thutmose IV, who clearly abandoned the site for a tomb in the main branch of the royal necropolis, KV43, which Carter had found and cleared for Davis in 1903.

32. Carter and Mace, *Tut·Ankh·Amen* I, 79.

33. James, *Path to Tutankhamun*, 176.

34. Ibid.

35. For Carter's own account of the circumstances leading up to and surrounding this adventure and discovery, see Carter and Mace, *Tut·Ankh·Amen* I, 79-82.

36. Ibid., 82. 37. Ibid. 38. Ibid., 82-83. 39. Ibid.

40. James, *Path to Tutankhamun*, 197.

41. Carter and Mace, *Tut·Ankh·Amen* I, 83.

42. Ibid., 84-85.

43. KV42, certainly early Eighteenth Dynasty in date, and undoubtedly royal in scale for that time, had once contained the burial of Sennefer, a mayor of Thebes under Amenhotep II. Clearly this was an appropriation approved by that king, of a royal sepulcher which stood unused. But for whom had it been hewn? The presence of Queen Meritre-Hatshepsut's foundation deposits not withstanding, there is the view that unfinished Tomb 42 originally was meant to be the final resting place of Thutmose II, inasmuch as it seems to fit rather nicely in the evolution of New Kingdom royal-tomb architecture between the putative original sepulcher of Thutmose I (KV38) and that of Thutmose III (KV34). Besides, no other tomb is identified with the second Thutmose; which does not answer the question of where he was buried if not in KV42.

44. In writing and speaking about the discovery of the Tomb of Tutankhamen, Carter never told the full story of this decisive June 1922 meeting with Carnarvon, especially his proposal to keep digging in the Valley of the Kings at his own expense. It is revealed by Charles Breasted in the biography of his father, James Breasted, *Pioneer to the Past* (New York, 1943), 328-329.

45. Carter and Mace, *Tut·Ankh·Amen* I, 87.

46. Ibid., 88. 47. Ibid. 48. Ibid., 89-90. 49. Ibid., 90.

50. Ibid., 91. 51. Ibid., 93.

52. Callender (1876-1936) was a British engineer and architect. He retired as manager of the Egyptian branch of railways in 1920 and settled in a house he had built at Armant, becoming a friend of Carter as a consequence. He was responsible for overseeing the building of the original Chicago House on the west bank at Luxor, and worked on excavations with Walter Emery, Sir Robert Mond and Victor Adda. He died at Alexandria.

53. Carter and Mace, *Tut·Ankh·Amen* I, 94. Apparently no photographs were made either of the passageway clearance in progress or of the miscellaneous objects found in the fill, *in situ* or later. Harry Burton's services as Carnarvon's and Carter's official photographer had not yet been acquired. When the existence of the wooden sculpture of a child's head on a lotus flower was made known (see Addendum One, "The Chronology of KV62," pp. 543-544), this was, of course, properly recorded by Burton.

54. Ibid., 95-96. Carter's *"Yes, wonderful things"* is perhaps the most evocative state-

ment in the entire history of archaeology; but his biographer T.G.H. James points out that the famous phrase may be the result of some editing by Carter's co-author of the first volume of *The Tomb of Tut· Ankh·Amen*, Arthur Mace. The excavator's own journal account has him replying to Carnarvon's inquiry, *"Yes, it is wonderful"* (Griffith Institute, Carter Notebook 1); whereas Carnarvon himself wrote of the moment (in an unpublished account preserved in the Metropolitan Museum of Art archives) that he asked his colleague, *"Well, what is it!?"* to which *"There are some marvellous objects here"* was Carter's reply.

55. From Carnarvon's fragmentary manuscript at the Metropolitan mentioned in note 54.

56. As stated in an interview with the London *Times* following the revelation of the quartzite sarcophagus within the nest of golden tabernacles. Thomas Hoving, *Tutankhamun: The Untold Story* (New York, 1978), 267.

57. For the full account of the secret exploration of the tomb the evening following the opening of the doorway to the Antechamber, see James, *Path to Tutankhamun*, 224-226.

58. Carter and Mace, *Tut·Ankh·Amen* I, 99-101.

59. Ibid., 102.

60. Ibid., 105. Carter rather overstates the case, inasmuch as both James Quibell and Ernesto Schiaparelli had been confronted with similar (if less extensive) challenges in their clearances of the considerable contents of KV46 (Yuya) and TT8 (Kha) several years earlier (1905 and 1906).

61. Ibid., 106. 62. Ibid., 107.

63. Ibid., 108. While Lythgoe's offer was generous, it probably was not without ulterior motive. During the years prior to, during and following World War I, both Carter and Carnarvon had had a close association with the Metropolitan Museum's Egyptian Department, in the acquisition of objects offered on the antiquities markets of Luxor and Cairo. Thus Lythgoe reasonably may have anticipated that — in exchange for the assistance of the Museum's Egyptian Expedition experts — the MMA later might be the beneficiary of the Earl of Carnarvon's own generosity: i.e., be given objects from his lordship's expected share of the Tutankhamen treasures. In fact, Lythgoe reported to Edward Robinson, director of the Metropolitan, that Carnarvon had personally assured him that the Museum would be *"well taken care of."* James, *Path to Tutankhamun*, 234-235.

63. Harry Burton (1879-1940), British photographer and archaeologist.

64. James, Ibid., 233.

65. Lindsley Foote Hall (1883-1969), American draughtsman.

66. Walter Hauser (1893-1959), American architect and archaeologist.

67. Arthur Cruttenden Mace (1874-1928), British Egyptologist.

68. Alfred Lucas (1867-1945), British chemist.

69. (Sir) Alan Henderson Gardiner (1879-1963), British Egyptologist and philologist.

70. James Henry Breasted (1865-1935), American Egyptologist and orientalist.

71. Carter and Mace, *Tut·Ankh·Amen* I, 127-128.

72. Ibid., 130. 73. Ibid.

74. This list is adapted from Helen Murray and Mary Nut, *Objects in Tut'ankhamun's Tomb* (Oxford, 1963), 4-5.

75. Carter and Mace, *Tut·Ankh·Amen* I, 134.

76. Ibid., 135.

77. One docket called for *"17* [unnamed objects] *of lapis lazuli color."* In the box were sixteen dark-blue faience libation vases, with a seventeenth located some ways off on the floor of the Antechamber. Ibid., 136.

78. In order to maintain the duplicity of that first night exploring the entire tomb, Carter necessarily feigned ignorance regarding the further state of the tomb vis-a-vis the tomb robbers in his first published volume on the tomb. Thus the balance of the present scenario is constructed from his remarks in volume three of *Tut·Ankh·Amen*, regarding the Treasury as found.

79. Although Carter gives the February 17th date in his first volume on the tomb, his biographer, T.G.H. James, places this event on February 16th (*Path to Tutankhamun*,

Above, below & opposite, Details of the Burial Chamber & Annexe clearance.

247), which is repeated by Nicholas Reeves in his *Complete Tutankhamun* (64, 210).

80. They included Lord Carnarvon, Lady Evelyn Herbert, H.E. Abd el Halim Pasha Suleiman (Minister of Public Works), Pierre Lacau (director-general of the Antiquities Service), Sir William Garstin, Sir Charles Cust, Albert Lythgoe, James H. Breasted, Alan Gardiner, Herbert H. Winlock, Reginald Englebach (chief inspector of the Department of Antiquities), Mervyn Herbert, Richard Bethell, three unnamed Egyptian Antiquities Service inspectors, an unnamed representative of the Egyptian Government Press Bureau, and Howard Carter and his staff (Burton, Mace, Lucas, Callender, etc.).

81. Carter and Mace, *Tut·Ankh·Amen* I, 179.

82. Ibid., 179-180. 83. Ibid., 185-186.

84. Or February 17th. See note 79 above.

85. Although Carter wrote "Alexander" in *Tut·Ankh·Amen* I (186). It is recorded elsewhere that the Belgian prince's name was Leopold.

86. In the biography of his father, *Pioneer to the Past*, Charles Breasted wrote that in a final argument Carter ordered his patron to leave his house (Carnarvon's money having paid to build "Castle Carter") and never enter it again (347). Which the earl did and did not.

87. Carter, *Tut·Ankh·Amen* II, 40.

88. Ibid. 89. Ibid., 44-45. 90. Ibid., 40-41. 91. Ibid., 48-49.

92. This group included Mohamed Zaghlûl Pasha and the (unnamed) governor of Qena Province, E.S. Harkness, James Breasted, the chief inspector of Antiquities for Upper Egypt, Albert Lythgoe, Percy Newberry, Alan Gardiner, Herbert Winlock, Norman de Garies Davies, Dr. Douglas Derry, Robert Mond, Georges Foucart, Bernard Bruyère, John Jacob Astor, Richard Bethell, the (unnamed) assistant curator of the Cairo Museum and Carter's associates, Mace, Callender, Lucas and Burton. Ibid., 50-51.

93. Ibid., 51-52.

94. Looped over these emblems was a delicate wreath composed of olive leaves and blue cornflowers braided together. Carter believed this had been a farewell offering made to Tutankhamen by his grieving widow at the close of the funeral ceremonies. He wrote, *"Among all that regal splendor, that royal magnificence — everywhere the glint of gold — there was nothing so beautiful as these few withered flowers, still retaining their tinge of color"* Ibid. 53.95. Ibid., 71 96. Ibid., 72. 97. Ibid., 73. 98. Ibid., 76-77

99. Ibid., 78. 100. Ibid., 79. 101., Ibid. 102., Ibid., 82-83. 103. Ibid., 83. 104. Ibid., 86.

105., Ibid., 86-87. See Appendix Four, "Abusing Pharaoh," p. 703, for the possible consequence of this *"trial."*

106. Ibid., 107. 107. Ibid., 108-109. 108. Ibid., 124.

109. The Middle Kingdom diadem is that of princess Sit-hathoriunut found by Flinders Petrie at Lahun; the Seventeenth Dynasty example belonged to an Atef king and was found by Theban tomb robbers in the mid-Nineteenth Century, eventually ending up in the Leiden Museum. A third diadem — also Seventeenth Dynasty — is mentioned in the records of the time of Rameses XI as having been among the objects stolen from the Tomb of Sobekemsaf.

110. The right side of the mummy's head was apparently not photographed in the cotton-batting setting, so its condition upon unwrapping cannot be known. In his remarks on the plates for the Griffith Institute "Tut™ ankhamun's Tomb Series" he authored (Volume V, *The Human Remains from the Tomb of Tut™ ankhamun*, 1972), F. Filce Leek wrote, *"The lobe of the right ear appears to have been detached along with the bandages, while the top of the left ear was broken* 111. Ibid., 8. 112. Ibid., 9.

113. Carter's diary entry for November 27th-December 14th. Ibid., 8

114. When assembling the canopy and shrine following Tutankhamen's interment, the necropolis workers misoriented two of the side panels of the shrine proper, vis-a-vis their relationship to the free-standing three-dimensional figures of the protective goddesses, so that the statuette of Nephthys faces the panel depicting Selket and

Qebhsenuef, and that of Selket faces the scene of Nephthys and Hapy.

115. These lids are thought by some scholars to represent a king other than Tut-ankhamen, although this conclusion is based solely on the fact that the facial features of each lid do not resemble the other certain portraits of the young king found in his tomb. If another king's, the obvious candidate is, once again, Smenkhkare.

116. Carter believed the two prematurely born infants (one certainly stillborn) probably to have been the ill-fated issue of Tutankhamen and Ankhesenamen (*Tut·Ankh·Amen* II, 88). This is a view subscribed to by most scholars of the post-Amarna period, although it has been proposed that the two fetuses' presence in the tomb was ritual in context (in some way connected to Tutankhamen's rebirth) rather than due to their personal relationship to the king himself. There are other examples of Eighteenth Dynasty royal children predeceasing their father and being interred in his tomb (i.e., those of Amenhotep II and Thutmose IV).

117. Carter was of the opinion (*Tut·Ankh·Amen* II, 89) that a small gilt-cartonnage mummy mask found by Theodore M. Davis in the Tutankhamen-related cache pit number KV54 (see this chapter, p. 322) had originally been intended for this infant mummy, but proved to be too small and so was discarded along with other refuse associated with Tutankhamen's mummification and funerary ritual (meal).

118. In his definitive (to date) popular study of KV62 and its contents (*The Complete Tutankhamun*, London and New York, 1990), Nicholas Reeves remarks that the second and larger of the fetal pair was examined by Prof. R.G. Harrison of the University of Liverpool (124); and he reproduces an x-ray of same (124), which purportedly reveals the condition known as Sprengel's Deformity (congenitally high scapula, spina bifida and scoliosis). Exactly when Harrison made this examination and x-ray is not indicated by Reeves; but it was that British anatomist's colleague, F. Filce Leek, who reported — in his 1972 *The Human Remains for the Tomb of Tut'ankhamun* (the Griffith Institute's "Tut'ankhamun's Tomb Series") — that the KV62 fetuses could not be located by Harrison and himself for the purpose of autopsying and x-raying (23).

119. Victor Loret had found several fragmentary deity and king figures in the Tomb of Amenhotep II (see Book One this series); Carter found ones in similar condition in KV43, the Tomb of Thutmose IV; and the Tomb of Horemheb, cleared under Theodore M. Davis, yielded yet additional, if fewer, examples. The chief difference between these and the KV62 assembly — aside from the fully intact condition of the latter — was the use of gilding on all but two of Tutankhamen's complete set, whereas the chronologically earlier and later royal ritual figures had all been coated in a thick layer of black pitch, without the benefit of even gold detailing. Gold and black have the same funerary-context color value, however, both symbolizing regeneration and rebirth.

120. Carter, *Tut·Ankh·Amen* III, 52.

121. For a detailed discussion of this problem, see Claude Vandersleyen, "Royal Figures from Tut™ankhamun's Tomb: Their Historical Usefulness," *After Tut'ankhamun: Research and Excavation in the Royal Necropolis at Thebes* (N. Reeves, ed., London, 1992), 73-81.

122. By a joint British-Dutch expedition under the direction of Geoffrey T. Martin. See his *Hidden Tombs of Memphis* (London, 1991).

123. Carter, *Tut.Ankh.Amen* III, 82.

124. Ibid., 83.

125. A great many of the royal *ushabtis* which have survived from the New Kingdom could be said to be rather crudely executed (e.g., those of Thutmose III, Amenhotep II, Thutmose IV, Seti I, Siptah, etc.), so the fact that numerous ones of Tutankhamen's worker substitutes are less than elegant would seem to have been the rule rather than the exception.

126. The fragmentary framework of such an "Osiris bed" was found in KV35 (Amenhotep II; see Chapter Two, p. 80) and a more complete one — quite similar to Tutankhamen's (if devoid of its soil and germinated grain) — survived in the debris littering KV57 (Horemheb). Cruder (non-royal) versions of the "Osiris bed" were also found in the Valley of the Kings tombs of Maiherpri (one example) and of Yuya and Thuyu (two examples; one for each tomb occupant, apparently).

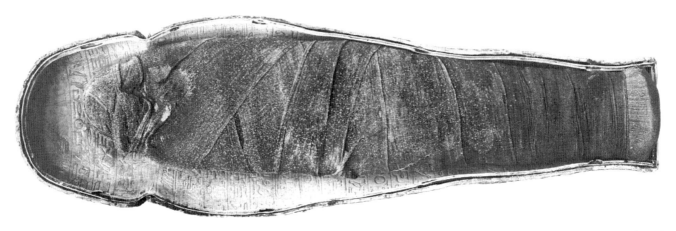

One of Tutankhamen's wrapped viscera bundles, resting within the basin of its solid-gold coffinette. Griffith Institute

In addition to the scenes of Tutankhenamen & Great Wife Ankhesenamen together on the small gold shrine, the gold throne & the inlaid ivory casket, there is the above ink depiction of them on one end of a game board found in the Annexe. Internet photo

The second of two similar feline-head appliqués found in chest No. 21. Made of gilded wood with crystal, glass & calcite inlays, it is associated with the fragment of a priestly robe sewn with tiny gold stars. Internet photo

127. The best known examples — indeed, the very best examples — are those found by the Metropolitan Museum of Art Egyptian Expedition in 1920, in the early-Twelfth Dynasty Tomb of Meketre at Thebes. See this author's article, "The Middle Kingdom Tomb Models of Vizier Meketre," *Kmt* 6:3 (fall 1995), 25-39.

128. Carter, *Tut·Ankh·Amen* III, 64.

129. Ibid., 70.   130. Ibid.

131. The parts of these two chariots (Nos. 332, 333) were jumbled together in much the same fashion as had been the three more elaborate "state" chariots and one hunting vehicle found in the Antechamber. They were both of light construction and apparently undecorated, save for leather side panels, which had largely decayed away. Carter wrote in the notes accompanying his sketch reconstructing the probable original appearance of the panels, *"the few fragments that remain of this leather covering show that it was highly coloured and decorated."* See Reeves, *Complete Tutankhamun*, 172.

132. This is inscribed to *"The king's son, the troop commander Thutmose, who repeats life."* Who was this Thutmose and what was his relationship to Tutankhamen? One guess is that he was a son of Thutmose IV and a younger brother of Amenhotep III, making him a probable uncle of one degree or another to the boy-king. More likely he was Crown-Prince Thutmose, the apparent eldest son of Amenhotep III and Queen Tiye, who was a high-priest of Ptah at Mennufer (Memphis) and whose premature death brought Amenhotep IV/Akhenaten to the throne, ultimately. In which case he would have been either Tutankhamen's elder brother or uncle, who died many years before the young king was born.

133. Carter, *Tut·Ankh·Amen* III, 98-99.

134. Ibid., 102-103.

135. Ibid., 106. Carter likewise suggested that the single large *ushabti* discovered positioned next to the small gold shrine in the Antechamber originally had been housed in one of the broken *ushabti* boxes in the Annexe (where others similar to it were found), and that it had been taken into the Antechamber by one of the thieves for no reason.

136. Ibid., 111.   137. Ibid., 115.   138. Ibid., 116.   139. Ibid., 118.   140., Ibid., 119.

141. The fact that these elaborate robes were found to have been treated so roughly suggests that they originally had not been in the box which contained them, and further likens the possibility that some straightening up of the Annexe had occurred after all, probably following the initial break-in of the oil-and-unguents thieves — at which time the headrests also were gathered up and placed together in the chest where Carter found them.

142. Carter, *Tut·Ankh·Amen* III, 130.

143. Ibid., 133-134.   144. Ibid., 134.

145. The "Tut'ankhamun's Tomb Series" at this writing consists of: (1) H. Murray and M. Nuttall, *A Handlist to Howard Carter's Catalogue of objects in Tut'ankhamun's Tomb*; (2) J. Cerny, *Hieratic Inscriptions from the Tomb of Tut'ankhamun*; (3) W. McLeod, *Composite Bows from...*; (4) W. McLeod, *Self Bows from...*;

(5) F. F. Leek, *The Human Remains from...*; (6) L. Manniche, *Musical Instruments from...*; (7) W.J. Tait, *Game-Boxes and Accessories from...*; (8) M. A. Littauer and J.H. Crouwel, *Chariots and Related Equipment from...*; and (9) D. Jones, *Model Boats from....* In press or forthcoming are: A.A-R.H. el-Khouli, R. Holthoer, C.A. Hope, O.E. Kaper, *Stone Vessels, Pottery and Sealings from...*; and A. Dodson, *The Coffins and Canopic Equipment from....* Also published by the Griffith Institute, in the same format but for some reason not included in the "Tomb Series" are: M. Eaton-

When the tabernacles sections had been removed from the KV62 Burial Chamber, it was noticed that there were four small plastered-over rectangular areas, one on each of the chamber's walls. Discovered behind these were four small objects, which had protective powers: Left to right above, An Osiris figure (No. 257); an Anubis jackal figure recumbent on a shrine (258); a wooden ushabti-like figure on a base (259); & a wooden djed *emblem (260).* Internet photos

Above, The gilded-wood lion-form bier which supported the great weight of Tutankhamen's coffins within the sarcophagus Griffith Institute *& Detail of one head.*

Author's photo

281

Krauss and E. Graef, *The Small Golden Shrine from...*; M. Eaton-Krauss, *The Sarcophagus in the Tomb of Tutankhamun*; and H. Beinlich and M. Saleh, *Corpus der Hieroglyphischen Inscriften aus dem Grab des Tutanchamun.*

146. As argued by Bob Brier in his *The Death of Tutankhamen: A True Story* (New York, 1998), where he posits Ay as the young king's murderer.

ADDENDUM ONE

The Chronology of the Tomb of Tutankhamen and Its Discovery

The following chronology of KV62 is adapted from four sources: *T.G.H. James,* Howard Carter: The Path to Tutankhamun *(London and New York, 1992); Nicholas Reeves,* The Complete Tutankhamun *(London and New York, 1990); Thomas Hoving,* Tutankhamun: The Untold Story *(New York, 1978); and Howard Carter's three-volume work,* The Tomb of Tut·Ankh·Amen.

Coregency of Amenhotep III/Amenhotep IV, c. 1365-1353 BC

Soon after being elevated to the throne alongside his father, Amenhotep IV commences a tomb for himself in the western branch of the royal necropolis at Waset (Thebes), where Amenhotep III's own tomb (today numbered WV22) is nearing completion. Work on Amenhotep IV's site (WV23) ceases when, in Year 8 of the coregency, that king — having embraced the exclusive worship of the sun disk and renamed himself Akhenaten — moves his court to a new capital, "Horizon of the Disk" (Akhetaten) located in Middle Egypt, where another royal tomb is begun.

Reign of Tutankhamen, c. 1343-1334 BC

After Tutankhamen has returned the capital to Mennufer (Memphis), following his accession to the throne at age nine or ten, he appropriates for himself the tomb begun by Akhenaten in the western branch of the Theban royal necropolis (WV23), resuming work on the site for use as his use as his own "mansion of eternity." In Year 9 of his reign (c. 1334 BC), the youthful Tutankhamen is critically injured, at eighteen or nineteen years of age (in a chariot accident?), and subsequently dies. Work on WV23 has not progressed beyond the long entry passage and the tomb is not suitable for the dead king's interment. Tutankhamen's successor, a non-royal relative named Ay, offers as a substitute his own nearly finished private tomb (KV62), also in the royal necropolis, which he has been preparing close by the tomb (KV46) of his parents, the royal in-laws Yuya and Thuyu. A yellow-quartzite sarcophagus originally prepared for his predecessor, Smenkhkare, but not used, is taken from storage and recarved for Tutankhamen, then introduced into KV62. The sarcophagus lid is damaged in the process and a replacement is hurriedly carved from granite. The king's canopic chest and enclosing baldachin/shrine are placed in a side room off the burial chamber. In March 1334 Tutankhamen's funeral rites take place, with King Ay presiding and performing the Opening of the Mouth ceremony. The nest of coffins and royal mummy are installed in the sarcophagus. When the latter's replacement lid is lowered into place, this cracks across its middle and must be repaired with plaster. Funerary furnishings are placed in the burial chamber side room. A nest of four gilded-wood tabernacles i erected around the sarcophagus and a partition wall is built; then the decoration of the burial chamber's four walls is executed. This space is blocked off and plastered, then stamped with the seals of Tutankhamen and the royal necropolis. A small side

Opposite, An artist's fanciful depiction of Antechamber objects being removed from KV62 in 1923. Internet photo

room off the antechamber is stocked with preserved food offerings, including wine and oils; and objects belonging to the king which would not fit in the burial chamber side room are installed here as well. The doorway to this chamber is blocked. The remainder of Tutankhamen's grave goods are introduced into the antechamber and its doorway is blocked, plastered and stamped. A few objects are left in the entry corridor, and its doorway is likewise sealed and stamped, the exterior stairwell being filled in with sand and rock debris. The interment of Osiris Nebkheperure Tutankhamen is completed.

Reign of Horemheb, c. 1330-1305 BC

At some point in the twenty-five-year reign of Tutankhamen's second successor, Horemheb, probably within the first five years, robbers remove part of the stairwell fill of KV62, break a hole in the outer doorway blocking, traverse the empty entry passage, break through the blocked doorway at its end, and enter the antechamber. These thieves are seeking valuable oils and unguents primarily, although anything portable of precious solid metals would be carried off as well. They penetrate the blocking to the entrance of the antechamber side room and ransack this space, emptying the several calcite vessels stored there of their liquid contents, pouring these into leather bags brought along for that purpose. Their colleagues, meanwhile, search the antechamber for portable solid metal, dumping the contents of chests and boxes onto the floor in the process. Possibly an alert is given by one of their cohorts who has remained outside the tomb on the lookout for necropolis guards, and the robbers quickly abandon the tomb with what loot they have gathered.

The break-in is discovered, the KV62 stairwell is emptied of its fill and necropolis officials — perhaps under the direction of one Maya, Tutankhamen's, Ay's and Horemheb's chief treasurer — put the ransacked chambers back in order, if somewhat hurriedly so, without real concern for returning dumped objects to their original containers. The robbers' hole into the antechamber side room is left gaping open. The doorway to the antechamber is repaired and its exterior replastered and restamped with necropolis seals. The entry passageway is filled with rock rubble, burying the few objects which litter its floor. The hole in the entry door is reblocked and replastered and stamped. The stairwell is filled in with rock debris and the "mansion of eternity" of Osiris Tutankhamen hidden once again.

But sometime later, perhaps years later, a determined group of necropolis thieves penetrate the tomb once again, clearing out most of the stairwell fill, making a hole in the outer doorway (in the same spot that the earlier thieves had broken through), tunneling along the blocked corridor just beneath its ceiling, and breaking into the antechamber (again through the repaired hole made by the earlier thieves). One or two of them make for the side room — which their torches reveal is invitingly standing open — and totally ransack the space a second time in a search for solid precious metals. While members of the gang begin to dump the contents of boxes and chests in the antechamber onto the floor, rummaging through the resulting piles of miscellany for portable solid gold, silver, etc., a couple more pry out stones at the bottom of the plaster-sealed large doorway at one end of the room, and crawl through the resulting hole into the burial chamber, making their way past the huge tabernacle nearly filling the space to the side room which is standing open. Once in this chamber, they open and ransack chests stored there, many of which contain the dead king's personal inlaid-gold jewelry.

Possibly their foray is cut short at this point by the arrival of necropolis guards, and the nefarious band is forced to flee with their bags of loot.

Once again those responsible for the royal cemetery enter the violated Tomb of Tutankhamen, this time having to gain access via the robbers' tunnel. Because the antechamber side room is in such a state of total chaos that there is not even any floor space in which to stand, the officials make no attempt to reorder the small room, nor do they bother to reblock the breach in its low doorway. The burial chamber side room is tidied up, the breach in the doorway between the burial chamber and antechamber is refilled with the blocks pried out by the robbers, but not replastered. The antechamber is neatened up again, and its door is resealed and replastered and stamped again. The tunnel in the corridor is filled in. The outer door is resealed, re-plastered, restamped, and the tunnel in the stairwell blocked with rock debris. KV62 is hidden once more — and its location this time forgotten.

Reign of Rameses VI, c. 1151-1143 BC

Workmen quarrying the Tomb of Rameses VI (KV6) construct stone huts directly over the buried entrance to the Tomb of Tutankhamen, totally unaware of what lies only a few meters below ground level.

The Twenty-first Dynasty, 1070-945 BC

The many burials in the Valley of the Kings, royal and non-royal, are officially dis-mantled by the revenue-poor government of the priest-kings ruling southern Egypt from Waset (Thebes). Most likely all of these already have been extensively robbed, but the effort is made to recover as much bullion as may remain among the debris of the tombs, in the form of gilding, gold leaf, etc. The Royal Mummies and others are recovered, rewrapped and recoffined, and placed together in at least two caches (DB320 and KV35). Four tombs escape this wholesale dismantlement, however, their locations having been forgotten: the Tomb of Maiherpri (KV36); the Tomb of Yuya and Thuyu (KV46); the reburial of Smenkhkare, the so-called "Amarna Cache" (KV55); and, of course, the Tomb of Tutankhamen (KV62).

1922 AD

November 1

English archaeologist Howard Carter commences one final season excavating in the Valley of the Kings on behalf of his patron, George Edward Stanhope Molyneux Herbert, the fifth Earl of Carnarvon. The two have been working Lord Carnarvon's exclusive concession in the Valley of the Kings since 1917, specifically seeking the location of the yet undiscovered burial place of the little-known Eighteenth Dynasty king Tutankhamen. Previous holder of the Valley concession, American Theodore M. Davis, believed he had come upon that site in 1909, a pit tomb which was num-bered KV58. Carter, however, was convinced that the latter was not a royal sepulcher and that Tutankhamen — whose remains were not among those royal mummies lo-cated in 1881 and 1899 — waited to be found. Three seasons had been spent without much to show for the effort and expense involved, and Carnarvon was ready to aban-don the seemingly fruitless project. Carter was determined to lay bare one last area of a triangular section in the central part of the Valley's main wadi, which he had been clearing to the bed rock. This was just below the entrance to the Tomb of Rame-ses VI (KV9), and was covered by the remains of stone huts built by the tomb cutters who had worked on the latter site in the middle of the Twelfth Century BC. Carnarvon acquiesced and agreed to finance Carter for one more season of digging in the Valley. On November 1, 1922, removal of the workmen's huts begins.

November 4

A step cut in the bedrock is uncovered. Carter is certain he has found a tomb and or-ders his workmen to clear away the mass of rubble overlaying the area.

November 5

Removal of the rubble continues and the upper edges of a stairwell are revealed. Step by step this is cleared until it becomes a roofed-in passageway, at the end of which the upper portion of a plastered doorway is uncovered, the visible area being stamped all over with the jackal-and-prisoners seal of the royal necropolis. Carter makes a small hole at the top of this doorway and observes that a rubble-clogged passageway lays beyond it. It is by now nightfall and he orders the stairwell completely refilled for protection.

November 6

Carter cables the following message to Carnarvon in England: *"At last have made wonderful discovery in Valley; a magnificent tomb with seals intact; re-covered same for your arrival; congratulations."*

November 8

Carter receives wire from Carnarvon, stating that the earl plans to arrive in Alexandria on the 20th.

November 18

Carter travels to Cairo to meet Carnarvon.

November 21

Carter returns to Luxor.

November 23

Lord Carnarvon arrives in Luxor, accompanied by his daughter, Lady Evelyn Herbert. They are greeted by Carter and the governor of Qena Province.

November 24

By the afternoon the whole stairwell of the tomb Carter has discovered is once more cleared and the entire plastered doorway is revealed. On the lower portion of the latter — which Carter had not uncovered earlier — stamped impressions bearing the nomen of Tutankhamen are discovered. Chief inspector of the Antiquities Service Reginald Engelbach arrives and witnesses the final clearance of rubbish from in front of the doorway. Carter orders a heavy wooden grille to be put in place to secure the latter, which he plans to take down the next day.

November 25

In the morning the seal impressions on the doorway are recorded and photographed. The stones forming the blocking are taken down and the rubble-filled descending passageway is revealed. Clearance of this corridor begins and by the end of the work day a considerable length has been freed up without encountering another doorway or the sign of a chamber.

November 26

Clearance of the corridor resumes in the morning and by the middle of the afternoon, some thirty feet from the outer door, a second sealed and stamped doorway is reached. Carter makes a tiny breach in the upper-lefthand corner of the blocking and candle tests for foul gases are conducted. Carter, with the aid of a candle peers through the hole and is *"struck dumb with amazement"* at what he beholds in the space beyond. When an anxious Carnarvon asks him if he can see anything, Carter purportedly replies, *"Yes, wonderful things."*

Lord Carnarvon, & his daughter, Lady Evelyn Herbert, at KV62 in late November 1922. Internet photo

The hole is enlarged and an electric lamp is inserted, revealing a largish, undecorated rectangular room very crowded with a multitude of objects large and small, many of them with the *"glint of gold."* The breach is further enlarged and the small party of excavators — Carter, Carnarvon, Lady Evelyn and Carter's first assistant, Arthur Callender, clamber through, entering the rectangular space which will be dubbed, appropriately, the "Antechamber." The four intruders thoroughly explore the room and its amazing contents, discovering as they do a gaping opening near the floor near a corner of the room. Through it their electric lamp reveals another, much smaller chamber beyond, this one so filled with a chaotic jumble of furniture and a miscellany of objects that no floor space is visible.

At the other end of the chamber — between two life-sized statues of a king, positioned in opposite corners facing each other — they determine that there is yet another plastered and stamped doorway. At the bottom of this, they notice that some of the blocking stones are loose, and Callender and Carter pry these out, so that an open space is revealed beyond, and what appears to be a wall of gold inlaid with blue tiles. Callender is too large to wiggle through this small breach, but the others, including Lady Evelyn, managed to crawl into what they soon determine is the tomb's decorated burial chamber. The rectangular, high-ceilinged space is all but filled, wall to wall, floor to ceiling, by an enormous shrine-shaped gilded-and-inlaid structure, with double doors at one end. Carter identifies this, no doubt, as likely the outermost of a series of "shrines" surrounding the tomb owner's sarcophagus.

In one corner of this chamber they come to a low doorway which is standing open. Flashing their lamp into the darkness, they behold yet another room, this also filled with objects, especially a tall golden shrine-like structure, which Carter probably suggests to his companions holds the king's canopic chest. They have decided, by now, that indeed they have found the seemingly intact burial of Nebkheperure Tutankhamen, the ephemeral late-Eighteenth Dynasty ruler for whom Carter and Carnarvon have been searching for five years.

But the hour is getting late, and the explorers squeeze back into the Antechamber, rejoining Callender waiting for them. He and Carter replace the loose stones, thereby once again blocking the doorway to the burial chamber, and they further disguise the presence of this breach by heaping loose reeds and a basket lid over it. The four leave the tomb, the outer doorway secured by the heavy wooden grille.

Returning to his house, Carter writes a note to Chief Inspector Englebach, inviting him to be present when the tomb is (officially) entered the next day.

November 27
In the morning Callender lays electric wiring into the tomb and Carter makes notes regarding the seal impressions, which will necessarily be destroyed when the door blocking is taken down. Englebach is away from Luxor, so in his place a local Antiquities inspector, Abraham Effendi, is in attendance when the doorway is removed block by block and the Antechamber is entered by the same quartet who had already secretly explored the tomb the night before.

November 29
The tomb is officially opened. In attendance besides Carnarvon and company are Lady Allenby (standing in for her husband who is in Cairo), the governor of Qena Province, the *mamour* of the district, and a number of other Egyptian notables and officials, as well as the correspondent for the London *Times*.

November 30
Pierre Lacau, director-general of the Antiquities Service. makes his official inspection of the Antechamber, attended by Paul Tottenham, adviser to the Ministry of Public works. The first reports of the tomb's discovery appear in the *Times*.

December 3
The entrance doorway secured with heavy timbers, the tomb's stairwell is once again filled to the surface level.

December 4
Lord Carnarvon and Lady Evelyn Herbert depart Luxor to return to England.

December 6 - 15
Carter travels to Cairo to make purchases of various materials (including an automobile) which will be required when clearance of the tomb begins upon Carnarvon's return to Egypt later in the month. He orders a steel gate to be made for the doorway to the Antechamber. While in Cairo (on the 6th or 7th) he receives a congratulatory cable from Albert Lythgoe, curator of the Egyptian Department of the Metropolitan Museum of Art; to which Carter replies, asking if he might borrow the services — *"for the immediate emergency, at any rate"* — of the Museum's Egyptian Expedition photographer, Harry Burton. Lythgoe responds in the affirmative and also offers Carter the assistance of any of the other members of the Expedition staff as he may need. Carter likewise manages to recruit the services of Alfred Lucas, who is just retiring as director of the Chemical Department of the Egyptian government. The steel gate is finished on the 13th and Carter returns to Luxor the next day. His purchases, including gate and automobile, arrive by train on the 15th.

December 16
The tomb stairwell is recleared and the tomb reopened.

December 17
The steel gate is installed by Callender.

December 18
Burton takes his first experimental photographs of the Antechamber. Metropolitan draughtsmen Lindsley Hall and Walter Hauser start making their plan of the space and its contents.

December 20
Lucas arrives in Luxor and at once begins experimenting with preservatives to be used with various classes of objects when they are removed from the tomb.

December 22
Bowing to clamor from the Egyptian and world press, Carter permits several native notables of Luxor to view the Antechamber, persons who had not received an invitation to the official tomb opening on November 29.

December 25
Arthur C. Mace of the Metropolitan Egyptian Expedition arrives in Luxor from Lisht,

Howard Carter (l.) accompanies Director of the Antiquities Service Pierre Lacau, as they exit KV62 following the Frenchman's first inspection of the tomb on November 30, 1922.

Egyptology Archives of the University of Milan

Above, below & both opposite, The removal of objects from the Antechamber in late February 1923 is captured in snapshots by a tourist on hand for the occasion. The items were then carried to the lab set up in close by KV15 (Tomb of Seti II), to be conserved & packed for shipping to Cairo.

where he had been working, to join Carter's team of experts.

December 27

The first of Tutankhamen's treasures is removed from KV62, the delicately painted wooden chest, object No. 21. It is carried on a specially prepared wooden tray to the Tomb of Seti II (KV15) some distance away. This large sepulcher has been allotted to Carnarvon by Pierre Lacau as a laboratory and storehouse, where the KV62 objects will be cleaned and conserved by Mace and Lucas, prior to the packing of these for eventual shipment to the Egyptian Museum in Cairo. Burton has been given use of Tomb 55 (the so-called "Amarna Cache") for his darkroom.

1923

January 9

In England Lord Carnarvon signs a fateful contract granting *The Times* of London exclusive rights to coverage of the clearance of the Tomb of Tutankhamen. He writes to Carter the next day, informing him of the decision, which he made without consulting the archaeologist. When this arrangement becomes public, there is a great outcry of protest from the Egyptian and world press.

January, 1923

Clearance of the Antechamber continues, as do protests about *The Times* situation

January 29

Lord Carnarvon and Lady Evelyn return to Luxor. Relations between earl and archaeologist appear strained.

Early February

Clearance and conservation continue. Arthur Mace writes in his diary that the *"Carnarvons are rather a nuisance"* and that *"Carnarvon makes all sorts of complications by doing things without thinking of the consequences."* He also notes that Carter seems on the verge of a nervous breakdown.

February 17

Dismantlement of the sealed doorway between the Antechamber and the rest of the tomb reveals the Burial Chamber and Treasury, the existence of which was already known by Carnarvon and company. In attendance for this event are: Lord and Lady Allenby; three Egyptian princes; the ambassadors to Egypt from France, Belgium and America; five ex-prime ministers of Egypt; three additional Egyptian officials; the *mudir* of Qena; the Herberts (Carnarvon, his daughter and brother); Sirs Charles Cust, William Garstin, John Maxwell and Alan Gardiner; Richard Bethell; Albert Lythgoe; Herbert Winlock; Arthur Merton of *The Times*; Pierre Lacau; Reginald Engelbach; James Breasted and his son Charles; Howard Carter and his associates (Burton, Mace, Lucas, Callender); three anonymous Egyptian inspectors of Antiquities; an unidentified representative of the Egyptian government; an unnamed representative of the Egyptian Press Bureau; and numerous Egyptian workmen.

February 18

Elisabeth, Queen of the Belgians, and her son, Prince Leopold, visit the Valley of the Kings and Tutankhamen's tomb.

February 22

Carter and Carnarvon reportedly have a heated exchange, and the archaeologist orders his long-time patron out of his house, telling him never to return.

February 26

The first season working in KV62 comes to an end. The tomb is closed and the stairwell is filled in.

February 27

The laboratory in KV15 is closed up. The clearance team disperses, Mace accompanying Carnarvon to Aswan the next day, as his guest. Carter shuts himself into his house to get some rest and quiet. Members of his team believe he is about to succumb to the nervous breakdown that has been pending in their view.

February 28

Either before or soon after his arrival in Aswan, George Herbert, Lord Carnarvon, is bitten on his cheek by a mosquito. He later inadvertently opens the swollen bite while shaving, thereby causing an infection and a fever to set in.

March 14

Having rejoined his daughter, Evelyn, in Cairo, then suffering a relapse following a momentary recovery from his fever, Carnarvon checks into the Continental-Savoy Hotel. His condition progressively worsens, with delirium resulting.

March 26

Almina Herbert, the Countess of Carnarvon, arrives in Cairo from England, to join her grievously ill husband.

April 5

In the early hours of the morning, the fifth Earl of Carnarvon, age fifty-seven, dies in his suite at the Continental-Savoy, Lady Carnarvon, his daughter and son (Lord Porchester) at his bedside. Purportedly at the moment of his death, the electric lights of Cairo are extinguished. Far away in England, the earl's three-legged terrier also suddenly drops dead at this same time. These bizarre coincidences quickly prompt a press rumor that Carnarvon is the victim of a "Pharaoh's Curse."

April 14

Carnarvon's embalmed body leaves Cairo to be returned to England, where it will be buried on the grounds of the family estate at Highclere.

April 16

Howard Carter returns to Luxor from Cairo, where he has been throughout the duration of his patron's illness. He turns his full attention to concluding the previous season's work, such as completion of conservation of the objects already removed from KV62 and their packing, and making arrangements for the security of the tomb over the coming summer. Carter still has with him Mace, Burton, Lucas and Callender.

May 14-15

Thirty-four packing cases containing eighty-nine boxes are transported from the Tomb of Seti II in the Valley of the Kings to the Nile bank, where they are loaded onto a river steamer in the presence of Chief Inspector Engelbach.

May 16-21

The steamer departs Luxor for Cairo and is met by Carter er at Cook's Wharf.

May 22-24

The crates are unloaded from the steamer and transported to the Egyptian Museum, where most are unpacked and the Antechamber objects immediately put on display.

May 25

Carter departs Egypt to return home to England.

June 16, June 23-July 2

Carter twice visits Highclere Castle to assist as he may Carnarvon's widow, Almina, in the settling of his late patron's estate, especially regarding the latter's collection of Egyptian antiquities, of which Carter was ostensibly the curator. Doubtless during these visits he discusses with Lady Carnarvon the future of the Valley of the Kings concession and the clearance of the Tomb of Tutankhamen. He is assured by her that she has every intention of continuing her husband's work there the following winter season.

July-September

Working with his colleague Arthur Mace, Carter completes the first volume of *The Tomb of Tut·Ankh·Amen*. Although on the surface seemingly written by Carter in the first person, the book in fact is largely the product of Mace's prose. It is published in the fall of 1923 by Cassell and Co. Also that summer several works on Tutankhamen by other authors are rushed into print, including: Sir E. Wallis Budge's *Tutankhamen, Amenism, Atenism and Egyptian Monotheism*; Jean Capart's *The Tomb of Tutankhamen*; G. Elliot Smith's *Tutankhamen and the Discovery of his Tomb by the late Earl of Carnarvon and Mr. Howard Carter*; and Arthur Weigall's *Tutankhamen and other essays*.

July 12

Pierre Lacau sends Lady Carnarvon the Egyptian Antiquities Service's authorization "*pour achever la déblaiement* ("to complete the clearance") *de la tombe de Tout. Ankh.Amon*." This permission was to remain in effect until 1 November 1924 and could be renewed if the work remained unfinished at that time. Conditions of the concession were to be the same as previously. The question of the division ("*partage*") of objects from the tomb was not addressed.

289

Additional tourist's snapshots of objects being carried from KV62 to KV15 in late February 1923. Author's collection

James Quibell

July 26

Carter attends a royal garden party at Buckingham Palace and is presented to King George V and Queen Mary. The king tells the archaeologist that he does not want the mummy of Tutankhamen removed from the tomb.

September 10

The Royal Scottish Geographical Society hosts Carter's first public lecture on the Tomb of Tutankhamen, given in Edinburgh to an audience estimated at over 3,000. He shows 145 color and black-and-white lantern slides of the Antechamber and its objects.

September 21

Carter's second lecture on the tomb is given at New Oxford Theatre. The audience invited by Lady Carnarvon includes several of the archaeologist's professional peers, among them Flinders Petrie, Percy Newberry, Sir Alan Gardiner and Arthur Mace. Carter shows motion-picture footage as well as his lantern slides.

October 3

The archaeologist departs London en route to Egypt by way of Trieste, where he meets up with members of the Metropolitan Egyptian Expedition staff.

October 8

Carter arrives in Cairo with plans to settle details concerning the fall-winter season's work at Luxor with James Quibell (about to retire as director of the Egyptian Museum), who is acting on behalf of an absent Pierre Lacau.

October 11

Carter meets with Quibell and two major problems are discussed: how news regarding the Tomb of Tutankhamen is to be disseminated; and the matter of visitors to the tomb — the frequency of visits, who shall be admitted, etc. It is decided that the London *Times* representative, Arthur Merton, will become a member of Carter's staff and will issue daily bulletins to *The Times* each evening and to the Egyptian press early the next day. Carter proposes that tourists be admitted to the tomb — whenever a convenient moment arrived and the work in the tomb could be suspended — by tickets obtained through the Public Works Ministry in Cairo.

October 12

Carter travels to Alexandria to present his proposals to the Minister of Public Works, Abd el Halim Pasha Suleiman. He is unable to meet with the minister, but is assured by R.A. Furness, the second secretary in the High Commission (which dealt with matters concerning the Antiquities Service) that Carter's proposals would almost certainly be acceptable to Suleiman and the Commission.

October 16

Carter meets in Cairo with Lacau and Quibell, and is informed that his proposals regarding Merton and visitors to the tomb has been agreed to. Lacau does not tell Carter, however, that — over the objection of the Egyptian members of the High Commission — the decision in favor of Carter had been forced by the Minister of Public Works, Suleiman, who wants no further discussion of the matter. Carter travels

to Luxor that same day.

October 18

Seventeen-hundred tons of sand and rock debris are removed from the stairwell of KV62 and the tomb is reopened. The retaining walls around the stairwell are repaired, electricity is reinstalled in the tomb's interior, and the roads leading between Tomb 62 and KV55 (Burton's darkroom) and KV15 (the laboratory/storehouse) are tidied up.

Late October

Carter receives a number of disturbing communications from James Quibell. In one the latter asks Carter to come to Cairo to assist in the unpacking of further objects from the Antechamber for display in the Egyptian Museum. In another marked *"confidential,"* Quibell informs Carter that A.H. Bradstreet, reporter for the *Morning Post,* has met with the Minister of Public Works and his undersecretary, Paul Tottenham, to protest the press arrangements which have been agreed to. As a consequence, it has been decided by the Ministry that Carter will be required to issue a daily bulletin to all newspapers and wire services, and that this will be done not later than 9:00 p.m. Quibell also confides that the minister has decided to put Egyptian surveillants in the Royal Valley to supervise Carter's work — this supposedly to avoid the criticism of his compatriots.

November 1

Bradstreet appears in the Valley of the Kings and Carter refuses to talk to him.

November 4

Carter travels to Cairo to meet, at his request, with Lacau, Quibell, Tottenham and the Minister of Public Works. The result of this meeting is a three-point agreement: (1) the Egyptian government will *"confide all duties of publication* [concerning the tomb] *to the diggers"*; (2) an Egyptian representative of the Antiquities Service will go to the tomb on a daily basis, in order to *"oversee the investigations"*; and (3) when the work of dismantling the Burial Chamber tabernacles has progressed to the point where it is *"materially practical for strangers to be admitted,"* a limited number of visitors holding dated and numbered tickets will be allowed into the tomb. There is some further discussion regarding the press situation, Lacau expresses reservations to Point 1 and the meeting is adjourned until the next day.

November 5

When the meeting resumes, Carter is angered to learn that Lacau will not sign the agreement. The Frenchman has decided that Carter should not be given the exclusive right to dispense information concerning KV62. The group decides to meet again the next day.

November 6

Carter presents Lacau, Quibell, Tottenham and the minister with a lengthy memorandum indicting the motives of the Antiquities Service and making a series of threats to expose to *"the world"* the full details of the negotiations surrounding the matter of the tomb. Tottenham agrees that Carter has made a good case; but Lacau and Quibell are both stunned and furious, and they refuse to express an opinion about

Howard Carter (l.) & Lord Carnarvon pose for Harry Burton's camera during the removal of the stone blocking wall between the KV62 Ante- & Burial chambers on February 17, 1923. Griffith Institute

Howard Carter & his team dining in the entry passage to the Tomb of Rameses XI (KV4). From Left to right" J.H. Beasted, H. Burton, A. Lucas, A.R. Callender, A. Mace, Carter & A. Gardiner. Griffith Institute

the memorandum.

November 12

After assurances over the telephone from Minister Suleiman himself that all would be settled in a satisfactory manner, Carter returns to Luxor.

November 14

Arthur Mace arrives in Luxor, carrying with him a letter from Pierre Lacau stating the points of agreement between the Ministry of Public Works and Carter. On the surface it appears that the archaeologist has won his argument; but on closer reading Carter realizes that the document is full of hedges and reservations — that everything agreed to is only *"temporary"* — and he declares it *"practically useless,"* firing off his objections in an insulting letter to Lacau. Carter insists that he be consulted in advance before any changes are made by the Antiquities Service to the three-point agreement. On receipt of this letter, Lacau is indeed insulted, regarding Carter's demands as high-handed interference with the operations of the Service; more than anything else this single communication from Carter turns Lacau fully against him.

November 16

Carter travels to Cairo to consult with the High Commissioner, Lord Allenby, regarding the matter of communiques about the tomb, visitor access, etc.; while in the capital, he grudgingly offers Paul Tottenham his own hedged acceptance of the three-point agreement.

November 17

Returning to Luxor, Carter is now ready to get back to matters archaeological, specifically, the dismantling of the gilded tabernacles in the Burial Chamber.

Late November

Work on taking apart the outermost tabernacle proceeds.

December 1

A seemingly innocuous letter is received by Carter from James Quibell, requesting that he submit a full list of all members of his staff. This appears to be the first move on Pierre Lacau's part to goad Carter into doing something rash, so rash that the director-general of the Antiquities Service will be justified in annulling the Carnarvon concession and ejecting Carter from the tomb. Carter, in fact, sees this *"extraordinary, outrageous"* government demand for the names of his staff as an attempt to disqualify and exclude *The Times* man, Arthur Merton, and thereby circumvent the press arrangements in the three-point agreement. He immediately responds to Quibell that he is *"thoroughly puzzled as to what the request can mean"* and that he is at liberty to employ whomever he wishes, as long as he adheres to the terms of the Carnarvon concession.

December 8

Lacau himself replies by letter to Carter, reiterating that the Minister of Public Works requires the list of *"all of* [Carter's] *collaborators"* so that he can exercise his right to exclude anyone who is not participating in *"scientific undertakings"* but rather only satisfying *"vain curiosity."* Lacau further states that the Egyptian government alone will grant permits for foreign visitors to the tomb, and that it will supervise all of Carter's activities and those of his staff and agents. And he emphasizes that, although the right to publish the *"scientific"* results of the tomb's clearance remained with Carter, the Egyptian government reserved the absolute right to publish at any time information of a general nature concerning the tomb and its objects. In conclusion, the director-general announces that any *"infraction or contravention"* by Carter or his people would result in the immediate cancellation of the Carnarvon concession.

December 13

Carter meets with Lacau in Luxor to discuss the matters in contention between them. Perhaps to discomfort the Frenchman, Carter has invited the Metropolitan's Lythgoe and Harkness, plus Mace and Callender, to be present for the interview. He bluntly informs Lacau that he is unwilling to accept the new official position in Cairo, considering this an encroachment on his work, and instead proposes that he continue the Tutankhamen clearance under the legal rights conferred by Lady Carnarvon's original concession. Lacau does not concede anything, telling Carter to present his views directly to Minister Suleiman; and the group goes to KV15 to inspect objects being conserved.

December 17

Carter is summoned to Cairo for a meeting with the minister and his assistant, Tottenham. It is at this time that Suleiman Pasha states directly that the root of the problem with the Ministry of Public Works and the Antiquities Service is, indeed, the presence of Merton of *The Times* on Carter's staff — who the bureaucrat emphasizes is not a scientist and cannot be disassociated from his London employer. Suleiman tells Carter that *"all difficulties"* can be resolved by Carter striking Merton's name from his list of collaborators. Carter attempts to defend the reporter, arguing that any news releases coming from him therefore have Carter's own stamp of approval. The minister refuses the flimsy logic of Carter's argument and instructs the Englishman that Merton is to be allowed in the tomb only on days reserved for the entire press corps. Carter leaves the meeting brusquely telling Suleiman that he will have to consult with his colleagues on the matter, and will reply formally in writing.

December 20

After discussing the situation with Lythgoe and the others of his associates — all of whom urge him not to concede to any of the Public Works minister's demands, or else a dangerous precedent will be set for foreign archaeologists wishing to work in Egypt — Carter dispatches a cable to *The Times* editors, warning them of the increasingly explosive situation; and he follows up the cable with a letter in which he includes all of the documents relative to the dispute. Then he sends his formal reply to Suleiman, in which he flatly notifies the minister that he cannot see his way to conform to the restrictions being imposed upon him. The same day he also writes a harsh letter to Lacau, complaining about the publication of information on the Tutankhamen objects in the official *Guide* to the Egyptian Museum, and he even threatens legal action in this regard.

Later that day, Carter receives a phone call from Paul Tottenham, who asks if he has reached a decision yet. When Carter tells him what has been decided, the bureaucrat begs the archaeologist not to send his letter to Suleiman and to reconsider his position. Carter replies it has already been posted and that he also has cabled London about the matter, thereby setting *"various machinery...in motion."* Tottenham pleads for Carter to make a small political compromise that might, in the long run, even be of benefit to himself. Carter, however, abruptly terminates the conversation.

December 23

In apparent open defiance of the Ministry of Public Works stipulation that only foreigners who have been issued a permit by the Ministry can enter the KV62, Carter invites Arthur Mace's wife, Winifred, and young daughter, Margaret, to visit the tomb. He also gives them a tour of the KV15 laboratory, so that they can see where

Almina Herbert, Lady Carnarvon (1876-1969), who continued her husband's Valley of the Kings concession. She remarried in 1923 & died at the age of 92.

La Domenica del Corriere

Anno . . . . L. 10,— L. 20,— Semestre . . . . . » 5,50 » 11,— Per le inserzioni rivolgersi all'Amministrazione del *Corriere della Sera* - Via Solferino, 28 - Milano.	Si pubblica a Milano ogni settimana Supplemento illustrato del " Corriere della Sera "	Uffici del giornale: Via Solferino, 28, Milano Per tutti gli articoli e illustrazioni è riservata la proprietà letteraria e artistica, secondo le leggi e i trattati internazionali.

Anno XXVI — Num. 8. **24 Febbraio 1924.** **Centesimi 20 la copia.**

La luce finalmente nelle tenebre trimillenarie di Tutankamen.
La scena culminante degli scavi di Luxor: il primo sguardo nel sontuoso sarcofago del re egizio.

(Disegno di A. Beltrame)

their husband and father works.

1924
January 3

With the first tabernacle and pall framework removed, and the objects which had been placed between them and the second tabernacle safely in the laboratory, Carter is now ready to open the second set of bolted and still-sealed doors, and to determine how many more such shrines surround the sarcophagus presumably within. At about 3:45 in the afternoon, with Chief Inspector Engelbach present, plus his own staff and a few chosen scholars who happen to be available (Lythgoe, Winlock, Newberry), Carter proceeds to reveal a third and then a fourth tabernacle, and, finally a massive yellow-quartzite sarcophagus, confirming that the King Tutankhamen's burial was, after all, intact. Carter formally wires Pierre Lacau that evening with news about the day's discoveries.

January 5

Lacau wires back his *"cordiales felicitations"* and asks to be informed when the sarcophagus might be opened. That same day Carter is visited by Paul Tottenham, who is the bearer of a double complaint from Minister Suleiman: that Carter has permitted another reporter from *The Times* other than Merton into the tomb; and that no Egyptian inspector was present when the Second, Third and Fourth tabernacles were opened. Carter flatly denies the first charge (which has been prompted by a malicious telegram to the minister from *Morning Post* reporter Bradstreet); and he argues that Engelbach was present for the opening, but if he had chosen not to bring along an Egyptian inspector as well, that was none of Carter's business. Tottenham returns to Cairo intending to advise his superior to take no action against the Englishman.

January 10

Lacau sends Carter a harshly worded letter which claims the right of the Egyptian Museum to publish descriptions of the Tutankhamen objects on display and implicitly states that KV62 and its contents are the sole property of Egypt — *"a part of the Public Domain"* — thereby prejudicing the possibility of a division of objects with the Carnarvon estate, once clearance of the tomb is completed. When Carter receives this letter, he calls in the services of a lawyer, F.M. Maxwell, to help him draft a response.

Latter Part of January

The Second, Third and Fourth tabernacles are carefully dismantled, the side and end panels leaned against the walls of the Burial Chamber, and the roof sections placed in the Antechamber.

It is during this same time that several of Carter's Egyptological associates begin to involve themselves in the dispute with the director-general of the Antiquities Service. Albert Lythgoe writes to the director of the Metropolitan Museum, Edward Harkness, suggesting that the American Secretary of State put diplomatic pressure on France to have Lacau removed from his appointed position. Likewise, Alan Gardiner and James Breasted, both in Luxor, are now plotting their own intervention with the Frenchman in Cairo. Enlisting the collusion of Albert Lythgoe and Percy Newberry, they draft a long, uncompromising letter to Lacau that emphasizes the danger to the scientific record of KV62 from the Antiquities Service interferences with Carter's work, and which directly attacks the director-general for what the authors consider his personal failures in the matter. This letter is taken to Cairo on January 30 by Gardiner, who then delivers it to Lacau in person. It is unclear whether Carter knows of his colleagues' intervention until after the fact.

February 3

Carter finally sends his lengthy, somewhat lofty reply to Lacau's letter of January 10. It reiterates in detail all of the points of his case and complains about the great amount of time which has been wasted on fruitless discussions — which would have better been spent on clearance of the tomb. Carter points out that between the beginning of the season, October 22, and December 17 (date of his most recent journey to Cairo) there have been fifty working days, one third of which were *"frittered away through departmental interference"* and Lacau's arbitrary demands. He charges that

Opposite, In February 1924 a Milanese newspaper reports on the opening of the gilded tabernacles which were nested around Tutankhamen's sarcophagus in the KV62 Burial Chamber. Because the Times *of London had exclusive use of Harry Burton's photographs, the article is illustrated by a color drawing depicting the scene, rather imaginatively based on Burton's black & white image.* Archival image

the Antiquities Service (i.e., Lacau) has *"ever since the death of the late Lord Carnarvon, not only been endeavoring to frustrate the rights of the Carnarvon family"* but also has *"tried to impede, hinder and delay the scientific work"* involving the clearance of KV62. Carter concludes by professing that he is at a complete loss to understand Lacau's motives, but that he has *"no doubt as to what will be the verdict of the World of Science on the issue between us."*

February 7

Summoned by Paul Tottenham, Carter travels to Cairo to meet with the new Minister of Public Works, Morcos Bey Hanna, a Nationalist who has a strong dislike for foreigners but particularly for the British. Thus Tottenham advises Carter to limit his discussion with the minister to the proposed date for the opening of Tutankhamen's sarcophagus. Carter apparently tries to abide by this advice, but Hanna — who has been irritated by a recent meddling visit from Alan Gardiner, who complained to him about the situation surrounding KV62 — raises several of the old problems. Lacau then joins the meeting, but somehow the rest of the conversation manages to focus on arrangements for the sarcophagus opening and subsequent visits by the press. A date of February 12 is settled upon for this event, press viewing on the 13th.

February 9

Carter returns to Luxor and begins to make arrangements for the official opening.

February 12

In the morning Carter meets with Pierre Lacau and Minister Hanna's representative, Mohammed Pasha Zaghlul, under-secretary in the Ministry of Public Works. The long list of those invited by Carter to attend the ceremonies later that day is reviewed and approved. Carter mentions that he plans to allow the wives of his colleagues to view the opened sarcophagus the next day, and Zaghlul expresses his surprise at this, but does not voice an immediate objection.

Just after 3:00 in the afternoon, the some twenty individuals who will witness the lid raising assemble in the tomb. The tackle is adjusted and the great (but broken) rose-granite slab forming the lid to the sarcophagus is hoisted slowly into the air, until it is suspended about two feet above the sarcophagus box. The ropes and tackle being secured, Carter and Mace roll back the shroud which covers the coffin just visible within the huge stone box. Everyone is astounded by the golden anthropoid figure which is revealed, the outermost of what will prove to be a nest of three coffins. The whole event takes approximately one hour and the entire party treks over to the Tomb of Rameses XI (KV4) for a celebration of toastings.

Late that evening, Under-Secretary Zaghlul receives a cable from the Public Works Minister Hanna forbidding the visit to the tomb which Carter has planned for the wives of his colleagues, so that they may privately view the opened sarcophagus and coffin within.

February 13

At 6:40 a.m. Carter receives word from Mohammed Zaghlul of the minister's order. Stunned he goes to Metropolitan House to confer with his museum colleagues. It is decided that Lythgoe and Mace will accompany Carter across the river to Luxor, there to attempt to see Zaghlul. En route Carter is shown two communications signed by Lacau: one repeating the refusal to allow the planned visit of the wives to the tomb and instructing the clearance team that three Egyptian inspectors are being assigned to guard KV62 and prevent unauthorized entries; the other expressing the Frenchman's regrets at the turn of events, but emphasizing that he has no choice but to see that the minister's orders are carried out.

A war council is held in James Breasted's room at the Winter Palace Hotel, with Carter, Lythgoe, Mace, Newberry, Gardiner, Breasted and others present. The regrettable situation is discussed and options considered. When it is not possible, finally, to see Mohammed Zaghlul, Carter goes to the hotel lobby and posts a fateful notice: Because of the *"impossible restrictions and discourtesies on the part of the Public Works Department and its Antiquities Service"* Carter and his collaborators refuse to perform any further work on the clearance of the Tomb of Tutankhamen; and following the viewing of the opened sarcophagus by the press that morning, the tomb will be closed and no further clearance will take place. In short Carter and company go on strike.

Carter and his colleagues return to the west bank and the Royal Valley and the tomb. As threatened, following the press viewing between 10 a.m. and noon, Carter padlocks both tomb and laboratory, leaving the stone lid of the sarcophagus poised perilously over the golden coffin with the mummy of the king inside.

February 15

Government soldiers are posted outside KV62, to make certain that Carter and his colleagues are not able to enter should they have a change of mind about their closure of the tomb. In fact, Carter does go to the Valley that day and is handed a government order forbidding entrance to both Tutankhamen's tomb and KV15 by any persons whosoever.

February 16-21

An exchange of recriminating notes, letters and telegrams between Carter and various government officials (including the Egyptian Prime Minister, Saad Zaghlul Pasha himself) transpires. Morcos Bey Hanna gives an interview in the Egyptian press justifying his actions in the matter. On the 18th Carter institutes legal proceedings in the Mixed Courts, and a hearing is scheduled for the 23rd. The tide of public opinion begins to turn against Carter and his associates. If they meant their strike as a bluff, thinking the government would back down, they discover they were terribly mistaken.

February 22

Pierre Lacau arrives in the Valley of the Kings, accompanied by an overkill entourage, including Reginald Engelbach, numerous local Egyptian officials, the *sheikh* of the Antiquities guards and their locksmith, plus thirty-three armed police, some on foot, others riding camels and horses. Carter's foreman *(reis)* and three of his workmen who have been posted by him nearby Tutankhamen's tomb are ordered to disperse, and they retreat to the expedition magazine (KV4). At Lacau's direction the smith cuts Carter's padlocks on KV62 and KV15, and both tombs are entered in

A rather glum Howard Carter (far left) poses with a delgation of Egyptian governmental officials, after they have visited KV-15, where the conservation lab for KV62 was located.

Archival photo

297

Herbert E. Winlock

turn by the Frenchman, Engelbach and the Egyptian delegation, wherein they make a thorough inspection of the status of things. The lid suspended over the sarcophagus is carefully lowered on its ropes and tackle back into place.

At the very moment Lacau is taking possession of the two tombs for the Egyptian government, Carter receives formal notice at his house that Morcos Bey Hanna has annulled the Carnarvon concession for the current season. Carter wires the minister back and threatens further legal action — in order *"to safeguard the contents of the tomb."* But he also states that if Lacau personally will apologize for the insult to his colleagues' wives, and if *"vexatious interference"* by the Antiquities Service ceases, he will reopen the tomb and resume his work therein. Carter receives no reply.

February 23
The hearing Carter has requested is held in the Mixed Courts in Cairo, presided over by an American judge, Pierre Crabites, acting as referee in this dispute between a foreigner and the Egyptian people. Following adjournment of the initial session, an offer for a renewed Carnarvon concession is made by the Egyptian government. James Breasted is invited to draw up a set of terms for same, for presentation to the court when it reconvenes on March 8.

March 6
A gala reopening of KV62, a *fantasiya*, is staged in the Valley of the Kings by the Nationalist regime, with 170 invited guests, including government ministers and High Commissioner Lord Allenby and his wife. The lid of the sarcophagus has been removed earlier and placed against a wall of the Burial Chamber. The high point of the event occurs when Pierre Lacau orders the overhead illumination to be extinguished and Tutankhamen's gilded coffin is left bathed by a single spotlight. A banquet celebrating the rightful claiming of the tomb by the people of Egypt is held afterwards in Luxor, and lasts until dawn of the next day.

March 8
The Mixed Courts reconvenes in Cairo and Breasted's terms for a renewed concession are presented, with certain exceptions to these being raised by the government. The lawyer representing the Ministry of Public Works suggests that if Carter will sign a renunciation to any claim to the objects from the tomb, the government will make its own concessions.

March 9
Against his better judgment, Carter is pressured into signing the following statement: *"I hereby declare that I for myself never have made, do not now make, and never intend to make any claim against the Egyptian Government or against anyone else to any of the objects found in the Tomb of Tutankhamen."* Coincidentally, Sir John Maxwell, lawyer for the Carnarvon estate, happens to be in Cairo at this time, and signs a like renunciation on behalf of the absent Almina Herbert, Lady Carnarvon. Breasted is now confident that the settlement he has worked so hard to accomplish will come about. However, when he presents the renunciation documents to Minister Hanna, the latter announces that he will not renew the concession until he has heard the judgment of the Mixed Courts in the matter, which is to be made the next day.

March 10
In his concluding argument before the reconvened Mixed Courts, for a new concession on behalf of Carter and the Carnarvon estate, Carter's lawyer, F.M. Maxwell, uses a word which proves fatal to his clients' case: he says that the government had come like a *"bandit"* and forced Carter from the tomb. The courtroom erupts in an uproar and even the presiding American judge is stunned. He asks Maxwell if the use of "bandit" is really necessary (it meaning "thief" in Arabic). The uncomprehending Maxwell replies that "bandit" is as good a word as any to describe the actions of the Minister of Public Works. This will be played in the Egyptian press as a vile insult to all the people of Egypt by Carter and company. Court adjourns without a ruling being rendered.

March 11-31
There ensues nearly three weeks of behind-the-scenes negotiations attempting to somehow salvage the situation for Carter. Despite reasonings, cajolings and pleadings

by any number of interested parties (Judge Crabites, Breasted, Winlock, American Ambassador Merton Howell, etc.) the personally offended and outraged Morcos Bey Hanna initially remains intransigent in his refusal to modify in any way his determination to keep Carter out of the tomb. Then, on the conditions that F.M. Maxwell will renounce his use of the word "bandit" in reference to Hanna, and that Carter will give his written assurance that he will *"cease forever"* his criticisms of the Egyptian government, the minister tells Breasted and Howell that he will issue a fully signed new concession to the Carnarvon estate (this perhaps because Hanna apparently can find no one who will agree to accept responsibility for resuming the clearance of KV62, including Lacau and Engelbach).

When, however, Breasted and Ambassador Howell appear at the appointed time to pick up the signed document of concession that the minister has promised, Hanna informs them that he has changed his mind (again) and, in fact, has filed an appeal in the Mixed Tribunal at Alexandria against any future decision by Judge Crabites which would force a compromise in Carter's favor. In short, the Egyptian Minister of Public Works has broken his word to the American ambassador; and a dispirited Merton Howell takes to his bed.

On March 31st, meddling journalist A.H. Bradstreet, reporting for the *New York Times*, posts a story that the United States has been affronted by Egypt in Minister Hanna's rebuff to Ambassador Howell; to which the latter issues an official denial, claiming that, to the contrary, he has been treated very courteously by the Egyptians with whom he has been interceding on behalf of Carter and the Carnarvon estate. Nonetheless Merton Howell is subsequently reprimanded by the American Secretary of State, Charles Evans Hughes.

On the same day, the 31st, the Mixed Tribunal at Alexandria rules on Morcos Bey Hanna's appeal and declares that the cancellation of the Carnarvon concession to the Tomb of Tutankhamen by the Ministry of Public Works is a fully legal act, over which the Mixed Courts in Cairo has no jurisdiction.

March 21

Howard Carter leaves Egypt for England, having persuaded Herbert Winlock to act as his proxy in the matter of the Tomb of Tutankhamen.

Winlock subsequently is presented with the Egyptian government's new terms for the renewal of the Carnarvon concession to KV62, which the American regards as impossible. Its fourteen provisions state, in part, that: (1) Carter will have the status of a *"supervisor"* for the Antiquities Service, and will need written permission from the government for each of his co-workers; (2) Five Egyptian *"apprentices"* will be assigned to the work; (3) Visitor permits will be issued by the government alone; (4) Lady Carnarvon can enter the tomb freely, but will have to report to the Antiquities Service every two weeks regarding how many visits she and the staff make; (5) She personally will have to make a record of all of the objects in the tomb and guarantee a scientific publication within five years of the completion of the clearance; (6) All objects from the tomb are government property exclusively; (7) Lady Carnarvon, Carter and everyone else associated with them vis-a-vis KV62 will have to sign an apology to the government about use of the word "bandit"; (8) Carter will have to state in writing that he will never again use language which is discourteous to the government and its ministers ; and (9) He will have to issue a personal apology for his purported claims that the government broke its promises to him.

March 29

A special commission of Egyptians, headed by Pierre Lacau and including Chief Inspector Engelbach, is in Luxor to make an *"inventory"* of all of the contents of KV62 and KV15, as well as the tomb being used as a magazine and occasional *"lunch room"* by Carter and his colleagues: KV4, the Tomb of Rameses XI.

March 30

This commission breaks down the wooden door securing KV4 and while casually examining its contents come across a wooden Fortnum & Mason wine case, within which is discovered, wrapped in surgical gauze and cotton batting, a painted-wood sculpture of the life-sized head of a child (the boy-king or perhaps one of the Amarna princesses, probably Ankhesenpaaten) emerging from a water-lily flower. Unlike the

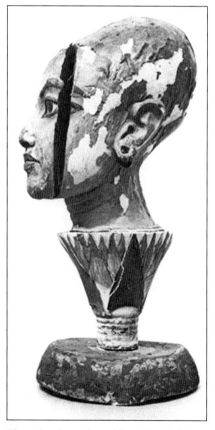

The painted-wood head found by the Egyptian commission who broke into KV4 hidden in a wine box. It had not been previously inventoried by Howard Carter, who the commission charged was plannng to steal the unique object. Internet photo

rest of the objects in the magazine, this is not labeled or inventoried. The Egyptian members of the commission become hysterical, charging that Carter was planning to steal this strikingly beautiful object. Although himself stunned by this potentially explosive revelation, Lacau attempts to calm his fellow commissioners by suggesting that perhaps the sculpture is, in fact, something which the excavator had purchased for Lord Carnarvon and which may have an El Amarna provenance, rather than coming from KV62. The Egyptians insist that Prime Minister Zaghlul himself be informed immediately of this situation, and that the sculpture be sent the next day by train to Cairo and the Egyptian Museum, to be held as *"evidence"* until the facts surrounding it can be determined.

Reginald Engelbach

March 31

Early in the morning of the next day, Engelbach pays a visit to Winlock and tells him of the situation with the wooden head (of which the American has already heard in the middle of the night, having been alerted by Carter's *reis*, Hussein). The chief inspector asks Winlock to obtain from Carter confirmation that he had purchased the object, and departs, harboring his own suspicions regarding the origin of the carving.

April 2

After pondering what to do, Winlock sends a coded cable to Carter in England, telling him of the problem and asking for an explanation. He follows this with a second cable which states that there are three theories being advanced about the sculpted head: (1) Carter purchased it on the antiquities market; (2) One of his workmen had inadvertently placed it in the magazine; or (3) It was found in the KV62 entry passage and Carter has simply forgotten to record its existence.

April 3

Carter cables Winlock from London that the sculpture belongs to material found in the filling of the corridor and that, although noted on the plan of same, had not yet been fully registered in the tomb index.

April 5

Winlock writes to Carter, informing him that Lacau is *"perfectly delighted"* with Carter's explanation. He believes the matter is closed. He further writes that everyone in the Antiquities Service wants Carter back in KV62, even Lacau; and he recommends that the archaeologist accept, for the present at least, any concession terms which the Egyptian government requires.

April 7

Carter writes to Winlock with a more detailed account of the finding of the sculpted head: which he and Callender discovered it in a *"very perishable condition"* and that it had been wrapped and stored in the magazine until *"the opportunity came for its correct handling."* He expresses displeasure that the head had been sent to Cairo before it received *"proper care."*

April 21

Howard Carter arrives in New York City aboard the *S.S. Berengaria*, to begin a lecture tour of the United States.

May-June

Carter travels to several U.S. cities and to Canada, giving his slide-show lecture on the Tomb of Tutankhamen to SRO audiences. He meets with and is commended by President Calvin Coolidge and presents his lecture in the East Room of the White House. He becomes Dr. Howard Carter upon receiving an honorary Doctor of Science degree from Yale University. In every way his spring in the States proves to be a personal triumph, as well as a financial success. And all the while, things continue to progress off stage in terms of smoothing out the problems in Egypt, so that a return to the Tomb of Tutankhamen in the fall seems almost inevitable.

Then, regrettably, a few days before he is to depart New York for England aboard the *S.S. Mauretania*, half-a-dozen copies of a Carter-authored seventy-four-page booklet intended for *"private circulation only"* comes off press in New York. This is titled *The Tomb of Tut-Ankh-Amen, Statement with Documents, as to the Events which occurred in Egypt in the Winter of 1923-1924 leading to the ultimate break with the Egyptian Government.* It is a scathing attack in the third person on Lacau, the Antiquities Service and the Egyptian authorities, setting down event by event, point by point, the whole unpleasant business that everyone who had been involved in it now thinks is finally behind them; and Winlock, in particular, is outraged at Carter, both for potentially restirring the hornet's nest and for having published without permission, as an appendix to this unfortunate dossier, Winlock's confidential (even secret) correspondences with Carter about the sculpted head discovered in the wine case. The American Egyptologist announces to Carter that he is disassociating himself from him in every way.

One of Carter's fellow passengers aboard the *Mauretania* en route to England is Edward Robinson, director of the Metropolitan Museum, who counsels the Englishman not to circulate his pamphlet attacking the Egyptians, and advises him that he should give them any apology the Egyptians require, only so that Carter can return to the tomb and complete his important work there. Perhaps surprisingly, Carter capitulates and decides to do as Robinson has suggested: he will abandon his struggle with Lacau and the Egyptians. He drafts his capitulation to the director-general of the Antiquities Service: *"I, the undersigned, Howard Carter, definitively renounce any action, claim, or pretension whatsoever, both as regards the Tomb of Tut-Ankh-Amen and the objects therefrom and also in respect of the cancellation of the authorisation and the measures taken by the government in consequence of such cancellation. I declare that I withdraw all actions pending and I authorise the representative of the government to apply for them to be struck out."*

September 13

After conferring with Carter and the executor of her husband's estate, Sir John Maxwell, the Countess of Carnarvon sends a letter drafted by them to Morcos Bey Hanna, in which she accepts (along with her *"agent"* Carter) the terms of a new concession to the Tomb of Tutankhamen, which have been worked out over the summer between the minister and the countess's representatives. She adds that she and Carter personally are willing to renounce any claim to objects from the tomb, but stresses that the executors of her husband's estate are of a different mind in that regard: inasmuch as the late Lord Carnarvon personally had spent some £45,000 during his years excavating in the Valley of the Kings, the executors are of the view that the estate should be compensated by the Egyptian government in some part for these expenses. The countess reminds Hanna that in the past such compensation to foreign excavators had been in the form of objects found, a share of which was granted to the excavator by the government. She therefore suggests to the minister that when the clearance of the tomb is complete and all of the *"actual contents...fully ascertained,"* a portion of these be given to the Carnarvon estate, as had been Lord Carnarvon's entitlement under the terms of his original concession to work in the Valley of the Kings. She goes on to propose that which objects would be awarded to the estate be determined by the arbitration of of two *"independent"* archaeologists, one representing the government, the other the estate, with an umpire, *"should it be necessary."*

Soon after, Lady Carnarvon receives a wire from her lawyer in Egypt that the ploy has worked: Hanna is willing to offer something rather than lose face. The Egyptian government will *"give at its discretion to Lady Almina a choice of duplicates as representative as possible of the discovery,"* as such duplicates can be *"separated from the whole without damage to Science."*

November 12

The second highest ranking British official in Egypt, Sir Lee Stack, commander-in-chief of the Egyptian Army and governor-general of the Sudan, is assassinated in Cairo; and as a consequence the Nationalist government of Saad Zaghlul Pasha resigns — including, of course, Morcos Bey Hanna — to be replaced by a pro-British regime with Ahmad Ziwar Pasha at this head. Ziwar is an old friend of Carter's, and the archaeologist is overjoyed at the unexpected turn of events in Egypt. He wonders how he may withdraw his and Lady Carnarvon's letters renouncing claim to objects from Tutankhamen's tomb.

December 15

Howard Carter is back in Cairo and within hours of his arrival he encounters Prime Minister Ziwar himself in the lobby of the Continental Hotel. Ziwar, in fact, brings up the matter of Tutankhamen's tomb at this time and tells Carter that he is most unhappy with the way the Zaghlul government has handled the matter and that his own cabinet is anxious that an arrangement fully agreeable to all parties concerned can be worked out as soon as possible. Carter assures his old friend that he himself wants nothing less than such a resolution, and that he could be ready to work in the tomb in two weeks' time.

This same day Carter queries his and Lady Carnarvon's lawyer in Cairo, Georges Merzbach, as to whether their letters of renunciation might be withdrawn; but he is counseled to leave well enough alone for the present, and to hope to alter such details over time, as possible. It seems best, Merzbach thinks, for them to accept the new concession to KV62 with the terms which had been worked out by him over the previous summer.

December 28

Carter finally gets his audience with Prime Minister Ziwar, makes suggestions as to how the dispute over the Tomb of Tutankhamen and its contents can be worked out, and requests that Ziwar arrange a meeting between himself, the lawyer Merzbach and the new Minister of Public Works. The Prime Minister seems sympathetic to Carnarvon's case and tells Carter to put his request in writing. Merzbach drafts a letter to this effect almost immediately.

1925

January 4

Carter finally receives notice that a meeting has been arranged, not with the Minister of Public Works, but with the Minister of the Interior, Sidky Pasha, and — much to Carter's chagrin — two additional negotiators, Pierre Lacau and the government's legal advisor when it took over the tomb, Bedawy Pasha. The meeting is to take place on January 7th.

January 7

A few hours before the negotiators convene, Carter meets privately with Prime Minister Ziwar, and is counseled by him to formally renounce any claim to objects from the tomb by the Carnarvon estate, including duplicates. He assures the excavator, however, that *"in time there would be objects"* and Ziwar gives Carter his personal pledge that Egypt will be *"exceedingly generous towards Lady Carnarvon and the estate, in the matter of duplicates which would not interfere with the over-all ensemble."* Carter is totally disheartened by this exchange, but does not attempt to argue with his old friend. The conference gets under way and things go badly at first, with Lacau and Bedawy being contrary. Carter's lawyer, Merzbach, however, turns things around, with an agreement being reached that the British side would renounce any claim to objects, but a separate letter would be issued by the Egyptians committing the government to a future division of duplicates.

January 13

Eleven months after Carter and company's strike and the Egyptian government's takeover of the Tomb of Tutankhamen, Lady Carnarvon is granted by Mahmoud Bey Sidky, the new Minister of Public Works, a one-year concession to continue the clearance of KV62, with Howard Carter acting as the *"archaeological agent"* on behalf of the countess and her late husband's estate.

January 19

Carter returns to Luxor and begins to make arrangements for a short campaign to ready the tomb and laboratory for a full-scale season, to commence the following September or October.

January 22

Going to the Valley of the Kings, Carter is distressed and angered to see that the great linen pall which was found between the First and Second tabernacles in the Burial Chamber has been left lying unprotected on the ground outside of KV15 (where it was undergoing conservation at the time of the strike and lockout), and that it is totally ruined by the sun and wind. The entrance to the laboratory tomb is found to be closed with a kind of lattice-work entirely covered over with white plaster, and KV62 itself lies under about one meter of accumulated rubbish. The "lunch tomb" (KV4) and Burton's photography darkroom (KV55) seem, from all outward appearances, to be in satisfactory condition.

January 25

Amidst much pomp and ceremony, the Government Commission and representatives of the Antiquities Service hand over possession of tombs 62, 15, 4 and 55 to Carter. In a letter reporting this to Lady Carnarvon, Carter writes, *"Lacau was not present. It would seem that he was ashamed to show his face."* The occasion is celebrated that evening at an official dinner hosted by the *mudir* of Qena.

Summer

Arthur Mace's health has been deteriorating, and he advises Carter that he will not be able to rejoin the team in the fall, nor, consequently, to contribute to the writing of volume two of *The Tomb of Tut·Ankh·Amen*. Carter thus enlists his old friend novelist Percy White to assist him in this task. The plan is to continue the narration from where the first volume left off, with inclusion of whatever the forthcoming season might reveal, especially the opening of the coffins and subsequent examination of the king's mummy. Carter will provide his notes and White will do the actual writing.

September 23

Carter leaves London to travel to Egypt via Trieste.

October 1

Carter calls on Campbell Edgar at the Egyptian Museum in Cairo, to confer about his plans for the fall-winter season. Edgar, an assistant curator, is filling in for Pierre Lacau — who is on leave in France, with intention to return to Egypt in early November. It is agreed that operations in KV62 will resume on October 11. Edgar informs Carter that Lacau expects to be on hand for the unwrapping of Tutankhamen's mummy. Before departing for Luxor in the company of Alfred Lucas, the archaeologist has *"an agreeable interview"* with the Ministry of Public Works' lawyer, Bedawy Pasha, who approves Carter's program for the coming season.

October 12

KV62 and KV15 are reopened and found to be in excellent condition.

October 13

The modern black shroud which Carter had placed over the open sarcophagus the previous January is removed, the lid of the outer coffin is lifted and a Second Coffin is revealed, this one gilded and inlaid all over, *rishi*-style, with chevrons of colored glass-paste. Carter is disturbed by the decayed condition of the shroud which covers this coffin, suggesting that dampness has penetrated therein and may have affected the mummy itself. The tomb is closed to await photographer Harry Burton's arrival in Luxor.

October 15-22

Burton photographs the still-shrouded Second Coffin. Then the entire coffin ensemble is lifted from the sarcophagus — using the same block-and-tackle arrangement employed to remove the sarcophagus lid — and rested on wooden planks passed under it and placed across the empty sarcophagus. The basin of the First Coffin eventually is lowered back into the sarcophagus box.

October 23

The lid of the Second Coffin is raised, revealing a red-shrouded Third Coffin inside. Burton photographs this, the shroud and a heavy floral collar are removed, and it is realized that this innermost coffin is made of solid gold. The basin of the Second Coffin and its weighty contents are carried into the Antechamber, where there is more room to examine the Third Coffin and what lies within.

October 28

The lid of the Third Coffin is raised and the fully wrapped mummy of Tutankhamen is revealed. Over the head and shoulders is an inlaid solid-gold funerary mask in the young king's likeness. A great deal of liquid unguents have been poured over the innermost coffin and the mummy as part of the funerary ritual in antiquity, and this has solidified, effectively cementing the mummy and gold mask to the interior of the basin of the Third Coffin, and the latter likewise to the basin of the Second Coffin.

November 1 & 2

In an effort to melt the unguents, Carter exposes mummy, mask and basins to the full sun for several hours each day, in temperatures reaching sixty-five degrees Centigrade (149° Fahrenheit). The mummy and mask stay firmly attached to the gold cof-

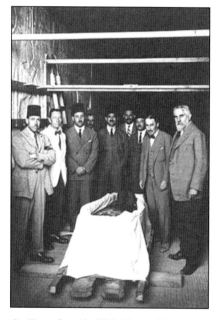

On November 11, 1925, Howard Carter & Pierre Lacau (on r.) assemble with a group of invited Egyptian government officials in the entry corridor of KV15, to commence the examination of Tutankhamen's mummy, still resting in the basins of the middle & innermost coffins. Dr. Douglas Derry is second from the left. Internet photo

Illustrated London News *artist's imaginary depiction of the mummy of Tuthankhamen being removed from KV62, to be examined by the excavators. When the king's remains were taken to KV15 for that purpose, the mummy was still wrapped & within the basins of the middle & innermost coffins.*

Archival image

fin, and the two basins remain stuck together, as well; so the "unwrapping" of Tutankhamen will have to be done *in situ*, as he lies within the two coffins.

November 11

The coffin basins with the mummy having been placed in the entry corridor to the laboratory tomb (KV15), at 9:45 a.m. an invited group gathers to formally observe the beginning of the dismantlement of the mortal remains of Tutankhamen. The assembly includes several Egyptian officials, Pierre Lacau, Carter, Lucas, Burton and Dr. Douglas Derry, who will perform the "autopsy" of the mummy. After the initial incision is made in the outer shroud enveloping the body, and the first sections of highly friable linen are lifted away, the group disperses.

November 11-15

Over four days the process of "unwrapping" the royal remains progresses to completion, with Burton photographing each stage as layer after layer of funerary and personal jewelry are revealed within the greatly decayed bandaging. In order to remove this jewelry, Carter and Derry literally take the almost carbonized royal mummy apart, removing both forearms and hands, severing the torso from the pelvis and legs, and decapitating the head, which is stuck to the back of the funerary mask. Subsequently the king's head is extracted from the mask and denuded separately.

December

The two coffin basins are eventually separated by the application of intense heat (968º F., 520º C.), using several Primus paraffin lamps burning at full blast. The gold mask is freed from the Third Coffin basin in the same manner. On the 31st Carter and Alfred Lucas accompany the solid-gold coffin and the solid-gold funerary mask to Cairo and the Egyptian Museum.

Posing for Harry Burton's camera with an Egyptian assistant in late October 1923, Howard Carter contemplates how to remove the third, solid-gold inner coffin which is cemented by long-dried unguents to the basin of the second coffin. Adapted Griffith Institute photo

  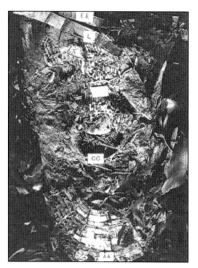 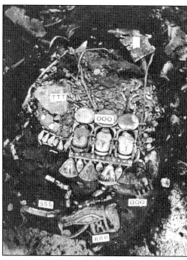

1926
Spring
Carter and Lucas work in the laboratory, cleaning and conserving the jewelry from the mummy. KV62 and the laboratory tomb are closed and handed over to the care of Antiquities Service chief inspector for Upper Egypt, Tewfik Boulos, on May 7. Carter is back in England on May 28.

Summer
Carter deals with the awkward issue of the sale of the Carnarvon collection of Egyptian antiquities. It ultimately is acquired in its entirety by the Metropolitan Museum of Art for the sum of $145,000. It is later claimed that a few of these objects, although uninscribed, may have come from the Tomb of Tutankhamen, perhaps removed by Lord Carnarvon himself, *"on account."*

September 29
Carter, back in Cairo, meets with Campbell Edgar at the Egyptian Museum, to go over his plans for work in KV62 during the 1926-1927 fall-winter season. It is agreed that beginning January 1, 1927, and continuing to mid-March, the tomb will be open to the public three days a week.

October 23
Having been reassembled on a specially constructed wooden tray filled with sand, and so photographed by Harry Burton, the mummy of Tutankhamen is lowered — with a minimum of formality by just Carter, Lucas and their workmen — into the gilded-wood First (outermost) Coffin, which earlier has been returned to the sarcophagus.

October 24
Work on the clearance of the Treasury commences and will continue until December 31.

1927
January 1-April 29
KV62 is opened to visits by the public, on Tuesdays, Thursdays and Saturdays, from 9:00 a.m. to noon, which continues until March 31. Carter and Lucas spend most of their time working in KV15, conserving and packing objects removed from the Treasury. On April 16 these crated objects are shipped to Cairo, with Carter following on the 24th. He departs Egypt for England on the 29th.

Spring
Volume two of *The Tomb of Tut·Ankh·Amen*, ghostwritten by Percy White, is published. Volume three will follow in 1933, also ghostwritten by White.

October 4-6
The Tomb of Tutankhamen is reopened by Carter and two days are spent completing the clearance of the Treasury, except for the canopic shrine and three boats.

October 30-December 15
Clearance of the Annexe.

1930s
The tabernacle elements are the final objects to be removed from the tomb, November 10, 1930. That same fall Egypt pays the Carnarvon estate £36,000 in lieu of duplicates. The last of the conserved objects will not be shipped to Cairo until the spring of 1932. Howard Carter dies in 1939.

Sequential Harry Burton photographs (left to right, p0777, p0778, p0781 & p0799) of stages in the the "unwrapping" of Tutankhamen's mummy over four days (Nov. 11-15, 1925), demonstrating what a nearly impossible task confronted Howard Carter in that operation. If all pharaohs' mummies were so loaded with gold jewelry & protective funerary amulets, it is not surprising they fell victim to ancient tomb looters. Griffith Institute

ADDENDUM TWO

"Pharaoh's Curse"

Three-quarters of a century after Howard Carter's discovery of the tomb now numbered 62 in the Valley of the Kings, the name of its occupant is well-known in every corner of the globe, and the solid-gold funerary mask which was found adorning his mummy has become something of an instantly recognizable icon symbolizing Egypt itself. But an intangible associated with the discovery of the Tomb of Tutankhamen and its clearance is also forever imbedded in the universal consciousness: the so-called "Pharaoh's Curse."

Simply put, this was the belief that any one who disturbed the eternal rest of Pharaoh would himself be struck down by death. It was of course the demise of George Herbert, Lord Carnarvon, on April 5, 1923 — six months after the discovery of Tutankhamen's tomb — which prompted the attribution of a "curse" as the cause of his ill fate following so close on the heels of the English earl's greatest success.

Of course two events allegedly occurring precisely at the moment Carnarvon died served to feed the press rumor that supernatural circumstances were involved: the dimming and total extinguishing for a short time of all electrical lights in Cairo; while, far away in England, at Carnarvon's Highclere estate, his three-legged female terrier, Susie, let out a yowl and dropped dead (this according to Herbert's son and heir, Lord Porchester). The apparently inexplicable coincidences of a city-wide blackout and simultaneously a dog's sudden death thousands of miles away were greater fodder for sensationalizing reporters on the scene in Luxor, scrambling to post stories which would sell newspapers at home, than the fact that the fifty-seven-year-old Carnarvon was already in frail health at the time KV62 was discovered, and that — after suffering an infection caused by blood poisoning resulting from a razor-nicked insect bite — he might fall prey to often-fatal pneumonia while bedridden.

Harry Burton's photograph of George Herbert, Lord Carnarvon, reading on the veranda of Howard Carter's house on the Luxor west bank. Adapted image colorized by Dynamchrome.

Feeding into the rumor of a curse was the other, earlier, coincidence of Howard Carter's pet canary purportedly being devoured by a cobra at "Castle Carter" on the Luxor west bank, while his owner was in Cairo to greet Lord Carnarvon upon the latter's arrival in Egypt following discovery of the long-looked- for Tomb of Tutankhamen. Carter's workmen had considered the yellow songbird as an omen of good luck, and they initiallly dubbed the find "The Tomb of the Golden Bird." Not missed by the press, subsequently, was the fact that the cobra from earliest times had decorated the brow of Egyptian kings (the ureaus), for the express purpose of protecting them from their enemies.

Disgruntled Egyptologist and former Antiquities inspector Arthur Weigall (intimately associated with the earlier discoveries of the Tomb of Yuya and Thuyu and of the so-called "Amarna Cache"), shut out of KV62 and watching from outside the comings and goings therein as an observer for the *Daily Mail* newspaper, is purported sarcastically to have remarked as Lord Carnarvon, in apparent good humor, entered the tomb for the opening of the doorway to the Burial Chamber, *"If he goes down in that spirit, I give him six weeks to live."* In almost precisely that period of time the earl was dead.

Two weeks before Carnarvon's demise, the novelist Marie Corelli had issued a newspaper warning that *"the most dire punishment follows any rash intruder into a sealed tomb."* Sherlock Holmes creator Arthur Conan Doyle attributed the English earl's fate to *"elementals"* which had been created by Tutankhamen's priests to safeguard the tomb. Other theories had Carnarvon pricking his finger (or cheek) on a poisoned arrow or other implement found in the Antechamber. And there was the suggestion of a deadly bacteria in the royal sepulcher which had fatally infected him.

Newspaper accounts told of an imaginary inscription carved over the entrance to the tomb: *"Death shall come on swift wings to him that toucheth the tomb of Pharaoh."* Another version of the same inscription had it reading: *"Let the hand raised against my form be withered! Let them be destroyed who attack my name, my foundation, my effigies, the images like unto me."* Carter is supposed purposely to have removed this dire warning and buried it in the desert. One reporter is said to have learned that a mud brick found in the entrance to the Treasury bore the hieratic in scription: *"It is I who hinder the sand from choking the secret chamber. I am for the protection of the deceased,"* to which was added by the reporter: *"and I will kill all those who cross this threshold into the sacred precincts of the Royal King who lives forever."* Other apocryphal inscriptions allegedly found in KV62 include one on a clay tablet from the Antechamber, which philologist Sir Alan Gardiner was claimed to have translated as reading: *"Death will slay with his wings whosoever disturbs the peace of the pharaoh"*; and supposedly on the back of one of the *ka* statues guarding the doorway to the burial chamber was to be read: *"It is I who drive back the robbers of the tomb with the flames of the desert. I am the protector of Tutankhamen's grave."*

Egyptologist-turned-journalist & former Antiquities inspector for Upper Egypt, Arthur Weigall (1880-1934) predicted Lord Carnarvon's demise in April 1923. Weigall was embittered from not having been allowed access to KV62, although he had been intimately involved with the discoveries & clearances of KV46 & KV55 several years earlier.

Studio portrait

Newspapers worldwide began reporting, as further evidence of the wrath of violated King Tutankhamen, a tally of all those, associated in some way with the tomb and its discoverers, who died post-Carnarvon. These included: the fifth earl's younger brother, Aubrey Herbert, in the same year, 1923; an Egyptian prince, Ali Kemel Fahmy Bey, shot to death at the London Savoy Hotel by his French wife, not long after he had visited KV62 as a tourist; an unnamed x-ray technician, who died en route to Egypt to examine Tutankhamen's mummy; Frank Jay Gould, the American railroad millionaire, who visited the tomb, contracted a cold, then succumbed to fatal pneumonia; Georges Bénédite, a French Egyptologist, who was killed in a fall subsequent to visiting KV62; an unnamed associate curator of the

British Museum who died in his bed after labeling objects from the Tomb of Tutankhamen (although nothing from the tomb was ever in that institution — until decades later); Carter's secretary, Richard Bethell, found dead in unusual circumstances at the Bath Club (1929), his father, Lord Westbury, who committed suicide subsequently, plus an eight-year-old who was run over by the late lord's hearse; and, perhaps most significantly, Egyptologist Arthur Cruttenden Mace — Carter's right-hand man during the first two seasons of KV62's clearance, and co-author of the first volume on the tomb — who withdrew from Carter's team due to ill health (pleurisy), dying in England at age fifty-three from a series of debilitating complications (stomach and heart problems) on April 6, 1928.

Tutankhamen, it seems, was rather selective in his retaliation. American Egyptologist Herbert H. Winlock (Carter's proxy during the later stages of the dispute with the Egyptian government over the tomb, who himself died in 1950 at age sixty-five), was to point out that of the twenty-six people present at the official opening of KV62, six had died within the following decade; of the twenty-two who attended the opening of the sarcophagus, only two were then dead (1934); and of the ten who witnessed the initial stage of the mummy's unwrapping, all were still alive. Indeed, the man who took the king's mortal remains apart, Dr. Douglas Derry, lived until age eighty-seven, and Carter himself, surely a prime target for royal revenge, only died in 1939, aged sixty-four. Finally, Evelyn Herbert, Carnarvon's daughter (later Lady Beauchamp), one of the first in the tomb, survived to age seventy-nine, dying in 1980.

ADDENDUM THREE

The Location, Architecture & Situation of Kings' Valley 62 The Tomb of Tutankhamen

Almost certainly not long after the reinterment of Smenkhkare in the unfinished private tomb Ay had been preparing for himself in the Great Place (KV55), the king's "right hand" began yet another (the third by count) site for his own eventual burial. This new tomb was situated only a few dozen yards diagonally across the wadi from the appropriated earlier sepulcher. Like the latter its first architectural feature was a steep, reasonably well-cut, rock-hewn stairwell, 1.68 meters (5 ft. 6 in.) wide, composed of sixteen steps and ending at a rectangular doorway, the jambs of which (reveals) were 95 centimeters (37.4 in.) thick.

Beyond this doorway, Ay's tomb-cutters tunneled a square-cut descending corridor measuring 1.68 meters wide and 2.0 meters high (5 ft. 6 in. by 6 ft. 7 in.) for a distance of 8.08 meters (26 ft. 6 in.). A second doorway was then hewn, its thickness being 1.05 meters (41 in.). Up to this point (stairwell and entry corridor), Ay's second Great Place tomb was similar in design to his first (KV55).

And the cutting of a squared-off, north-south-oriented largish rectangular chamber on the perpendicular to the axis of the stairwell and corridor — measuring 7.85 long by 3.55 meters wide and 2.68 meters high (25 ft. 9 in. by 11 ft. 7.8 in. by 8 ft. 9.5 in.) — repeated, if enlarged, the basic plan of Ay's earlier tomb. As in the latter, the floor of this first chamber is several centimeters lower than the floor of the corridor. While the walls, floor and ceiling of the chamber are as smoothly dressed as possible, no finishing plaster was applied for decoration.

Whatever function Ay's architect intended this large chamber to have served, it was not as the burial chamber, proper. In the short north wall of this space, the stone masons continued their cutting, ultimately extending the first chamber into an "L" shape with the addition of a second "chamber" or large wing, the floor of which was 94 centimeters (37 in.) lower than the main space. This "addition" measured 6.37 by 4.02 meters (20 ft. 10.8 in. by 13 ft. 2.27 in.) and was 3.63 meters (11

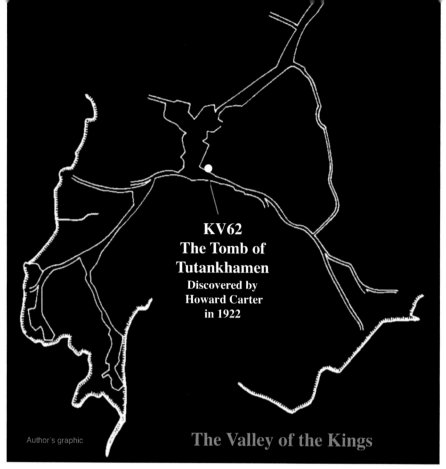

KV62
The Tomb of
Tutankhamen
Discovered by
Howard Carter
in 1922

Author's graphic

The Valley of the Kings

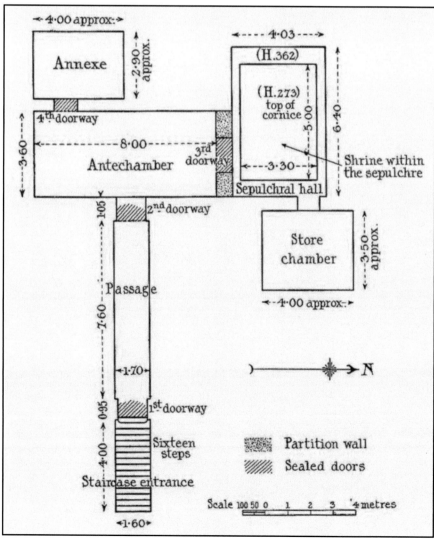

Howard Carter's "sketch-plan" of KV62, which he included in volume one of The Tomb of Tut·Ankh·Amen *(1923), although at that time he was able to only approximate the dimensions of the side rooms. Note that he designates the space he later called the Burial Chamber as the "Sepulchral hall" & his "Store chamber" here subsequently was renamed the Treasury. Carter never published an elevation of KV62.*

The scene painted on the upper portion of the east wall of the KV62 Burial Chamber. It depicts the mummy of Tutankhamen being drawn on a canopied sledge by a dozen men wearing white head bands, two shaved bald & attired in the peculiar high-waisted, sleeveless garment which identifies them as the viziers of Upper & Lower Egypt. The individual last in line may possibly be the dead king's regent, General Horemheb. The low doorway on the left side of the wall opens onto the side room which Howard Carter called the Treasury.

Griffith Institute

ft. 11 in.) high, the ceiling on the same level as that of the first-hewn chamber.

(Whether or not it had been his architect's intention to have extended the one chamber of Ay's KV55 into a similar L-shaped space can only be speculated on — but this seems unlikely, given the elevated squared-off "door" which had been introduced into the short north wall. In any case, the cutting beyond the initial chamber in the earlier tomb had only proceeded as far as the so-called "niche" when work was terminated to receive the jerry-rigged reburial of Smenkhkare.)

If further hewing of Ay's new tomb had occurred by the time of King Tutankhamen's untimely death, this cannot be known. The two side rooms opening off the "L" chamber(s) already may have been cut (or at least begun) when the dramatically changed circumstances at court found the elderly Ay, the faithful retainer, the "gray eminence," suddenly Horus, king, successor to the childless teenage "Osiris Nebkheperure," who was now undergoing mummification and would soon need a place to be laid to rest.

It is probable that Tutankhamen's own tomb — WV23 in the western branch of the Great Place — consisted of little more than the stairwell and long entry corridor, and so was wholly unsuitable for the interment of the last legitimate male of the great Thutmosid line. So, once again, Ay offered up his own modest tomb in the Great Place as a humble (if just barely suitable) "mansion of eternity" for his young predecessor. This solution, while expedient, did not reflect any extraordinary generosity on the part of the new king: Kheperkheperure Ay-itnetjer (*"Ay, Father of the God"*) himself no longer had any need for the space; he would simply continue work in the West Valley sepulcher which Tutankhamen had only begun, for his own kingly burial in time (which would come much sooner than he may have imagined).

As the period of mummification and mourning progressed through its sev-

311

Decoration of the long north wall of the KV62 Burial Chamber is comprised of three separate scenes. On the far right is a representation unique to royal-tomb decoration, in which the teenaged Tutankhamen's elderly successor, Ay, is depicted in the role of "son" Horus (king) performing the "Opening of the Mouth" ceremony for his "father," Osiris (here the mummiform Nekheperure Tutankhamen). Ay wears the Khepresh *crown & the leopard skin of a* setem-*priest. Both kings' prenomen & nomen cartouches identify them.* (Continues opposite)

enty-day duration, there was a great rush to ready KV62 for its new royal owner. Whatever had been Ay's plan for the tomb's ultimate employment, certain "royal" adaptations were now made. If they had not been begun or finished already, two side rooms to be used for storage of grave goods were commenced and/or completed. Situating the sarcophagus crypt was obviously the primary concern of those responsible for burying Osiris Nebkheperure. It was decided to employ the lower-elevated "wing" of the L-chamber for this purpose, with a masonry dry wall to be installed ultimately, which would define and separate this area from the higher, longer portion of the original chamber. The resulting space, the "burial chamber," would have to incorporate as best as possible the necessary Osiride funerary decoration which traditionally — since Thutmose III, at least — immediately surrounded the dead king in his coffins and sarcophagus. Clearly the four walls of the KV62 burial chamber/crypt did not have the necessary room for the *Amduat* texts which had been employed in the tombs of Thutmose III, Amenhotep II and Amenhotep III (the burial chamber in the Tomb

In the middle scene, the revivified Nebkheperure (identified by just his prenomen), in the costume of a living king, is greeted in the realm of the deities by the sky-goddess, Nut. The far-left scene shows Nebkheperure — wearing the Nemes head covering & followed by his ka (spiritual double) — embracing Osiris, lord of the Unerworld, with whom he had become united. Griffith Institute

of Thutmose IV was undecorated, for whatever reason). Thus, to ready the four walls of the room in which Osiris Nebkheperure would lie for eternity, a thick coat of gypsum plaster was applied and smoothed. The actual painting of the surfaces would not take place until after the funeral rites, when the coffined dead king was installed within his sarcophagus and several free-standing tabernacles were erected around the latter (more about these below).

At some point during the seventy days of mourning for Tutankhamen, the yellow-quartzite sarcophagus which he would use was brought into the tomb. This originally had been prepared for (and probably was occupied briefly by) King Smenkhkare; but when the latter's burial was dismantled at Akhetaten, the decision was made to appropriate this particular monument for eventual use by his successor. It thus likely was transported to Waset (Thebes) and placed in storage until such future, presumably far-off, time as it would be needed.

That time had come rather sooner than might have been expected and now

313

Decoration of the west wall of the KV62 Burial Chamber is a depiction of an extract from the Amduat. *The uppermost of the four registers shows the solar barque of Kheper-Re preceded by five funerary deities. Below are a dozen baboons representing the 12 hours of the night, through which the solar barque had to pass.* Griffith Institute

the inscriptions were carefully recut to transfer ownership of the sarcophagus to Tutankhamen, and it then was taken with considerable effort to the Great Place for installation in that king's tomb being readied there. But before the huge stone receptacle was lowered down the steep stairwell of KV62, it was discovered that the sarcophagus was both too high and wide to go through the doorway separating the stairs and the corridor. Thus it was necessary to level out the bottommost six steps and to cut away the jambs and lintel of this entry, enabling tight passage of the yellow-quartzite box.

At some point in its transfer (from Akhetaten to Waset, or Waset to the Great Place — more likely the latter) it would seem that the matching lid of the Smenkhkare/Tutankhamen sarcophagus was irreparably damaged, making the hurried manufacture of a substitute necessary (this carved out of an available slab of granite and then painted to "match" the quartzite box).

In the Theban royal workshops where Osiris Nebkheperure's funerary equipage was being rushed to completion, one of the greatest tasks almost certainly was the construction and decoration of four nested gilded-wood tabernacles which would surround the dead king's mortal remains. Whether such tabernacles (or "shrines") were employed for kings earlier in the Eighteenth Dynasty is not known, as none, if they existed, have survived. (The earliest example of such a funerary

314

structure is that found dismantled in KV55, which presumably had been made for the burial of Queen Tiye, and which — very likely unused by her — was employed for Smenkhkare's two sequential interments.) But Tutankhamen's tabernacles, with or without kingly precedent, helped solve the lack of available wall space in KV62 for the rendering of the necessary royal funerary texts inscribed in the burial chambers of most of his pre-Atenist predecessors. These texts (and accompanying vignettes) were carved, instead, in sunk relief on gesso which was then gilded; and they literally covered the exterior (and some interior) side, end and door panels of three of the king's four tabernacles (the outermost of these being decorated rather in an all-over motif of several registers of alternating pairs of *djed* pillars and *tyet* knots in gilded sunk relief on a background of inlaid blue faience).

When the time came to begin stocking the Tomb of Tutankhamen with the grave goods to be interred with the king (undoubtedly in the days just preceding the funerary rites themselves), it is almost certain that the largish storeroom opening off the sarcophagus chamber was the first to be so furnished. This space measures 4.75 by 3.8 meters (15 ft. 7 in. by 12 ft. 5.6 in.) and is 2.33 meters (7 ft. 7.73 in.) high. It is accessed by a low doorway 1.12 meters (3 ft. 8. in.) wide, which opens in the eastern short wall of the burial chamber (close to its northeast corner). In this space were

Decoration of the long south wall of the KV62 Burial Chamber depicts the deceased king — identified by his prenomen & Horus name — in the presence of three other Underworld deities. The jackal-headed Anubis (center) presents Nebkheperure to Hathor (far right), who raises an ankh *to the king's mouth. The lefthand portion of the scene — painted on the masonry partition wall dividing the Burial Chamber from the Antechamber — depicts the goddess Isis greeting the king in a fashion similar to Nut on the north wall. Seated behind her in three registers are minor Underworld deities, Because Howard Carter ultimately had to demolish the partition wall (in order to remove the tabernacles from the Burial Chamber), the painted plaster on which the Isis figure & the minor deities were shown could only be partially salvaged. These fragments were reassembled on a sand tray & placed in storage (perhaps one day to be properly conserved, mounted & displayed in KV62, or even the Luxor Museum).*

It has been suggested that the two artists who painted the north & south walls of the KV62 Burial Chamber (& there do seem to be different hands reflected in the rendering of the figures on these opposing walls) were the same painters who subsequently decorated the burial chamber of King Ay's tomb, WV23. Neither artist's treatment of the squat figures adheres to the canon of proportions followed at the time. Perhaps this was due to the cramped space (only two-feet wide) in which the painters were forced to work, inasmuch as the wall decorations were not executed until after the nest of four tabernacles had been installed.

Interestingly, while the painted surfaces of all four plastered-limestone walls of the Burial Chamber were found to be heavily mottled with fungal growths, the fragmentary painted-plaster of the area which covered the masony partition wall seems generally free of such organic growth.

placed the king's canopic equipment (housed in a gilded-wood shrine-like structure) and other objects of a ritualistic nature, including numerous *naoi* containing gilded-wood small statues of deities and a king (probably not Tutankhamen, but one of his predecessors), and a flotilla of model river-vessels. The low doorway to this chamber was not sealed — likely due to the magical nature of its contents and the need for supernatural access to and from the sarcophagus chamber proper.

Following the last rites of Tutankhamen and the subsequent funerary banquet partaken of by the late king's widow, his successor Ay, and a half-dozen other principals of the royal court and Amen priesthood (the setting for which may have been the still-empty first chamber of the tomb), Tutankhamen's mummy was installed in its nest of coffins (the basins of which likely were already in place within the sarcophagus). Unfortunately, when the replacement lid of the sarcophagus was lowered into position, this cracked across its middle from side to side and had to be quickly patched with plaster.

Now the numerous sections of the gilded-wood tabernacles were brought into the burial chamber and leaned against the walls. Assembly of these proceeded from innermost to outermost, with various objects of the king's grave goods being left on the floor between the fourth and third tabernacles, and the second and third tabernacles (a single bow), and in the space between the doors of the second and first (outermost) tabernacles. A framework supporting a huge, coarsely woven linen pall sewn all over with gilded-bronze marguerites, was positioned between the outer two tabernacles.

Once these "shrines" were in place, artists entered the now-crowded burial chamber and began the task of decorating the space with painted large-scale vignettes of the sort — on the two long walls, any way — which had previously been relegated to the upper walls of the so-called well chambers in the tombs of Thutmose IV and Amenhotep III. In general, these depicted the deceased king in the presence of var-

316

ious funerary deities (Osiris, Isis, Hathor, Anubis). An innovation in this previously established decorative scheme was made in the portrayal of the new Horus (king), Ay, performing the "Opening of the Mouth" ceremony for the mummiform Osiris Tutankhamen Nebkheperure.

Innovations were also made in the decoration of the two short ends of the chamber. On the east wall, at a level just above the open low door of the side store-room, the funeral cortege of Tutankhamen was shown, with the royal mummy on a canopied sledge being drawn by a dozen men wearing white head bands, two of whom would seem to be the viziers of Upper and Lower Egypt. On the west wall was painted an excerpt from the *Amduat*, showing the solar barque preceded by five deities and a dozen squatting baboons (in three registers), representing the twelve hours of the night. The background for all of these scenes was painted yellow (as was the case in the similar Thutmose IV and Amenhotep III tomb paintings) and the figures themselves were rendered relatively simply, with some distorted proportions caused by the cramped quarters in which the artists were forced to work.

While this painting was under way (completion of the scenes must have taken several days), a partition wall was built between the crypt and the large outer chamber. Constructed of limestone splinters reinforced with timber then plastered over on both sides, this wall was pierced in its middle part by a squarish doorway with a rough beam of wood serving as its lintel. When decoration of the crypt was completed, the doorway was filled up with rough stones, thus sealing the burial chamber. The outer side of this blockage was then thickly plastered and stamped repeatedly with the deceased king's elaborated nomen and the "jackal-and-prisoners" seal of the Great Place.

It is likely that while the crypt was being decorated and the dry wall constructed the objects destined for the small side room opening off the outer chamber were brought into the tomb and placed accordingly. This space (4.35 by 2.6 meters

The KV62 Burial Chamber today, with the First Coffin of Tutankhamen resting in situ *in the lidless sarcophagus, protected by plate glass. Two details are of interest: (1) in the closeup of the figure of Ay officiating as a* setem-*priest (opposite) the rope of the funerary sledge depicted on the adjoining east wall wraps around the corner & intrudes into the north-wall scene; a similar effect is found in the burial chamber of WV23 (Ay), suggesting an artist's hallmark in both tombs; & (2) The niches which contained three of Tutankhamen's "magical" bricks are visible in the south, west & north walls; these had been plastered & painted over by the decorators of the Burial Chamber.*

George B. Johnson photos

and 2.55 meters high — 14 ft. 3.25 in. by 8 ft. 6 in. by 8 ft. 4.39 in. — with its floor level 0.9 meters/2 ft. 11.43 in. lower than that of the large outer chamber) was intended to house the foodstuffs, oils, wine, etc., which Osiris Tutankhamen would require in the Hereafter. Strangely, however, numerous ritualistic/magical objects (especially *ushabtis* and model boats), which more properly should have been placed in the inner storeroom housing the canopic equipment, also were left in this space, as were several storage chests and furniture pieces, especially the king's beds. Once the small room was filled to its reasonable capacity, the low rectangular doorway to it (1.95 meters wide by 1.3 meters high; 6 ft. 4.7 in. by 4 ft. 3 in.) was sealed with masonry and plastered over.

First hewn, last filled, the large outer chamber was now provisioned with the balance of Tutankhamen's grave furnishings. Two life-sized *ka* statues of the king were positioned, like guardian figures, on either side of the sealed door to the crypt. Three high animal-form "ritual beds" were positioned head to tail against the room's long west wall opposite the doorway opening onto the corridor. Under, on and in front of these were placed a quantity of storage chests, various furniture items and numerous cases of mummified meat (that more properly should have gone into the adjoining storeroom with the other foodstuffs). Finally, several of the king's dismantled chariots were carried into the chamber and stacked in the southeast corner.

With everything now situated to the satisfaction of the Great Place officials in charge, the doorway to the outer chamber was filled up with rough masonry and its outer surface thickly coated with mud plaster and stamped all over with royal and necropolis seals. Next several objects were placed in the corridor, chief of which were a series of large ceramic storage vessels which contained the leftovers from the king's embalming (chiefly bags of natron), plus the dishware and refuse from the meal which had been consumed by the mourners following Tutankhamen's last rites. Then the repaired outer doorway (the cut-away jambs having been rebuilt with masonry and plaster, and a lime-washed wooden-beam lintel installed) was also closed with rough slabs of limestone and the outer surface of this blockage coated with mud plaster and stamped repeatedly. Finally, the stairwell was filled in with rock debris, gravel and sand, so that the location of the resting place of the last Thutmosid was lost for all time.

Or until the first burglary of the "mansion of eternity" of Osiris Nebkheperure Tutankhamen occurred, perhaps within only months of the king's funeral. Having dug out enough of the filling of the stairwell to expose the upper part of the blocked doorway, the band of thieves breached the upper-lefthand portion with a hole large enough to permit them to step down into the empty corridor. At the far end of the latter, they came to the second blocked doorway, which they also broke through at its top, thereby gaining access to the large outer chamber. These thieves may have been necropolis workers who had participated in the installation of the grave goods in the tomb in the first place — because the exact location of the plastered-over blocked doorway to the outer side room was apparently known to them. This they broke through and one or two of them began to empty the numerous calcite vessels stored there of the precious oils and unguents which these held — pouring the liquids into leather bags brought along for this purpose. Meanwhile their cohorts proceeded to ransack the storage chests in the outer chamber, looking for portable objects of solid metal, preferably gold and silver, but copper and bronze as well. It is likely that objects were passed out to a fellow thief or thieves who had remained in the corridor; and on closer inspection, some of these things were tossed aside when lack of any real intrinsic value was determined.

Whether this gang of robbers completed their foray or were interrupted by Great Place guards and fled (or were apprehended) cannot be known. In any case, their break-in was discovered and necropolis officials entered the Osiris Nebkheperure's "mansion of eternity" in the robbers' wake and reordered the outer chamber and its side room, although they did not refill the robbers' hole gaping in the blocking of the doorway to the latter space. The large forced opening in the top part of the blocked doorway between the outer chamber and the corridor was closed, however, and plastered and stamped repeatedly with the jackal-and-prisoners necropolis seal.

To protect the tomb from further intrusion, the decision was made to fill the entire corridor with rock rubble. The several large storage vessels which had been placed in this passageway by the burial party (containing mummification and funerary-meal refuse) were removed and subsequently buried in a pit not far away from the tomb. The miscellaneous small objects littering the corridor floor, discarded by the tomb robbers, were ignored and thus came to be covered over by the rock-chip and gravel fill which was brought into the long space by the basket load, until this passageway was finally thoroughly plugged along its entire length. The stairwell was once more buried and the location of this particular royal "mansion of eternity" forgotten again.

Until, that is, a second band of thieves, probably several years later, risked another forced entry into the burial place of that now-barely remembered Horus, Nebkheperure Tutankhamen. This time the stairwell was also cleared of enough of its fill to expose the upper portion of the resealed outer doorway. Another hole — smaller than that of the first break-in — was made in the upper left-hand part of the doorway blocking, and perhaps as much as seven or eight hours then were spent penetrating the limestone chips and gravel plugging the corridor — basket after basket of this rubble being passed out along a chain of diggers. The resulting tunnel finally reached the second blocked, resealed doorway. Once again this was breached below its lintel by a hole just large enough to permit the intruders to wriggle through and drop down several feet to the floor of the outer chamber.

The second tomb robbery saw the thieves penetrate all of the sepulcher's spaces. The outer side room gaped open and invited further exploration of its partially reordered contents. One of the robbers left his dirty footprints on a bow box he stood atop while ransacking whatever could be reached and opened.

As he wrecked further havoc in the side room, and a couple of his cohorts rerummaged through chests in the outer chamber, other thieves breached the bottom of the large sealed doorway at the far end of that space, making a hole just large enough to permit them to worm into the sarcophagus chamber. Almost immediately they found themselves ducking through an open doorway and standing in an inner side room, where they began pulling off the lids of half-a-dozen large chests arranged side by side in a row, to discover that the contents of these included, in part, large quantities of royal jewelry and solid-gold or -silver libation vessels. While they were thrusting handful after handful of these precious objects into the cloth sacks they carried, an alarm may have been sounded by one of their fellows who had stayed outside the tomb as a lookout for patrolling Great Place guards. The entire gang would have then scrambled out of the tomb, scurrying like rats through their tunnel up into the (night?) air — to slink away or be apprehended is anyone's guess.

Once again necropolis officials entered the "mansion of eternity" of little-remembered Osiris Nebkheperure. And once again they set about, perhaps only half heartedly, reordering the chaos left behind by the tomb robbers. Objects littering the floor were scooped up and dropped into whatever open chest or casket was at hand. Lids were replaced on these containers, but none was resealed. This time no attempt was made to enter the outer storeroom, as it was now wholly jumbled, with no exposed floor space in which to stand. The hole in the blocking of the doorway between the crypt and outer chamber was refilled with loose limestone splinters, but not replastered. The opening into the outer storeroom was left gaping. Crawling back into the robbers' tunnel and emerging into the fresh air and daylight, the necropolis officials ordered their workmen to refill and replaster the breach at the top of the inner doorway. When this was done, the wet mud-plaster was stamped with the "jackal-and-prisoners" seal. Then the tunnel was plugged with rock rubble, and the larger breach in the outer doorway was filled, plastered and stamped. The stairwell was reburied once more; and the necropolis restoration party departed the Great Place, hoping, no doubt, that the king who rested there never again would be disturbed.

And so he was not, for over three millennia, until the English archaeologist Howard Carter in 1922 AD finally succeeded in his long hunt for the burial place of a barely known king who reigned briefly at the end of the Eighteenth Dynasty. For convenience of reference, Carter gave names to the four rooms he found filled with Tutankhamen's grave goods. The long rectangular outer or first space beyond the corridor he called the Antechamber, and its side room he dubbed the Annexe. Quite rightly he called the room housing the royal mummy in its series of coffins, sarcoph-

Isometric Plans of KV62, Showing Blockages & Placement of Contents

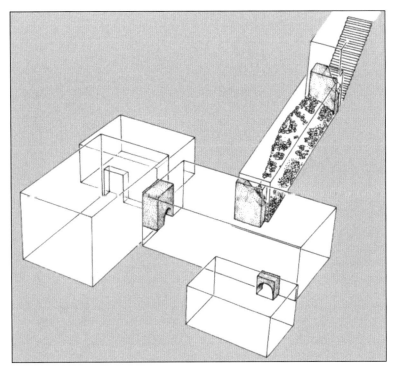

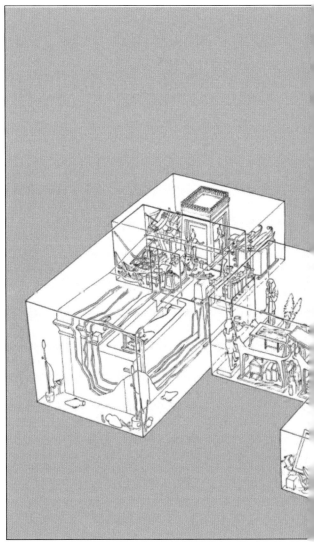

agus and sheltering tabernacles the Burial Chamber; and its side room became the Treasury (because so much jewelry was found there).

The Englishman felt that Tutankhamen's modest last resting place could be equated with the basic layout of New Kingdom royal tombs up to that time, if on a highly abbreviated scale. He saw the KV62 Antechamber — if pivoted around so that it was on the same axis as the entry corridor — corresponding to the multi-pillared chamber ("Chariot Hall") first seen in the Tomb of Amenhotep II and duplicated in the sequential tombs of that king's successors, Thutmose IV and Amenhotep III. This space, however, had only one side room (the Annexe) instead of the two located on opposite sides of the pillared hall in each of those three earlier sepulchers. The Burial Chamber, on its lower level than the Antechamber, Carter saw as an imitation of the sunken crypts containing the sarcophagi of Tutankhamen's trio of ancestors. Again, instead of two side-rooms of the original royal plan, the KV62 sarcophagus chamber had only one largish side-room (the Treasury).

This attempt to contort the plan of KV62 into something much more elaborate seems to be wishful thinking rather than reality. In fact, it would be more logical to not reposition the Antechamber in such a hypothesis, as the entry corridor being perpendicular to the former is more in keeping with the right-angled "bent" axis of the earlier royal sepulchers (conflating their multiple corridors and antechambers into a single passageway).

Carter thought, for no very good reason, that Maya, Tutankhamen's treasurer, was the architect of KV62. Since it is highly probable, as posited above, that the young king's makeshift tomb was designed for the intended use of a private person (Ay), it is unlikely that Maya — who otherwise had no known architectural credentials — would have played any role in its conception or adaptation.

Where KV62 Objects Were Found

Author's adaptations of
Garth Denning drawings

STAIRWELL
Boxes, Chests
Amulets, Beads, Jewelry
Sealings
Vessels
Wine Jars

CORRIDOR
Archery Equipment
Flora
Gaming Equipment
Amulets, Beads, Jewelry
Labels
Royal Figure (?)
Sealings
Toiletries
Ushabtis, Related Objects
Vessels
Wine Jars

ANTECHAMBER
Amulets, Beads, Jewelry
Archery Equipment
Basketry
Beds
Boomerangs, Throwsticks
Boxes, Chests
Chairs, Stools, Footstools
Chariots & Equipment
Clothing
Flora
Gaming Equipment
Hassock
Labels
Lamps, Torches
Naoi with Divine Figures
Musical Instruments
Preserved Food & Containers
Portable Canopy
Ritual Couches
Ritual Objects
Two Royal Figures
Royal Regalia
Sealings
Shrine
Sticks & Staves
Toiletries
Tools
Ushabti
Vessels
Writing Equipment

ANNEXE
Amulets, Beads, Jewelry
Archery Equipment
Basketry
Beds
Boomerangs, Throwsticks
Boxes, Chests
Chairs, Stools
Chariot Equipment
Clothing
Cuirass
Fans
Flora
Gaming Equipment

ANNEXE, *cont.*
Hassock
Labels
Model Boats
Musical Instruments
Portable Canopy
Preserved Food & Containers
Ritual Objects
Royal Regalia
Sealings
Shields
Shrines
Swords
Toiletries
Tools
Ushabtis, Related Objects
Vessels
Wine Jars
Writing Equipment

TREASURY
Amulets, Beads, Jewelry
Archery Equipment
Boxes, Chests
Canopic Equipment
Chariots, Equipment
Clothing
Coffins
Fans
Flora
Human Remains
Lamps, Torches
Model Boats
Model Granary
Naoi with Divine Figures
Naoi with Royal Figures
Ritual Objects
Royal Regalia
Sealings
Sticks & Staves
Toiletries
Tools
Vessels
Writing Equipment

BURIAL CHAMBER
Amulets, Beads, Jewelry
Archery Equipment
Bier
Clothing
Coffins
Daggers
Divine Figures
Fans
Gold Mask
Labels
Lamps
Mummy
Musical Instrument
Pall & Framework
Ritual Objects
Royal Figures
Royal Regalia
Sarcophagus
Sealings
Sticks & Staves
Tabernacles
Vessels
Wine Jars

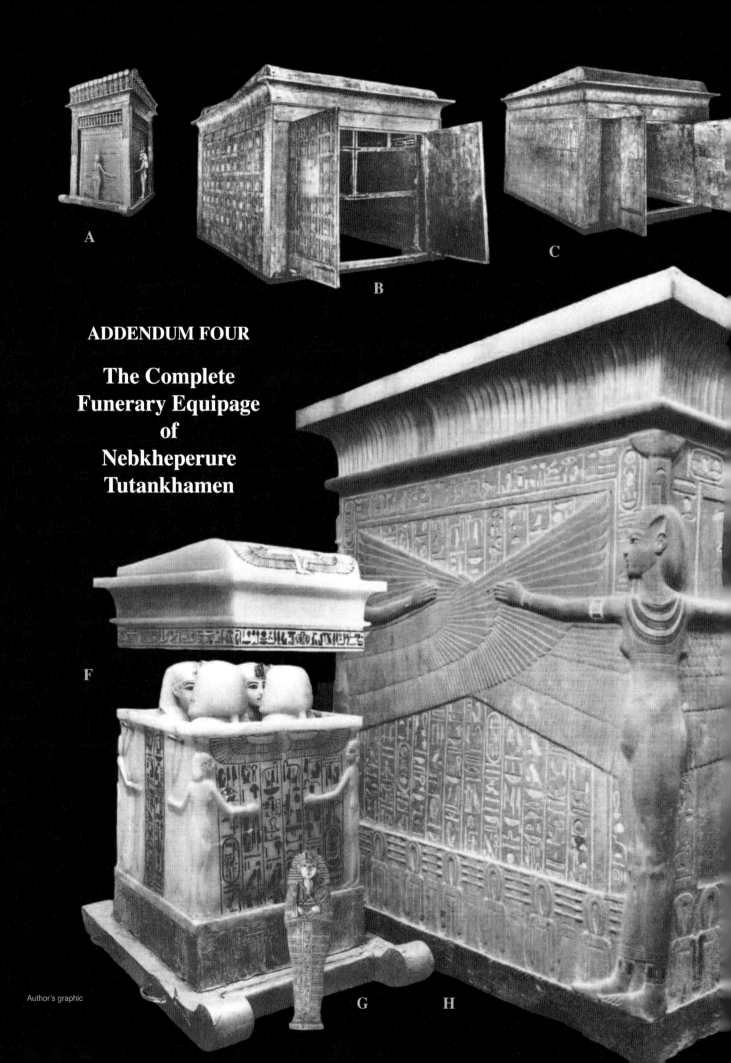

A

B

C

ADDENDUM FOUR

The Complete
Funerary Equipage
of
Nebkheperure
Tutankhamen

F

G

H

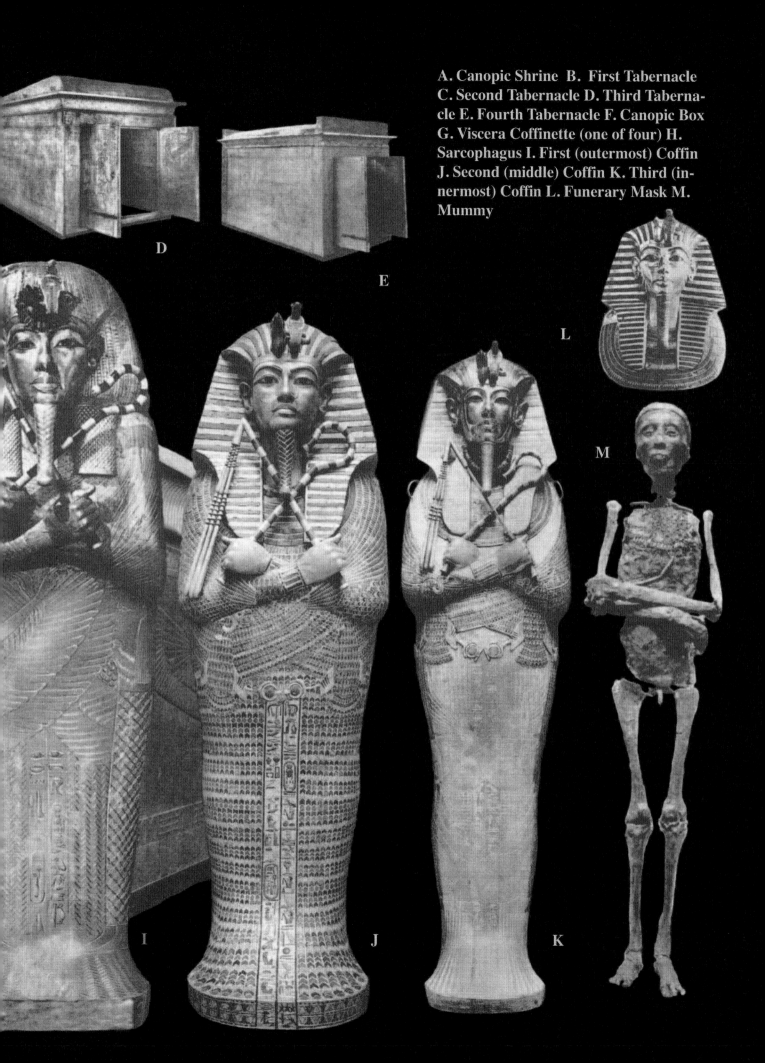

A. Canopic Shrine B. First Tabernacle
C. Second Tabernacle D. Third Taberna-
cle E. Fourth Tabernacle F. Canopic Box
G. Viscera Coffinette (one of four) H.
Sarcophagus I. First (outermost) Coffin
J. Second (middle) Coffin K. Third (in-
nermost) Coffin L. Funerary Mask M.
Mummy

D

E

L

M

I

J

K

ADDENDUM FIVE

CT-Scanning & DNA-Testing Nebkheperure Tutankhamen's Mummy

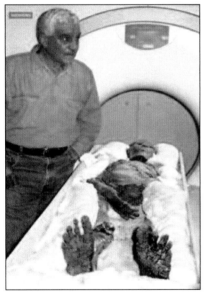

Top, The mummy of Tutankhamen as it appeared following the CT-scanning in 2005, its several parts reassembled, albeit without the arms folded over the torso mid-section as they had been when re-interred by Howard Carter in 1926. Above, Zahi Hawass, then director of the Supreme Council for Antiquities, with the king's mummy positioned for CT-scanning in the Seimens machine donated to Egypt for mummy scanning by the National Geographic Society. Internet photos

Other than Amenhotep II, Tutankhamen is the only New Kingdom pharaoh to have been found resting in his original place of interment; but, unlike his great-great grandfather (whose mummy had been stripped of its adronments by tomb robbers and then rewrapped and returned to his sarcophagus in a cheap replacement coffin), Tutankhamen was still lying within his ornate nested original coffins and funerary mask, his bandaging quite literally loaded with amulets and funerary jewelry. It was, however, this totally undisturbed condition which apparently contributed to the prematurely deceased teenaged ruler's mummy being among the most poorly preserved of his royal peers (allowing that Amenhotep III and the KV55 individual are skeletal today, and Rameses VI had been torn into several bundled-together pieces). It is thought by scholars and researchers that the friable state of the Tutankhamen remains when finally revealed by Howard Carter is the consequence of the freshly bandaged mummy having been excessively anointed with a great quantity of liquid unguents — and the innermost coffin as well — which effectively served to thoroughly char the hermetically enclosed dead king.

But Tutankhamen's mummy has suffered like no other at the hands of its discoverer — and subsequently. It is well documented that Howard Carter (assisted by anatomist Dr. Douglas Derry) literally decapitated, bisected, quartered and amputated the royal body — their butchery justified as necessary in order to free the mummy from the funerary mask and inner-coffin basin to which it was glued by the hardened unguents, and to remove the many bracelets adorning the king's forearms.

Carter and Derry merely wrote summary anatomical descriptions of the king's mummy, then re-interred Tutankhamen in his outermost coffin in 1926, the several parts reassembled and resting supine on a long tray filled with sand, the lidded coffin being returned to the sarcophagus in the Burial Chamber, protected by a cover of thick plate-glass. But the boy-king's second final rest was apparently unofficially disturbed sometime between the 1926 re-interment by Carter, at which time the

Left, Tutankhamen's mummy displayed in a glass case positioned in the Antechamber of KV-62, following the 2005 CT-scannings & DNA-testing. Above inset, Closeup of the mummy's head, with punched-in eyesocket & missing left ear. Inset above left, Two views of the 2005 French forensic reconstruction of how Nebkheperure Tutankhamen may have appeared in life, but bearing no resemblance to the many contemporary depictions of the teenage ruler in both the round & relief. Internet photos

Egyptian government permitted British anatomy professor R.G. Harrison to disinter the mummy for the purpose of x-raying the skull and torso, to determine Tutankhamen's exact age and cause of death.

The 1968 disinterment immediately showed that the cotton batting with which Carter had covered the king's remains in 1926 to be in disarray and that, while the corpse was still lying supine on the sand tray, the severed forearms were no longer crossed at the torso's mid-section, but rather resting fully extended along the body's sides. Also the beaded bib and skull-cap which Carter had left on the mummy were now missing, the frontal rib-cage and sternum as well, and the clavicals disarranged. Additionally the king's eye-sockets seemingly had been punched in, and the right ear and penis were gone, the left ear broken. It has been proposed that possibly during World War II, when the Valley of the Kings was only minimally attended, the KV62 occupant had been surreptitiously exposed for the purpose of stealing any jewelry left on the corpse. It was at this time that the frontal rib cage would have been sawed off, the sternum coming with it, in order to recover the beaded bib which was adhered to the chest by a carapace of resin. Getting little of value for their effort, the thieves returned Tutankhamen to his coffin and sarcophagus, for Harrison to officially redisturb a couple of decades later.

When American orthodontist James E. Harris was x-raying the Royal Mummies in 1978, for the purpose of studying their dentition and morphological relationships, it was decided that Harrison's decade-old radiograph of the Tutankhamen skull was of inferior quality, so Harris was permitted to disinter the king yet one more time for new x-raying, with Egyptian government officials in attendance for the one-day activity. Unofficial photos taken at that time reveal that the royal corpse appeared even blacker and more-charred looking (Dr. Derry had discribed the mummy's skin as grayish colored).

Harris's x-ray confirmed that two boney fragments (first noted by Carter) did, indeed, appear to be embedded in a resinous mass at the back of Tutankhamen's otherwise-empty cranium (the brain having been extracted as part of the mummification process). This prompted a slue of theories regarding how the young king had died prematurely, chief of those being that he had been purposely murdered by a sharp blow to the back of his head. This would be disproven, however.

With the advent of computerized tomography, it was decided by then Egyptian Antiquities chief Zahi Hawass — as part of his Egyptian Mummies Project (EMP) — to have the Tutankhamen mummy CT-scanned. So on January 15, 2005, the royal remains were yet again exposed, this time actually removed from KV62 altogether — albeit still resting on the sand tray — and taken to a trailer parked nearby the tomb, which housed a Seimens scanner donated to the Egyptian government by the National Geographic Society. The scanning process took just thirty minutes and resulted in some 1,700 generated images. Tutankhamen was then returned to his sarcophagus and the coffin resting within; the plate-glass cover was replaced; and Hawass and his all-Egyptian team returned to Cairo, to study and ponder the results of their CT-scan of the king. Based on the latter, three forensic reconstructions of Tutankhamen's head were commisioned, none of them looking very much like his contemporary depictions.

The scan showed that there was no traumatic injury to the head (ruling out death by a blow thereto), that Tutankhamen had a slightly cleft palate (which caused him no problem in life) and that the elongated skull was within the normal range and appeared to be a family trait. Bone maturity and presence of wisdom teeth confirmed the king had been about nineteen at his death. There was no premortem injury to the body, save for a fracture of the left femur (thigh) near the knee; presence of embalming material on the edges of this break (perhaps caused by a fall from a chariot?) suggested that it had occurred shortly before death, which may have resulted from subsequent blood poisoning. The only other anomoly to the mummy was a congenital deformity of the left foot (a variety of clubfoot), which possibly caused the young king mobility impairment (and Hawass saw as the reason for so many canes and walking staves found in KV62).

The Egyptian Mummies Project segued in 2007 into Hawass's Family of King Tutankhamun Project, and the CT-scanning and DNA-testing of eleven royal (or royal-related) mummies thought to have been relatives of the boy-king, a pedigree spanning five generations. This study lasted until 2009 and resulted in a second examination of Tutankhamen's CT-scan data, which indicated that the young pharaoh had been infected (even multiple times) by *malaria tropica*, as had three others of the mummies in the study; but in none of the cases would any one infection have necessarily been fatal. The DNA-tests also indicated that Tutankhamen was most likely the son of the individual whose skeletal reamins were found in KV55 (Akhenaten, or more probably Smenkhkare) and the Younger Lady mummy discovered in KV35, who was also a daughter of Amenhotep III and Great Wife Tiye and so a full sister of the father. Since the identity of the KV35 female is in question, it has been suggested that she might be the royal pair's granddaughter, instead, thus Meritaten the eldest child of Akhenaten and Nefertiti, and wife of the ephememral Smenkhkare.

Tutankhamen's mummy rests (at this writing) in a glass case in KV62's Antechamber.

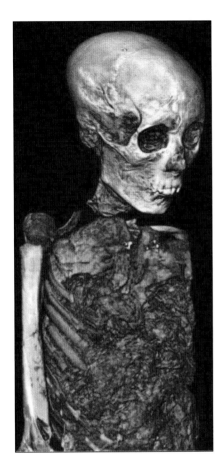

The CT-scan of the mummy of Tutankhamen reveals the absence of a sternum, as well as the frontal rib-cage (irregularly sawed-through left ribs still in place), & the thorax solidly packed with intrusive materials, disquising the fact that the king's heart is also missing. Internet photo

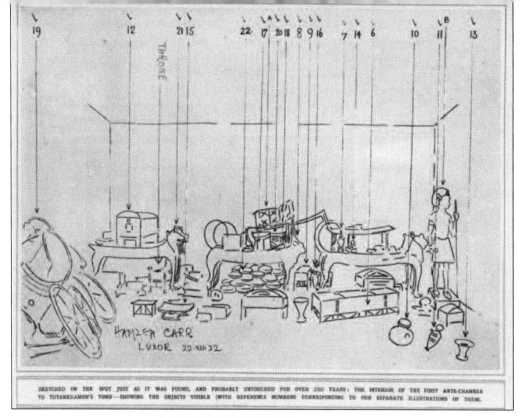

SKETCHED ON THE SPOT JUST AS IT WAS FOUND, AND PROBABLY UNTOUCHED FOR OVER 3000 YEARS: THE INTERIOR OF THE FIRST ANTE-CHAMBER TO TUTANKHAMEN'S TOMB—SHOWING THE OBJECTS VISIBLE (WITH REFERENCE NUMBERS CORRESPONDING TO OUR SEPARATE ILLUSTRATIONS OF THEM).

Hamzeh Carr was an Anglo-Egyptian artist & illustrator of Middle Eastern & Buddhist subject matter active in the 1920s, an example of his work seen in the full-page illustration above for a 1926 edition of the Rubaiyat of Omar Khayyam.

ADDENDUM SIX

The First Record of KV62: Sketches of the Antechamber & Contents by Hamzeh Carr, Made December 22, 1922

In its edition of January 6, 1923, *The Illustrated London News* published five full pages of sketches of the just-discovered Tomb of Tutankhamen, with the following accompanying text: *"These deeply interesting sketches were made by the artist, Mr. Hamzeh Carr, on December 22, when the tomb of King Tutankh-amen, discovered by Lord Carnarvon and Mr. Howard Carter, was reopened after having been closed for a time since the first inspection, to allow of due preparations being made to guard it and clear the contents. Representatives of the Press were allowed to view the ante-chamber, the only one so far opened, from the thresh- old, by the light of a powerful electric lamp. 'Mr Carr', we are informed by our correspondent, was very fortunately able to obtain Mr. Carter's permission to sketch, and was the only artist present at the opening of the tomb.*

No. 17

PROBABLY FOR THE KING'S HEAD-DRESS: A BOX BEARING THE THREE ROYAL CARTOUCHES AND DECORATED WITH PAINT, BEATEN GOLD, AND INLAID STONE.

"Immediately after the Press view, the tomb was closed again, except to members of Lord Carnarvon's staff. The sketches obtained by the artist are absolutely exclusive and unique. No photographs were then allowed to betaken of the interior of the tomb. Our sketches show objects as they were found, absolutely untouched. Many objects, including the king's throne, are so concealed behind others as to be impossible to sketch. The chariots lay in a heap in a corner, and the wheels have all been taken off, apparently to get them into the tomb"...

Lord Carnarvon himself, describing the Antechamber, writes: *"Between two of the couches we noticed four of the most beautiful alabaster vases ever found; nothing to touch them has ever come to light before... At the northern end are two life-sized portrait statues of the king in bitumenised wood. The features are most delicately carved... The first thing one noticed against the wall facing the door were three gigantic carved gilt wooden beds, the ends of the beds having carved heads, one head, in particular, with a large ivory tongue and teeth looking most weird. Upon these beds were heaped chairs, boxes, smaller carved couches, and some wonderful sticks beautifully carved and inlaid... Everywhere was a mass of boxes, some opened and plundered, others seemingly untouched. At the present moment, owing to the profusion of articles, we have not a notion of a thousandth part of the contents of even this chamber."*

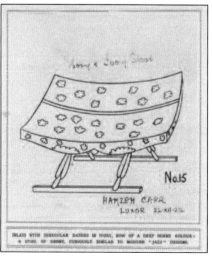

No. 15

HAMZEH CARR
LUXOR 22-XII-22

INLAID WITH IRREGULAR DAISIES IN IVORY, ROW OF A DEEP OCHRE COLOUR: A STOOL OF EBONY, CURIOUSLY SIMILAR TO MODERN "JAZZ" DESIGNS.

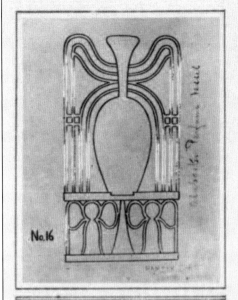

CARVED FROM A SINGLE PIECE OF ALABASTER:
A PERFUME-VESSEL (ABOUT 16 IN. HIGH).

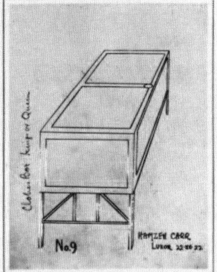

HOW EGYPTIAN ROYALTY KEPT THEIR GARMENTS 3000
YEARS AGO: A BLACK AND WHITE CLOTHES-BOX.

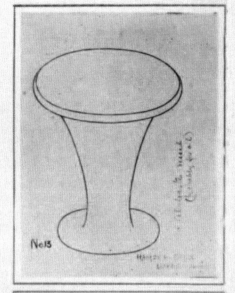

ALSO BELONGING TO THE UNIQUE SET OF ALABASTER
VESSELS: ONE PROBABLY USED FOR OIL.

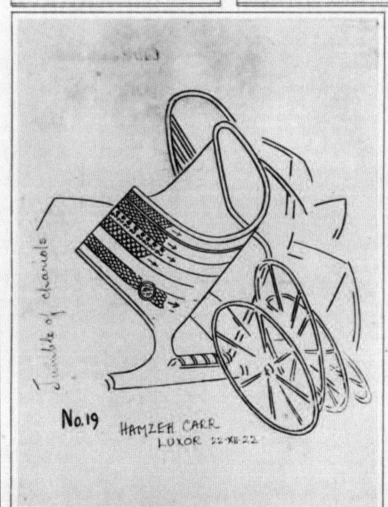

DECORATED THROUGHOUT IN BEATEN GOLD, INLAID STONE, AND PAINT (THE ARROWS INDICAT-
ING CONTINUATION OF DESIGN): CHARIOTS WITH WHEELS REMOVED TO GET THEM INTO THE TOMB.

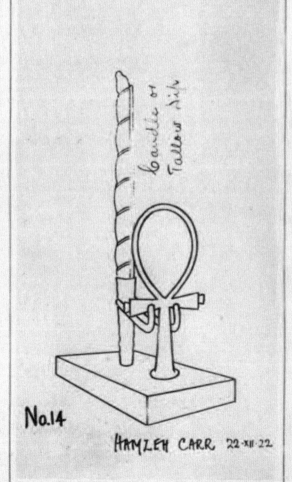

SAID TO BE THE FIRST EXAMPLE OF SUCH LIGHTING IN EGYPT: A CANDLE
OR TALLOW DIP IN A GOLD SOCKET, WITH IRON OR BRONZE SUPPORT.

TUTANKHAMEN: DIRECT DRAWINGS OF OBJECTS FOUND.

BY HAMZEH CARR, BY PERMISSION OF MR. HOWARD CARTER.

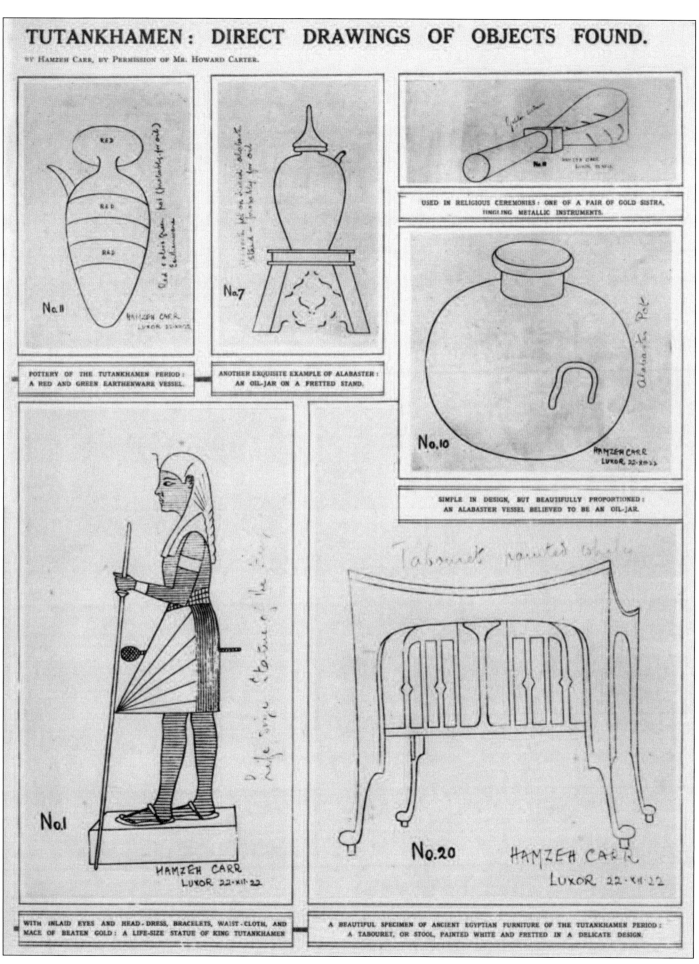

USED IN RELIGIOUS CEREMONIES: ONE OF A PAIR OF GOLD SISTRA,
TINGLING METALLIC INSTRUMENTS.

POTTERY OF THE TUTANKHAMEN PERIOD:
A RED AND GREEN EARTHENWARE VESSEL.

ANOTHER EXQUISITE EXAMPLE OF ALABASTER:
AN OIL-JAR ON A FRETTED STAND.

SIMPLE IN DESIGN, BUT BEAUTIFULLY PROPORTIONED:
AN ALABASTER VESSEL BELIEVED TO BE AN OIL-JAR.

WITH INLAID EYES AND HEAD-DRESS, BRACELETS, WAIST-CLOTH, AND
MACE OF BEATEN GOLD: A LIFE-SIZE STATUE OF KING TUTANKHAMEN

A BEAUTIFUL SPECIMEN OF ANCIENT EGYPTIAN FURNITURE OF THE TUTANKHAMEN PERIOD:
A TABOURET, OR STOOL, PAINTED WHITE AND FRETTED IN A DELICATE DESIGN.

DRAWINGS MADE SPECIALLY FOR "THE ILLUSTRATED LONDON NEWS"

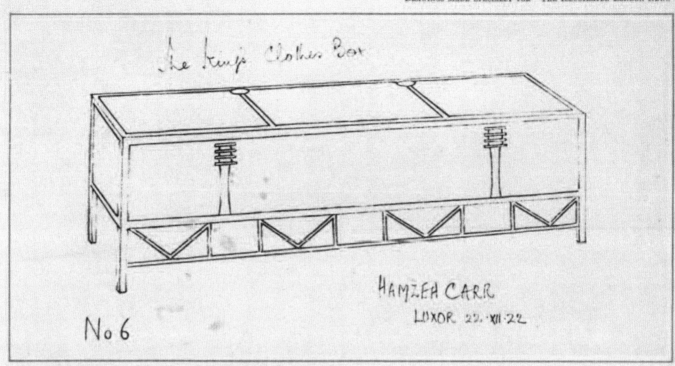

DECORATED ON THE SIDES WITH THE TET SIGN (OR OSIRIS' BACKBONE): KING TUTANKHAMEN'S CLOTHES-BOX, IN A DESIGN OF BLACK AND WHITE, WITH BROWN WOODWORK AT THE BASE.

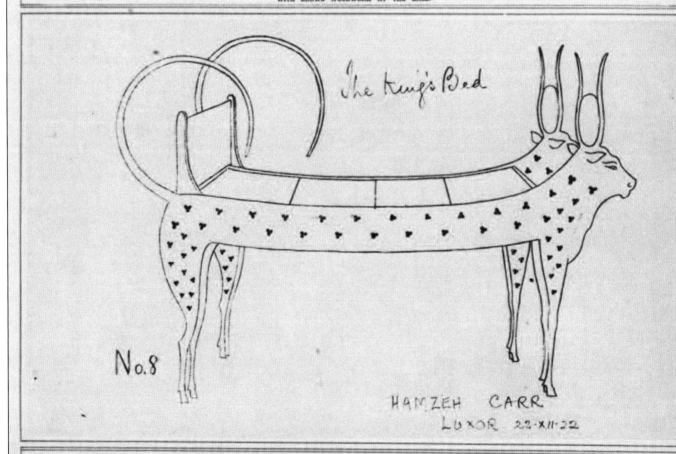

IN AN EXQUISITE DESIGN OF HORUS FIGURES COVERED WITH BEATEN GOLD AND DECORATED WITH A PATTERN OF STALKLESS TREFOIL: A MAGNIFICENT COUCH FOUND IN THE FIRST ANTE-CHAMBER OF THE TOMB.

BEDS AND WARDROBES OVER 3000 YEARS OLD.

BY HAMZEH CARR; BY PERMISSION OF MR. HOWARD CARTER.

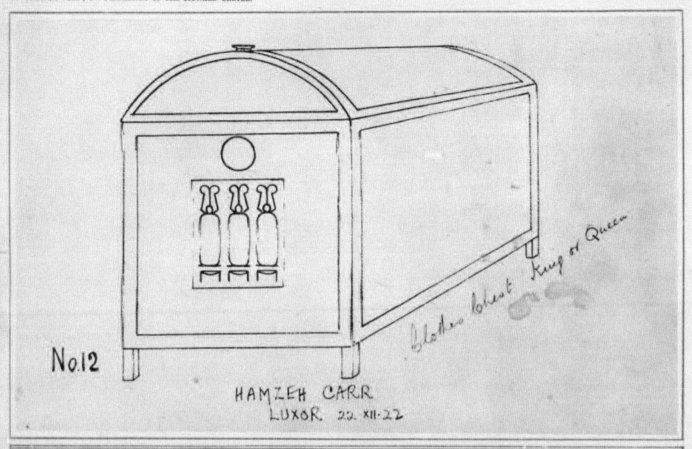

No.12

Clothes Chest King or Queen

HAMZEH CARR
LUXOR 22. XII. 22

DECORATED AT THE END WITH THE SUN DISC AND UNDER IT THREE CARTOUCHES — THE FIRST AND THIRD BEARING THE NAME OF THE KING
AND THE CENTRE ONE THAT OF THE QUEEN: A BLACK AND WHITE CLOTHES-CHEST.

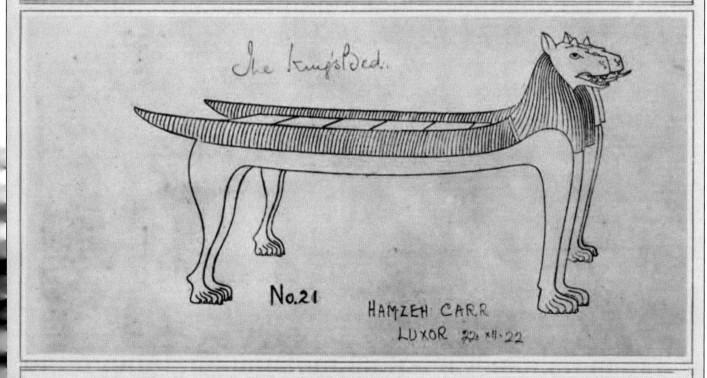

The King's Bed.

No.21

HAMZEH CARR
LUXOR 22. XII. 22

ENTIRELY COVERED WITH BEATEN GOLD AND IN PERFECT PRESERVATION — EVEN THE TEETH AND TONGUES OF THE HEADS BEING UNBROKEN:
ANOTHER SPLENDID ROYAL COUCH IN THE ANTE-CHAMBER OF TUTANKHAMEN'S TOMB.

ADDENDUM SEVEN

If Harry Burton Had Photographed
KV62 in Color

All Images © Dynamichrome

Opposite, The king' mummy with its gold mask, as first revealed in the solid-gold Third Coffin. Date November 1925.

Above, Carter examining the Third Coffin still resting in the basin of the rishi-*style Second Coffin. Date October 1925.*

The Metropolitan Museum of Arts Egyptian Expedition's generous loan of its staff photographer, Harry Burton, to fellow Englishman Howard Carter, for the purpose of the excavator accurately recording KV62's contents as found and the lengthy process of the tomb's clearance, resulted in an Egyptian archaeological site being fully scientifically documented for the first time. Earlier efforts at photographing tomb contents in place had been minimal at best (e.g., TT8, Kha and Merit, in 1906; and KV55, the Amarna Cache, in 1907). Working with a tripod in cramped circumstances, skillfully using electrical lighting on tripods and then processing his large-format glass-plate negatives in an improvised dark room in nearby KV55, Burton made over 2,800 exposures of the tomb spaces and individual objects (these photographed against seamless backgrounds in the conservation lab which had been set up in KV15. The resulting black-and-white images are crystal clear and capture infinite details and textures.

In conjuction with the "Discovering King Tut" KV62 replicas exhibition, in co-operation with the Griffith Institute, Jordan J. Lloyd and his team at Dynamichrone, a company specializing in reconstructing and colorizing historic black-and-white photographs, numerous ones of Harry Burton's images have been colorized, and a selection of these presented here.

View of the southwest corner of the Antechamber, contents in *situ. Date De-cember 1922 or January 1923.*

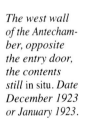

The west wall of the Antecham-ber, opposite the entry door, the contents still in situ. Date December 1923 or January 1923.

Above, The northwest corner of the Antechamber, the numbered contents still in situ. Date December 1922 or January 1923. Below left, Detail of calcite vases between the lion & cow couches, the Antechamber. Date December 1922 or January 1923. Below, Detail of the numbered objects on & under the lion couch in the Antechamber. Date December 1922 or January 1923.

337

Opposite, Arthur Mace (standing) & Alfred Lucas performing conservation on one of the guardian statues from the Antechamber. Date probably January 1924. Left, Carter & Carnarvon at t he opening of the Burial Chamber. Date February 16, 1923. Below, Carter & Callendar wrapping one of the guardian statues. Date unknown.

Opposite, View into the Treasury with contents in situ. Date probably 1923.

Right, Detail of four chests in the Treasury, inventory numbers in place. Date probably 1923.

Below, View of the south wall of the Treasury, with bitumen-coated deity shrines & model boats in situ *Date probably 1923.*

341

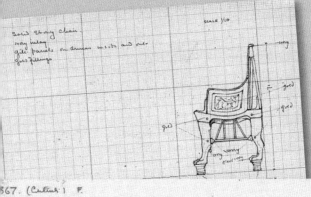

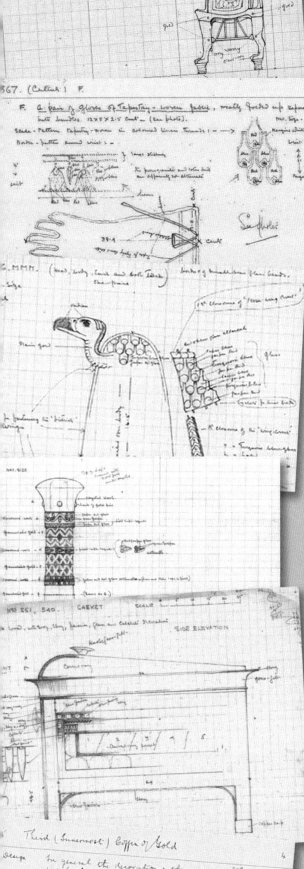

Tombs discovered with their contents for the most part intact in the Valley of the Kings during the years prior to KV62 (Maiherpri, KV26, in 1899; Yuya and Thuyu, KV46, 1905) regrettably were not photographed by their discoverers with those burial goods in place; the totally undisturbed TT8 (Kha and Merit, 1906) warranted only three such photographic interior general-views. And the funerary objects themselves, in those few instances, were only photographed individually once they had been removed to museum contexts. Thus Howard Carter's enlisting of Metropolitan Museum of Art Egyptian Expedition photographer Harry Burton to fully record KV62's plethora of contents *in situ* — and then each object separately — was a first for Egyptian archaeology and set the standard for all future discoveries. Burton made some 1,850 glass-plate negative exposures, which were developed and then printed in the improvised darkroom of KV55, close by KV62.

After the carefully lighted *in situ* views were completed, Carter (presumably with the assistance of Arthur Callender) then placed small cards printed with numbers 1 through 620 on each major object in the tomb's four chambers (and entry passage, after the fact). A great many of these objects consisted of multiple parts (such as the contents of boxes, chests, etc.), which were further subdivided with letters of the alphabet: e.g., 256 a, aa, aaa, b, bb, bbb, etc. (in the case of the royal mummy). Burton then made additional photographs of detailed areas of the clearance, so that the object numbers were in view (as in the close-up of the Annexe clearance at far right). When individual objects were subsequently photographed in the "studio" Burton had set up in the KV15 laboratory, the number cards were included in each exposure.

In addition to the object photos, every KV62 piece was recorded (usually by Carter himself or, in the early stages of the clearance, by Arthur Mace) on a handwritten index card, which included the object's position in the tomb, its material(s) and measurements, and a description of its main physical characteristics. Some objects required multiple cards and even attachments of small sheets of gridded paper, especially when a schematic drawing of the recorded object (and its details, in many cases) was included. Alfred Lucas also added notes regarding the on-site conservation or restoration of objects, in addition to which he kept his own detailed records of the laboratory work. Archived today at the Griffith Institute, Oxford, are some 3,150 of the KV62 object cards. These have been digitized and are available online to researchers and interested persons. Burton's original photographic negatives are likewise housed at the Institute, with a duplicate full-set maintained by the Metropolitan in New York.

Carter also kept a journal, in which he described in some detail (or not) the daily activities of the tomb clearance, although these entries rarely add significant information to the other records. He likewise kept personal pocket-diaries, which are of little real archaeological value, but do serve to document the excavator's feelings regarding the many interruptions occurring and the "politics" of the excavation.

Detailed plans of the four tomb chambers, showing the contents *in situ*, were also made, by Metropolitan Museum draughtsmen L. F. Hall and W. Hauser. (see their plan of the Antechamber, pp. 58-59). Carter himself drew the plan of the Burial Chamber (see p. 110). Reports on certain aspects of the tomb's contents (e.g., the botanical materials) were provided by various experts.

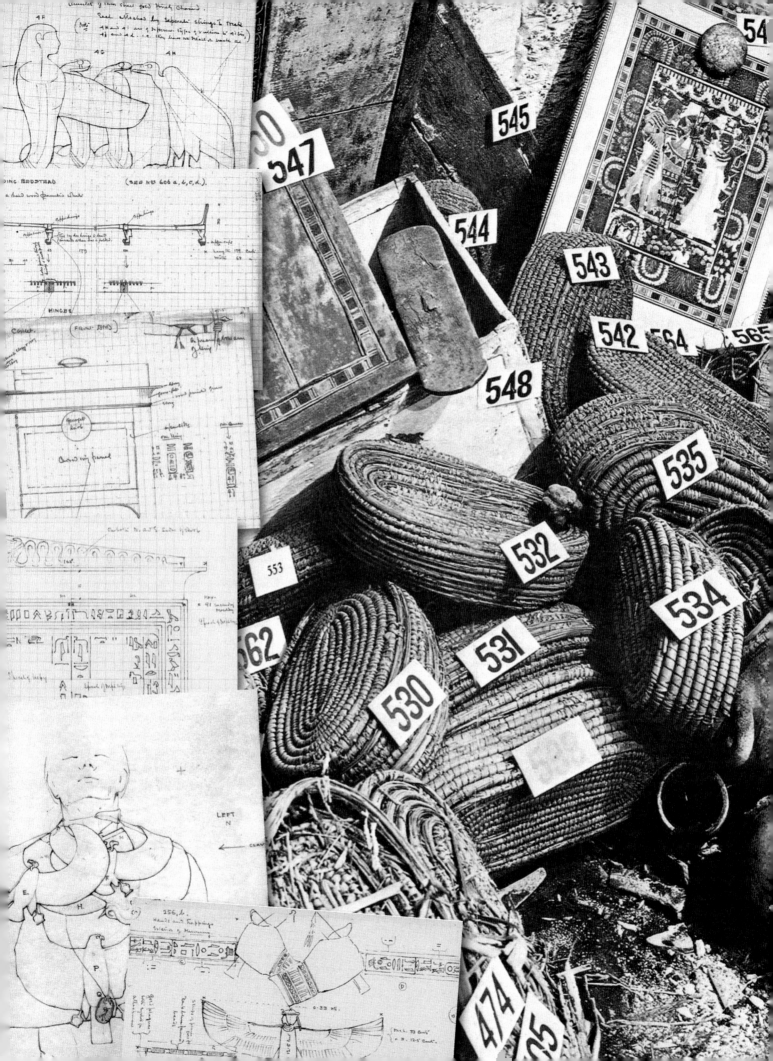

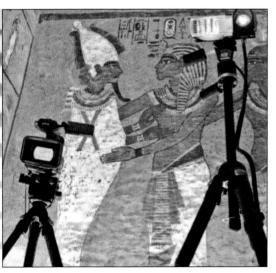

Top, Completed installation of the KV-62 Burial Chamber and sarcophagus. Above, Factum Arte photographic equipment in chamber during the recording, with a technician in the middle view matching color swatches to the north-wall paining.

Factum Arte photos

ADDENDUM NINE

Creating a Full-scale Facsimile of the KV62 Burial Chamber

Coinciding with the Ninetieth Anniversay of the discovery of the Tomb of Tutankhhamen, exact replicas of the Burial Chamber and sarcophagus were presented to the Arab Republic of Egypt, a gift from the Factum Foundation (Madrid, Spain), the Society of Friends of the Royal Tombs of Egypt (SFRTE, Zurich, Switzerland) and the University of Basel. They were exhibited in Cairo on November 13-14, 2012, during the EU Task Force Conference on Tourism and Flexible Investment.

Creator of the accurate-in-every-detail KV62 facsimiles was Factum Arte, a Madrid-based workshop specializing in to-scale exact copies of large art works and historical monuments, made possible by the latest developments in digital-photographic repliction. The company has focused on this innovative approach to monument conservation. An exhibition of Factum Arte's work was held at the Sir John Soane's Museum, London, in 2013.

The royal tombs in the Valley of the Kings are especially vulnerable to deterioration, due to their popularity as tourist sites; they were never meant to accommodate vast numbers of daily visitors. Factum's involvement with Egypt and the VOK began with the duplication of certain chambers of the Tomb of Seti I (KV17) in 2001, in collaboration with many Egyptologists, technicians, cultural-heritage managers, the former Egyptian Supreme Council for Antiquities (SCA) and the current Ministry of State for Antiquities (MSA). Factum has also duplicated at full scale the decorated burial-chambers of tombs KV34

(Thutmose III in 2002) and KV35 (Amenhotep II in 2017) for museum exhibitions of pharaonic treasures. The five-venue Thutmose III exhibition was visited by over 3,000,000 people. The MSA supports Factum Arte's approach to the conservation of the Valley of the Kings royal tombs in the form of future full-scale facsimiles of certain chambers, if not the entire sepulchers.

The exact replication of Tutankhamen's Burial Chamber and sarcophagus took Factum Arte over three years to complete, using the most advanced 3-D technologies for recording the painted surfaces of the chamber's walls — and the sarcophagus's raised- and sunk-reliefs — in astonishing detail and then reproducing them physically in three dimensions without any significant loss of information. (Factum Arte uses photogrammetry of 100-million measured points per square meter.) The scanned images were then printed on "skin" fabric for seamless attachment to support panels. Part of the process included matching color swatches to multiple points on the painted decorations, to assure absolute color-resolution.

Above, Factum Arte technicians digitally photographing the KV62 Burial Chamber. Below, a digital scan of the king's mummy on the funerary sledge in process.
Factum Arte photos

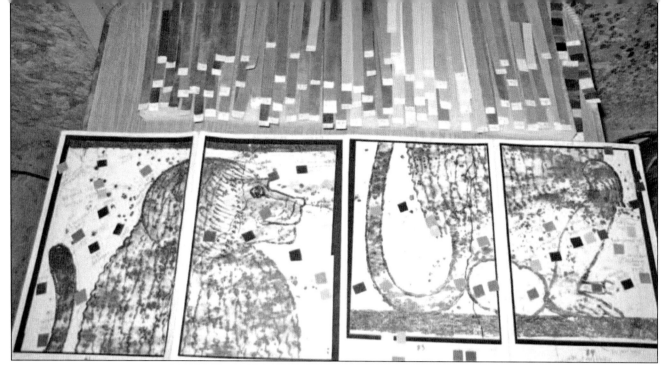

In May of 2014, the Factum Arte replicas of the KV62 Burial Chamber and sarcophagus opened as a tourist attraction in a specially constructed £420,000 subterranean site close by Carter House on the Luxor west bank, not far from the entrance to the Valley of the Kings, where the actual tomb monument is now closed to the public (and undergoing restoration at this writing).

Opposite, The Factum Arte replication of the section of the KV62 Burial Chamber south wall, which Howard Carter had to partially destroy in order to remove the larger funerary objects from the tomb. The original painted fragments were reassenbled on a sand tray by Carter & are stored in the KV62 Treasury. Factum Arte photos

Opposite, Factum Arte replication of the torso of one of the raised-relief four goddesses guarding the corners of Tutankhamen's sarcophagus (inset, the sarcophagus being digitally scanned). Above, The Factum Arte printed panels of the Burial Chamber west wall being installed temporarily on a framework in the company's workshop. Below the panels of the east wall being permanently installed in the fired-brick chamber constructed to display the Burial Chamber facsimile close by Carter House. Factum Arte photos

Right, Entrance to the facsimile subterranean site, open to the public since 2013; Carter House is on the hill in the background.
Internet photo

ADDENDUM TEN
Tutankhamen's Treasures on Tour

Since their discovery in Valley of the Kings Tomb 62 in 1922 and their removal to the Cairo Egyptian Museum (1923-1930), the funerary "treasures" of Nebkheperure Tutankhamen have been the exclusive property of the Egyptian government; and many Egyptians are of the belief that the some 5,000 objects should always remain displayed only in Egypt (in reality just the major pieces have ever been on view, the balance in Cairo Museum storage, some things on view and in storage at the Luxor Museum and in storage on the Luxor west bank). However, beginning in 1961— to produce revenue for the Egyptian government — select ones of the Tutankhamen treasures began to be displayed in special exhibitions outside of Egypt, worldwide, periodically until most recently (at this writing) in 2013. Thus, they have become the most widely traveled and viewed artifacts in the world, and Egypt's best good-will ambassadors. The tours are as follows:

TUTANKHAMUN'S TREASURES
1961-1965

UNITED STATES: Washington, DC, 11/3-12/3/61; Philadephia, PA, 12/15/61-1/14/62; New Haven, CT, 2/1-2/28/62; Houston, TX, 3/154/15/62; Omaha, NE, 5/1-5/31/62; Chicago, IL, 6/15-7/15/62; Seattle, WA, 8/1-8/31/62; San Francisco, CA, 9/15-10/14/62; Los Angeles, CA, 10/30-11/30/62; Cleveland, OH, 12/15/62-1/13/63; Boston, MA, 2/1-2/28/63; St. Louis, MO, 3/15-4/14/63; Baltimore, MD, 5/1-5/31/63; Dayton, OH, 6/15-7/15/63; Detroit, MI, 8/1-9/1/63; Toledo, OH, 9/15-10/15/63; Richmond, VA, 11/1-11/30/63; Pittsburgh, PA, 12/19/63-1/15/64; CANADA: Montreal, 1/64-2/23/64; Ottawa, 3/5-4/5/64; (1964 New York World's Fair, NYC, 4/22-10/18/64); Tortonto, 11/6-12/6/64; Winnipeg, 12/64-1/65; Vancouver, 1/29-2/28/65; Quebec, 3/1-4/1/65

Top, Crowds queue in front of the British Museum in London, for the Tutankhamen exhibition in 1972. Inset, The Tutankhamen gold funerary mask being unpacked in Paris for the 1968 exhibition there. Internet photos

THE TUTANKHAMUN EXHBITION
1965-1966
JAPAN: Tokyo, Aug-Oct/65; Kyoto , Oct-Nov/65; Fukuora. Dec/65-Jan/66

TUTANKHAMUN AND HIS TIME
1967
FRANCE: Paris, 2/2-8/4/67

TREASURES OF TUTANKHAMUN
1972
GREAT BRITAIN: London, 3/29-11/4/72

U.S. President Jimmy Carter & First Lady Roslyn study the gold funerary mask of Tutankhamen during the 1976-'77 exhibition at the National Gallery in Washington, DC. Below, Crowd viewing one of the KV62 Antechamber chests in the same exhibition. Internet photos

TREASURES OF TUTANKHAMUN'S TOMB
1973-1975
UNION OF SOVIET SOCIALIST REPUBLICS; Moscow, Dec/73-May/74; Leningrad, July-Nov/74; Kiev, Ukraine, Jan-Mar/75

TREASURES OF TUTANKHAMUN
1976-1981
UNITED STATES: Washingto, DC, 11/17/76-3/15/77; Chicago, IL, 1/14/-8/14/77; New Orleans, LA, 9/16/77-1/15/78; Los Angeles, CA, 2/15-7/15/78; Seattle, WA, 7/15-11/15/78; New York, NY, 12/15/78-4/15/79; San Francisco, CA, 6/11-9/30/79; CANADA: Totonto, 11/1-12/31/79; WEST GERMANY: Berlin, 2/16-5/26/80; Cologne, 6/21-10/19/80; Munich, 11/22/80-2/1/81; Hanover, 2/20-4/26/81; Hamburg, 5/15-7/18/81

TUTANKHAMUN
AND THE GOLDEN AGE OF THE PHARAOHS,
2004-2013
SWITZERLAND: Basel, 7/4-10/3/04; GERMANY: Bonn, 4/11/04-1/5/05; UNITED STATES: Los Angeles, CA, 6/13-11/20/05; Fort Lauderdale, FL, 12/15/05-4/23/06; Chicago, IL, 5/26/06-1/1/07; Philadelphia, PA, 2/3-9/30/07; UNITED KINGDOM: London, 11/15/07-8/24/08; UNITED STATES: Dallas, TX, 4/27/09-3/10/10; San Fraancisco, CA, 6/27/09-3/28/10; New York, NY, 4/23/10-1/11/11; AUSTRALIA: Melbourne, 4/8-11/1/11; JAPAN: Osaka, 3/17-6/3/12; Tokyo, 8/4/12-1/20/13

Staff preparing to unwrap KV62 objects for the 1977 Tutankhamen exhibition at the Chicago Field Museum. Below, Entrance to the Field Museum in Chicago, with banners advertising the "King Tut" exhibition there in 2007. Internet photos

TUTANKHAMUN: THE GOLDEN KING
AND THE GREAT PHARAOHS,
2008-2013
AUSTRIA: Vienna, 3/9-9/28/08; UNITED STATES: Atlanta, GA, 11/13/08-5/16/09; Indianapolis, IN, 6/25/09-10/28/10; CANADA: Toronto, 11/24/09-5/2/10; UNITED STATES: Denver, CO, 6/2910-1/9/11; Saint Paul, MN, 2/28-9/5/11; Houston, TX, 10/13/11-4/15/12; Seattle, WA, 5/24/12-1/6/13

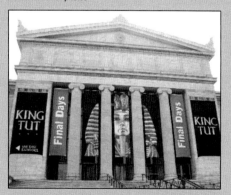

ADDENDUM ELEVEN
Exhibitions of KV62 Replicas

The first exhibition of a replication of Tutankhamen's tomb was staged by Arthur Weigall for the "British Empire Exhibition" at Wembley, U.K., in 1924. Permanent modern exhibitions of facsimiles of KV62 and its contents exist in Dorchester, Dorset, U.K.; Las Vegas, Nevada, U.S.; and even in Cairo. It must be pointed out that a good many KV62 objects in these exhibitions leave a great deal to be desired in their exactness of replication and accuracy of presentation.

A traveling exhibition of KV62 replicas, created by SC Exhibitions in 2015, has (at this writing) visited Johannesburg, South Africa; Munich, Dresden, Graz, Stockholm and other European cities; plus San Diego, Grand Rapids and New York City in the U.S.

Titled "The Discovery of King Tut," this latter presentation is comprised of over 1,000 remarkably precise re-creations of KV62 treasures and presents two sets of objects, allowing exhibition visitors to experience the jumble of the tomb's contents in their archaeological context (through simulations of the Antechamber, Burial Chamber and Treasury) and displayed separately as select individual objects. Using the latest in replication technology, the "Discovery" objects were handmade in Cairo by Egyptian craftsmen. While the above-mentioned replicas exhibitions include depictions of Tutankhamen's unwrapped mummy, only the "Discovery" presentation shows the king's pathetic remains as they actually appear today.

In addition to the tomb chambers and objects, the "Discovery of King Tut" exhibition includes Harry Burton photographs of KV62, colorized by Dynamichrome (see pp. 334-341).

"Discovery" is the official replica-exhibition as endorsed by the Egyptian Ministry for Antiquities and Heritage.

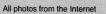
All photos from the Internet

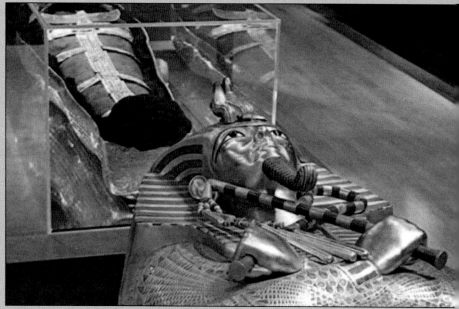

353

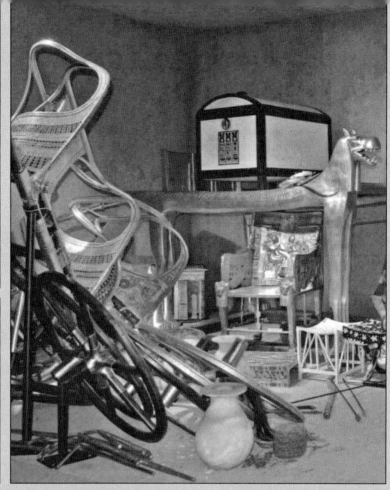

All photos from the Internet

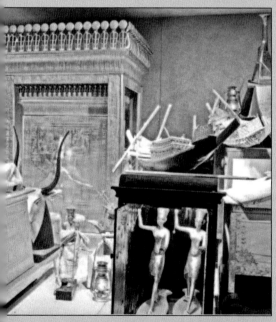
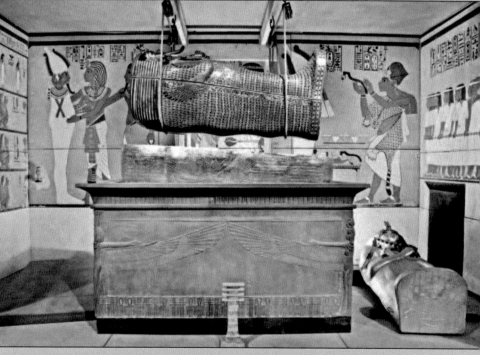

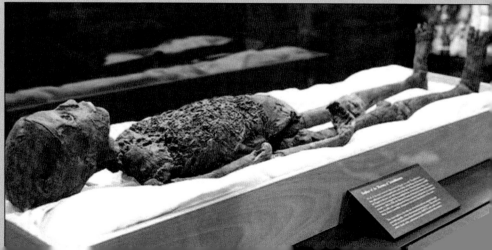

ADDENDUM TWELVE

Hidden Chambers in KV62?

Dr. Nicholas Reeves
Internet photo

British Egyptologist Nicholas Reeves has a long association with Nebkheperure Tutankhamen, having written popular books on both Howard Carter (*Howard Carter Before Tutankhamun*, with John H. Taylor, 1992) and KV62 (*The Complete Tutankhamun*, 1990), as well as having served as the curator of the Egyptian collection at Highclere Castle (1988-1998). Between 1998 and 2002, he co-directed with fellow British Egyptologist Geoffrey T. Martin the Amarna Royal Tombs Project in the Valley of the Kings, excavating — without success — for possible burial-sites of members of Akhenaten's family. The Project was re-initiated in 2014 by the University of Arizona, although at this writing no further Valley excavations have been undertaken by Reeves.

He did, however, set the world of Egyptology on its ear when, in July 2015, Reeves published (through the auspices of the University of Arizona) the Amarna Royal Tombs Project Occasional Paper No. 1, *The Burial of Nefertiti?*, in which he proposed his theory that KV62 contains two additional "hidden" chambers, one of which possibly holds or leads to the undisturbed burial of Queen Nefertiti, interred as King Ankhkheperure Neferneferuaten Smenkhkare — for whom KV62 had originally been hewn then subsequently appropriated and altered for interment of her successor, Nebkheperure Tutankhamen, he having died prematurely without a ready tomb-site of his own.

Reeves based his theory — which was met with considerable scepticism by fellow Egyptologists — on what he preceived from studying Fac-

356

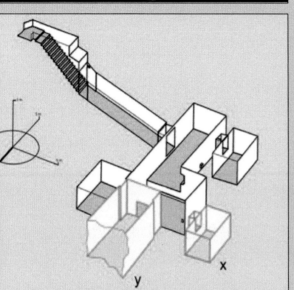

Opposite page, The painted decoration of the north wall of the Burial Chamber of KV62. It was proposed that a hidden doorway leading to a further chamber or chambers lay hidden behind the righthand scene of King Ay preforming the Opening of the Mouth ceremony for Tutankhamen. Left, Figure 15 from N. Reeves's The Burial of Nefertiti? *reproducing the Factum Arte hi-resolution scan of the Burial Chamber north wall with numbered anomalies noted by Reeves. Below left, Isometric plan of KV62, with indications of the additional chambers (in yellow) proposed by Reeves.* The Burial of Nefertiti? frontispiece & Fig. 15

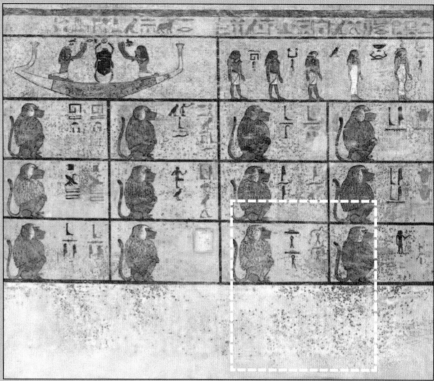

tum Arte's 2010 three-dimensional scans of the KV62 Burial Chamber walls (done for the purpose of creating a fullscale facsimile of that space; see Addendum Nine, 344-349). He detected what he interpreted as indications of sealed and plastered over small doorways in the short west wall of the chamber, and the long north wall. He decided the west-wall "doorway" opened onto an additional store room, contemporary with the stocking of Tutankhamen's burial; the north-wall hidden portal would, more importantly, give access to a passageway which would lead to another, unviolated burial chamber, which in all likelihood would prove to house the long-sought-after mummy of the famous Nefertiti. Further study of the present layout of KV62 convinced Reeves that it conforms to what is known for the standard plan of New Kingdom queens' tombs, with its Antechamber originally having been the beginning of a second, right-turning passageway leading to additional chambers (or single chamber) further north. To accomodate the Nefertiti tomb for Tutankhamen's interment, this passageway was expanded to the west to create the present Burial Chamber — with the addition of the Treasury and the Annex store rooms. While the doorway to the so-called Treasury was left unsealed (and the funeral-cortege wall painting adapted to the narrowed space above it), a third store-room added off the west end of the new Burial Chamber was sealed and plastered and painted over, for whatever reason — but perhaps to allow adequate room for the *Amduat* twelve-baboons scene subsequently decorating that wall.

A further case for a Nefertiti original ownership of KV62 was made by Nichols Reeves. In a late-2015 online interview with the Egyptian news-

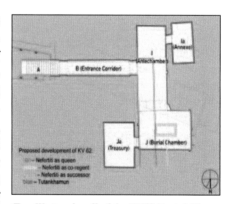

Top, West end-wall of the KV62 Burial Chamber, with painted-plaster decoration refering to the Amduat*), location of the proposed "hidden" doorway indicated.* Author's graphic
Above, N. Reeves's plan of the four stages of suggested development of KV62.
Fig. 30, Reeves, *The Burial of Nefertiti?*

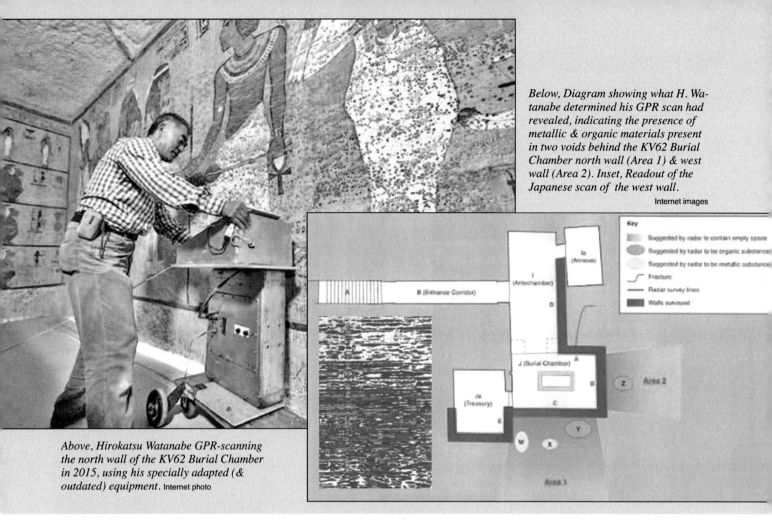

Below, Diagram showing what H. Watanabe determined his GPR scan had revealed, indicating the presence of metallic & organic materials present in two voids behind the KV62 Burial Chamber north wall (Area 1) & west wall (Area 2). Inset, Readout of the Japanese scan of the west wall.

Internet images

Above, Hirokatsu Watanabe GPR-scanning the north wall of the KV62 Burial Chamber in 2015, using his specially adapted (& outdated) equipment. Internet photo

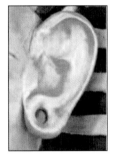 

Above, left & right, Pierced ear of the Tutankhamen funerary mask & the same pierced ear of his mummy.

Archival & Harry Burton photos

paper *Al Ahram*, he posited that eighty percent of the burial goods found by Howard Carter in KV62 belonged originally to Nefertiti (as King Ankhkheperure Nefeneferuaten Smenkhkare), which seems preposterously high in this writer's opinion. He said he believes that the famous gold funerary mask adorning Tutankhamen's mummy was originally made for Nefertiti, citing its pierced ears as proof, then making the blantantly erroneous assertions *"Tutankhamen did not have pierced ears, but a depression that shows he wore earrings only as a child"* and *"Egyptian kings never wore earrings."* One has but to look at Harry Burton's photos of the king's mummy's head to see that, in fact, the boy-king did, indeed, have pierced ears, the holes every bit as large as those on the mask; plus there are dozens of other depictions of him in the round and relief showing his ears pierced (if not, in fact, wearing earrings). And what about the several pairs of such adornments found in KV62 inscribed with his name?

Another argument Reeves put forth as evidence for a Nefertiti presence in KV62 is that the Burial Chamber wall-figure labeled with cartouches as King Ay (the unique Opening of the Mouth scene) is actually Tutankhamen performing that funerary ritual for the deceased Nefertiti. He sees in the "Ay" figure's facial profile a correspondence to the small wooden head showing the youthful Tutankhaten emerging from a water lily (see pp. 48-49). But it seems to this writer the same profile (sloping forehead, pointed nose, full lips, bulbous small chin, with "under" chin) is more readily mimicked in the profile of the plaster "mask" found at El Amarna (now in Berlin), which is often identified as Ay, due to its similarities to relief depictions of him in his El Amarna tomb, as well as to a small "anonymous" king's head in the collection of the Cairo Egyptian Museum, which has often been cited as evidence of Ay's facial resemblance to Queen Tiye, his purported sister.

`   While most Egyptologists scoffed at Reeves's proposal (many remembering he had once suggested that papyri were hidden in the aprons of the two KV62 "guardian" figures — although none were found upon examination), Egyptian Antiquities authorities were intrigued by what new discoveries in Tutankhamen's tomb would mean for re-invigorating Egypt's revolution-depleted tourism. Thus, the Ministry of State for Antiquities authorized a Ground Penetrating Radar (GPR) of the two walls in question.

        A Japanese radar-scientist was engaged by the Ministry to undertake the KV62 scans. With the world watching, in late November 2015, Hirokatsu Watanabe used a specially adapted GPR device to make horizontal scans of the Burial Chamber's walls (normally GPR scanning is done vertically). While the resulting images were indecipherable to the layperson, it was announced by the Egyptian Minister for Antiquities that *"the results are very promising and amply warrant continuation of...investigations to the next stage."* Watanabe returned to Japan to further study his scans and then make a formal report of his analysis to the Ministry of what these showed regarding voids in the bedrock. When this was finally forthcoming, Watanabe was certain that there, indeed, were two voids, and even projected that the one in the west wall evidenced something organic and beyond the north wall a metallic presence. Discussion immediately shifted as to how these voids would be accessed without damage to the Burial Chamber's painted decorations, with suggestions of drilling small holes in the plain dados of the walls, for insertion of an endoscopic camera, as well as breaking through into the northern void from the undecorated Treasury. Certainly cutting a hole large enough for human access through the undecorated west wall of the Treasury would make examination/exploration of the "Nefertiti tomb" possible. But how would any sizeable grave goods (e.g., funerary shrines) be removed from there, if such existed?

In his argument that the KV62 Burial Chamber north-wall vignettes represent Nefertiti rather than Tutankhamen, N. Reeves drew comparison between profiles of the Osiride king and a sculpture of the queen, as well as the king performing the Opening of the Mouth & the head of young Tutankhaten found in the tomb (above). Figs. 27 & 28 from *The Burial of Nefertiti? The plaster study from El Amarna widely believed to depict Ay (below) offers a better comparison, however.* Internet photo

Above & opposite, Views of the Turin 3rd GPR-scan of the KV62 Burial Chamber north & west walls, which confirmed the National Geographic scan that there are no voids present. Internet photos

All second guessing was premature, however. In the spring of 2016, there was a major shuffle in the cabinet of Egyptian President Abdel Fattah el Sisi; and Mamdoud Eldamaty found himself ousted as Antiquities Minister, replaced in that role by a former director of both the Cairo Egyptian Museum and the National Museum of Egyptian Civilization, a repected scholar, Dr. Khaled Elanany. It was speculated that Eldamaty has been too outspoken in his enthusiasm for moving ahead with further KV62 exploration, under his direction. It was assumed that low-keyed Elanany would take a much more measured approach to the conundrum. At a subsequent press conference, the new Antiquities minister stated that the purpose of any future scans of KV62 would be to determine the thickness of the walls, in order to decide the next steps to be taken in accessing the detected spaces.

Thus in March 2016 — without media fanfare — the Antiquities Ministry engaged a team of National Geographic radar technicians to conduct a follow-up second GPR scan of the KV62 walls in question. Although the results also were not at the time released for peer review, the NatGeo scan failed to find any indications of the voids purportedly detected by Watanabe.

At the early-May 2016 2nd Annual Tutankhamun GEM Conference, the fact of the second KV62 scan was announced, with fully contradictory results from the first scan: the Burial Chamber walls concealed no voids. Former Antiquities czar Zahi Hawass was present at the conference and was obviously delighted that his belief there were no "hidden" chambers waiting to be found in KV62 had been confirmed by the NatGeo investigation. *"If there is any masonry or partition wall, the radar signal should show an image,"* Hawass said. *"We don't have this, which means there is nothing there."*

Hawass and Eldamaty were sharing the stage (seated side by side, despite there allegedly being "bad blood" between them) and a heated argument

in English by the two ex-ministers ensued, Hawass charging Eldamaty with having secretly submitted paperwork to the Egyptian authorities, seeking permission to drill holes in KV62 for insertion of a fiber-optic camera; and Eldamaty countering that Hawass had himself, during his brief tenure as Antiquities Minister, drilled a hole in a pyramid, only asking permission to do so after the fact.

On the final day of the GEM Tut conference, Antiquities Minister Elanany announced, *"Until now we don't have a conclusive result* [from the KV62 scans]*,"* calling for further radar and other hi-tech examinations of the tomb. His parting words were, *"That is my message — that science will talk."*

Following the Tutankhamen conference, National Geographic released the raw data from its GPR negative-results for peer reviews in the United States and Egypt. Watanabe — who is in his mid-seventies — also made available some images of his scans; but not the raw data, protesting that, after forty years of customizing it, the information his equipment produces is unreadable by anyone other than himself, so there would be no point in sharing it for review. He has stated that he trusts his data "completely."

A number of experts criticized Watanabe for using Koden-brand GPR machines, which have not been on the market for more than twenty years. Supporters said that Watanabe — who has an industrial background rather than an academic one — relies more on his long per- sonal experience than on cutting-edge technology. He apparently has had successes conducting other archaeological GPR scans, including making possible excavations of Sicán-culture tombs on the northern coast of Peru.

An American geophysicist — who has developed GPR software — examined the NatGeo scans raw-data and found no evidence of voids behind the KV62 walls. All of the other analysts of the same scans came to like conclusions, one saying, *"If we had a void, we should have a strong reflection. But it just doesn't exist."* Another expert stated that GPR could not detect organic material, as Wa-tanabe claimed to have seen in both phantom chambers. It was allowed that reading radar data is often subjective, but with KV62 such is not the case.

One thing which was ignored, or at least not addressed, publically, in the two contradictive GPR scans of KV62 was the fact that both investigations employed their differing technologies in an inadequate way. An American Egyptologist — who shall go unnamed, but with a vested interest in the KV62 situation and with personal experience in using GPR archaeologically — has told this writer that the only way *Ground Penetrating* Radar can fully record subterranean voids and determine their size and shape (and so whether they are, indeed, man made) is by shooting vertically into a bedrock surface, not horizontally as had been done in both the Watanabe and NatGeo scannings. He said that GPR can penetrate at least thirty feet of bedrock, and so easily enough could be used in the case of KV62.

Twenty Seventeen came and went with only interview claims by Zahi Hawass that a third GPR scan of the Tutankhamen tomb would be done, sooner or later, possibly by a Russian team. This would be accompanied, he said, by a scan of the entire Valley of the Kings, in a focused effort to find previously unknown tombs there (so, presumably shooting vertically through Valley bedrock limestone). Meanwhile Hawass personally would be directing excavations in the West Valley of the Kings, close by the Tomb of Ay (WV23), to locate what he predicated would be the intact Tomb of Ankhesenamen, widow of Tutankhamen and putative second wife of his successor. (Although he did, indeed, excavate in the West Valley, Hawass did not find any such tomb, or at least did not make public its finding.)

It was later announced by the Antiquities Ministry that, in fact, a team of radarologists from the Polytechnical University of Turin, Italy, would be conducting the third scanning of KV62.

Again without media fanfare, that promised re-scanning took place over seven days, from January 31 to February 6, 2018. The joint Egyptian-Italian team — under the direction of Dr. Franco Porcelli and obervation by former Antiquities Minister Mamdoud Eldmaty — consisted of nine technical experts and researchers, not only from the Turin university, but also two private Italian companies, 3DGeoimaging and Geostudi Astier. The scanning was done by four different radar-systems, covering low to high frequencies. The multiple scans were of the north and west walls of the Burial Chamber; the west wall of the Treasury; the north wall of the Annexe; and even the floor of the Burial Chamber. The preliminary report of the Egyptian-Italian work did not indicate that any external, vertical scanning of KV62 had been done at the time.

There was mixed reaction when Dr. Porcelli presented his paper at the 5th Annual GEM Tutankamun Conference in early May 2018, announcing that thorough analysis of the multiple-walls scans by the Turin team made three months earlier conclusively had determined that there are no voids, of any nature, behind any of the walls of the Tomb of Tutankhamen. Case closed. Disappointed of course were those optimists who had hoped that the mystery of Nefertiti's fate would have been solved had her burial indeed been discovered in KV62. Perhaps those promised GPR vertical scans of the entire Valley of the Kings (and West Valley, too) might one day yet come upon where she reposes, remaining to be revealed. Meanwhile, the argument can continue that she has already been found in the mummy KV21-B.

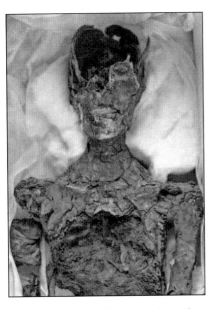

Photoshop-enhanced Internet photo of badly mutilated mummy KV21-B, DNA identified as the grandmother of the KV-62 fetal mummies, so in all probability Nefertiti.

ADDENDUM THIRTEEN
A Little Beeswax & Good to Go

It must have been quite a shock to Cairo Egyptian Museum staff when, in Augsut 2014, the false beard of the golden funerary mask of Tutankhamen became detached during cleaning of the artifact while it was displayed as the centerpiece of the Museum's Tutankhamen galleries. In an immediate effort to disguise this situation, the beard was quickly and unprofessionally reaffixed to the mask's chin using epoxy, some of which smeared onto the latter. This was scraped off, subsequently, leaving several small scratches on the ancient gold. As would happen the Egyptian press learned of the situation and there was instant scandal that Tutankhamen's treasures were not being properly cared for.

Over a year later, in October 2015, a German expert in glass and metal conservation, Christian Eckmann, was engaged by the Museum to rectify the epoxy damage and to properly reattach the beard. At the same time, a full-scale study of the mask was undertaken, using Museum archives as reference. Records showed that the beard was originally detached by Howard Carter's team (see Burton's photograph of a beardless mask, p. 157) and it was not reattached until 1946, using a soft soder. One of the surprises when the beard was re-detached during the 2015 conservation was the discovery that it has an internal tube which connects with the chin.

The restoration process began with a 3-D scan of the mask, followed by a millimeter-by-millimeter removal of the inadequately applied epoxy, using wooden tools and raising the temperature of the artifact. This took more than four weeks of meticulous effort. It was announced by the German Archaeological Institute in Cairo (which had cooperated with the Museum in the restoration process) that the 2014 damage to the mask had been "exaggerated." A 3-D hologram of the iconic treasure was on display in the Museum during the restoration.

When it came time to rejoin the mask and beard, Eckmann and his Egyptian team decided to apply ancient technology and used beeswax, which had been employed as an adhesive in ancient Egypt.

During his close examination of the mask, Eckmann determined that suggestions it had been originally created for Nefertiti (as King Ankhkheperure) were mistaken. He observed that the face piece and helmet were made from the same gold and that there was no evidence of overwriting of an earlier cartouche by that of Nebkheperure (Tutankhamen).

Bottom left, Close-up of the 2014 botched epoxy reattachment of the beard to the mask. Center & right, German restorer Christian Eckmann working on the mask in 2015.
Internet photos

Select Bibliography

Aude Gros de Beler, *Tutankhamun*, (New York, 2002)

Julia Bertsch, Katja Broschat, Christian Eckmann, Salima Ikram, Nicole Reifarth, Florian Ströbele, André Veidmeijer, authors, *Tutankhamun's Unseen Treasures: The Golden Appliques* (Cairo, 2017)

Arnold C. Brackman, *The Search for the Gold of Tutankhamen* (New York, 1976)

Charles Breasted, *Pioneer to the Past; The Story of James H. Breasted, Archaeologist* (Chicago, 1943)

Bob Brier, *The Murder of Tutankhamen. A True Story* (New York, 1998)

Earl of Carnarvon and Howard Carter, *Five Years Exploration at Thebes* (London, 1912)

Elizabeth Eliot Carter, *The Valley of the Kings: A Novel of Tutankhamun* (fiction, New York, 1977)

Howard Carter and A.C. Mace, *The Tomb of Tut-Ankh-Amen*, Vol. 1 (re-print, New York, 1963)

—(with Percy White) *The Tomb of Tut-Ankh-Amen*, Vol. 2 (reprint, New York, 1963)

—(with Percy White) *The Tomb of Tut-Ankh-Amen*, Vol. 3 (reprint, New York, 1963)

—*The Tomb of Tut-Ankh-Amen: Statement*, with introduction by John A. Larson (Brockton, MA, 1997)

—*Tut-Ankh-Amen. The Politics of Discovery* with introduction by Nicholas Reeves (London, 1997)

Michael Carter, *Tutankhamun. The Golden Monarch* (New York, 1972)

Theodore M. Davis et al., *The Tombs of Harmhabi and Tout'ankhamanou* (London, 1912)

Christiane Desroches-Noblecourt, *Tutankhamen, Life and death of a pharaoh* (New York/Boston, 1963)

Aidan Dodson, *The Coffins and Canopic Equipment from the Tomb of Tut'ankhamun* (Oxford, forthcoming)

— *Amarna Sunset: Nefertiti, Tutankhamun, Ay, Horemheb and the Egyptian Counter-Reformation* (Cairo/New York, 2009

— "Were Nefertiti & Tutankhamen Coregents?" *Kmt* 20:3, fall 2009, 41-49

Elaine Edgar, *A Journey Between Souls; The Story of a Soldier and a Pharaoh* (Lafayette, CO, 1997)

I.E.S. Edwards, *The Treasures of Tutankhamun* (New York, 1973)

— *Tutanhhamun: His Tomb and Its Treasures* (New York, 1977)

Earl L. Ertman, "Under the Disk & Crescent: The Use of the Symbols of the Moon and the God Khonsu in the Reign of King Tutankhamen," *Kmt* 20:1 spring 2009

Dennis C. Forbes, "Abusing Pharaoh," *Kmt* 3:1 (spring 1992), 58-67

— "Ritual Figures in KV62. Prototypes and Correspondences," *Amarna Letters* 3 (San Francisco, 1994), 110-127

— "A New Take on Tut's Parents," *Kmt* 8:3 (fall 1997) 85-87

— *Tombs.Treasures.Mummies. Seven Great Discoveries of Egyptian Archaeology* (Sebastopol/Santa Fe, 1998), 319-351

— "Beyond the Tomb: The Historical Tutankhamen from His Monuments," *Kmt* 16:2 summer 2005, 38-50

— (with Salima Ikram & Janice Kamrin) "Tutankhamen's Missing Ribs," *Kmt* 18:1 (spring 2007), 50-56

— "Tutankhamen's Family Ties Full of Knots!" *Kmt* 21:2, summer 2010, 18-35

— "Abusing Pharaoh: Mistreatment of the Mummy of Tutankhamen in Antiquity & Modern Times," Addendum Two,; "Re-imagining Tutankhamen: Three Forensic Reconstructions of How He May Have looked in life," Addendum Three; & "FKTP: The Family of King Tutankhamen Project," Addendum Seven: Book Five, *Complete Catalogue of the Royal Mummies, Tombs.Treasures.Mummies.* (reprint 2016), 162-173, 174-75 & 198-215

— "New 'Virtual Autopsy' Creates a Grotesque Tutankhamen," *Kmt* 25:4, winter 2014-15, 24-25

— "Tut TV: Six-Hour Miniseries to Love or Loathe," *Kmt* 26:3, fall 2015

Penelope Fox, *Tutankhamun's Treasure* (London/New York, 1951)

Christopher Frayling, *The Face of Tutankhamun* (London, 1992)

Rita Freed, Yvonne J. Markowitz, Sue H. D'Aria, eds., *Pharaohs of the Sun: Akhenaten, Nefertiti, Tutankhamen* (Boston/NewYork/London, 1999)

J.R. Harris, "Akhenaten and Nefernefruaten in the Tomb of Tut'ankhamun" in C.N. Reeves, ed., *After Tut'ankhamun. Research and excavation in the Royal Necropolis at Thebes* (London, 1992) 55-72

M. Eaton-Krauss, "The Sarcophagus in the Tomb of Tut'ankhamun" in C.N Reeves, ed., *After Tut'ankhamun; Research and excavation in the Royal Necropolis at Thebes* (London, 1992)

— T*he Sarcophagus in the Tomb of Tut'ankhamun* (Oxford, 1993)

— (with E. Graef), *The Small Golden Shrine from the Tomb of Tut'ankhamun* (Oxford, 1985)

— "Seats of Power: The Thrones of Tutankhamen," *Kmt* 19:2 summer 2008, 18-33

— "The Burial of Tutankhamen" Part One, *Kmt* 20:4, winter 2009-10, 34-47

— "The Burial of Tutankhamen," Part Two, *Kmt* 21:1, spring 2010,18-36

— *The Unknown Tutankhamun* (Bloomsbury, 2014)

— "Tutankhamen's Iron Dagger: Made from a Meteorite?" *Kmt* 27:3, fall 2016. 30-31

— "The Third International Grand Egyptian Museum Tutankhamen Conference," *Kmt* 28:3, fall 2017, 10-12

Zahi Hawass, *The Golden Age of Tutankhamun: Divine Might & Splendor in the New Kingdom* (Cairo/New York, 2004)

— "King Tut Returns: Tutankhamun & the Golden Age of the Pharaohs," *Kmt* 16:2, summer 2005, 20-38

— *Tutankhamun & the Golden Age of the Pharaohs* (Washington, DC, 2005).

— *King Tutankhamun: The Treasures of the Tomb* (New York, 2008)

— *Discovering Tutankhamun: From Howard Carter to DNA* ((Cairo/New York, 2013)

— (with Sahar N. Saleem) *CT Imaging of the New Kingdom Royal Mummies* (Cairo/New York, 2016)

Fiona Herbert, *Carter & Carnarvon" The Story of the Two Englishmen Who Discovered the Tomb of Tutankhamun* (Highclere, 2007)

Thomas Hoving, *Tutankhamun: The Untold Story* (New York, 1978)

Salima Ikram and Aidan Dodson, *The Mummy in Ancient Egypt: Equipping the Dead for Eternity* (London/New York, 1998)

T.G.H. James, *Howard Carter: The Path to Tutankhamun* (London, 1992)

— *Tutankhamun* (Vercelli, Italy, 2008)

George B. Johnson, "KV62, Its Architecture & Decoration," *Kmt* 4:4 (winter 1993-1994) 38-47

— "Circa 1365 BC or 1912 AD? Reconsidering the Queen Tiye-as-Sphinx Bracelet Plaque in the Collection of the Metropolitan Museum of Art," *Kmt* 21:4, winter 2010-11, 18-29

W. Raymond Johnson, "Tutankamen-Period Battle Narratives at Luxor," *Kmt* 20:4, winter 2009-10, 20-33

Andy Joose, "Tutankhamen's Perplexing Calcite Bar-

que (& the Secret of the Sloppy Painter)," *Kmt* 16:1, spring 2005, 34-39

Michael R. King & Gregory M. Cooper, *Who Killed King Tut: Using Modern Forensics to Solve a 3,300-Year-Old Mystery* (New York 2004)

Peter Lacovara , "Tutankhamen: The Golden King & the Great Pharaohs," *Kmt* 19:3, fall 2008, 34-43

F. Filce Leek, *The Human Remains from the Tomb of Tut'anhhamun* (Oxford, 1972)

Jaromir Malek, *Tutankhamun: The Story of Egyptology's Greatest Discovery* (London, 2009)

Kamal El Mallakh & Arnold C. Brackman, *The Gold of Tutanhhamen* (New York, 1978)

Jo Marchant, *The Shadow King: The Bizarre Afterlife of King Tut's Mummy* (New York, 2013)

Helen Murray and Mary Nuttall, compilers, *A Handlist to Howard Carter's Catalogue of Objects in Tut'ankhamun's Tomb* (Oxford, 1963)

Robert B. Partridge, "Tutankhamen's Solid-Gold Coffin Was Altered in Antiquity," *Kmt* 8:1 (spring 1997) 64- 68

James Patterson & Martin Dugard, *The Murder of King Tut: The Plot to Kill the Child King, a Nonfiction Thriller* (New York, 2009)

Alexandre Piankoff, *The Shrines of Tut-Ankh-Amon* (Princeton, 1955)

C.N Reeves, *Valley of the Kings; The decline of a royal necropolis* (London, 1990)

— *The Complete Tutankhamun* (London/New York, 1990)

— ed., *After Tut'ankhamun. Research and excavation in the Royal Necropolis at Thebes* (London, 1992)

— (with Nan Froman) *Into the Mummy's Tomb* (New York, 1992)

— & John H. Taylor, *Howard Carter Before Tutankhamun* (New York, 1993)

— (with Richard H. Wilkinson) *The Complete Valley of the Kings* (London/New York, 1996)

— "The Gold Mask of Ankhkheperure Neferneferuaten," *The Journal of Ancient Egyptian Inter connections* (Tucson, 2015), 77-79

— "The Burial of Nefertiti?," *Amarna Royal Tombs Project, Valley of the Kings Occasional Paper No. 1* (Tucson, 2015), 1-16

John Romer, *Valley of the Kings* (New York, 1981)

Phillis Saretta, "The Discovery of King Tut: Made-in-Egypt Replicas Dazzle in Manhattan," *Kmt* 27:1, spring 2016, 24-35

— "If Harry Burton Had Photographed KV62 in Color," ibid., 36-43

Alberto Siliotti, *Guide to the Valley of the Kings* (New York, 1997)

David P. Silverman, Josef W. Wegner, Jennifer Houser Wegner, eds., *Akhenaten and Tutankhamun: Revolution & Restoration* (Philadephia, 2006)

Irene and Laurence Swinburne, *Behind the Sealed Door: The Discovery of the Tomb and Treasures of Tutankhamun* (New York, 1977)

G.R. Tabouis, *The Private Life of Tutanhhamen* (New York, 1929)

Joyce Tyldesley, *Tutankhamen: The Search for an Egyptian King* (New York, 2012)

Philipp Vandenberg, *The Golden Pharaoh* (New York, 1978)

Claude Vandersleyen, "Royal Figures from Tut'ankhamun's Tomb: Their Historical Usefulness" in C.N Reeves, ed. *After Tut'ankhamun, Research and excavation in the Royal Necropolis at Thebes* (London, 1992), 73-81

Arthur Weigall, *Tutankhamen and Other Essays* (London, 1923)

H.E. Winlock, *Materials Used at the Embalming of King Tut'ankh-Amun* (New York, 1941)

H.V.F. Winstone, *Howard Carter and the discovery of the tomb of Tutankhamun* (London, 1991)

André Wiese, Andrea Brodbeck, eds., *Tutankhamun: The Golden Beyond: Tomb Treasures from the Valley of the Kings* (Basel, 2004)

William Wise, *The Two Reigns of Tutankhamen* (New York, 1964

Barry Wynne, *Behind the Mask of Tutankhamen* (New York, 1973)

Detail of Tutankhaten's nomen cartouche on the armrest of the golden throne. Internet photo *Opposite, Detail of inlaid-gold pectoral element of a winged Kheper beetle formng a rebus of Tutankhenamen's prenomen (Nebkheperure). See p. 224.* Cairo Egyptian Museum

Dennis C. Forbes, the author, has been an ardant Egypto-phile since childhood. In 1990 Forbes created the quarterly *Kmt, A Modern Journal of Ancient Egypt*, & he continues today as its editorial director, having contributed numerous articles, photographs & graphics to the Journal during its 29 years of publication. In addition to *Tombs.Treasures.Mum-mies.*, he is the author of *Imperial Lives, Biographical Sket-ches of Famous New Kingdom Egyptians* (2005); & seven volumes of his black & white photography of the Egyptian monuments are published as *Intimate Egypt* (2009-2016). A native of Des Moines, Iowa, & for a quarter century resident in San Francisco, Forbes has lived for the past 19 years in rural North Carolina near Asheville. George B. Johnson photo

Made in the USA
San Bernardino, CA
14 February 2020